STRUCTURE, STYLE AND INTERPRETATION

IN THE

RUSSIAN SHORT STORY

STRUCTURE, STYLE AND INTERPRETATION

IN THE

RUSSIAN SHORT STORY

L. Michael O'Toole

YALE UNIVERSITY PRESS

NEW HAVEN AND LONDON

1982

Designed by Stephanie Hallin
and set in Compugraphic Bembo
by Red Lion Setters, London.
Printed in Great Britain by
Ebenezer Baylis and Son Ltd,
The Trinity Press, Worcester and London.

Published in Great Britain, Europe, Africa and Asia
(except Japan) by Yale University Press, Ltd,
London. Distributed in Australia and
New Zealand by Book and Film Services, Artarmon,
N.S.W., Australia; and in Japan by Harper & Row,
Publishers, Tokyo Office.

Library of Congress Cataloging in Publication Data

O'Toole, L.M. (Lawrence Michael), 1934–
Structure, style, and interpretation in
the Russian short story.

Bibliography: p.
Includes index.
1. Short stories, Russian – History and
criticism. 2. Russian fiction – 19th century –
History and criticism. I. Title. II. Title:
Russian short story.
PG3097.085   891.73'01'09   81-11650
ISBN 0-300-02730-3   AACR2

CONTENTS

PREFACE

I HAVE CHOSEN to focus in this book on a group of Russian short stories of a particular seventy-year period, using an analytical model derived from the work of the Russian Formalist critics and their successors in the Soviet Union, France, the United States and Britain. The narrative theory is universal, however, and can be applied to the short fiction of any culture, in the analysis of individual stories, the contrasting of pairs or groups of stories from the same or different literary traditions or periods, or level-by-level as a test for the method as I have attempted here. Thus, although I hope the book will be of interest to Russian specialists, it is by no means designed for them alone. Teachers and students on courses in Comparative Literature, Literary Theory and the Sociology of Literature may find it a useful starting point for discussion and wider analyses; in fact, the concentration on a single literary culture should itself raise many interesting problems for these disciplines: to what extent is the code underlying all narrative universal? how far is comparison across cultures meaningful without a systematic and consistent description of the works of each particular culture? how far is the evolution of a genre dependent on—or even relatable to—a particular progression of historical circumstances, modes of government, patterns of social hierarchy and differentiation?

I have not attempted to frame the discussion within a general semiotics of literature. Wherever it has seemed appropriate I have experimented with a semiotic treatment of particular narrative techniques: character contrasts; spatial relations; perception through different sense codes; oppositions between light and darkness, or culture and nature; parallelisms on various levels within texts, and between the texts and other genres and texts that they imply; the tensions created by the interplay of narrative levels or language registers, and so on. All these and many other signifying patterns emerge from the rich texture of the stories I have chosen. Perhaps one day semiotic theory will be coherent enough (and I will be brave enough) to undertake a fully semiotic analysis of such a group of stories as these. For present purposes I have preferred to enrich the structural and stylistic analysis with occasional semiotic insights.

The basic theoretical principle of the method tested here is that the study, teaching and serious discussion of literature must start with the 'text' itself. This is not to deny the simple reader who has no studious intentions when he picks up a piece of fiction his proper pleasures; it is merely to re-assert that anyone who claims to be 'studying' literature, in addition to enjoying it, should base his study and discussion on a systematic analysis of the patterns of meaning created within the text. As I hope has been made clear, I believe that the reader's actual *enjoyment* of the text is enhanced by the processes of analysis and synthesis that I have illustrated. The 'immanent' study of the text of the literary work is, of course, fundamental not only of Formalist and Structuralist approaches, but of rhetorical analysis, Anglo-Saxon New Criticism, *explication de texte*, stylistics, modern hermeneutics, practical criticism, and the best of 'Leavisite' English criticism. Where these approaches will differ is in the degree to which they believe that the patterns of meaning can be related to each other, prior to being related to extra-textual matters such as the writer's biography or psychology, or the society of his day, or larger questions of literary evolution.

My indebtednes to the Russian Formalist critics will be evident on nearly every page of this book. The writings on narrative techniques of Shklovsky, Eikhenbaum and Tomashevsky, and the rigorous concern for the relationship between poetic language and everyday language of Jakobson and Tynyanov are reflected here even when I have deliberately reinterpreted in the light of later structuralist theories—or inadvertently misinterpreted them.

Three outstanding contemporaries of the Formalists—Bakhtin, Propp and Vinogradov—have also had a profound influence, the first two through their own highly original theories and through the later extensions of these theories by Barthes and Todorov and others, the last through his direct and highly sensitive response to the functioning of style in Russian literary texts.

Nearer home, the two groups whose help I must acknowledge with sincere gratitude are, firstly, my colleagues and friends in the Neo-Formalist Circle, especially Joe Andrew, Andrew Barratt, Leon Burnett, John Ellsworth, George Hyde, Susan Knight, Robin Milner-Gulland, Robert Russell, Ann Shukman, Gerry Smith and Dennis Ward; and, secondly, the groups of students at the University of Essex who joined so enthusiastically in collective analysis of the stories.

My wife Myra and Dan and Holly have been wonderfully patient as each living-room became a study and as the moods of anxiety or preoccupation distracted Dad from family pastimes.

NOTE

Most of the stories discussed in this book are readily available in two anthologies: *Great Russian Short Stories*, edited by Stephen Graham, London: Ernest Benn Ltd, 1959, and *The Short Stories of Russia*, edited by David J. Richards, Harmondsworth: Penguin Books, 1981. All the passages quoted have been newly translated by the author in order to bring out specific points of style. However, the translations in these anthologies are accurate and readable and are a good introduction to Russian literature for the English reader.

1

REFRACTIONS:

Interpretation Through Structural Analysis

I

'REFRACTION' will sound to many readers like yet another term borrowed from the so-called 'exact sciences' to lend an aura of scientific respectability to the study of literary form which by its very nature eludes, even derides, precise categories and frameworks. Provided, however, that we do not invest too many assumptions in the borrowed word and tie ourselves to an inflexible method, the relative precision of a term used in physics may help us to clarify, for ourselves as well as others, those elements which can be described out of the enormously complex, subtle and shifting process whereby two minds meet—in the reading of fiction.

Webster defines refraction as: 'The deflection from a straight path suffered by a ray of light, heat, sound, or the like, in passing obliquely from one medium into another in which its velocity is different, as from air into water or from a denser to a rarer layer of air.' This seems to offer a more flexible and multi-dimensioned model of the reading process than the starkly presumptuous *'emitter-message-receiver'* model that many literary structuralists, like most linguists, have borrowed from the discourse of communication theory. It envisages a source of energy (the writer's ideas, feelings, attitudes and intentions) existing in one medium (the form of the printed work) and passing obliquely (and who will deny that reading is a highly oblique process?) into another medium (the reader's mind, with its permanent or transient predispositions, moods and degrees of attentiveness) where its velocity changes and it is deflected to a greater or lesser extent from its original path. We will not go so far as to propose measuring the relation between the 'angle of incidence' (the writer's position in relation to some 'vertical' norm) and the 'angle of refraction' (the degree to which his intentions are deflected as they change velocity in the normally denser medium of the reader's mind). Indeed, the refractive model we need is not so much that of a single ray of light being deflected as a complex array of energy sources passing into the new medium and being variously refracted, some of them—if the writer is lucky in gauging the density of our minds correctly—coming together in a focal point like rays of light through a lens, others deflecting away and lighting up the dark recesses of the mind.

Our model should remind us of two important aspects of literary interpretation: firstly, we have no way of studying the original source of energy except through its refraction in our own perception, so, hopefully, we will avoid the 'intentional fallacy', and secondly, the mind and current mental state of every reader is different, so that it is futile to seek interpretations which fully coincide. What we need is a consistent mode of analysis and a coherent and common language for discussing our findings with other readers.

This book is a modest attempt to apply a single analytical framework to twelve well-known Russian short stories of the nineteenth century, using as consistent a terminology as possible. Although I have chosen to focus on one country's short stories over a mere seventy years, I believe that the method is relevant and fruitful in the analysis and interpretation of short stories from any culture and period.[1] Thus the book should be of as much interest to students of the short story in other languages and to students of comparative literature and literary theory as to strictly Russian specialists. Despite the flourishing of structuralist theory in the last two decades, most published attempts at a structural description have either been carefully chosen fragmentary examples to illustrate or prove a theoretical point, or analyses of a single work. One of the best ways to test—and to teach—a theory and the methodology based on it, however, is to apply it to a corpus of data which is similar enough to keep the method consistent, say, a specific literary genre, and diverse enough to prove the theory's general applicability.

As a student and teacher of both Russian and English literature, I have been acutely conscious of the lack of a method and a common vocabulary with which the student of literature could approach a work on which he is required to make some original and intelligible pronouncement in essay, tutorial or examination. For the student of poetry there is a tradition, or rather a set of conflicting traditions, which offer separate procedures for analyzing metre, rhythm, rhyme, line structure, verse structure, syntax, semantic patterning, imagery and so on, and yet little enough advice on how to move from the sets of findings on these separate levels to some kind of synthesis which could even begin to account for the unity of form and meaning which we must take as one of the defining characteristics of the aesthetic product. When he turns to narrative prose forms the student finds even less guidance available: on the one hand, massive tomes of theory about the nature of narrative with occasional partial texts as illustrations. On the other, essays in criticism of individual novels or short stories involving a wide range of critical approaches, some of them explicitly disavowing theory and method as something unworthy of the critical enterprise, while resorting to a metaphorical mode of exposition which is presumed to convey the unique quality of the critic's insights into the work, but usually serves to overlay the patterns of meaning within the work with all kinds of further patterns contained in the explicatory metaphors. Small wonder, then, that the student comes to rely on the received opinions about specific works to be gleaned from biographies of the author or surveys histories of literature, hopefully spicing these with his own *ad hoc* comments on aspects of style and technique that he happens to notice on a single first reading.

II

The method of analysis we propose to adopt for each of the twelve Russian short stories involves six different levels:

Figure 1

Narrative Structure —	Point of View
Plot —	Fable
Setting —	Character

There are a number of questions which the student can ask about the workings of these levels in any short story he is analyzing. These will be the same questions for every story, though the answers will produce different kinds of groupings pointing to the distinctive features of any particular story. (None of the levels and very few of the questions to be asked on each level are new: some of them were outlined by Aristotle, others were partially explored by the Russian Formalists in the 1920s and by their structuralist successors both in Russia and elsewhere; some, like character and setting, will be regarded as the common coinage of critical discourse about narrative in most times and places. What may be more novel is the insistence in this book on the interrelationship between the levels and on the need for synthesis as a corollary to analysis.) The student will find himself faced with six sets of answers to questions as a result of this analytical stage; does he just record these for posterity—or his next week's essay? No, because this stage of analysis is only the starting-point for our enterprise. Since we presume the short story to be one of those literary forms which best represents the unity of the aesthetic whole (we will be discussing this issue later), our interpretation of the work is going to depend on the quality of the synthesis which follows the analysis.

The point of working systematically through an analytical framework of this kind is not to ignore our own original and unsystematic intuitions. It is rather to try to establish where intuition and formalization fit in the whole reading and re-reading process. For our reader is not merely the one who picks up a short story for entertainment and to be taken out of himself, though these pleasures are a good starting-point, but the one who 're-reads' the story, either actually, or in the sense of mulling over the whole work or details of it afterwards, and more particularly, the student of literature—of whatever age or academic seniority— who is called upon to articulate his responses to the story and compare notes with others. At the analytical stage there should be considerable consensus over the answers to the questions we propose to ask on each of the six levels. Where answers differ radically, we first have to clear up any misunderstandings and then consider whether the differences imply differing interpretations of the theme or plot or character. Considering one level at a time and focussing on specific questions should help the discussants to 'stay on the same wavelength', so that differences of opinion will be due to genuine disagreements and not a result of talking at cross-purposes.

At the analytical stage, then, the discourse is for the most part logical; at the synthesizing stage it is far more analogical, intuiting relationships between the levels analyzed. Not that, being analogical, they can only be expressed in metaphors which may or may not mean the same thing to all the participants in the discourse (under 'discourse' here we include not merely class or tutorial discussion, but the whole gamut of possibilities from scholars corresponding in learned journals to informal discussion and even, of course, the internal dialogue within the solitary reader which is one form of 're-reading'). However intuitive the insights, they must be referred back to relevant levels of analysis, using as far as possible the agreed terminology. In other words, analysis-synthesis is not a single cycle: our very decision to read a work, our response to even its title involves a sort of provisional interpretation which gets modified in the reading process. Long before shutting the book and opening our mouths we are engaged in a vigorous internal dialogue with the text. We read both linearly, within time, and pictorially, outside time, i.e. at any stage in the story we have established for ourselves—without stopping to do so deliberately—a picture of what is going on; this is incomplete and may be full of errors but gets modified as we read on. Words, phrases, sentences, ideas, paragraphs, episodes, characters, descriptions, chapters, plot lines offer a constant flow of data to the 'scanning device' in our minds which frames them, forms mental constructs and 'comprehends' the story in an expanding series of manageable wholes.

If the very reading process consists of the interplay of synthesis and analysis, then surely the production of 'a reading', either in discussion or contemplation, must also involve the same interplay. Whereas the interplay is *implicit* in the act of reading, it should be *explicit* in the study of literature. The 'levels' of analysis are ultimately a heuristic device to make possible a consistent method of analysis and to offer a framework and terminology for discourse about the text. Within the real literary text they are not ultimately separable and the student will be committing himself, as in all academic (or 'purely academic') enterprises, to a willing suspension of disbelief.

The first stage, then, is a 'refracturing' of the text which we have perceived as some kind of whole, breaking it down into manageable units with a clearly perceivable structure. This cannot be the reverse of the synthetic process by which we made that whole, since, although a fascinating psychological problem, it is not a process that can be reproduced. What we can do is to break the text down into manageable levels which seem to represent universal features of the narrative. Each chapter of this book is devoted to a detailed discussion and illustration of the workings of narrative at each level, but some sense of how they relate may be appropriate here. (In the final chapter we will discuss some of the structural relationships involved in the synthesis of the analytical levels, as well as some general problems concerning the short story as a genre, its evolution in nineteenth-century Russia and the recurrence of particular topics (*topoi*) and themes.)

Narrative Structure is the dramatic trajectory of the story's 'action' from its initial situation, through a complication, a *peripeteia*, or turning point, a dénouement which represents some kind of reversal of the complication, to a closing situation. It is the mechanism by which the theme, which may be stated statically as some sort of contrast, is given dynamic form. In linguistic terms, it is the way an underlying meaning, often a semantic opposition (despair/hope; illness/health; pride/humility; rejection/acceptance; solitude/integration; nature/culture), is given syntactic form. In psychological terms, it is the way we are moved from recognition of a problem to involvement with it, from a stance where we can dispassionately view a situation with the intellect to a feeling that we have sympathetically experienced the situation and its outcome. And yet narrative structure allows us to have it both ways: our sympathies are personally engaged for the hero or heroine or victim, yet the very aesthetic balance of the form at the same time forces us to stand back and view their fortunes impersonally.

If narrative structure is the outline of the story in terms of its *action, Point of View* is the level on which we perceive the story as *discourse*. It is the way supposedly objective events are already refracted through the consciousness and perception and tone of voice of the narrator. This, perhaps, is the 'angle of incidence' which governs the 'angle of refraction' through which the story is deflected in the denser or rarer medium of our mind. To continue our earlier linguistic analogy, if narrative structure is akin to the propositional structure of a sentence, then point of view is akin to its modal structure. (This will be discussed further, with examples, in the relevant chapters.)

In Figure 1 (p. 3) narrative structure and point of view were set apart as levels which define the whole work and to which all the other levels are, in some sense, secondary (I hope it will become clear that by 'secondary' I mean 'defined by', not 'less important'). The two levels we will consider next are *Fable* and *Plot*. These are the essential chaining structures of the narrative, relating events 'horizontally' through the text in terms of time and causation. (The difference between my use of these terms and the use of the terms *fabula* and *syuzhet* by the Russian Formalists will be discussed in the chapter on fable.) The fable is the dispositional sequence of the events which form the narrative structure, i.e. what actually happened in its original chronological sequence and at its original natural tempo. It is a paradox, of course, to speak of the fable as if it were some kind of raw material for the story, since, with most stories, it did not happen in reality either and can only be reconstructed in the reader's imagination on the basis of the information we are actually given in the story. However, we undoubtedly have a strong impulse as we read to reconstruct a natural time sequence for events and to relate them to a realistic measure of duration and this temporal prism should provide one of the media through which our mind refracts the story the author presents us with. Similarly, the plot is the causal unfolding of the narrative, the degree to which actions, events, thoughts and impulses are motivated, that is, related to each other in terms of cause and effect, either through deliberate, sometimes explicit, clues left by the author, or through our own reconstruction as we read of the most probably motivation. Once again, in analyzing plot we will have to try to discriminate between our own interpretations of causal relationships and the information the author has actually given us. Frequently this will be a matter of style.

A scrupulous reconstruction of the fable and plot will have revealed to us much of the linear structure of our short story and will clarify how the author has used temporal and causal relations in constructing the narrative structure and refracted these relations through his choice and variation of point of view. A great deal of the meaning of most short stories, however, is transmitted by means of the direct associations which we make between discrete fragments of text without reference to the sequential and consequential relationships of the linear text. The main field where the associations of this kind can usefully be traced is that of *Character*. Students and critics of narrative genres have always been aware, of course, of the subtle and varied ways in which the characters in a story are created, develop and function and the very human interest of character—our identification with the hero and alienation from the villain—tends to make this the level of structure which is easiest to explore and describe. We are likely to reach agreement quite quickly on technical questions about the significance of physical description, speech and actions, or explicit psychological comment in the delineation of a character; we will agree fairly readily about which characters are 'flat', part of the décor, and which 'round' and capable of development; we may even agree —or agree to differ—in our moral evaluation of the motives and actions of each character. All such discussion is useful and necessary, yet isolated from the other levels of structure it may tell us comparatively little about how the story works in aesthetic terms and by its very preponderance in discussion may distract from important but less obvious aspects of the theme. In addition to reconstructing the means by which the character is drawn, we must focus on his (or her) function in the narrative structure, his significance for our perception of the structuring of time in the fable, or of cause and effect in the plot; we should particularly attempt to account as fully as possible for the interplay of character and point of view, since in many stories we are dependent on the thoughts and speech and reactions of the characters for our knowledge of what is going on. Refraction is at its most complex here because a character may be our only source of information, yet viewing him objectively we know that we can only trust him so far and that his opinions and predilections are highly selective. A kind of dialectical interplay will be going on throughout the story between our trust in the character's objectivity and our suspicions about his subjectivity: we will be looking for the flaws in the prism. And since the author may have put in our way not just one, but many such prisms, and since the prisms may be arranged in parallel—each separately refracting the same sets of information—or in series—one refracting the next one's refraction, and so on—the interplay may be complex indeed.

Setting, too, is largely developed through associations between different and widely separated parts of the text even though some of its temporal and spatial features—changes of time, season or historical circumstances and movement from place to place—may also have important implications for the continuity of the fable and plot. Given the close and integrated texture we are claiming for the short story form, we should beware of assigning to setting a purely ornamental function as some critics have done. The choice of a time and place within which any part of the action is set is rarely arbitrary and will affect the shape of the narrative structure and the choice of character. It may permit a variation in place of the story telling or may make the rapid passage of time more acceptable; it may motivate a flashback or a prophetic dream, and it may lead a character to take some fateful decision. Most crucially, a paragraph of description of a place, or even a passing reference to it, may have moral implications, providing a kind of neutral and universal touchstone by which we (partially) judge the behaviour of the characters. It may even, as I hope to show, become an active agent in the plot in its own right, raising all kinds of philosophical questions about the relation-ship between man and 'his' world. With any of these functions, setting, whether real or fantastic, historical or outside time, passive or involved, will be one of the essential prisms through which our sensibility refracts the narrated world.

III

These, then, are six levels of narrative structure in the short story that we will be exploring in some depth. The isolation of these six raises some questions, how-ever:

1. How do each of these levels of structure, taken singly, relate to the theme of a story?

2. How 'structuralist' can the approach outlined and explored here claim to be?

3. If we only isolate such broad structural features as these, the macrostructure of the work, how are we to account for the microstructure of linguistic features which we normally term 'style' and which must play an important part in any close reading of a text?

4. How close a relationship can be established between style and theme, or style and structure? Is there such a thing as a stylistic dominant which will account for the overall tone of a story and which might be said, as the Formalists put it, to 'organize the composition of a work and subjugate to itself all the other devices required to create an artistic whole'?

5. Does the rigorous (not, we hope, rigid) application of a mechanistic

structure rule out the workings of intuition? Are we guilty of 'reduction-ism' before we even start? Are we likely to end up discovering, as Emily Dickinson put it, 'the facts, but not the phosphorescence'?

6. If we focus to such an extent on re-reading, that is, if we impose our analyt-ical frames on the whole story, perceived after the event as some kind of totality, to what extent can we say anything useful about the dynamics of the reading process as we read the story for the first time?

7. Can a structured approach of this kind offer any useful generalizations about the nature of the short story genre?

8. Can it indicate any features peculiar to the *Russian* short story or tell us how that genre evolved in the course of the nineteenth century?

None of these questions can be answered in the abstract, in purely theoretical terms, and I have set out in this book very deliberately to test these kind of theor-etical problems of narrative structure in terms of real, complex, interesting texts which for many lovers of literature have established themselves as 'works of art'. Some of the more theoretical issues will be reserved for the final chapter, where an attempt will be made to relate the method outlined here to other approaches to the study and criticism of literary narrative. Meanwhile, I hope that the whole book will serve as a kind of model for the method.

IV

All the stories discussed in this book are well known to the lover of Russian liter-ature and the ones by Pushkin, Gogol, Turgenev and Chekhov are regarded as classics (i.e. to be found in international anthologies of the genre and in student syllabuses). Their accessability in translation and their pedagogical relevance were not, however, the major reasons for their selection.

The stories are analyzed and discussed in pairs for each chapter and were chosen because the stories in each pair offer a significant contrast in the workings of the level of structure explored in the chapter while having similar or broadly related themes. We hope, therefore, that the interpretation of each story will be refracted not only through the structuring of the given level within itself, but in the contrast with features of the structure of the story with which it is paired. Often, I believe, this parallel treatment will point to some important character-istics of the narrative art of the individual author and occasionally, as with Dostoevsky and Tolstoy, or Turgenev and Chekhov, it may help to pin down some specific features in the writing of authors who are frequently compared in a more general way.

A brief summary of the reasons for choosing each pair of stories may provide a context for their detailed discussion in the relevant chapters.

Narrative Structure may be simple, focussed on a single line of action in a physical sphere, as in Leskov's *The Man on Sentry Duty*, or complex and constructed on a psychological or metaphysical plane as, I will argue, is the case in Gogol's *The Overcoat*. The complexity of the play with Point of View in a story like *The Overcoat* may be such that the story is lifted out of the narrative plane where the reader mainly responds to *what* is told to the plane of discourse where he responds to *how* it is told.

This transfer of focus from the narrative plane to the discourse plane will be central to my discussion of point of view in Dostoevsky's story *A Gentle Spirit*, though, once again, we will see that this play with point of view can not be divorced from the underlying narrative structure. Dostoevsky's story shares the same theme with Tolstoy's *Father Sergius*, that is, the quest for God through contact with one's fellow men, but the treatment could hardly be more different. The extreme subjectivity of Dostoevsky's first person narrator-hero encompasses a wide range of other voices all subversive to the narrator's authority, while the objectivity of Tolstoy's third person narrator slips from nicely balanced dialogue into a doctrinaire and monologic harangue.

At the level of Fable we will be contrasting the complex time structure of a story set in the tangibly real world of *The Post-Stage Master* with the naively linear time sequence followed by the hero of *Makar's Dream* whether in reality, a drunken stupor or a dream world.

Pushkin's much-studied story from the *Tales of Belkin, The Pistol Shot*, offers a nice study in Plot, with its complex patterns of individual motivation, as interpreted for us by a prominent narrator, while Gorky's *Twenty-Six Men and a Girl* purports to represent the consequences of group motivation as told by a narrator from within the group who cannot, however, completely mask his own individuality.

Turgenev's romantic classic *Asya* and Chekhov's symbolic *The Black Monk*, create Character in strongly contrasting ways, even though they both stem from Romantic models of human psychology.

Nature, which provides the Setting in so many of Turgenev's *Sportsman's Sketches* becomes an active force in that most powerful story of the series, *Bezhin Meadow*. In Chekhov's *Peasants*, on the other hand, the agency for good or evil is all too evidently human, while nature plays an important role in the story on the discourse plane as mute judge and arbiter of human morality.

The summary here of the underlying argument of each chapter has necessarily been schematic. It begs many questions which I hope will be answered in the course of the analysis and in Chapter 8 where the dynamics of the analysis-synthesis process will be discussed in detail.

V

Refraction turns out to be a rather complex process, far more than the deflection of a single ray of light through a medium denser than air, such as glass or water.

A complex of energy sources—fictive characters, actions, settings, etcetera—is refracted through a narrative structure and then refracted again by a more or less complex point of view. The medium of language, refractory enough for the writer, further refracts the energies as it transmits them to the reader. But readers' minds, moods and receptivity differ markedly and, for that matter, so do those of any one reader at different times. And our *re*-reader refracts and *re*-fracts. Nevertheless, groups of readers, societies and the literate world at large do reach some kind of consensus in their reading of individual works that seems to be due to more than social and academic convention. Students of literature must surely concern themselves with exploring and describing those universal elements in narrative that make possible both focus and diffraction. And we may need a good deal more description before we indulge in further theorizing.

NOTES TO CHAPTER 1

1. The author has published analyses of stories by James Joyce and Conan Doyle and has used the method in teaching stories by such diverse writers as Petronius, Maupassant, O. Henry and a modern Japanese writer.

2

NARRATIVE STRUCTURE

Leskov: *The Man on Sentry Duty*
Gogol: *The Overcoat*

I

NARRATIVE STRUCTURE is the shape of a story's trajectory. Every story is projected from a state of rest by a force of some kind in an arc of rising tension until it reaches the apogee where it begins to fall towards a point of impact. Russian criticism has tended to use a vincular metaphor in preference to a ballistic one to describe this movement: an initial *zavyazka* (tying up, or ravelling) leads to a central *uzel* (knot) after which the story is resolved in a *razvyazka* (unknotting, or unravelling). English has tended to mix its metaphors and source languages and speak of the 'complication' leading to a 'crisis' and 'peripeteia' which makes possible the 'dénouement'. Each of these metaphors has its own virtues—and problems—as a way of describing narrative structure, but they all have some important elements in common.

They all start by assuming a previous state of rest or equilibrium or normality which is disturbed by an outside force of some kind. The condition initiated by this force gets worse until it reaches an extreme degree. The story cannot be left at this point, however: another force comes to bear which reverses the process and allows for the gradual resumption of normality or the establishment of a new equilibrium. In each metaphor the prior and ultimate states of rest are only implied or hinted at and the main focus is on the extended processes of complication and resolution with the peripeteia as a crucial turning-point between them.

It may seem rather platitudinous to devote so much attention to this pattern of rise-and-fall or tension-and-release which is common to so many types of human experience, whether in nature (the sun's course, the seasons, growth and decay, a storm) or in society (bargains, arguments, wars, orgasms). Indeed, narrative structure might be taken as a metaphor for the course of life itself. The point is, however, that narrative is *not* life: it allows us to experience the tension and relief at one remove. A major function of art, according to some psychologists, is, in fact, to produce tensions in the perceiver which will match in their variety and diffusion his residual tensions but which are specific enough to be resolved within the context of the art experience, thus channelling the residual tensions into a manageable framework and allowing for their vicarious relief. This rather crude homeostatic model has been refined by some psychologists who allow for a cognitive dimension to the aesthetic experience, so that we both undergo the experience of tension-and-release offered by works of art and stand back and contemplate the experience.[1]

Now the short story, like the dream, the anecdote, the fairy tale and the ballad, is designed to be experienced at one sitting, so that unity of form is crucial to its definition: it is centripetal. Most forms of the novel also have a centre—a relationship, a character, a state of mind or a philosophical idea—but the novel tends to be centrifugal. The fundamental characteristic of the short story as a genre is the tightness, unity and coherence of its structure. Edgar Allen Poe, one of the greatest of early short story writers, expressed this well in a famous review of Hawthorne's *Twice Told Tales* (1842)

> A skilful literary artist has constructed a tale. If wise, he has not fashioned his thoughts to accommodate his incidents; but having conceived, with deliberate care, a certain unique or single *effect* to be wrought out, he then invents such incidents—he then combines such events—as may best aid him in establishing his preconceived effect. If his very initial sentence tends not to the outbringing of this effect, then he has failed in his first step. In the whole composition there should be no word written of which the tendency, direct or indirect, is not to the one pre-established design.

The central point around which the whole narrative structure pivots is the peripeteia, so that pinpointing the peripeteia should help us to ascertain the nature of the conflict in the story. I would argue a strong relationship between the narrative structure and the theme (Poe's 'unique or single preconceived effect'), and hence believe that our interpretation of the story as a whole is going to depend in the first instance on where we perceive the peripeteia and on what level we consider it is taking place. Several of the stories analyzed here present problems as to the placing of the peripeteia. The turning-point on the level of physical action may offer a possible theme (realized in terms of a movement towards that action in the complication and its resolution in the dénouement), yet the essential theme may be on a deeper psychological or metaphysical level, of which the overt action is only a manifestation or illustration, and will be recognized through the central significance of a quite different peripeteia in the mind or spiritual life of the hero, in the relation between our reality and other spheres of reality. As we shall see, the crucial turning-point may be a complex set of turning-points, related but on different levels, may link two subordinate plot structures or may occur outside the story line altogether. These, however, will be special manifestations of the writer's art which gain their extra significance by being deviations from a recognizable norm whereby we expect to find the peripeteia at the centre of the narrative structure.

The reader may well ask what determines our selection of one turning-point in preference to another and why, in a particular story, the psychological or metaphysical should be regarded as taking precedence over the level of physical action, or vice versa. The answer is that we have other criteria pointing in the same direction: lines of cause and effect in the plot, tendencies in a character or in the relationship between characters, the way the story is refracted to us through point of view. Most frequently it is a matter of style. In virtually every story studied here the moment of peripeteia is signalled by a change in the language, whether a marked shift in the referential field, a bunching of certain features of cohesion, or an intensification of certain interpersonal elements such as modality, lexical weight, modal particles, or even rhythm. The linguistic features may be small but they are not trivial, and the shift in tone can be clearly felt. We will draw attention to the specific features involved when we discuss individual stories.

Whereas the peripeteia is usually a single moment or a brief series of moments which is crucial to the re-reading and interpretation of a story, the complication normally takes up the bulk of the fable and plot structure and provides our main sense of the text as we read it for the first time. Here we will be concerned with the play with time (flashbacks for essential prior information, or description and digressions to slow down the action) and will be building up a picture of the patterns of motivation in the plot which lead to the crisis. The balance between elements of narration, description and dialogue and the way they relate may help us to account for changes in narrative tension and pace. They will probably also be worth studying for the play of point of view, both in terms of the characters' awareness of what is going on and of the author's—or, rather, his narrator's—stance towards both events and characters. Some authors convey most of the essential information through direct narration, some in descriptive passages and some in dramatic scenes involving mostly dialogue. A tendency to rely on one of these narrative modes in preference to the others may be an important factor in defining both an individual writer's poetics and the poetics of a school with well-established norms.

Digressions may be trivial and purely ornamental; they may help to define the author's/narrator's stance; or they may, as in *The Overcoat*, be a crucial element in the narrative structure.

Since crises in all spheres tend to resolve themselves, for better or worse, far more rapidly than they develop, we may expect the dénouement to be briefer than the complication. Most authors seem to prefer a narratorial mode at this stage in the story. Occasionally an author deliberately refrains from resolving the crisis. Although Chekhov is often cited in this regard, he very rarely leaves his stories completely 'open-ended' in the way that Maupassant or some modern American writers do.

The central phases of narrative structure are normally framed by elements of prologue and epilogue, in each of which we can distinguish two phases, the general and the specific. The general prologue provides some glimpses of the total social scene into which the action of the story fits, while a special prologue gives us some essential background information about the past and present lives of the main characters. It may, in fact, be a mistake to refer to these as 'framing' elements, since they are more often than not presented in flashback form after the story proper has started and since they constitute not so much a 'frame' as the state of equilibrium which is disturbed by the onset of the complication. They are matched at the end of the story by a special epilogue, which tells us anything we need to know of the subsequent lives and fate of the main characters, and a general epilogue which restores a sense of the general social equilibrium. Occasionally an author deliberately adds an artificial epilogue in order to reveal a moral or point up some hidden design. Leskov does this in *The Man on Sentry Duty*.

II Leskov: *The Man on Sentry Duty (1839)*, 1887;[2] *(Chelovek na chasakh (1839)*

The narrative structure of this story is classically straightforward and symmetrical. The narrator explicitly introduces his story to us in a general prologue encapsulated in Chapter 1, self-consciously aware of his readers, his hero, the social and historical signficance of the events narrated and even what he terms the originality of the dénouement. He refers obliquely to his own role as narrator in claiming that the story is totally free of invention. The story is rounded off in an equally neat general epilogue where the narrator stylishly hesitates to speculate on the Almighty's view of what has transpired but claims that true lovers of goodness among his readers must be pleased by the performance of the humble hero of his accurate and unartificial tale.

The plot itself opens with a special prologue in which we find the young and humane Guards Officer, Miller, settling down as duty officer on a winter's night in 1839 in St Petersburg. The complication follows in three ascending stages (in terms of rank and intensity of reaction): Postnikov, the sentry, is faced by a crisis of conscience, having to choose between deserting his post to save a man drowning in the river or loyally staying at it and letting a fellow human-being drown. His humane decision presents Miller, his immediate superior, with a crisis of regimental reputation, since the other external complicating agent, a vain and stupid officer of the Invalid Corps has meanwhile presented himself to the police as the rescuer in the hope of gaining a medal. For Colonel Svinin, the regiment's commander, this becomes a crisis in his career because such desertion of a post by one of his men could only be due to the commander's 'softness', a fatal stain on his hitherto unsullied reputation. Only Kokoshkin, the Chief of Police has the confidence, the knowledge of the workings of the corridors of power and the understanding of human nature to resolve these crises: Postnikov must be punished, the Invalid Officer duly, if cynically, rewarded, the victim of drowning admonished, and Svinin reassured.

In the dénouement we find Postnikov humbly content with only receiving two hundred strokes of the lash, Miller resigned to suppressing his liberal principles and administering the punishment, the Invalid Officer bemedalled, and Svinin apparently satisfied with the survival of his reputation and his own paternalism in rewarding Postnikov with some tea and sugar to help him get over his flogging: a completely symmetrical narrative structure appropriate for historical anecdote of half a century before. But such mechanical neatness of structure, such predictable resolution of all the complications would hardly make the story worth telling forty-eight years after the events described, and certainly not worth re-reading nearly a century and a half later. And at this point we find the saving flaw in the narrative structure: in place of the special epilogue we are given a detailed account of a very curious conversation between Svinin and a high Church dignitary (based on the real Metropolitan Philaret) whose curiosity has been whetted by rumours of the events and who demands a first-hand account. In the course of this interview we find that Svinin, for all his callous careerism, has some lingering humane doubts about having punished Postnikov for his brave and charitable act, while the Metropolitan soothes away all doubts and questionings with mumbled aphorisms, scriptural quotations and the click of his rosary beads. Soviet critics have, of course, invariably focussed on the anti-clerical satire of this episode as epitomizing what they take to be the central theme of the story: the cynicism of the established church in justifying and even sanctifying the inhumanity of an autocratic, oppressive and bureaucracy-ridden régime.[3] And indeed this is a somewhat simplistic and tendentious interpretation of the overt theme of the story.

As we have seen in Chapter 1, the narrative structure is the compositional realization of a fundamental semantic opposition, a pattern of process-participant relationships analogous to that which operates in a transitive sentence to express a shift from one state to a contrasting state. The very title juxtaposes the opposing elements *chelovek* ('man'; with stronger connotations in Russian than in English of human being, humane, philanthropic) and *na chasakh* ('on sentry-duty'; representing the institutional, controlled, potentially anti-human, with the possibility of an unconscious pun on *chasy* (clock/duty watch) underscoring the conventional and regulatory which tends, particularly for the Russian mind, to exclude or smother the human response). The juxtaposition comes to the fore in Postnikov's moment of decision, which, though it could only have lasted a few seconds, is dramatized as an elaborate internal dialogue between his 'better' self and his habit of obedience to orders. The language of this dialogue highlights the juxtaposition: on the one hand, the ponderous, sometimes archaic, sometimes jargon-ridden register of army regulations or court-martial depositions 'he was a sensible and exemplary soldier of sound mind and understood perfectly well that to abandon his post was such a dereliction of duty by a sentry as to lead at once to a court-martial, then running the gauntlet of the guard, and penal servitude and perhaps even a "firing squad".' On the other hand, the directness of colloquial speech, with ellipsis, particles, colloquial lexis, the vividness of the present tense, exclamations, etcetera

but from the turbulent river the groans were once more drifting closer and closer and he could hear a gurgling and a desperate floundering.

—I'm dro-ow-ning! . . . Help, drowning!

And just nearby there's[4] the Jordan pipe . . . It'd be all over. Postnikov took another quick look or two all round. Not a soul in sight, just the street lamps trembling and winking in the wind, and borne on the wind, intermittently, that cry . . . perhaps his last . . .

Again a splash, again a monotone wail and a gurgling in the water.

The sentry couldn't stand it and abandoned his post.

(See Russian Texts, No. 1)

The same register contrast is used in describing, through indirect speech, the Invalid Officer's report to the policeman on duty and the episode in the dénouement (matching the one we have quoted in the complication), where Postnikov is punished for his 'crime'.

The main characters, too, seem to be arranged along a scale of humanity—roughly in order of their appearance in the story—from Postnikov[5] with his self-sacrifice for another to the Metropolitan with his total moral cynicism. In between these extremes stand Miller with his liberal, 'so-called humane' intentions, but his indecisiveness in taking action; Svinin with his careerism and ability to take formal action, but his residual moral doubts; and Kokoshkin for whom moral considerations are irrelevant.

It would seem, then, that a narrative structure which matches a complication caused by private humanity with a dénouement resolved by institutionalized inhumanity, an almost schematic arrangement of the characters according to the degree of humanity which they manifest in the crisis, and the juxtaposition of colloquial and institutional styles all point clearly to the theme of man's inhumanity to man when he responds only to the inertia and insensitivity of an autocratic régime. If, as we have proposed, the narrative structure gives dynamic form to a static contrast, turns a basic semantic opposition into a process of shift from one state of affairs to another, then the theme of *The Man on Sentry Duty* should be this rather naive social message, a rather mechanical fable. But the conversation between Svinin and the Metropolitan, as we have seen, breaks the symmetry of this narrative structure and suggests a rather more complex and interesting theme. For although Svinin is seeking a resolution for his moral disquiet from the highest possible authority, his Reverence is preoccupied with something quite different. He has become interested in the Postnikov case after hearing an inaccurate rumour about it (a version, incidentally, which allows a far more rational interpretation of the rewarding of the Invalid Officer and the punishment of Postnikov than the true facts allow!). Being 'not indifferent to events in society' the inquisitive Metropolitan wants to tie up a few loose threads in the story (*Pronitsatel'nomu vladyke kazalos' neyashym skazaniye o vystrele*).[6] He conceives it as his ecclesiastical duty to seek out the truth from the 'idle gossip' (*suyesloviye*) of the world at large 'In the world people accept a great deal with great frivolity and "spread gossip", but those living in retreats and at the court take a much more serious view and know the veritable truth about worldly matters.' All of his first questions and comments to Svinin (in typical, ponderous, archaic language) concern this problem of relative truth

—Hence one must conclude that not everything was everywhere reported in accordance with the total truth? . . .

. . . One must distinguish what is lies and what is incomplete truth . . .

. . . The incomplete truth is not lies. But about this the less said . . .

. . . The sacred is God's concern, but corporal punishment is not harmful to the common folk and contradicts neither the custom of nations nor the spirit of Holy Writ.
(See Russian Texts, No. 2).

And the Metropolitan concludes with a firm instruction about maintaining discretion '—But most of all in this whole matter one must preserve caution about this whole affair and nowhere in any wise mention who for any reason has been told about it.' But Leskov, of course, has been so indiscreet as to tell us the story, and the truth as we know it from the glimpses he vouchsafes us into the minds of Postnikov, Miller, the police duty officer, Svinin and Kokoshkin is constantly at odds with the relative interpretations each of them gives of the circumstances as they know them. In a sense, this is akin to our other 'naive' theme: truth, like mercy, becomes a very relative value in a society as terrorized and corrupt as Russia in the latter years of Nicholas I. But the texture of the story which we enjoy so much as we read *The Man on Sentry Duty* is created by these contrasts of interpretation as they emerge through patterns of narrative and comment, of direct speech, indirect speech and soliloquy, of contrasting registers in the language. And we notice that the author has added the date (1839) to the title, thus immediately creating a resonant context for the events narrated in the mind of any reader who knows even a little Russian social history, and he comments in his 'prologue' that the outcome of the affair is so original that anything similar would scarcely be possible outside Russia. Moreover, his anecdote is 'partly one belonging in Court circles as well as historical': in other words, we may expect both historical truth and relative interpretation. And although the time sequence of the events narrated is purely linear (see the chapter on fable), the narrative is punctuated by references to the time of narration, forty-eight years later

. . . of an extremely poorly studied period in the thirties of this century which nears its completion. (Chapter 1)

. . . N.I. Miller (subsequently a full general and principal of a lycée.)[7] (Chapter 2)

. . . there occurred an altogether extraordinary and troubling event, which is now scarcely recalled by a few of the men of that time who are now living out their lives. (Chapter 2)

... of the Invalid Corps (subsequently disbanded). (Chapter 4)

... 'a service type' (of the kind people now again remember with regret). (Chapter 7)

... there were some people out of sympathy with Svinin's views because at that time 'humanism' and other fads (*zabluzhdeniya*) like it had still not been entirely got rid of. (Chapter 7)

and so on.

Two further points emerge from these quotations: on the one hand, they are part of the narrator's attempt to persuade us of the authenticity of his story, and on the other, the use of quotation marks and loaded words such as 'fads' (*zabluzhdeniya*) constantly remind us of the conventionality of the genre and the relativity of the truth it depicts. This brings us to the core of the dilemma which critics of Leskov have found themselves in: most of his writing is on the border between history and fiction. Leskov's career had brought him into close contact with peasant life, the workings of the bureaucracy both in the provinces and in the capital and the intricacies of the Court, the Church and the Army. With his enormous appetite for facts, his memory for historical events and his ear for specific speech styles he could rarely refrain from mixing the authentic and the invented. Since he wrote in the period when psychological realism, which did not depend on external authenticity, was the dominant mode, critics and readers have found it hard to assign him to a convenient niche. Yet it is a narrow view of genre that sees psychological realism as the ultimate in narrative fiction. Leskov was reviving the 'empirical' element in narrative at the expense of the 'fictional',[8] thus continuing the eighteenth-century tradition of Sterne, Smollet, Voltaire, Montesquieu and Radischev and presaging its revival in new 'mixed' genres explored in our own time by Norman Mailer, John Berger and others.

Like these writers, Leskov is well aware of the ironic potential that this blending of fact and fiction offers. He begins and ends tongue-in-cheek: 'There is no invention whatever in the story we are about to tell ...' (Chapter 1) ... 'of my accurate and artless tale' (Chapter 18); certainly none of the external facts and events narrated are invented, but the story delights us with its interpretations of the characters' motivation, inner conflict and final reaction which can only be invented. The single word 'humane' (*gumannyi*) acquires four interpretations in the context of the delineation of Miller's qualities

He was a man of so-called 'humane' tendencies, which had long been noted and which had had a slightly harmful effect on his prospects in the services in the view of the authorities.

In fact, however, Miller was an exemplary and reliable officer...'

(See Russian Texts, No. 3)

Here we are presented with: 1) the actual meaning of the word 'humane' (*gumannyi*); 2) the popular view of the word expressed ironically by the quota-tion marks, the 'so called' (*tak nazyvayemym*) and 'tendencies' (*napravleniyem*)—even by the alien 'Westernness' of the word itself (cf. *chelovechnyi*)—; 3) the offi-cial army view that this humanity was to the detriment of his career as an officer (though only 'slightly', the narrator feels qualified to assure us!); and 4) the narrator's rational, unprejudiced view introduced after 'In fact, however . . . ' (*Na samom zhe dele . . .*) Even more clearly, the long introduction of Svinin, the main vehicle for the story's moral dilemma, to which the whole of Chapter 7 is devoted, is woven of many different viewpoints: (1) the 'objective' narrator's voice 'Lieutenant Colonel Svinin did not have that sympathetic and soft-hearted nature that had always distinguished Nikolai Ivanovich Miller.' (2) the ironic comment of the quotation marks round 'professional' (*sluzhbist*), 'humanism' (*gumanizm*), 'humanists' (*gumanisty*). (3) the Tsar's presumed view of weak officers and dissolute men 'His Majesty would be infuriated, of course, and would be sure to tell the regimental commander that he had 'weak officers' and that the men under them were "debauched".' (4) Svinin's own view expressed mainly in comical largely meaningless army clichés

in the service all faults are faulty;

like hard-tempered steel;

to make sure that it was as clear as his dress uniform of the least speck;

they would trip him up to make way for one of their pals;

an ineridacable stain would remain on his, Svinin's, reputation;

not to be able to leave behind his portrait in the gallery of historic names of the Russian state
(See Russian Texts, No. 4)

and (5) the view of their colonel which the men in his company held as expressed in the gossip about the Postnikov affair: 'So that everyone in the Sentry Corps knew what Private Postnikov would have to suffer for abandoning his post, that he would take it like a man, and that Svinin would not have any sleepless nights over it.' In three paragraphs, then, Leskov has woven a highly complex skein of conflicting and interacting points of view which sums up superbly the interplay of public and personal views of people and events and reminds us in practically every phrase of the relativity of truth.

This theme might seem rather far removed from the one which first presented itself through our examination of the narrative structure of *The Man on Sentry Duty*, i.e. the conflict between the humanity of man acting as an individual and the inhumanity of man as a cipher in a fundamentally amoral or immoral society. Whereas the opposition humanity/inhumanity seems to belong to the *histoire*, that between absolute and relative truth seems to work at the level of *discours*.[9]

But Leskov has united the two themes in the apparently superfluous conversation between Svinin and the Metropolitan, that supposedly supreme arbiter of morality who is actually only pre-occupied with versions of the truth ranging from current rumour through individual opinion to Holy Writ. Leskov's two key virtues (as D.S. Mirsky—perhaps Leskov's most perceptive critic—has pointed out[10]) are as a narrator of vivid anecdotes and as a socio-linguist. In *The Man on Sentry Duty* this curious conversation and Leskov's virtuosity with language which it typifies becomes a bridge between the two themes producing a 'meta-theme' whereby humanity depends on man's individual awareness of truth and inhumanity grows out of the distortions of truth produced by corrupt public institutions.

III Gogol: *The Overcoat*, 1839-1841; (*Shinel'*) [11]

Another story which we may presume to be set in the year 1839, since Nikolai Gogol began writing it in that year, apparently about contemporary events, is *The Overcoat*, perhaps the most well-known and elaborately analyzed story in the whole of Russian literature. Many critics, from Belinsky onwards, have taken the theme to be similar to that which can be found on a first reading of Leskov's *The Man on Sentry Duty*: the plight of the 'little man' in the face of an impersonal and inhumane society prevailing under the autocratic rule of Nicholas I. But if an analysis of the narrative structure ultimately proved this theme inadequate in the case of Leskov's story, in the case of Gogol's it makes such a theme appear a travesty of the story's real essence.

The basic plot of *The Overcoat* appears straightforward: a poor and pathetically limited copying clerk, Akakiy Akakiyevich, finds his old coat inadequate protection against the cold of the St Petersburg winter, skimps and saves to have a new one made, has a brief moment of triumph as the toast of his colleagues but is robbed of the prized overcoat as he makes his way home from the celebration. He summons up the confidence to ask a certain Person of Consequence to intercede with the chief of police and help to recover the stolen coat, only to be shouted at and sent packing into the street where he catches cold, goes home to bed and dies. After his death, rumours are rife about a ghost resembling Akakiy who snatches overcoats from the backs of citizens with so little respect for rank that he finally appears in the carriage of the Person of Consequence and demands back 'his' overcoat.

These bare bones yield a nicely symmetrical structure:

Figure 2

General Prologue	:	the St Petersburg background and Akakiy's past
Special Prologue	:	Akakiy's present job, private life and poverty
Complication	:	the lack of a coat and gradual acquisition of the new one
Peripeteia	:	the theft of the new coat

Dénouement   : attempts to recover the coat and death
Special Epilogue : 'revenge' by Akakiy's ghost
General Epilogue : a widening circle of rumour about ghosts in St Petersburg

But such a naive narrative structure, while accounting for the socio-humanitarian theme, leaves almost completely out of the account several important elements in the story: the complex pattern of digressions, including the so-called 'lyrical digressions', the strategic importance of the Person of Consequence, the richness of Akakiy's inner life, the recurrent interventions by supernatural forces and the intricate verbal play which becomes a dynamic force in the story in its own right. We must consider each of these elements in turn before finally committing ourselves to a final statement of the narrative structure which (by definition) is a dynamic working out of the story's deep theme.

The digressions in *The Overcoat* fulfil many functions. Moreover it is rare for any digression to have only one function. Some of them operate as elements in the narrative structure: the comment about the hero's surname, Bashmachkin, and the long anecdote about the choice of his Christian name contribute to a rather piecemeal general prologue whereby we learn some vital facts about Akakiy's past through a series of flashbacks. Vital? Well, in so far as the fate of Gogol's characters is partly determined by their names (or lack of a name, as with the Person of Consequence), the naming of Akakiy is important: as Gogol assures us, it was through this bizarre naming procedure that Akakiy 'came into being' (*Takim obrazom i prozoshet Akakiy Akakiyevich*). So the fantastic account of how he received such a very pedestrian name turns out to be more significant than a straightforward account of significant moments in his earlier life. But this flashback is also an exercise in Shandyesque digression for its own sake, part of an elaborate effort on the part of the author to downgrade plot, narrative structure and characterization as important aspects of narrative and present the fortuitous recollection as if it were logically motivated. As many of Gogol's most brilliant critics have shown, the naming episodes are as much elaborate games with words and sounds as anything else. The rather idiotic etymological pun about the surname Bashmachkin not implying that his forefathers wore 'shoes' (*bashmaki*) prepares the way for another etymological pun whereby the narrator assures us that despite its 'recherché' (*vyiskannym*) strangeness, the name Akakiy was not 'sought' (*yego ne iskali*)—and then goes on to relate the frantic search through the calendar of saints' names which led to his 'late' mother choosing Akakiy in desperation. Even 'the late' (*pokoinitsa*) is a rather gruesome temporal pun, since his mother is referred to as recently expired all the time she is struggling to choose. Not that the boundary between living and not living is so very clearly defined for Gogol, since this digression ends with two matching sentences where an animate masculine verb-ending only too easily slips into an inanimate neuter ending (this time a grammatical pun!): 'So this is how Akakiy Akakiyevich came about' (*Takim obrazom i proizo**shel** Akakiy Akakiyevich*). Then a short account of

Akakiy's first signs of animation—tears and a grimace of fearful foreboding, then: 'And so this is how all this came about' (*Itak, vot kakim obrazom proizo***shlo** *vse eto*).

We are in a grotesque world where names, puns, rumours and reputations become reality and the real is diminished, distorted or magnified to fantastic proportions. The very archaic and exotic sonority of all the alternative possible names gives way to the flat and unsonorous 'Akakiy' which manages to combine a Russian child's word for faeces, the Greek word for humility, a humbly obedient sixth-century saint,[12] and the anguished repetition of the existential question *kak?* (How?) A detailed analysis of this infinitely rich word play of this passage would show to what extent the *kak* root, or its answer *tak* figures in the frantic search for a name:

Kakoye *ona khochet vybrat'* . . .	*which* she wanted to choose . . .
Net, imena-to vse **tak**iye . . .	No, the names were all *the sort* . . .
kakiye *vse imena, ya, pravo,*	*What sort of* names they all were
nikogda ne slykhivala **tak**ikh . . .	I really never heard *such a sort* . . .
vidno, yego **tak**aya *sud'ba* . . .	obviously *such* was his fate . . .
kak *i otets yego* . . . **Tak**im *obrazom* . . .	*like* his father . . . And *so*

In one digression, then, Gogol has succeeded in combining apparent plot motivation, temporality, philosophical import, etymological, lexical and grammatical puns and pure phonetic sound play, to say nothing of the syntactic rhythms and intonation curves. And these functions are not fulfilled separately. They are fused so inextricably that the verbal play becomes part of the narrative structure: life is not separable from the act of talking about life: like Akakiy himself, life is a verbal coincidence. In the same way, digressions which appear to function primarily as a mode of characterization, such as the descriptions (despite the author's intentions!) of Petrovich and his wife, of Akakiy's speech mannerisms or the family life of the Person of Consequence, or those where the prime intention appears to be the depiction of social setting, such as the vignette of how the clerks of St Petersburg spend their evening or the tale of the titular councillor who made himself a waiting-room around his desk to ape his superiors, are equally examples of verbal play in their own right. As Boris Eikhenbaum pointed out,[13] there is no neutral intonation in Gogol. The description of the clerks' evening pursuits makes its impact less through the accuracy or vividness of social detail than through the fact that it is conveyed in a single sentence nearly a page long which sets up syntactic-intonational expectations which are thwarted by the bathos of the negative reference to Akakiy's way of spending his evenings: 'in a word even at the time when everything is striving to enjoy itself,—Akakiy did not give himself over to any enjoyment.'

While some of the digressions clearly serve to convey the framing elements of narrative structure, then, this is far from being their primary function. By their vigour, verbosity and virtuosity they have become more important than the story itself. As with *Tristram Shandy*, the reader begins almost to resent the way anything as prosaic as plot distracts from the poetry of the digressions. The so-called 'lyrical digressions'—for there are at least two—are not different in kind from the other digressions in *The Overcoat*. Only critics (from Belinsky onwards), who feel reassured if they can find a prominent and explicit moral or political motif in a work, have given the lyrical digressions in *The Overcoat* a particular significance for the theme of the story. If, however, we see them as excursions into an emotional-moral dimension, comparable with the excursion into a 'sociology-of-literature' dimension of the digression with which the story opens, or the excursion into the dimension of naming rites and word-play of the digression concerning Akakiy's christening, then we may recognize that they are on a par with the other gambits Gogol uses to amuse and distract his readers. Naturally, the degree of emotionality expressed is different, but the manner in which the digressions are constructed is not. As so often, Gogol allows a phrase to generate the digression: 'something could be heard in him of the sort that inclines one to pity' and the abstract notion of something inclining one to pity inevitably brings into being a person thus inclined: 'so that one young man suddenly pulled up sharp as if pierced through . . . ' This is the same mechanism as that whereby the general proposition about every private citizen considering the whole of society insulted generates a police superintendent who does feel insulted, and whereby the pun on *iskat* (to search) in *vyiskannym* (recherché) generates the desperate search for a Christian name by Akakiy's mother and godmother.

Moreover, the stylistic mannerisms of the 'lyrical' digressions are not significantly different from those which sustain or vary the tone of the other digressions: (1) the vagueness: 'one young man who had recently been appointed' (*odin molodoi chelovek, nedavno opredelivshiisya*), 'all but permitted himself' (*pozvolil bylo*), 'as if pierced through' (*kak budto pronzennyi*), 'as if everything had changed before him' (*kak budto vse peremenilos' pered nim*), 'some kind of unnatural force' (*kakaya-to neyestestvennaya sila*); (2) hyperbole: 'suddenly' (*vdrug ostanovilsya*), 'everything' (*vse peremenilos*), 'unnatural' (*neyestestvennaya sila*), 'for a long time after at the merriest moments' (*dolgo potom, sredi samykh veselykh minut*) 'many times' (*mnogo raz sodrogalsya on potom na svoyem-veku*), 'how many' (*kak mnogo*) . . . 'and even in that man' (*kak mnogo . . . i bozhe! dazhe v tom cheloveke*). Of course, the emotional tone of the vocabulary, the inversions (*predstavlyalsya, zakryval sebya rukoyu bednyi molodoi chelovek, sodrogalsya on*) the diminutives (*nizen'kii, 's lysinkoyu*) and the exclamatory '*bozhe!*' are distinctive to the 'lyrical' digression, but our sensitive young clerk has no greater claims to credibility as representative of the author's views than the touchy captain or Akakiy's godmother. All the digressions in the story, whether 'lyrical', 'linguistic', 'sociological' or 'philosphical' contribute to the story's rich verbal texture and to the flirtatious relationship between the author/narrator and his readers; none can claim any priority as 'thematic'.

In our search for the essential theme of *The Overcoat* we will have to return to the narrative structure and in particular the role of the Person of Consequence in that structure. In our schematic analysis of the narrative structure we assigned the role of the Person of Consequence only to the dénouement and the special epilogue, i.e. Akakiy's attempts to recover the coat lead him to beg the Person of Consequence to help and the latter's arrogant refusal leads Akakiy (or leaves him no option but) to catch cold and die. The threads of this injustice then get nicely tied up in the epilogue where Akakiy's ghost robs the Person of Consequence of *his* overcoat and changes his way of life and attitudes. But as Frederick Driessen pointed out in his subtle analysis of *The Overcoat*,[14] there are important parallels between the Person of Consequence and both Petrovich and Akakiy which make his role a much more prominent one.

Both Petrovich and the Person of Consequence are tyrants in their own sphere who boost their own morale by browbeating and disheartening the weak and dependent like Akakiy who turn to them for help. Significantly, the same phrases are used about them: Petrovich is pleased not to have let himself down by giving in to Akakiy's pleas: 'satisfied that he had both not let himself down and had also not betrayed his tailor's art . . . ' (see Russian Texts, No. 5) while the Person of Consequence is always held back from being sociable by the thought of 'letting down his consequence': 'he used to be pulled up sharply by the thought of whether he might through this be letting down his consequence' (See Russian Text, No. 6). And, of course, they are both much concerned with the effect their words have, as they look sideways (*iskosa*) at their hearers: 'He (Petrovich) was very fond of powerful *effects*, loved suddenly to throw a person into confusion in some way and then *glance sideways* at what sort of funny face the person would pull after such words.' (See Russian Texts, No. 7) 'While the Person of Consequence, satisfied that the *effect* had exceeded even his expectations . . . *glanced sideways* at his friend to discover how he viewed the matter.' (See Russian Texts, No. 8) Such parallelism of the syntax of these two quotations and the very words used could not be a coincidence. Moreover, Petrovich and the Person of Consequence are the only characters in the story whose early life, background and rise to their present position of authority are related (in flashbacks), and whose wives are described (accidentally, as it were, in digressions). There is even much playful discussion of the way they have acquired their present titles. Would it be too fanciful to see the general portrayed on Petrovich's snuff-box—albeit with his face pasted over with a scrap of paper—as the General of Consequence, ('face' or 'personnage') the *litso* who has become 'faceless' through bureaucracy and rank? As Driessen points out, Gogol was well aware of the parallel and wished to highlight it further in his penultimate version of the story where Akakiy dreams about Petrovich making a pistol-coat which will frighten the general. Fortunately he saw that such proximity would reduce the impact of the parallel and omitted it in the story's final version.

Structurally, then, Petrovich and the Person of Consequence represent Akakiy's encounters with authority. They frame the episode of his life with his coat: his new life begins to take shape with his visits to Petrovich; it loses all shape and meaning with his visit to the Person of Consequence. Matching complication and dénouement? Yes, but while Petrovich is not changed by his encounter with Akakiy, the Person of Consequence is. For him the conversation has as far-reaching consequences as Akakiy's first visit to Petrovich had for Akakiy. The parallels and contrasts between the Person of Consequence and Akakiy are even more striking and significant.

The Person of Consequence is introduced first by one of Gogol's negative throw-away lines: 'Exactly what the Person of Consequence's official position was and what it involved has remained unknown to this day.' which is not unlike the 'Bashmachkins who always wore boots' in tone. Then by a long digression on how he acquired his title, having started as a 'Person of No Consequence'. This digression depends on some elaborate punning and morphological word-play with the word *znachitel'nyi* which, outside the set phrase *znachitel'noye litso*, means 'significant'. This is a mirror image of the digression concerning how Akakiy came by his pathetically *in*significant name. The mirror-image contrast continues with an account of the general's abuse of his supposed power at his office. Even the three phrases he uses to browbeat his subordinates: 'How dare you? Do you know with whom you are speaking? Do you realize who is standing before you?' although so different in tone, seem to echo rhythmically and in their insistence on the second person Akakiy's haunting question: 'Leave me alone, why do you insult me?' (See Russian Texts, No. 9) Their speech habits in general are remarkably similar: as soon as the Person of Consequence finds himself in the company of anyone just one rank below him, he is prone to lapse into a pitiful silence and utter only occasional unclear and monosyllabic noises (cf. Akakiy's reaction to anyone faintly superior when 'he would express himself mostly in prepositions, adverbs and the sort of particles which have absolutely no meaning'). Both, it is made clear, are prisoners of rank at their respective ends of the hierarchy in bearing, behaviour and speech

> Seeing Akakiy's humble look and ancient uniform, he suddenly turned to him and said: 'What do you want?' in a sharp, firm voice, that he had deliberately practised previously in his room at home, alone in front of the mirror, a whole week before he even got his present post and general's rank. Akakiy promptly experienced the appropriate shyness, got a bit embarrassed and, as best he could, insofar as his tongue would allow him, explained with the addition of the particle 'um' even more than usual, that there had been this overcoat which was quite new . . .

Two further details: as Driessen points out, [15] Akakiy never even glances in the mirror, whereas the Person of Consequence studies himself in the mirror (almost as if Akakiy is too faint an object to have a reflection, while the general is almost nothing but reflected image, as the quotation above and the scene with his old acquaintance show); while Akakiy's entry to the office is never noticed, even by the doorkeepers, the Person of Consequence deliberately engineers meetings on the stairs. As with the mirrors, they both seem to stand on a line between reality and imagination, with Akakiy constantly trying to fade out and the Person of Consequence constantly trying to fade in.

We have needed to enumerate many details of the story here which would properly be analyzed on the level of characterization, but the parallels between these two characters are crucial for the narrative structure. (In any case, as we have pointed out, the analytical 'levels' are constructs to aid the systematic analysis: within the work itself they have no separate meaning and interact constantly.) The point is that the Person of Consequence is of considerable consequence for our interpretation of *The Overcoat*. I want to argue that our earlier schema of the narrative structure, the one which most commentators assume implicitly to be accurate, [16] is in fact quite inadequate, offers only an impoverished interpretation of the theme, and fails to integrate many of the features we are considering: the digressions, the role of the Person of Consequence, the inner life of Akakiy, the role of the supernatural and, above all, the style.

The Overcoat falls clearly into two parallel parts, each with its own narrative structure:

Figure 3

	Akakiy	*Person of Consequence*
Prologue	(Underdog) Naming, background, present life	(Top dog)
Complication	Acquisition of coat	Acquisition of Akakiy's problem
Peripeteia	Loss of coat	Loss of coat
Dénouement	Failure to find coat; death	Change of heart; humility
Epilogue	The supernatural takes over	

Thus the turning-point in each part of the story is the robbery of a coat, which for both Akakiy and the Person of Consequence is an object essential to their confidence and self-esteem, a buttress to their personality. What is more, the robbery takes place in both cases after a supper-party at which the central characters had drunk two glasses of champagne which make them 'merry' and when both of them were motivated by erotic plans, however subconscious: the general, though happily married, plans to visit his mistress; Akakiy, though wearing his 'life's companion', the new coat, 'even made as if to run, for no known reason, up to some lady or other who rushed past him like lightning, every part of her body filled with extraordinary movement'. Both react to the robbery by going home and shutting themselves away, greatly chastened.

By stressing all these parallels we must not, however, obscure the crucial contrasts between the two narrative structures: for the Person of Consequence status, respect from others, self-respect, family-life and a love-life on the side are real aspects of life, underwritten by the prevailing social order and social attitudes. For Akakiy all these things are temporary figments of an imagination which has been inspired by the acquisition of the overcoat, that symbol of status, companionship and love. Yet is the objective reality of the general's authority, power, family and mistress any more *real* than the subjective reality of these elements which the coat conjures up for Akakiy?

The story may divide up rather readily, as we have shown, into two distinct episodes, each with a clearly defined narrative structure. But they do relate. In terms of character, plot and setting, the two episodes are mirror images of each other. They meet in the visit of Akakiy to the Person of Consequence which resolves (however tragically) Akakiy's crisis and initiates the general's crisis. This scene, I would maintain, becomes the peripeteia of an overarching meta-structure in the narrative where Akakiy's subjective reality and the general's objective reality clash. Which is more real: the live Akakiy's wraith-like figure suffering every indignity that fate and his fellow-men inflict on him or the dead Akakiy's sturdy ghost wreaking vengeance on the mighty of this world? Which is more real: a little clerk's pride and dignity in doing his chosen job to perfection, virtually *living* his sad little vocation, or a bumptious general's status and 'consequence' which depend on rehearsals in the mirror, a chain of command at the office and three fierce but meaningless phrases? Which is more real: the love Akakiy feels for his coat which raises his whole life to a new plane and even makes him capable of an erotic awareness as he gazes at a saucy painting in a shop window or glimpses a lively young woman passing, or the cynical way the Person of Consequence takes his wife and family for granted and subscribes to the prevailing morality by keeping a mistress on the side?

Reality is on the borderline between life and death, between the objective and the subjective. For that matter, it is on the borderline between the real and the supernatural. James Holquist and Victor Erlich have both demonstrated decisively the extent to which Gogol's world is balanced on a tight-rope between the real and the supernatural.[17] Erlich puts it well: 'An Akakiy Akakiyevich-like specter starts haunting the city. At one point he seems to confront the "Person of Consequence" and brusquely to claim "his" overcoat—an experience which allegedly both frightens and chastens the overbearing official. I'm saying "seems", since we cannot be absolutely sure that this is what actually happens. So fluid is the boundary between reality and delusion in the murky world of this St Petersburg tale, so dense the fog of absurd rumors which thrive on the metropolitan muddle, that the "ghostly clerk" might well be a figment of the overbearing bureaucrat's frightened imagination, a phantom emerging from the vapors of his bad conscience.'[18] For Gogol the supernatural is characteristically demonic in form. The devil is clearly at large in the fantastic scenes at the end of the story where a policeman in Kolomna is prevented from giving chase to a ghost by a pig which rushes out and knocks him off his feet (like the demonic pig in the story of the two Ivans which steals the deposition), and when he catches up with the ghost is threatened by a monstrous fist of inhuman size belonging to a tall figure with enormous moustaches who disappears without trace into the darkness. No doubt the wind which bothers the Person of Consequence ('suddenly springing up from God knows where and for no earthly reason') is the same one which whistled along the streets from all four directions and blew the tonsillitis germ into Akakiy's throat. But the devil is lurking in wait for Akakiy from the very beginning. He cannot walk along the street without a chimney-sweep (from Hell?) brushing soot on him, or a builder spilling lime (for burning corpses?) on him. It is the devil that prompts Petrovich to ask such a fiendish price for a new coat, perhaps a devil who lurks in Petrovich's snuff-box with the obliterated general on the lid, for in Gogol's world snuff-boxes are coffins, sneezing really does warrant a 'God bless you!' and every lonely square is inhabited by a policeman who, despite his protective halberd, is usually caught in the act of taking snuff on his calloused fist, which, like Petrovich's tortoise-shell toe-nail, may evoke the Devil's hooves.

As Holquist sums up: 'The devil, the "unnatural power", is still at work, but he is now a symbol for the cruel, impersonal disorder of the city.' This element is certainly present in the story, yet to make it central is once again to stress a narrowly socio-moral theme. Holquist's earlier remarks about the St Petersburg setting are far more convincing in the light of our interpretation here

> The setting is again the fantastic city Gogol called Petersburg. It is once again a place where things get lost; but this time it is not a nose, or even just an overcoat, that disappears, but the 'hero' himself. He is lost not only in the sense of losing his way (although he does this, too), but also in the sense that his very being is brought into question . . . Lest it be objected that such confusion is explainable due to the simple nature and lowly rank of Akakiy, it should be remembered that the 'exalted personage' to whom he appeals after his coat is stolen is no more secure.[19]

The demonic setting brings us once more to our theme of the blurring of boundaries between the real and the supernatural, between the 'dead' world of bureaucratic ritual and the 'living' world of human hopes and aspirations, between 'objective' and 'subjective' views of reality, between the physical and the spiritual, between the two halves of a 'looking-glass' world.

But the boundary that Gogol blurs most brilliantly of all is that between the actual and the verbal, between what is said and the way it is said. Vladimir Nabokov has overstressed the point: 'The real plot (as always with Gogol) lies in the style', which sounds good, but ignores the notion of linear development which is essential to the plot. It would be more accurate to say that what impinges most on the reader is the verbal play, pushing the more conventional mechanisms of plot and narrative structure into the background. As we observed earlier of the digressions, so linguistic invention itself has become more important than the mere story: *histoire* turns to *discours* in a special way—the plot usually depends on some verbal association, a pun, a syntactic twist or a switch of intonation to advance at all. Nabokov again sums up the process in a memorable phrase about *Dead Souls*: 'In this dizzyingly centrifugal orgy of subordinate clauses, language is on the rampage.'[20]

Language in Gogol's stories becomes an independent, impersonal force which takes over the personality and will of mere human beings. This is made explicit in the descriptions of the two 'protagonists' of *The Overcoat*, Akakiy and the Person of Consequence. Akakiy is totally dominated by his inability to express himself meaningfully or even to finish a sentence he has started

> The reader should know that Akakiy expressed himself for the most part in prepositions, adverbs and, finally, the kind of particles that have absolutely no meaning. But if the subject was very difficult he even had a habit of not ending his sentences at all, so that quite often, having begun his speech with the words: 'That's really absolutely sort of...' there would be nothing further, and he himself would forget, thinking that he had already said everything.
> (See Russian Texts, No. 10)

A demonic force, a kind of incipient chaos, lurks in wait for Akakiy not only behind every corner of the St Petersburg labyrinth, but behind every thought that begins to shape itself in the mists of his mind. Nor does the Person of Consequence fare better with words. Despite his ability (and need) to inspire awe and obedience in all his subordinates, with a whole range of bureaucratic power gambits and three terrifying, but meaningless questions, he becomes pathetically speechless in the company of anyone below him in rank

> If he happened to be with his equals he was just as one should be, quite a decent chap and in many ways not even stupid; but as soon as he happened to be in company where there were people just one rank below him he would get quite out of control: he would fall silent and his state would arouse pity, particularly since he himself would even feel that he might have been spending the time incomparably better. Sometimes you could see in his eyes a powerful desire to join in some interesting conversation and circle, but he would be pulled up sharp by the thought: wouldn't this be just a bit much on his part, wouldn't it be too familiar, and wouldn't he be letting down through this his consequence? And as a result of these considerations he would remain all the

time in the same silent state, only occasionally pronouncing some monosyllabic sounds, and thus he acquired the reputation of being the most tedious of men. (See Russian Texts, No. 11)

Not only the social conventions and bureaucratic hierarchies, then, but real linguistic impotence reduce both Akakiy and the Person of Consequence to a state of monosyllabic gibbering.

But they are not the only characters in *The Overcoat* to be dominated by language; the narrator himself seems to be as much at risk from the verbal torrent which threatens all the time to sweep away out of control his plot, his characters and his narrative structure. If Akakiy and the Person of Consequence are victims of linguistic drought, however, the narrator is a victim of sheer intoxication with words. Our last quotation provides some good examples: 1. *Balance and rhythm*: the two halves of the first sentence combine similarity and contrast: 'If he happened to be with his equals . . . ; but as soon as he happened to be in company . . . ' (*Yesli yemu sluchalos' byt's rovnymi sebe . . . ; no kak tol'ko sluchalos' yemu byt'v obschestve . . .*). Similarly the three 'thoughts' that disturb the Person of Consequence in the second sentence are beautifully matched: 'wouldn't this be just a bit much on his part, wouldn't it be too familiar, and wouldn't he be letting down through this his consequence?' (*ne budet li eto uzh ochen' mnogo s yego storony, ne budet li famil'yarno, i ne uronit li on chrez to svoyego zhacheniya?*). While the conditional clause in the first sentence appears to end quite logically and appropriately, however, the main clause combines at least three features which are absolutely crucial to Gogol's style: 2. *alogism*, 3. *hyperbole*, 4. *bathos*. In this case the three are inextricably linked: the hyperbolic 'he simply got totally out of control' is not logically related to the absurd illustration of his uncontrolled state—'he kept silent'. But if we look more closely, we find a similar, if less startling play with alogism, hyperbole and bathos in the apparently logical first clause: after 'very decent' and 'in many respects' we might have expected something more positive than 'not a stupid man'. Gogol typically heightens the bathos of this alogism by throwing in the word 'even' (*dazhe*) which, as Chizhevskiy pointed out in a famous article[21] is the key word underlying a whole range of effects in *The Overcoat*. The tendency towards colloquialism in the narrator's choice of language—which Chizhevskiy refers to as an impoverishment but which we would rather view as an enrichment of the prevailing literary norm—is well illustrated by the particles in the phrase 'simply got totally out of control' (*prosto khot' iz ruk von*), in the self-interrogation of the free indirect questions in the second sentence quoted above.[22] The shift in point of view signified by this increased colloquialism is, of course, made explicit by the shift to the supposed internal monologue or thoughts of the character contained within the narrative mode, but the pun with which the sentence ends involves a more typically unmotivated Gogolian shift, recalling the narrator's long digression on the word 'significant' (*znachitel'noye*), set in train by the first mention of the Person of Consequence

What exactly the official position of the Person of Consequence was and what it involved has remained unknown to this day. The reader should know that a certain person of consequence recently became consequential, and up to then had been a person of no consequence. However, his post even now has not been counted as of any consequence in comparison with others far more consequential. But a group of people is always to be found for whom whatever is inconsequential in others' eyes is for that reason consequential. However, he strove to bolster up his consequence by many other means . . .
(See Russian Texts, No. 12)

Here sheer verbosity, a sort of intoxication with the endlessly expanding morphological and semantic frontiers of the pun, has driven out rational linear narrative. Language has become a demonic force in the story in its own right: it is indeed 'on the rampage'. The pun, like the alogism and the hyperbole-bathos mechanism offers a sort of verbal mirror dividing the 'real'-world of denotational meaning from the looking-glass world of infinitely receding connotations into which the reader risks falling with the narrator at every turn in the syntax.

So far we have illustrated some of the essential stylistic tricks Gogol plays on his readers on the basis of two short extracts, but examples of the same devices abound throughout *The Overcoat*. Hyperbole, for example, far from being expressed only by 'even' (*dazhe*) exploits a whole variety of syntactic and lexical devices and many other adverbial intensifiers as well. (See Russian Texts, No. 13, for all the examples below.)

1. *Hyperbole*
   (a) *Adverbial:*
   altogether quite recently; in some places *even totally* drunk; and *even* his brother-in-law and *absolutely all* the Bashmachkins; He would take it and get down *there and then* to writing it; they would tell *right there* in his presence all sorts of . . . stories; and inflict stinging flicks *indiscriminately* on *all* noses; have no idea *whatsoever*;
   not to finish off sentences *at all*, so that *very* often . . . and then *nothing at all* would follow and he *himself* would forget;

   (b) *Morphological* (particularly verb prefixes and suffixes), (see Russian Texts, No. 13; these cannot, of course, be translated);

   (c) *Syntactic* (particularly intensified negative contrast)
   nothing gets angri*er than all kinds* of departments;
   they weren*'t in the least* looking for the name . . . *there was no way* they could give *any other*;
   The porters *not only didn't* stand up . . . they *didn't even* look up;
   Hardly anywhere could you find a man who would live *like that*;
   It wasn't just . . . No . . . ;
   not just titular councillors, *but even* privy . . . *indeed even* those;

She was emitting *so much* smoke that you *couldn't even* see the cockroaches;

2.   *Qualification* (a mirror-image of hyperbole):
     a) *Morphological* (particularly diminutive and other modifying suffixes):
     Short*ish* in height, *somewhat* pock-marked*ish*, *somewhat* ginger*y*, *apparently*
     even *somewhat* short-sighted*ish*, with a *slight* bald-patch above his forehead;
     a uniform that wasn't green, but of *a kind of* gingery-mealy colour. Its *tiny*
     collar was narrow*ish* and low*ish*;
     and *something or other* would stick to it . . . either a *scrap of hay* or *some little*
     thread *or other*;

     b) *Syntactic*:
     A clerk that *you wouldn't exactly call* remarkable;
     When and at what season he had come to the department and *who* had appoin-
     ted him *was something no-one* could recall;
     our northern frost, *although, for all that, there are some who* say that it's very
     healthy;
     for some time he had *begun* to feel that he was *somehow getting* particularly hard
     stung in the back;
     he wondered finally whether *there mightn't be just the odd* fault;

3.   *Anti-climax* (often as much rhythmic as lexical after a graded hyperbole):
     shortish in height < somewhat < somewhat < somewhat even > haemor-
     rhoidal;
     His father < and grandad < and even his brother-in-law < and absolutely
     all the Bashmachkins > had worn boots;
     he burst into tears and made such a face < as if he had a premonition > that
     he would be a titular councillor;
     took to drinking rather heavily every feast-day, < at first on the main ones,
     < then indiscriminately, < on all church feasts, > wherever there was a little
     cross marked in the calendar, < so much smoke, > that you couldn't see >
     even the cockroaches;

     (The best example of this mechanism is the one we have already mentioned,
     quoted by Eikhenbaum,[23] where a complex fantasy nearly a page long about
     the multifarious ways St Petersburg clerks spend their evenings collapses in
     the abrupt negativity of Akakiy's emptiness:
        In a word, even at that time when everything is striving to amuse itself,
        > Akakiy Akakiyevich did not commit himself to any amusement.)

4.   *Incongruity* (involving many of the other devices we are examining):
     The potential names available (vs.) Akakiy's actual name;
     A stark imperative: *perepishite* (copy it) (vs.) an over-gracious euphemistic
     request: *vot interesnoye, khoroshen'koye del'tse* (here's an interesting, nice little
     matter);

The clerk's vision of Akakiy's relationship with his seventy-year-old land-
lady;

Such semantic non-sequiturs as:

> He was particularly skilful (vs.) at arriving under a window just in time;
> only perhaps if, coming from goodness knows where, a horse's muzzle
> came to rest on his shoulder . . . (vs.) only then would he notice . . . ; up
> the stairway, which, to do it justice . . . (vs.) was all awash with water and
> slops . . . ;

> the landlady was emitting so much smoke in the kitchen, (vs.) that you
> couldn't even see the cockroaches;

> slightly tipsy (vs.) or as his wife used to put it: 'he's up to his eyes in
> vodka, the one-eyed devil'.

The typically Gogolian device of confusing animate and inanimate phenomena, and so on.

5. *Puns.* If the other stylistic devices we have mentioned normally involve a
relationship between parts of sentences, the special virtue of the pun is that it
sets up an incongruity within a single word. We have mentioned some of
the most obvious and frequently cited examples:

(a) *Etymological:*

Bashmachkin	→	*bashmak* (shoe)
vyiskannym	→	*ne iskali* (seek)
sovetnikam	→	ne dayut *sovetov* (council)
znachitel'noye litso	→	ne uronit li *znacheniya* (would he not lose importance)

(b) *Semantic:*

proizoshel Akakiy Akakiyevich → *proizoshlo vse eto*
(Akakiy Akakiyevich came about → all that came about)
kto opredelil yego (who had appointed → defined him)
ne na seredine stroki → *skoree na seredine ulitsy*
(not in the middle of the street → rather in the middle of the line)
yel kusok govyadiny c lukom → *yel vse eto s mukhami*
(ate a piece of beef with onion → ate all that with flies)
kholod propekal v spinu → *on byl raspechen generalom*
(the cold burned his back → he was grilled by a general)

and so on.

Boris Eikhenbaum, in perhaps the most famous study of *The Overcoat*,[23] conclu-
ded from his analysis of these and other stylistic devices that, with the plot
reduced to a minimum and the centre of gravity switched to the devices of quasi-
oral narration (*skaz*), the personal tone becomes the organizing principle for the
story. Eikhenbaum was taken to task by his fellow Formalist, Viktor Shklovsky,
for his error in separating the style from the plot. The plot, says Shklovsky,[24] is
not reduced to a minimum. It is small-scale, but highly complex. The value of

the *skaz* is in preserving the scale: the author uses it to examine all the details through a magnifying glass. He accepts Akakiy's thought system and at the same time never loses sight of the triviality of that system. The *skaz* discourse has the same random, alogical, spasmodic rhythm as Akakiy's thought and speech processes. Despite the somewhat tendentious socio-political conclusion this leads Shklovsky to draw, his view of the relationship between the plot and the narrative mode seems to have a richer potential.

Our own analysis of the narrative structure of *The Overcoat* has revealed the central shift in the story from the dead world of the living Akakiy to the lively world of his ghost; from an impersonal world which dominates the little man to a world of personalities dominated by his spirit; from a 'real' world constantly threatened by demonic forces to a world of rumours where the demon spirits have taken over. We are in the realm of the 'grotesque' which, according to Kayser, is 'Not only something playfully gay and carelessly fantastic, but also something ominous and sinister in the face of a world totally different from the familiar one—a world in which the realm of inanimate things is no longer separated from those of plants, animals and human beings and where the laws of statics, symmetry and proportion are no longer valid.' [25] The metaphor which has presented itself time and again to describe this turning-point is the surface of a mirror. But we are never sure, ultimately, whether the original object or its reflection in the distorting glass is more real. As with narrative structure, so with plot: which are more real—the episodes which advance the action or the digressions which retard it? So with character: who is more real—Akakiy Akakiyevich, the named protagonist who acquired his name by a quirk of fate or the anonymous Person of Consequence, whose 'consequence' is constantly threatened by a pun? So with setting: which is more real— the mirage-like St Petersburg peopled by faceless bureaucrats or the rather solid city through which Akakiy's ghost pursues his vengeful course? So, finally, with narrative mode and style: which is more real—the story or the manner in which it is told, the denotational meaning of the words or their infinitely receding or demonaically interacting connotations? For in Gogol's grotesque world language is as much at risk as causality, personality and action.

NOTES TO CHAPTER 2

1. This model of the psychological and cognitive functions of art is excellently discussed in H. Kreitler and S. Kreitler, *Psychology of the Arts* (Durham, North Carolina, 1972).
2. The text used is from the eleven volume edition of Leskov's works: N.S. Leskov, *Sobranie sochinenii v 11 tomakh*, 8 (Moscow, 1956-1958, pp.154-73; author's translations).
3. See for instance, M.S. Goryachkina, *Satira Leskova* (Moscow, 1963, p.92) or A.G. Tseitlin in D.D. Blagoi, *Istoriya russkoi literatury*, III, pp.588-9.
4. The essence of the contrast is even contained in the quite different syntactic function of *yest'* (is/ was) in these passages.

5. Even Leskov's choice of a name for his hero is a pun on *post*, meaning 'fast' (*postnik*—'one who fasts')—the symbolic act of Christian renunciation, and *post* in the obvious, institutional (and non-Russian) sense of 'sentry post'. He highlights the pun by ending the passage quoted with the word and immediately beginning the next chapter describing the sentry's Christian act of mercy: 'Postnikov rushed to the steps . . .'

6. A typical Leskovism: the modern neutral word *rasskaz* has become *skazaniye* (archaic, high-flown) through reference to the Metropolitan.

7. The time actually referred to here is, of course, intermediate between 1839 and 1887, but by drawing our attention to his own knowledge of Miller's subsequent career the narrator reminds us of his own position in the time scale.

8. For an explanation of the significance of these terms see Robert Scholes and Robert Kellogg, *The Nature of Narrative* (Oxford, 1966, pp.13-14).

9. The distinction between *histoire* and *discours* was discussed by Roland Barthes in his 'Introduction à l'analyse structurale des récits' and Tsvetan Todorov in 'Les catégories du récit littéraire', both articles in *Communications*, 8 (Paris, 1966, pp.1-27 and 125-51 respectively). We will be considering it in greater detail in the chapter on Point of View.

10. ' . . . Leskov is read today for his qualities of form, style and narrative, and less than ever for his ideas. In fact very few of his admirers realize what his ideas were. Not that his ideas are at all obscure or concealed, but simply that the attention is concentrated on something different.

    'Leskov's most striking originality lies in his Russian. His contemporaries wrote in a level and even style, avoiding anything too striking or questionable. Leskov avidly absorbed every unexpected and picturesque idiom. All the various forms of professional and class language, every variety of slang, were welcome to his pages. But his special favorites were the comic effects of colloquial Church Slavonic and the puns of "popular etymology" . . . Another striking peculiarity that Leskov alone of all his contemporaries possesses is a superlative narrative gift. His stories are mere anecdotes, told with enormous zest and ability . . . His most original stories are packed with incident and adventure to an extent that appeared ludicrous to the critics, who regarded ideas and messages as the principal thing . . . This taste for verbal picturesqueness and rapid and complicated narrative is in striking contrast to the habits of almost every other Russian novelist.' (D.S. Mirsky, *A History of Russian Literature*, London, 1949, p.315)

11. References and quotations are taken from the text of *The Overcoat* in the six volume edition of Gogol's works: N.V. Gogol, *Sobranie sochinenii v shesti tomakh*, Gos. izd. Khudozhestvennoi literatury, III (Moscow, 1952, pp.129-60; author's translations).

12. 'St Akaky lived in the sixth century. He lived for nine years in the service of a certain evil *starets* (elder) and suffered all insults without complaint and performed scrupulously everything he was ordered to do. When he died, he answered to the question "Is he dead?" from the grave, "I am not dead, for it is impossible for one who is a doer of obedience to die". The elder then repented his hardness and for the rest of his days led a life which was pleasing to God'. (I. Bukharev, *Zhitiya vsekh svyatykh*, Moscow, 1892, p.624; quoted by F.C. Driessen, in *Gogol as a Short Story Writer*, The Hague, 1965, p.194)

13. B. Eikhenbaum, *Kak sdelana 'Shinel' Gogolya* (Poetika, 1919; reprinted in *O proze*, 1969, pp.206-26; translated in *The Russian Review*, XX, 1963, pp.277-99).

14. F.C. Driessen, *Gogol as a Short Story Writer* (The Hague, 1965, pp.182-214).

15. *Ibid.* p.208.

16. With the notable exception of Driessen.

17. James M. Holquist, 'The Devil in Mufti: the *Märchenwelt* in Gogol's short stories' (*PMLA*, 82, Oct. 1967, pp.352-62); Victor Erlich, *Gogol* (New Haven, 1969).

18. Erlich, *op. cit.* p.145.

19. Holquist, *op. cit.* p.361.

20. Vladimir Nabokov, *Nikolai Gogol* (New York, 1958, p.83).

21. D. Cizevsky, 'Zur Komposition von Gogol's "Mantel"' (*Zeitschrift für slavische Philologie*,

XIV, 1937, pp.63-94). Chizhevsky starts from a thorough and imaginative exploration of the curious range of functions fulfilled by *dazhe* in *The Overcoat*. Firstly, it is an 'impoverishment', a way of bringing literary language nearer the vernacular. Secondly, and more significantly, the many comic effects he achieves with the word are based on a 'kind of strange antithesis of what is significant and what is not': after *dazhe* we expect a climax—which Gogol does not give us. Sometimes we get the opposite of what we expect, i.e. an alogism. Thirdly Gogol makes his narrator approach the sphere of thought of his hero and tries to view the world through the little man's eyes. He sees the world from below, as it were: what is small becomes large. The reader constantly has to change his point of view and become aware of the insignificance of what is so vital to Akakiy.

The effects studied by Chizhevsky—in effect, colloquialism, alogism, hyperbole and bathos—are by no means only achieved by varying the functions of *dazhe* as we hope to show, but this curiously ambiguous modal word is an apt epitome of these aspects of Gogol's style.

22. Some good examples of 'free indirect style' are discussed by Michael Gregory in 'Old Bailey Speech in *A Tale of Two Cities* (*Review of English Literature*, VI, 2, 1966, pp.42-55). The best recent discussions among the proliferating literature on this problem are: Brian McHale, 'Free indirect discourse: a survey of recent accounts' (*PTL: A Journal for Descriptive Poetics and Theory of Literature*, 3, 2, 1978, pp.249-88); and Roy Pascal, *The Dual Voice: Free Indirect Speech and its Functions in the Nineteenth Century European Novel* (Manchester, 1977).

23. Boris Eikenbaum, *op. cit.*

24. Viktor Shklovsky, 'Shinel' (in *Povesti o proze*, II, 1966, pp.92-103): 'The string of events is not impoverished, but exaggeratedly small-scale; the number of things happening, however trivial, is actually considerable' (p.94).

25. Wolfgang Kayser, *The Grotesque in Literature and Art* (Bloomington, Indiana, 1963, p.224). Quoted by Erlich in his excellent study: *Gogol, op. cit.* p.3.

3

POINT OF VIEW

Dostoevsky: *A Gentle Spirit*
Tolstoy: *Father Sergius*

I

THE UNDERLYING central theme of a story is refracted, as we have seen, through the trajectory of the narrative structure. But the image is further refracted by the workings of point of view, and the particular pleasure that reading provides seems to be due largely to the play with point of view. This is not simply a matter of large-scale decisions on the writer's part about whether he will use a first person or third person narrator and how omniscient that narrator will be, or the degree to which the narrator will be a character in his own right. Any decisions on the structural level will permeate every sentence and phrase of the text. Every 'fact' in the world of the story will become fiction as it is mediated through a consistent point of view. Consistency is crucial here, as at all levels of the text; we normally perceive the narrated events and the characters' reactions to those events from one point of view at a time and the language of the text must be consistent with the personality and perceptions of the vehicle of that point of view, whether that is a character or a narrator figure. Of course, all kinds of variations are possible, involving rapid switching of point of view within a scene, the merging of two characters' points of view upon some event or the ironic interplay between the contrasting points of view of character and narratorial voice, but these complications demand an even greater degree of consistency and linguistic control of the dissonant 'voices'. It should be possible to relate elements in the language of an episode to a particular point of view, or, if there is ambiguity, to locate the source of the ambiguity in linguistic and rhetorical terms.

In spite of the significant work in this field by modern critics like Wayne Booth, Boris Uspensky and Gérard Genette,[1] there is still no adequate theory of point of view that can: (1) describe it as a coherent and rule-governed system; (2) relate it to other dimensions of narrative structure; or (3) relate the structural options of point of view to specific elements in the language of a work.

Perhaps we can make a start by distinguishing between syntagmatic and paradigmatic relations in a text. This is originally a linguistic notion, postulated by de Saussure and Jakobson, for discriminating between the two major axes of sentence relations, those of *chain* and *choice*. Roland Barthes[2] has usefully extended this distinction as it operates in literary texts, claiming that we may distinguish two types of function: (a) those, properly labelled 'function', which relate units in sequence through the narrative (i.e. syntagmatically) and (b) those which he labels 'indices' which relate a given unit to the more general, abstract purposes of the story (i.e. paradigmatically). We will be discussing this distinction in some detail in the chapter on plot, but for the moment we may note that some elements of point of view locate the 'sentient centre', or perceiving consciousness, at different points in time and space in the *sequence* of the story, while other elements have an 'indicial' significance in specifying the attitude of the narrator to other characters, to himself, to his audience and to the act of narration itself. Thus, in terms of the categories of analysis we are using in this book, point of view operates syntagmatically in relation to fable and plot and those elements of setting in time and place that vary in the course of the work, while it operates paradigmatically in relation to character and the fixed features of setting.

The relation between point of view and narrative structure is more complex since the units of both these categories act simultaneously as functions *and* indices. A shift in point of view may merely mark a point in the sequence of the narrative (e.g. a shift from the prologue to the initial complication) or it may take place at the very point of peripeteia in the narrative structure that defines the story's theme (as we shall see in Dostoevsky's *A Gentle Spirit*).[3] Here the distinction made by French semioticians[4] between *l'histoire* (the events narrated) and *le discours* (the manner of their transmission) is important both theoretically and for our description. As we saw in our discussion of Gogol's *The Overcoat* and as we shall see even more dramatically in our account of Dostoevsky's *A Gentle Spirit*, the very theme of the story involves a shift from *histoire* to *discours*.

Like all the aspects of point of view, this shift is manifested in features of the language of the text and we will attempt to enumerate some of the linguistic elements that normally realize each aspect of point of view and to account for these in terms of a theory of language use. Hopefully, the examples arising from our two strongly contrasting stories will help to clarify some of the distinctions we are making and to provide some check on their descriptive validity.

Figure 4 is an attempt to show in diagrammatic form the main relations between the 'sentient centre' of the point of view, whether character or narrator, or both, and the elements it is mediating, or refracting, namely, time, place and objects, other characters, self, the audience and the narrative act itself. Column 2 suggests some of the ways that these relations are manifested, 'objectively' as it were, in terms of the focus and memory of the perceiver, in the language and structure of the text. Here a camera analogy might be appropriate, since we are concerned with the apparent physical limitations on perception such as angle and distance from the subject, aperture (receptiveness), focus (clarity of vision) and shutter speed (intelligence). The author may adjust any of these at different points in his story and the pattern of his adjustments will probably bear some relation to the pattern of elements in the narrative structure and will certainly be manifested in the language. Column 3 attempts to indicate some of the more subjective and interpersonal elements of the language and rhetoric that reveal the perceiver's degree of involvement and sympathy with the elements he is relating to. We would emphasize that this is a very provisional schema, a kind of checklist

Figure 4.   Point of View Relations and their Realization

STRUCTURAL AND TEXTUAL
MANIFESTATION

1. Relation to	2. Focus and Memory	3. Degree of Involvement and Sympathy
TIME		
Rapid	Explicit dates and times	Adverbs of pace or tedium
Slow	Temporal adverbs	Rapid switches (*suddenly*)
Variations	Description/Scene	Contrasts in temporal deixis (*now/then*)
PLACE AND OBJECTS:		
Sight	Verbs of perception and	Personal/Impersonal forms
Hearing	sensation	Adjectives and adverbs of
Smell	Active/Passive voice	degree
Touch	Nominative/Dative case	'Loaded' lexis
OTHERS		
Opinions	Full rendering	Comments and comment
Personality	Depiction	adjuncts
Character	Interpretation	Explicit judgement
Moods	Direct/Indirect speech	'Slanted' depiction
Speech		Free indirect speech
SELF		
Opinions	Explicit/Implicit	Assertiveness
Personality	Self-awareness	Comparison with Others
Character	Honesty	Pride/Shame
Moods	Shifts of mood	Mood adverbs
Speech	Self-quotation	Self-irony
AUDIENCE		
Unperceived	Impersonal tone	Explicit comment
Mediated through	Characters as audience	Interpersonal features
characters	to narrative	(mood and modality,
Personified	Direct address	comment adjuncts,
Actual	Foregrounding of	lexical loading, particles,
	'phatic elements'	punctuation)
NARRATIVE ACT		
Causality	Explicit reference to	Degree of specification
As text	organization of plot	Stress and anxiety
As statement	Quotation, Cohesion,	Play with quotation
As revelation	Beginning—End	Sentence adverbs
	Control of facts	Attitude to reported speech
		Dramatic delays and exposés.

of the main types of point-of-view relations and their realization in structure and language. It is not a rigorously structural model with well-defined and comparable categories. It is doubtful whether the theory of point of view is sufficiently advanced in either linguistic or literary terms for this.

The linguistic model which has the most to offer poetics here is Systemic-Functional Grammar which distinguishes clearly between experiential elements in language on the one hand (Column 2) and interpersonal and textual elements on the other (Column 3).[5] If we can extend this distinction to the main rhetorical figures and the structural devices through which the story is refracted we will go some of the way towards relating the micro- and macro-level workings of point of view.

It may be useful to illustrate the point of view relations and their manifestations shown in Figure 4 from a number of stories considered in the book before we go on to study point of view in two stories in detail. In relation to *Time*, the explicit reference to dates in *The Man on Sentry Duty* or periods that have elapsed in *The Pistol Shot* or *Father Sergius* and the basic opposition between narrated description and dramatized scene vary the objective focus on a syntagmatic axis, while stress on the pace of events in *Makar's Dream* or the endless tedium of life in the bakery in *Twenty-Six Men and a Girl* express a degree of involvement. In terms of *Place*, the opening paragraphs of *Bezhin Meadow* are a model of succinct spatial orientation of an observer in both objective terms—the season of year and time of day—and subjectively as he responds to sounds, scents and the bitter cold. The ironic response of the sentient centre to *Others* (e.g. the post-stage master and his daughter) in the Pushkin story contrasts nicely with the emotionally involved view of the characters in Chekhov's *The Peasants*. The hero's view of *Himself* that is induced by the vision of the black monk in Chekhov's story combines both objective and subjective features, whereas the objective features of Dostoevsky's narrator-hero can only be gleaned, as we shall see, from the account that he gives of himself which is biased in every detail. Similarly, a first person narrative like that in *A Gentle Spirit* is likely to show a far greater preoccupation with the *Audience* and the very *Act of Narration* than the 'cooler' exposition of Pushkin or Turgenev, although Tolstoy, writing with a moralistic purpose, reveals his attitude to these through both structure and style more than we would expect in a third person omniscient narrative.

The inevitability of a point of view—an act of narration, *discours*, refracting a sequence of events, *histoire*—makes the short story and the novel essentially 'dialogic' in character. Bakhtin's term is relevant not only to the 'polyphonic' novels of Dostoevsky, which he explored so profoundly in his book on that writer,[6] but to all narrative genres which presuppose, and to some extent incorporate, an audience, a view of self and of others and a dialectical relationship with place and time.

II Dostoevsky: *A Gentle Spirit*, 1876; (*Krotkaya*)[7]

We may end a first reading of *A Gentle Spirit* totally bewildered, at a loss to pin down any one theme, or we may be tempted to restate the standard set of polarities through which the relationships in Dostoevsky's novels may be stated. In this power-game between the pawnbroker and his wife we may recognize all the antithetical pairs of the Dostoevskian dialectic that we perhaps recognized in Raskol'nikov and Sonia in *Crime and Punishment*, or Nastasia Fillipovna and Myshkin in *The Idiot*: pride/humility, power/submission, sadism/masochism, physical love/platonic love, corruption/purity, self-hate/self-love, wealth/poverty, society/the individual, alienation/atonement, rejection/acceptance, anomie/order, the irrational/the rational, and so on. Plenty of evidence could be adduced to prove any of these pairs was a prominent theme, yet none of them singly seems to represent 'the axis that maintains the unity and consistency in the work'. Any single choice of one of these pairs as theme, or even some global antithesis which embraced all of them, such as 'godliness/ungodliness' or §906/§907 of Roget's *Thesaurus*, would have to assign all the 'godly' features to the meek wife and all the 'ungodly' to the proud husband. But it is the essence of Dostoevsky that both characters have symptoms of, or at least a potential for, the antithesis of their primary features. (As Bresson makes clear in his film of the story (1969), the 'gentle spirit' has an instinctive sensuality which her husband is slow to recognize, while there is a purity of motive underlying his thought and behaviour which none of the other characters can penetrate to.[8])

In other words, the dialectic is not in the surface structure of the relationship, but in the deep structure of the character of both husband and wife. And this alters the whole relationship between author, narrator and reader. We are not presented by the author with a conflict between two characters embodying opposing forces which he eventually resolves in favour of one or the other. That would be the pattern of what Bakhtin characterizes as the 'monologic novel' of Dostoevsky's predecessors. Dostoevsky's 'polyphonic novel' embodies a conflict between two autonomous characters which may never be resolved, and this has implications for all the levels of structure and style.

It would be wrong, then, to interpret the story as the resolution of a conflict between any of the antithetic pairs we have enumerated, even though they are all manifestly present in the story. The theme, indeed, seems to operate at a rather curious point in the line of the communication process between the writer—his narrator—the created image of the reader—the real reader. As Wayne C. Booth expresses it: 'It is only as I read that I become the self whose beliefs must coincide with the author's. Regardless of my real beliefs and practices, I must subordinate my mind and heart to the book if I am to enjoy it to the full. The author creates, in short, an image of himself and another image of his reader; he makes his reader, as he makes his second self, and the most successful reading is one in which the created selves, author and reader, can find complete agreement.'[9] In *A Gentle Spirit* the essential theme is not, as in classic short stories by Pushkin,

Turgenev or Chekhov, confined to the facts and relationships narrated (*histoire*), but spills over into the process of narration (*discours*).

It certainly involves a conflict between all the warring forces that have been enumerated, but a conflict so complex and multi-dimensional, so utterly language-bound and so finally unresolvable that we should rather call it a *dialogue*: on the level of *histoire* the hero carries on a dialogue with the girl, with a set of social mores, with his past, with his future and with conflicting sides of his own nature. On the level of *discours* he carries on a dialogue with the chaos of his own unmanageable thoughts and with his readers, whom he addresses as his judges, and hence with mankind in general and ultimately with God. At a rather transitional level between *histoire* and *discours* are the various symbolic objects (icon, bed, revolver), acts (laughter, tears, silence, song) and literary references (*Faust, Gil Blas*, some themes from Pushkin, Dostoevsky's own earlier works) which all play their part in the *histoire* but whose very ambivalence enables the author and his narrator to carry on an implicit dialogue on the level of the *discours*. (Perhaps symbols and literary references are alike in that, while playing a role in the narrative, they have direct reference to outside the narrative, are both functions and indices, and thus link *histoire* and *discours*.)

This complex web of dialogues achieves coherence only through the artistic form of the story. A major preoccupation of the hero is collecting his thoughts together in some sort of coherent order: 'I just can't get my thoughts together I'll simply tell it all in order (order!)' until the end when the terrible truth shines only too clearly in his final despairing question: 'But no, seriously, when they take her away tomorrow, what will I be then?' A hint seems to lie in a note from Dostoevsky's notebooks: 'Throughout his life a man does not live, but composes himself, *autocomposes*' (*samosochinyayetsya*).

Robert Louis Jackson sees the quest for form, in a classical, ideal sense, as a subjective need of several of Dostoevsky's heroes such as Devushkin, Myshkin and Dmitrii Karamazov, all of whom struggle, like the hero of *A Gentle Spirit* to emerge from chaos: 'All his life Dostoevsky worshipped ideal form as the symbol and embodiment of moral and spiritual transfiguration'. [10] And Jackson examines the significance of *obraz* in Dostoevsky's thought: 'The moral-aesthetic spectrum of Dostoevsky begins with *obraz*—image, the form and embodiment of beauty—and ends with *bezobrazie*—literally that which is "without image", shapeless, disfigured, ugly. Man finds pleasure (he also calls it beauty) in *bezobrazie*, in the disfiguration of himself and others, in cruelty, violence, and, above all, sensuality—and "sensuality is always violence". Aesthetically, *bezobrazie* is the deformation of ideal form (*obraz*). The humanization of man is the creating of an image, the creating of form (*obrazit'*).' [11] Seen from this point of view, *A Gentle Spirit* turns out to be central to Dostoevsky's moral and aesthetic philosophy, for the crucial symbol in the story is an *obraz*: [12] the icon which the girl as a final resort has to pawn, in itself a symbol of holiness, purity, inviolability, healing (making whole); it represents a part of her which the pawnbroker senses he can never touch with his financial power, his pride or his sensuality; and clutching the icon to her breast as she jumps to her death, she is depriving the hero of that integration, that wholeness, which he had sought through his relation with her. It was in fact the icon mentioned in the newspaper report [13] that so fired Dostoevsky's imagination and provided the crucial link with the theme of the retired officer-pawnbroker-underground man which had been lying dormant in his artistic consciousness: 'It added that she threw herself out and fell to the ground *clutching an icon*. That icon in her hands is a strange feature—quite unheard of in suicides'. [14]

Tentatively, then, we may define the theme of *A Gentle Spirit* as man's search for form, wholeness, integration. The hero must fulfil an intellectual need to pull all the threads of his thoughts together, an emotional need to establish a relationship with another human being, a moral-aesthetic need to synthesize the warring antitheses of his formless (and therefore *bezobraznyi*) nature.

One way in which the narrator-hero hopes to pull the threads together is by imposing a time structure on the story. He has a point of view in relation to time and, like him, we have to make a considerable effort to recreate the fable accurately because the temporal sequence is so dislocated. (We will be discussing in the next chapter the reasons for needing to reconstruct the fable in a work of fiction.)

We begin at the end: the heroine is dead and the narrator is trying to tell everything in its order. This foreknowledge we have of the heroine's death colours our response to each stage of the story: 'Through an attribute of my nature' he wrote in his *Writer's Diary* in 1881, 'I begin from the end and not from the beginning, present my whole thought at once. I have never been able to write gradually, making measured approaches and presenting my idea only after having previously chewed it over and proved it as far as possible.' [15] Jackson, who quotes this note, comments: 'To present a whole thought at once, of course, is to present an image.' [16]

The image of the dead girl laid out in her coffin, lined with white *gros de Naples* (the exotic south the hero never attained?) and resting on two card tables (the world of gambling and finance conquered by the purity of death?) provides an unspoken comment to all the hero's explanations and protestations. Bakhtin most aptly characterizes Dostoevsky's 'dialogic soliloquy' as 'speech glancing over its shoulder at another's speech' (*slovo s oglyadkoi na chuzhoye slovo*). [17] A vital part of the 'other's speech' here is the silent comment of the body in the coffin. Several times the chapter divisions become meaningful because they hinge around the recollection of this image: the past he is narrating is directly and ineluctably linked to his present predicament.

Certain of the shifts in temporal sequence are mere mechanical consequences of Dostoevsky's choice of a first person narrator. The girl's past life and present predicament are outlined through facts he manages to glean during their business conversations and a longish flashback, presented as Lukeriya's answer to his investigations (such as any author might resort to). The pawnbroker's own past is presented in a more complex way: his better birth and circumstances are directly contrasted with hers and then a series of hints about becoming a pawnbroker to revenge himself on society prepare us for the 'Efimovich episode', which, although it represents the first blow his wife strikes in *their* duel, her first assertion of independence, is primarily a device to uncover for her and the reader the terrible secret in her husband's past. First we learn from the narrator that Efimovich had played a sinister role in his disgrace, then his wife challenges him with the few facts she has managed to glean from Efimovich about his disgrace and later poverty. The full story only emerges later in an orgy of self-justification he treats us to in recalling her illness which followed the revolver incident (her second abortive blow for independence). Thus the memory of his disgrace in refusing to fight a *real* duel has become the chink in his armour which gets probed each time he is threatened in the imaginary duel he initiates with his wife, the 'gentle spirit' (the only duel this Russian Mephistopheles knows how to fight).[18]

While the reconstruction of the fable reveals to what degree the time sequence of mere events is dislocated, the narrator is nonetheless obsessed with time; we are given exact times for his attempts to get his thoughts straight (6 hours), her age (3 months under 16), her visits to the shop (next day, 2 days later), the period since her parents' death (3 years), since the fat grocer had had his eye on her (a year), his age (41), the number and frequency of their visits to the theatre (3 times, once a month), the frequency of her excursions with Efimovich (the next day, the day after, 2 days later), his period of poverty (3 years), the length of his eavesdropping session (a whole hour), the time he took to glance up at her after the revolver episode (5 minutes), the length of her illness (6 weeks), the season when she started singing (mid-April) and many other precisely noted moments and periods which create the illusion that the narrator and we have a firm grasp on structured time. But note the complexity of the tense-switching as the narrator's fevered thoughts move from his present predicament back to past events, partially forward to hints at the present consequences of those events, further back to the roots of it all in the distant past, forward to a present challenge to his audience and forward again to his fears for the future: the flight of Dostoevsky's time machine is vertiginous and the glimpses of signs like adverbials of time that we pass on the way only make us dizzier: 'at this point—for the first time—then —for the next day—then—now—a few days ago—in five minutes', etcetera (*tut-to—v pervyi raz—togda—nazavtra—potom—teper'—neskol'ko duei nazad—cherez pyat' minut*, etcetera).

The narrator's dialogue is with time itself. His attempts to create order (*poryadok!*) to gather all the threads together, to give form to the anarchy of his thoughts and memories, are constantly thwarted by the speed and multidimensionality of human thought. But the reader (one of the addressees in the dialogue whose presumed assumptions provide one element in the 'other's speech') is not an uninvolved spectator. He is drawn into the maelstrom despite himself and must struggle to create order out of the chaos. We are challenged not only on the level of *histoire*, as in most prose fiction, but on the level of *discours*.

Booth discusses the battle with time in *Tristram Shandy* as a prototype for that of modern narrators among whom we must include the hero of *A Gentle Spirit*

> Sterne faces, like the reader, the world of chaos in fleeting time as it threatens the artist's effort to be true to that world without lapsing into chaos itself. It is hardly surprising that modern critics have tried to account for the whole book as a battle with time, or as an effort to ascend from the world of time into a truer world. It is more than that, but in the valiant figure of the little eccentric we do have a prefiguring of the many modern narrators ... who dramatize James's message by fighting the reader's battle against time. [19]

If the stylistic dominant on the level of the Fable is the conflict between rapid & extreme switches of tense & temporal adverb (dislocation of *time* structure) and a pedantic accuracy in giving us exact figures for ages, periods, etcetera (attempts to reimpose a time structure), on the level of *Plot* is the conflict between a vague & enigmatic, often self-contradictory imprecision as to motives & consequences (dislocation of *causal* structure) and the pseudo-precision of the conjunctions and parenthetical phrases & certain syntactic structures (giving the illusion of comprehending the underlying causal patterns).

A narrator who prefaces so many sentences with 'the main thing is; the crucial point is; that's it; that's just the point; the fact is that; it wasn't just that; in a word; here's what it was; here's how it was; but that's just how it was; that is to say; precisely; of course; naturally; precisely'; etcetera (*glavnoye—samoye glavnoye —v tom-to—vot v tom-to i—delo v tom, chto—malo togo—odnim slovom—vot chto—vot tak—ved' eto tak i bylo—to yest'—imenno—konechno—razumeyetsya— toch'v toch*, etcetera), must, we feel, have a firm grasp on the thread of events. The same impression is conveyed by the negatively introduced antitheses: 'But for me the main thing was *not that ... but* that ...' (*No glavnoye alya menya bylo ne v tom ..., a v tom, chto ...*); or by the intensification device noted by Vinogradov in his article on *The Double* (his classic example is 'with anxiety, with great anxiety, with extreme anxiety' (*s bespokoistvom, s bol'shim bespokoistvom, s krainim bespokois- tvom*). The device is usually less obvious in *A Gentle Spirit*: at its simplest we have intensifying series of near-synonyms:

I believed in this blindly < crazily < horrendously

just looking for trouble < absolutely begging for trouble

Oh, I was never liked even at school < always and everywhere I've been disliked.

She was a tyrant < the unbearable tyrant over my spirit < a torturer

Oh, I still didn't understand then! < At that time I still didn't understand anything at all! < I still haven't understood a thing to this very day!

But this is the truth < I mean the very truest of truths.
(See Russian Texts, No. 14)

There are two slightly more complex forms of the same device: the merging of two notions which intensifies them both: 'But I wanted breadth + I wanted to graft breadth on her very heart → to graft it onto her heart's glance, don't you see?' and 'She was a wild beast + she was in a fit → she was a wild beast in a fit.' (See Russian Texts, No. 15) and the rhetorical pedantry of the shift from modal to finite verb in: 'I want to judge myself and I am judging. I must speak *pro* and *contra* and I am speaking.' (See Russian Texts, No. 16)

On the other hand the narrator's grasp on reality often slips and the vague pronouns: something, someone, (*chto-to, kto-to*), adverbs: sometime, thus, not like that (*kogda-to, tak, ne tak*) and conjunctions: as though, it wasn't as if (*kak budto, neto chtoby*) proliferate, particularly when he is under stress, as when he tries to justify his treatment of the girl soon after the marriage: 'But you see I understand now that I was wrong about something! At this point something turned out wrong . . . Here was a plan. But then I forgot something or left it out of account. There was something here I couldn't do' (see Russian Texts, No. 17) or when he tries to describe her singing: 'But now her little song was so weak—Oh, not exactly mournful (it was some romance or other), but something seemed to have cracked in her voice and broken, as if her little voice couldn't cope, as if the song itself was sickly.' (See Russian Texts, No. 18) He would like to explain her singing as due to some external force that had possessed her, just as he had been the victim of Fate at the time of his banishment from the regiment. Here we have a semantic shift from the neutral meaning of *sluchai* (event, happening) to its deeper sense (chance, fate) which the adjective *sluchainyi* (accidental) preserves: the first sentence shows the pun is deliberate

Although *what happened* in the regiment was due to my unpopularity, it was undoubtedly a matter of *chance*. I might add that there's nothing more insulting or unbearable than to be ruined by some *contingency* which might and might not have been due to some *unfortunate* piling up of circumstances which might have floated past like clouds. For an intelligent person it's degrading. What *happened* was as follows.
(See Russian Texts, No. 19)

This sense of chance governing his actions extends to his marriage: 'But then I got married. Whether by *chance* or not, I don't know' and to the revolver episode: 'For example, how could I, without *the chance assistance* of that terrifying revolver catastrophe, convince her that I wasn't a coward and that I'd been accused of cowardice in the regiment unjustly? But the catastrophe brought things to a head *just right*' (i.e. also as chance would have it).

The narrator-hero seems to oscillate between extremes of wilful choice of his actions and an irresponsible abdication of will and responsibility: 'Everything turned out just as I had anticipated and presupposed, even though I was unaware that I was anticipating and presupposing it.' (Very modern to blame it all on one's sub-conscious!) Of course the hero gives the trick away in his afterthought: 'I don't know if I am expressing myself comprehensibly.' As always, the problem has been shifted from the *histoire* to the *discours*, and this is one of the riddles we have to solve as we read the story.

Consider how many causal/linguistic relationships we have to pin down in the title and the first short paragraph alone

> Who was I (*why 'was', if he is writing?*) and who was she (*again 'was'? and why both anonymous?*) . . . (*why a pause?*) Just as long as she's here (*where?*)— everything's still alright: (*why?*) I go up and look every minute or so; (*at what?*) but they'll take her away tomorrow (*ill? dead?*)—and how will I remain on my own? (*why does this worry him?*) Now she's in the hall (*which one?*) on a table, (*she must be dead!*) they put two card tables together (*of all things!*) and tomorrow there'll be a coffin and white, white satin, and yet that's not the point . . . (*why the interruption? Why is the coffin lined with white satin not the point? Must we focus on the body itself? Or do mere factual details distract from the main task—rationalizing it all—and the main focus—the narrator himself?*)
>
> (See Russian Texts, No. 20)

We have defined *Plot* as the causal unfolding of the narrative, the selection and arrangement of events in such a way that they form a logical sequence. But how confident are we in tracing events back to their causes? Becoming a pawnbroker was, it seems, something to do with wanting to revenge himself on society which was due, it appears, to his disgrace in the regiment, due to his morbid pride, due to the fact nobody had ever loved him . . . But each part of this train of causes must be reconstructed out of a series of guesses. And did his wife commit suicide because his early cold neglect of her had turned to a hysterical longing, or because she was too ill to recover her strength, or because her gentle nature could no longer bear the battle of wills he imposed on their relationship, or because this was a last, trump card (or a Last Trump card) she had to play to achieve victory over him? There are two possible reasons we might reconstruct for the wilful destruction of causality in *A Gentle Spirit*, both of course, anticipated by the narrator. On the one hand: 'Perhaps this never happened, perhaps I didn't even think all that even then, but all that must have happened, even without the thought because I've done nothing but think about it every hour of my life since then' (i.e. a thing is true because he thinks it—the ultimate in solipsism). On the other hand: 'So perhaps in order to pose a riddle I did all that nonsense.' (i.e. he wants to torment us as well as himself with the riddles which obsess him. But *histoire* and *discours* have merged and these two reasons are really the same: the narrator needs us to help him pull all the threads together and achieve integration, but at the same time we are figments of his own imagination.)

In analyzing the stories by Leskov and Gogol in the previous chapter we found it useful to start by presupposing a symmetrical structure hinging on the peripeteia, or moment of reversal, which is motivated by the *complication* and resolved by the *dénouement*, these normally being 'framed' by a specific prologue and general prologue and a specific epilogue and general epilogue.

If our analysis there was valid it seems that the most revealing way of uncovering the narrative structure may be to find the peripeteia and work backwards and forwards from there. Our search for the peripeteia in *A Gentle Spirit* might focus on three possible moments of reversal.

The revolver episode is the first moment in the story where the relationship seems to shift key: the complication would then be the battle of wills between husband and wife, won at this point by the husband's phenomenal strength of will in continuing to pretend to sleep, and resulting in the girl's surrender, 'beaten but not forgiven' (*pobezhdena, no ne proschena*), her illness and eventual suicide. This, in a sense, is the most *physical* possible peripeteia, with the conflict brought to the surface in a highly dramatic encounter. It also occurs conveniently at the end of Chapter I. The theme, however, is not the progress of their relationship as such, but the hero-narrator's response to it, and the outward calm he manages to maintain in his wife's presence is not reflected in either the content or the style of his subsequent thoughts. Chapter 2 opens with the highly significant 'flash-forward' to his present predicament, his attempts to pray and to sleep, and the most ambiguous reference to condemned men who sleep exceptionally soundly on their last night (he cannot sleep, so, by a perversely false syllogism, he must be innocent!). When he reverts to the narrative, too, there is no release from his tension: 'it was horribly fascinating for me to try and guess: what exactly is she thinking at this moment?' Two consecutive sentences involving chiasmus seem to keep the tension high rather than resolving it:

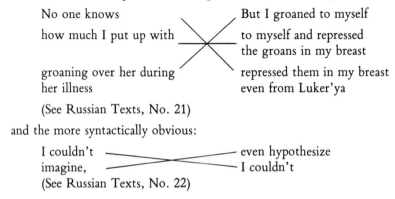

No one knows ⟋ But I groaned to myself

how much I put up with ⟍⟋ to myself and repressed the groans in my breast

groaning over her during ⟋⟍ repressed them in my breast
her illness even from Luker'ya

(See Russian Texts, No. 21)

and the more syntactically obvious:

I couldn't ⟍⟋ even hypothesize
imagine, ⟋⟍ I couldn't
(See Russian Texts, No. 22)

Moreover, the long flashback which follows is a full recapitulation, a reliving almost, of the circumstances of his disgrace in the army, with a welter of protestation and self-justification in which the narrator seems even to lose control of the language he uses. Vinogradov[20] speaks of the automatized, puppet-like style of Golyadkin as his schizophrenia develops. Here, too, the narrator turns into a regimental parrot, reverting from his highly subtle, tortuous and often ambiguous style to a parody of the cliché-ridden vocabulary and syntax of the career army officer

> he had it in for Bezumtsev; it was not a personal matter but concerned the regiment as well and since of all the officers of our regiment only I was there he thereby proved to all the officers and spectators who were present in the buffet that there might be certain officers in our regiment who were not so touchy as to their own honour and that of the regiment; 'after a brilliant career in uniform'; And so—if it had to be shame, let it be shame, if disgrace, then disgrace, if downfall, then downfall, and the worse it was, the better. (See Russian Texts, No. 23)

The latter sentence—a repetitive string of clichés—becomes a substitute for thought.

The revolver episode, then, resolves nothing on the *psychological* plane. A far more convincing peripeteia is the physically undramatic, but psychologically tension-fraught, moment when the girl sings to herself. The complication here is the relationship which has up to now been dominated and controlled by *his* will, so that all her attempts at self-assertion—offering clients more money, refusing to go to the theatre, pretending to have an affair with Efimovich, contemplating shooting her husband in his sleep—are bound to fail. All these forms of revolt are too conventional and her husband rejects all conventions: the challenge of the seduction of his wife was as false and pointless as the challenge to a duel over a trivial insult to the regiment. When he eavesdropped on Efimovich and his wife, he was motivated by curiosity, not by anger and revenge. Here are two people playing a relationship game with incompatible rules and as long as she follows the normal social rules he can continue to win their duels. But her illness is partly psychosomatic: her body has discovered the power of passive resistance and her husband's usual weapons of negligence and irony are blunted. When the girl begins to sing she is half-consciously using this unconventional form of resistance as a defence. In a sense, too, she has discovered herself and reverted to her own true nature. This humility, passivity and gentleness represent the real 'gentle spirit' and she no longer needs his tyrannical pity; her very completeness is a total defence against the cruel aunts, fat grocers, and sadistic pawnbrokers of the world she was born into. Her husband is stupefied: she is capable of ignoring him as he ignored her: 'She is singing, and in my presence. *Has she forgotten about me, then?*' The blindfold has fallen from his eyes, conveniently anticipated in the preceding section: 'But a blindfold hung before me and blinded my mind. A fateful, terrible blindfold!' and signalled for us in the title to this section and in his reactions 'I noticed suddenly', 'and suddenly it struck me at that moment', 'it hit me extremely and all at one instant', 'blindfold!' His style becomes imprecise and over-anxious as he tries to define the sound of her voice in complex concessive and qualifying clauses: 'At that time her voice was still *fairly* strong and clear, *though* uncertain, *but* terribly pleasant and healthy. But now the little song was so frail—Oh, *not exactly* mournful (it was some romance or other) but *as if* there was *something* cracked and broken in her voice, *as if* the song itself was ailing.' (See Russian Texts, No. 24) If the right adjective eludes him in describing her voice, his attempts to define his own reactions are quite frenetic: 'People will laugh at my anxieties, but nobody will ever understand why I got so anxious. No I wasn't sorry for her yet, but this was something quite different again. At first, at least for the first few minutes, there was a sudden onset of puzzlement and a terrible astonishment, terrible and strange, morbid and almost revengeful.' The dénouement resulting from this peripeteia, then, represents their roles reversed, with the girl calmly being her meek but self-sufficient self and ignoring her husband, while he searches desperately for ways of penetrating her armour. Her suicide holding the icon of Virgin and Child becomes her ultimate defence, her final victory over him and the supreme symbol (*obraz*) of her meekness.

Thus the singing episode is certainly the moment of reversal for the girl and for the abstract power of those blessed in the Sermon on the Mount. But what is its significance for the narrator-hero? Within their relationship it reverses his role but as far as his relationship with himself and the world is concerned it leads nowhere. It only deepens his predicament and intensifies his loneliness. The girl's suicide is not *her* tragedy but *his*! (so even the 'tragic irony' of our foreknowledge of her death was ironic). He is left totally alone with his dialogue. In other words, the attempt to establish a real relationship has failed and he is left trying to establish a dialogue relationship with us, his readers and judges. The reversal is from *histoire* to *discours*, and the peripeteia is her death, the fact with which the story ends—and begins. Our attempt to discover a neatly symmetrical narrative structure for this story has, to our delight, failed. There is a symmetry in the surface structure, within the *histoire*, but in its deep structure the story is about the relationship between *histoire* and *discours* and this is not symmetrical but cyclic: the narrator finds no answer to the tragic question at the end: 'When they take her away tomorrow what will become of me?' except to retell his story starting with the same question. In his particular circle of hell he must spend eternity rolling his story up the hill only for it to roll down on top of him; retelling it in an attempt to gather his thoughts together and to create a relationship with his audience, only to be faced with 'inertness' and the loneliness of man: 'Men are on their own on earth—that's the trouble!' Only his readers succeed in recreating a whole out of the chaos of the story.

Dostoevsky manages to illustrate that 'the medium is the message' in a sense more profound than McLuhan intended. Is he teasing us when he pretends in his preface to the story that he has achieved something miraculous in presupposing a stenographer who could note down every thought in this soliloquy, just as Victor Hugo's condemned man had every thought noted to the very last? For the miracle of *A Gentle Spirit* is not in this fairly obvious device, but in the subtlety of structure which hinges on a switch from *histoire* to *discours* and in the dialogic complexity of style in which *histoire* and *discours* are in constant tension and interaction.

Barthes says of the modern psychological novel: 'Nowadays writing is not narrating, but saying that one is narrating and relating the whole referent ("what is said") to the act of saying; this is why part of contemporary literature is no longer descriptive, but transitive, enabling one to achieve in the word a present so pure that the whole discourse becomes identified with the act of delivering it, the whole *logos* being brought together—or extended—into a *lexis*'.[21] On these grounds *A Gentle Spirit* is unmistakably an ancestor of the modern psychological novel.

This interaction between the narrative and the act of narration, between *histoire* and *discours* is crucial to our analysis of point of view. Although we have gained some insights into the play with point of view within and across the story line, so far we have not even approached the question of the 'tone' of the narrative, and most readers would probably agree it is the narrator's tone that we most recall after our first reading of the story. 'Tone', of course, is a notoriously vague word which is often used as a substitute for analysis; we must attempt to be more precise. Here we mean the way the language of the *discours* conveys the narrator's attitude to his narrative, to his audience and to himself. His attitude to other characters and to society at large is conveyed rather through the *histoire* (in so far as the two are separable), and it will be better if we examine these in relation to character and setting. The narrative and discourse are so closely intertwined that extracting phrases which are indisputably discourse from their immediate context is a rather artificial procedure, but one to which we must resort in order to illustrate the pressure of discourse on the narrative.

The narrator's key preoccupation, with regard to his narrative, as we saw in our study of plot, is with creating order out of chaos: 'I want to get it clear for myself.' This is made difficult for him by the pressure of time: 'For six hours already I've been trying to clarify things and still can't gather my thoughts together'; 'But what's the matter with me. If I go on like this, when will I pull everything together? Quick, quick—no that's not it at all, oh God!'; 'I'll summarize this scene.' Besides these explicit references to time, the whole of *A Gentle Spirit* has an urgency of tone which we must consider again when we attempt to define the stylistic dominants of the story. The unreliability of memory also threatens the coherence of the narrative

I'll simply tell it in order (order!)

I remember, I've forgotten nothing!

Here was a plan. But then I forgot something or left it out of account. I didn't manage to do something at this point.

But I remember, I remember!

I can only recall . . . I recall as through a fog . . . I can recall only . . .

The horror of what has happened and what he knows about himself makes full rationalization impossible. As he tells us at the start, at a subconscious level he understands only too well

That's exactly my horror that I understand everything!

I want to capture it all, all that filth. Oh, the filth!

Oh, how terrible is truth on this earth!

and note the title of the suicide section: 'I understand too well.' (*slishkom ponimayu*). But the narrator claims that his biggest problem in reconstructing the story is his confusion and inability to recognize causes and consequences, so on the one hand we have

The crucial thing was . . .

You see the main thing was . . .

But, you see, I understand now.

And I understand my despair fully. Oh, I understood it!

Oh, that was the most crucial thing of all.

The main thing was, I didn't believe . . .

I could see it all, all down to the smallest detail.
(See Russian Texts, No. 25)

On the other hand, in total contrast: 'Oh then I didn't understand! I still didn't understand anything at all then! To this very day I didn't understand! And even now I don't understand, even now I understand nothing' (see Russian Texts, No. 26) where the escalating clauses we noticed earlier twice reveal his anxiety

And yet . . . and yet, what am I saying! Stupid, stupid, stupid!

Oh, madness, madness! A misunderstanding, an unlikelihood, an impossibility!

But why not? Was that really so unlikely?
Could one really say that was possible?
(See Russian Texts, No. 27)

The narrator is much concerned with this question of the authenticity of his story. He begins self-consciously: 'Gentlemen, I am far from being a literary type, as you can see, and let that be, but I'll tell it as I understand it.' (See Russian Texts, No. 28) The authenticity of the seduction scene with Efimovich is tested by literary standards too: 'The wittiest author of a high society comedy could not have created this scene of mockery.' The irony of this attitude to his narrative and his readers is carried too by several literary references. He alludes to the callousness of youth with a misquotation from Pushkin's *The Demon* (1823) and another in close succession from Lermontov's 'Believe not, believe not yourself, oh youthful dreamer' (*Ne ver', ne ver' sebe, mechtatel' molodoi*) (1839). The titles of operettas they saw on their few monthly visits to the theatre are a clear comment on her motivation (or his?)—*Hunting after Happiness*, and on the submerged symbol of a caged bird, *The Song Bird*, which becomes so significant with the 'psychological' peripeteia (although characteristically, the narrator tries to cover his tracks with qualifications: on the one hand he is not sure (*kazhetsya*); on the other, these details are 'not important' (*O, naplevat', naplevat'!*)).

There are echoes of Pushkin which are unmarked—and may have been unconscious—but which seem too strong to ignore. For all the social and psychological differences in the protagonists, the shadow of Onegin and Tatyana seems to hang over the pawnbroker who refuses the love of an innocent girl only to find it is beyond his reach when he comes to recognize what he was refusing. In a sense, Dostoevsky has dared to uncover the logical consequences of the wilfulness and alienation which in Onegin were contained by social restraints or diverted into aimless travel. The entrance of Efimovich, its effect on the hero and his reminiscences of their relationship in the regiment, even the melodramatic exit from the potential duel situation and the ever-ready revolver, all irresistibly recall Silvio in *The Shot*, while our hero's eavesdropping on the seduction scene echoes *The Post-Stage Master* witnessing the attempted seduction of his daughter. The very differences in the situation seem to increase the significance of these allusions: beyond the unspoken reference to the Pushkin story there seems to be an unspoken comment which at once reminds us of the paternalistic element in our pawnbroker's attitude to his much younger wife and the almost uxorious jealousy of the station-master for his daughter. As with a metaphor, the comparison can be almost infinitely extended.

These references, in fact, play very much the same role in the story as do such metaphors as the girl 'pawning' herself, the 'icon' of her integrated and unassailable spirituality, the 'duel' of wills, the 'theatricality' of the hero, the symbolic 'rape' by revolver, the 'song' of the free spirit, the drop of the dead girl's 'blood' with which the narrator is 'sullied'. These references and metaphors have acquired a symbolic function because their significance is not confined to a given moment, but pervades the whole story. They are what Barthes defines as *indices*: 'here the unit relates not to a complementary and consequent act, but to a more or less diffuse concept, still necessary, however, to the meaning of the story: indices of character concerning the protagonists, information relating to their identity, indications of "atmosphere", etcetera; the relation of the unit and its correlate is no longer distributional, but integrative.' [21] They are units that burst out of their context in the *histoire* because the author is committing us to them in his *discours*.

The clearest examples of this two-dimensional function are firstly the quotation from Goethe's *Faust* and secondly the reference to Le Sage's *Gil Blas*. Syntagmatically, in the flow of the narrative, they seem to represent stages in the power relationship between the pawnbroker (who would like to seem Mephistophelian) and the girl (who eventually unmasks his bogus power, just as Gil Blas, to his detriment, unmasked that of the Archbishop of Granada). As usual, Dostoevsky's narrator tricks us into thinking that the *Faust* reference is there primarily to indicate how educated he is—a trap Grossman falls straight into in his notes to the story. [22] Paradigmatically, however, this quotation has implications for the story at almost every point and on every level. Like a key phrase in music, having played its part in the continuous flow of notes of one passage, it recurs throughout the movement, striking an echo in other passages, even when tempo, key and the order of the notes in the phrase are changed. A study of the hero of *A Gentle Spirit* as a Russian Mephistopheles would yield an interesting figure. Dostoevsky's meek heroine has many affinities with *Faust*'s Gretchen: her youth ('she must be turned fourteen'), [23] her poor background and purity ('And poverty enriched by innocence,' 'I mean that true souls hardly guess/The sacred worth of their own innocence;/Yet simple love and meekness are sublime'); her refuge and reassertion in song ('An old refrain,/"Were I a bird"/ Comes, as she sees the clouds drift by/Over the city wall, to mock her pain./ Except for that, her only song is sighing'); even the motif which brings the hero and her together—the game with the jewellery played by Mephistopheles (and, by a nice twist, Gretchen's mother engaged in pawnbroking!); most importantly, the girl's inviolability ('over her the devil has no power'). The pawnbroker combines features of both Faust and Mephistopheles. He shares with Faust his grandiloquence ('Prating with definitions all aglow,/Grandiloquent of words and bold of breast'); but this is undermined by doubts ('And now look close: if truth must be confessed/You understood as much as now you know.' 'the tendrils of my joys that start,/Cankered with doubts, the mind's self-conscious tares'). He mocks the girl—and us—for suspecting that he quoted *Faust* to impress: he really shares with Mephistopheles 'the spirit that endlessly denies', he too feels himself 'Part of a power that would/ Alone work evil, but engenders good'. By the end, Faust and Mephistopheles have merged inseparably ('The bliss you have bestowed/ To bear me ever nearer to the gods/ Binds this companion to me: doomed I am/ To need the help of him whose impudence/ Ensures the cheap abasement of myself/ In my own sight'). We are back with Dostoevsky's doubles, Ivan Karamazov and his nocturnal visitor, the two Mr. Golyadkins, but this time the relationship is manifested in the very structure of the story, in the interaction between the pawnbroker, hero of the *histoire*

(Faust), and his *alter ego*, the narrator, the centre of the *discours* (Mephistopheles).

The complexity and ambivalence of the narrator's point of view comes out
most clearly in his attitude to his audience. Every piece of writing has an implicit
set towards a group of readers which is traceable ultimately to certain linguistic
features, but here the device is, to use a favourite Formalist term, 'laid bare'. The
phatic, intercommunicative aspect of the discourse is 'foregrounded' and the
narrative is constantly interrupted or linked by direct forms of address to the
unseen audience

> Gentlemen ... if you want to know ... Oh, listen, listen! ... Stop, gentle-
> men! ... That is, you see ... Wait ... Well? What do you think? ... Listen
> ... How can I start ... You see ... You see ... You must agree ... Just note
> ... Would you believe it ... You say ... You see, gentlemen ... I don't
> know if I'm expressing myself comprehensibly ... I repeat, and repeat again
> ... I'll say once more: Oh, of course, nobody knows ... I'll just add one thing
> ... Just a couple of words first ... You know ... Listen and take it in ... Oh,
> believe me ... etcetera.
> (See Russian Texts, No. 29)

This is what Jakobson characterizes as 'set for contact'

> There are messages primarily serving to establish, to prolong, or to discon-
> tinue communication, to check whether the channel works ('Hello, do you
> hear me?'), to attract the attention of the interlocutor or to confirm his
> continued attention ('Are you listening?' or in Shakespearian diction 'Lend
> me your ears!'—and on the other end of the wire 'Um-hum!'). This set for
> CONTACT, or in Malinowski's terms PHATIC function, may be displayed
> by a profuse exchange of ritualized formulas, by entire dialogues with the
> mere purport of prolonging communication. [24]

While this statement is an adequate account of phatic function in genuine
dialogue between two speakers it does not get near the problem of the dialogue
element in soliloquy and monologue. Bakhtin, writing in 1929, but only republished in full in 1963, showed that all speech and writing is potentially dialogic
and that the 'polyphonic' novels of Dostoevsky are essentially dialogic in relation
to man, society and even language itself

> Dialogic relations are possible not only between relatively complete utter-
> ances, but any meaningful unit, even the single word, may be considered
> dialogically, if it is considered not as an impersonal unit of language, but as a
> sign of another's semantic position, as representing another's utterance, i.e. if
> we hear another's voice in it ...
>   On the other hand, dialogic relations are possible too between linguistic
> styles, social dialects, etcetera, if they are apprehended as particular semantic

positions, as a kind of linguistic view of life (i.e. beyond a purely linguistic view of them).

Finally, even one's own utterance may be considered dialogically as a whole, in parts, even word-by-word, if we somehow separate ourselves from it, speak with some inner reservation (*ogovorka*), distance ourselves from it, limit, or, as it were, duplicate our authorship of it.[25]

Dostoevsky's hero in *A Gentle Spirit* is not content merely to grapple with his own sense of guilt: he must project it in some human form with which the dialogue becomes explicit. His inner censor is given the status of a group of judges. Thus he does not simply address them, he confesses to them, feels bound to present them with all the necessary evidence. The whole of the revolver scene is presented as a *procès-verbal* with a minute description of every move made by the participants and a digression to discuss motives. As to the matter of the revolver: 'Note: she knew about the revolver . . . '—full details as to why he keeps a loaded revolver—'Please make a note of all this'. Under the pressure of insistent (imagined) cross-examination, he is forced to confess to certain errors of judgement: 'I'm not arguing, I won't contradict like some lunatic . . . It's true, indisputably true, that I made a mistake. And perhaps there were even a lot of mistakes . . . I could see, of course, that I was a burden to her, don't go thinking that I was so dumb and such an egoist as not to be able to see that . . . And after all she even perked up once or twice. You see, I remember, I remember. Why do you keep saying that I looked and saw nothing?' all of which leads up to the circumstantial account of the suicide which involves evidence from Lukeria and other eye-witnesses.

We are presented, more or less explicitly, with the evidence of the accused and of witnesses, with speeches by counsel for the prosecution and counsel for the defence and observations from the bench. For the narrator can play (or cannot help playing) all the roles in his own trial—including our own. As Bakhtin says of the original Underground Man with whom the pawnbroker has so much in common

> There is nothing we can say about the hero of *Notes from the Underground* that he does not know himself and which he cannot anticipate our efforts to express. He obstinately and painfully dredges up for us his social and historical typicality, a sober psychologist's, or even psychopathologist's definition of his mind, a characterization of his own consciousness, his comic and tragic features, his moral code. He is most concerned about what others think of him, so he strives to be one step ahead. He has spent forty years eaves-dropping, learning to do this.[26]

Not that any of the characters in this courtroom drama are infallible. The discourse has an extra ambivalence, an extra dimension of irony, in that he can turn on his judges and question their competence or even accuse them (whereas 'contempt of court' is a notion belonging to the monologic, authoritarian world of real courts)

> No, listen, if you're going to judge a man, then at least judge him knowing his case . . . Listen!
> No, just take some noble deed, a difficult, secret, unannounced, unflashy, slandered deed with lots of sacrifice and not a drop of glory,—where you, a shining paragon, are shown up as a swine for all to see while you were the most honest man on earth, go on, just you attempt such a deed, oh no, my dear sir, you'd turn it down!
> (See Russian Texts, No. 30)

The particles -ka, -tka, -c, add an extra colloquial defiance, impudence even, which he maintains on the following page 'Well, you see, gentlemen . . . So am I supposed to justify myself? . . . Well, if you'll excuse me . . . , (*Vidite-s . . . Ne opravdyvat'sya zhe? . . . Pozvol'te-s . . .*) and he even makes the device explicit ('lays it bare') in recounting the conversation following his proposal: 'Of course, she thought for a long time right there by the gates before she said yes. She got so carried away thinking about it that I was just on the verge of asking: "Well then?"—and couldn't resist, I asked ever so stylishly "Well then, mademoiselle?", adding the little term of address.' (See Russian Texts, No. 31) It should not be assumed that a stylistic feature of this type is some kind of universal of Dostoevsky's style, a sort of trait which we may encounter anywhere in his language without reference to the thematic-structural context. This implicit assumption vitiates the otherwise excellent studies of Dostoevsky's style by Vinogradov,[27] Tynyanov,[28] Bitsilli[29] and others. The point is that the significant page numbers we have cited turn out to be the same as those illustrating the linguistic reflections of dislocation of time and causality we noted under fable and plot. That is, memories of some particularly crucial, testing moments in their relationship (the proposal, her discovery of the details of his past, the revolver episode) lead to his disorientation to which he reacts by challenging his judges in this curiously vulgar, colloquial way. At the moment of recollecting the cold steel of the revolver touching his temple he is prepared to be judged: 'You ask whether I held firm hopes of being spared? I will answer you, as before God . . .' but he is not going to be judged arbitrarily: 'But I will ask . . . But you will put the question again: why did you not spare her the evil deed? Oh, I've put that question to myself a thousand times since then . . . I was dying, I myself was dying so who could I save? And how do you know whether I would have wanted to save anyone just then. How can you know what I could have been feeling just then?'

It is, of course, her suicide that induces the most agonized bout of self-interrogation which turns into the most spirited attack on his judges and the relevance of the laws by which, he assumes, they are judging him

What are your laws to me now? What's the point of your customs, your manners, your life, your state, your religion? Let your judge judge me, let them bring me to the court, to your court of appeal, and I will say that I admit nothing. The judge will shout: 'Silence, Officer!' And I will shout back at him: 'Now where have you got the power to make me obey? Why has gloomy inertness shattered all that was dearest. What do your laws mean to me now, then? I withdraw.' Oh, what the hell!

What the narrator of *A Gentle Spirit* fears even more than judgement is laughter, because laughter is as undefinable and ambivalent as his own reasoning, yet it is beyond reasoning. Within the story he has no weapon with which to oppose the irony of his wife's tapping foot, the crease of her smile and the mockery of her song. She discovers this ultimate defence through the Efimovich affair which prompts her to a sarcastic response to his explanations: 'Oh, now you're a some-body—a great financier!' The discourse, too, is full of references to laughter, from his own parody of the triumph of the ruthless villain: 'Surely this triumph over her wasn't worth two hundred roubles? Hee-hee-hee!', through the begin-nings of self-doubt: 'though it's funny talking to oneself in mysterious phrases'; or, 'I said just now "the most noble of men". That's funny, and yet that's just how it was.'; to the more paranoiac: 'They'll laugh at my anxieties, but no one will ever know why I got so anxious!' and, 'I know, I know, don't prompt me: you find it funny that I complain of chance and of five minutes.' His very last question pleads for the laughter to stop: 'No, seriously, when they take her away tomorrow what will become of me?'

Bakhtin sets the laughter in Dostoevsky in a tradition of 'carnival' and 'Menippic satire'. The open laughter is largely suppressed in all but the earlier stories

> but the trace of the aesthetically organizing and world-illuminating power of ambivalent laughter in which Dostoevsky was steeped is there in all his novels. We find this trace in the structure of his images, in many plot situations and in certain lexical peculiarities of his style. But the main, and one might say decis-ive expression of this suppressed laughter is in the author's ultimate position which rules out all possibility of one-sided dogmatic seriousness or absolute fixing on one point of view or one pole of life and thought. All one-sided seriousness and all one-sided feeling is invested in the heroes, but the author, making them all collide in the 'larger dialogue' of the novel, leaves the dialogue open, without a resolving full-stop. . . . [30]

A rough sketch for a story that Dostoevsky made in 1869,[31] seven years before he wrote *A Gentle Spirit*, shows how important this fear of mockery was for his vision of the hero: 'A real underground type, the nooks and crannies in life. Irrit-able, boundless vanity . . . His wife can't help but notice that he's educated, but then discovers that he's not so educated, every jibe (and he takes everything as a jibe) infuriates him, mistrusts everyone.' The hero's 'boundless vanity' is compounded of alternating self-love and self-destructiveness. His attitude to *himself* is an important aspect of the point of view of the story. On the one hand, he dismisses himself as 'a cheap egoist' (*deshevyi egoist*) and constantly mocks himself with ironic self-quotation

> an honest man, they'll say, and he's studied every aspect of the matter.

> But you see I was 'revenging myself on society', really, really, really!

> Wait: naturally I never even uttered a syllable to her then about generosity; on the contrary, quite on the contrary: It is *I*, I would say, who remain loaded with benefits, and not *you*!
> (See Russian Texts, No. 32)

(where the very pomposity of the participle in the last sentence is a further element of self-parody); the impersonality of a school report: 'Stern, proud, in need of no-one's moral comforting, suffers in silence;' and the explicit wounded vanity of: 'At first, at least in the first minutes there was perplexity and a terrible astonishment, terrible and strange, morbid and almost vengeful: "She's singing, and in my presence! *Has she forgotten all about me then?*" Similarly, he frequently dismisses his own preoccupation with his own reactions with: 'Still, never mind about me, we'll get to that later . . . '. And yet he is not sure: perhaps the answer to the question lying on the table is in himself: 'And anyway, what is there for me now—is the whole business inside me or not?'

On the other hand, he is often motivated (vis-à-vis his readers as well as vis-à-vis his wife) by vanity and self-love. He is vastly proud of the cat-and-mouse game he plays with the girl when she pawns her humble trinkets and his three 'special thoughts about her': 'After all I wasn't badly brought up and have some manners.' a thought which develops with the proposal into: 'But I spoke not only decently, that is revealing myself as an educated man, but with originality, and that's the main thing.' He nourishes his conceit with a deliberately enigmatic silence in her presence: 'To her delight I responded with silence, benevolent, of course . . . but still she soon saw that we were different and that I was an enigma. And the main thing was, I played on the enigma! In fact perhaps I carried out the whole stupid business in order to pose an enigma' (a comment which, as we have seen, relates as much to the discourse as to the story . . .). The mere thought of his triumph over the girl keeps him warm all winter and he admits to deliberately delaying the dénouement of their conflict

> In her eyes I could no longer be a villain, but merely a rather strange man, yet even this thought doesn't give me as much pleasure as it might after all that has happened: strangeness is no vice, in fact to the contrary it sometimes attracts a woman. In a word, I deliberately postponed the dénouement: what had happened was for the moment too much for my peace and quiet and contained too many scenes for my daydreams.

And he confesses: 'The hideous point is that I'm a day-dreamer.'

The closer we come to the hero-narrator's point of view on himself the more strongly the whole story becomes analogous to an act of masturbation. On the surface we have the obvious sexual themes of domination through marriage, the denial of conjugal rights after the revolver threat, and Dostoevsky's perennial fetish over kissing women's feet and being fascinated by their boots and shoes. More symbolically, the duel is a competition in virility (from which he always retreats when the challenge comes from men), the revolver threat becomes a threat of rape (the reversal of conventional sexual roles here adds force to this symbolic act since his duelling opponent is now his wife); the suicide itself becomes (for both of them?) a sort of orgasm, an ecstasy. Above all, the alternations of self abasement and deliberate cruelty—he himself admits to her: 'a personal notion of self-flagellation and self-eulogy' (*lichnaya ideya samobichevaniya i samovoskhvaleniya*) which reveals a sado-masochistic pattern which is sexual in origin as well as in manifestation. And underlying all this perhaps is his awareness, or fear, of impotence: as his pawnbroking was an impotent punishment of society, so his silent bullying is an impotent attempt at male dominance.

In *A Gentle Spirit*, the whole process of telling his story becomes an act of psycho-moral self-stimulation, a symptom of his alienation and yearning for re-integration which is denied him through normal sexual intercourse and which he must seek through verbal discourse, through the very act of narration. By a converging of *histoire* and *discours* the merely physical has become metaphysical, the merely sexual has become spiritual (and, since we are in Dostoevsky's 'dialogic' world, vice versa).

We must avoid seeming to reduce our narrator to a psychological 'case', however, since Dostoevsky has taken care to reveal the social man, not least in the language he uses. The language the girl is made to speak is the plainest, most direct and most neutral standard Russian, in total contrast to the tortuous mixture of colloquialisms, slang, high literary-philosophical style, and special jargons (military, pawnbroker's) of which *his* speech and writing are composed. The conversation about his disgrace illustrates the contrast: she asks, without any beating about the bush (*s dubu sorvav*): 'Is it true that you were dismissed from the regiment for cowardice in not fighting a duel?' His answer consists of qualifications and euphemisms: 'Well, it's true; according to the verdict of the officers I was requested to remove myself from the regiment, although, in any case I had already handed in my resignation some time earlier.' (See Russian Texts, No. 33) His answer to her next interrogation: 'You were dismissed as a coward?' (*vygnali kak trusa?*) adds to the qualifications and euphemisms a characteristically tortuous and pompous aphorism

> Well, yes, I was sentenced for cowardice. But I refused the duel not as a coward but because I didn't want to submit to their tyrannical verdict and challenge someone to a duel when I couldn't myself see any offense. You

know,—here I couldn't restrain myself,—to stand up against such tyranny by action and to take all the consequences meant showing far more courage than in any duel you like to mention.
(See Russian Texts, No. 34)

The intriguing thing about the pawnbroker's character is that, despite his sharply critical intelligence, his simultaneous grasp of every point of view through layer after layer of irony, his scorn for social and moral convention, he is imprisoned by his own conventionality. He likes to interpret his becoming a pawnbroker as his revenge on a society which rejected him, but, apart from refusing duels, his overt, non-verbal acts are all totally conventional: he superstitiously refuses to pledge the icon in the icon frame and puts it in his icon corner in the shop with the lamp burning; he requires a go-between (Lukeriya) to make a proposal; despite his wish for a quick quiet wedding (à l'anglaise) he ends up satisfying the aunts' wish for the normal niceties; his obsessive miserliness is for the sake of the most conventional of Russian bourgeois dreams—a modest estate on the south coast of the Crimea with vineyards and a wife and family ('If God sends us any') with a little charitable work among the locals; even this dream can only be replaced, when she falls ill, by the equally conventional trip to Boulogne suggested by the doctor; when she lies dead in the courtyard he is more concerned with the reactions of the neighbours and the stranger who points at her blood than with the victim herself. Even his hope that his wife might come to understand him better when she sees the books on his shelves is borrowed from *Eugene Onegin*! If the dialogue in his soul between good and evil, between what man can know and what only the devil and God can know, between renunciation and the will to dominate, is a dialogue between Faust and Mephistopheles, then the Mephistopheles is patently Goethe's cheap, moth-eaten, pathetic demon, spouting resounding axioms in vulgar rhyming doggerel.

His language betrays his concern for respectability: 'I permitted myself a giggle at her things. That is to say, don't you see, I never permit myself such a thing, I maintain a *gentlemanly tone* with my clients.' (See Russian Texts, No. 35) The pseudo-gentility of foreign words often betrays him whether borrowed straight from English (*ton gentlemenskii*) or as French-style euphemisms: 'I entered into *graceful* conversation *with the utmost courtesy*. After all *I wasn't badly brought up* and have *good manners*. I appeared as if *out of some higher world*.' (See Russian Texts, No. 36) He is a master of euphemism; there are the sexual undertones in

It was now that I noticed her for the first time in a particular way and thought something about her in that way, I mean precisely something in a particular way.

for you, I particularly stressed and precisely in a certain sense.

I suddenly had certain thoughts running round my head about her. That was

my third *particular* thought about her.
(See Russian Texts, No. 37)

The euphemistic language of advertisements where the 'governess' and 'companion' mean 'mistress' and 'kept woman' is something he has real feeling for: 'and then: will agree to anything, teaching, companionship, housekeeping, caring for an invalid, and can sew, etcetera, etcetera, Oh the whole tarradiddle!' (See Russian Texts, No. 38) He may affect to despise regimental mores, but his use of officers' mess jargon in a whole page (p.405) rings true to the last cliché.

The hero of the *histoire* is committed to silence as the mode for his revenge on the world

> But I'm a pastmaster at speaking in silence, I've talked my life away in silence and lived through whole tragedies with myself in silence. Oh, I was miserable too, you know! I was cast out by everyone, cast out and forgotten, and nobody, but nobody knows that! . . . I kept silent and was especially, especially silent with her, right up until yesterday,—why was I silent? Well, as a proud man, I wanted her to recognize this for herself, without me, but certainly without stories from scoundrels, but so that she might guess about this man and reach him!

But his protestations about silence are expressed loudly and repetitively, with every sentence a series of graded synonyms ending in an exclamation. For the hero of the *discours* is a babbler whose ironic role is the constant betrayal of his *alter ego*.

In our analysis of *A Gentle Spirit* we have discovered linguistic features which reflect or realize the structural features. Collecting our examples together, we might say that we have found a stylistic 'dominant' for the work which can, at least partly, account for the prevailing 'tone' of the whole work. We might follow Shklovsky in his study of *Tristram Shandy* in finding *retardation* (*tormozheniye*), a sustaining of the reader's appetite through constant interruption, as the dominant device. The main types of retardation we have noted were: 1. Interruptions, 2. Interjections, 3. Direct address, 4. Digressions, 5. Qualifications, 6. Time-switching, both backwards and forwards, 7. Riddles, whether thematic or linguistic—the particular thought (*osobennaya mysl*)—etcetera), 8. 'Stepped structures', both in the action and in the syntax, 9. Repetition and echoing, 10. Subject-Predicate interruption and inversion, 11. Eccentric syntactic sequence, 12. Positive notions introduced with their negativized opposite, 13. Mounting comparatives—'more and more' (*vse bol'she i bol'she*); 'I wanted more and still more irresistibly . . . ' (*mne vse bolee i neuderzhimee khotelos*). These linguistic devices certainly help to create and sustain tension in the way Shklovsky suggests, but our structural analysis would suggest that this is not their main function in this story. What virtually all these lexical and syntactic complexities have in common is that they must be accounted for within the *interpersonal* component of Halliday's 'Functional Model'.[32]

Lexically, the dominants we have picked out express levels of formality (e.g. foreign words, complex slavonicisms, army jargon, slang) and degrees of expressiveness (e.g. diminutives); the adverbial groups tend to belong to classes of 'comment' adjunct ('not only decently but with originality'—*ne tol'ko prilichno, no i original'no*); nominal groups are heavily marked by attitudinal modification ('a rather cheap egoist'—*dovol'no deshevyi egoist*) or intensification ('gave me only the tiniest drip of time'—*tol'ko samuyu kapel'ky vremeni dali*); verbal groups frequently express modality ('I must speak for and against and do speak'—*ya dolzhen govorit' pro i contra, i govoryu*) or a marked polarity ('but I softened nothing quite the reverse, in fact, seeing she was afraid, I deliberately put it more strongly'—*no ya ne smyagchil nichego, malo togo, vidya, chto boitsya, narochno usilil*).

The degree to which the interpersonal function in the style predominates over the experiential and textual, the degree to which *histoire* has become *discours*, the degree to which the whole *logos* is brought together—or extended—into a *lexis*, substantiates our statement of theme. Bakhtin synthesizes Vyacheslav Ivanov's (1916) insights into Dostoevsky's heroes' predicament as follows

> He defines Dostoevsky's realism as based not on objective perception, but on penetration (empathy). The principle of Dostoevsky's world-view is to assert the alien (other's) 'I' not as an object, but as another subject. To establish the other's 'I'—'thou art' (*ty yesi*)—is the crucial problem which, according to Ivanov, Dostoevsky's heroes must try to solve in order to overcome their ethical solipsism, their isolated 'idealist' consciousness and to turn another person from a shadow to a true reality. Behind Dostoevsky's tragic catastrophes there always lies a solipsistic isolation of the hero's consciousness, an imprisonment in his own world.[33]

This is an excellent interpretation of one of Dostoevsky's central themes. The structure and style of *A Gentle Spirit* suggest that in this story at least the formula must be extended: the hero's attempt to discover the truth of 'thou art' (*ty yesi*) has failed and the *narrator* is condemned to an eternal dialogue between 'I am' (*Ya yesm'*) and 'you are' (*vy yeste*)[34] from which only the reader can attempt to make a synthesis.

III Tolstoy: *Father Sergius*, 1890-98; (*Otets Sergii*)[35]

The identity of narrator and hero with which Dostoevsky plays in *A Gentle Spirit* permits a richness and complexity of point of view that has implications on every level of the story's structure and, as we have seen, even calls into question the very nature of the narrative act. We must recognize, however, that this technique was relatively uncommon in nineteenth-century fiction and even in Dostoevsky's own works; technically as well as philosophically, Dostoevsky was anticipating many key features of avant-garde fiction in the twentieth century. For a more typical treatment of point of view in the tradition of the realist novel we must turn to one of its greatest exponents, Lev Tolstoy.

Third person narration[36] brings into play whole dimensions of the narrative process that are untouched by first person narration. In the first place it forces us to discriminate between the process of perception and the process of telling. In first person narrative only the workings of memory or anticipation provide a distance between the perceiving of an event and its telling, but the third person voice provides an extra consciousness through which objects and events perceived, sensations felt, or thoughts thought by one or more characters are refracted through the narratorial voice. This voice may itself belong to an autonomous character in the story, as in the 'Maxim Maximych' chapter of Lermontov's *A Hero of Our Time*; it may belong to a figure whose prime function is narration, although he is strongly characterized by his style, as with the army officer who narrates *The Pistol Shot* in Pushkin's *Tales of Belkin*; it may belong to a 'frame narrator' whose outlines are barely sketched in; or it may be a more or less 'omniscient' voice which knows not only every event, but every reaction, thought and plan of the story's 'sentient centre'. However omniscient this latter voice, of course, he will still select to tell us only a portion of what he 'knows' and, as we shall see in the chapters on *fable* and *plot*, will rearrange the temporal and causal sequence of what he tells us for intrigue and suspense.

If we look again at Figure 4 (p. 39), we may see a relationship between the type of narratorial voice and the elements in the story he relates to. The 'objective' third person narrator will focus on elements of the *histoire* which are relevant to the experience and perception of his hero,[37] such as Time, Place and Objects, and Other Characters. 'Objectively', he will transmit, in language which is primarily referential in function, the experiential details of the world in which the hero moves (Column 2). Depending on the degree to which he wishes to convey the 'subjective' response of the hero, he will 'load' the lexis, modification and grammar to express his degree of involvement and sympathy with the hero's responses to people and situations (Column 3).

A highly self-conscious, 'subjective' narrator, on the other hand, will focus on elements of the *discours* which seem relevant to his perception of the narrative act, such as aspects of himself, his audience and the very act of narration itself. If he maintains a cool relation to the narrative act his attitude will be conveyed in largely referential language (Column 2). If the very act of narration has become a source of emotion or anxiety for him—if it has become a 'trial' to him as in *A Gentle Spirit*—the language will become strongly interpersonal, overheated even, as it manifests the degree of his involvement with himself, his audience and the story-telling process.

We may thus perceive a two-dimensional scheme implicit in Figure 4, as delineated by the broken lines superimposed on the rows and columns. In a simplified form this might be represented as a grid-and-group diagram (Figure 5):

Figure 5

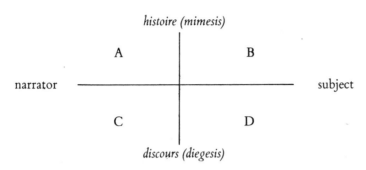

The narratorial stances we have just delineated and the language in which they are conveyed will then be located in the quadrants as follows:

A : focus on story : objective information : referential function of language

B : focus on story : information as perceived by hero : expressive function of language

C : focus on narrative act : objective voice : textual function of language

D : focus on narrative act : subjective involvement of narrator : interpersonal function of language.

We may see this in terms of Plato's opposition between *mimesis* (perfect imitation) and *diegesis* (pure story) if we adopt Genette's formula suggesting that 'the quantity of information is inversely proportional to the presence of the informer; so that *mimesis* represents the maximum of information with the minimum intrusion of the informing voice, while *diegesis* represents the maximum intrusion of the informing voice with a minimum of information'.[38] I believe, however, that the additional dimension of degree of subjectivity provided by Figures 3 and 4 has important effects on both the structure and the style of a story.

We must also bear in mind that the point of view never remains static throughout a story. Frequently the sentient centre is introduced as from the outside before we are drawn into his inmost thoughts and sensations. Even when a story opens within the hero's consciousness, as in Chekhov's *The Student*,[39] there are moments when the narrator draws back to create an ironic distance, or perspective, between the perceiver and the teller. And when the whole focus of the story has been shifted to the *discours*, as in *A Gentle Spirit*, the narrator creates his audience of listeners or judges (creates us, his readers) to achieve the ironic distance.

Perhaps it is characteristic of the novelist that he expects to be able to shift his point of view rather freely between characters and in and out of his main sentient centre, whereas the short story writer will aim for a more unified point of view. Certainly Tolstoy contrasts strongly with Chekhov in this respect. In *Father Sergius* he moves rapidly from a collective social view to an individual one, from biographer to social historian to anthropologist, and from the consciousness of one protagonist to that of another. Even more striking, and perhaps more questionable aesthetically, are the sudden shifts that Tolstoy makes out of the narratorial mode, i.e. what we can only take as the explicit moralistic opinions of the author himself are allowed to intrude into the diegetic world of the story.

One of the major themes of *Father Sergius* is the conflict between social man and the individual conscience. We can trace this theme in the play with point of view in the first two sections of the story. The opening sentence is a summary of the background and events leading to Kasatsky's decision to become a monk as it might be presented objectively by a social historian, while the second sentence contrasts society's conventional view of this decision with a hint at the hero's view as an individual: 'This event seemed extraordinary and inexplicable to people who were unaware of its inner causes:/for Prince Stepan Kasatsky himself, however, it all happened so naturally that he could not imagine how he might have acted in any other way.' Once Tolstoy has named his hero, he adopts the voice of the biographer presenting a more detailed account of his boyhood, schooldays and army career. Here the social view prevails with the tone occasionally approaching that of the hagiographer, so conventionally perfect is the young man in breeding, upbringing and abilities. And yet there is a flaw in his character, nicely exposed by the adversative clauses in the structure of three consecutive sentences: '*In spite of* being taller than average,/he was handsome and agile. Moreover, in his behaviour he *would have been* a model cadet/*had it not been for* his quick temper. He didn't drink or go whoring and was remarkably truthful./*The one thing that prevented him* from being a model was the flare ups of anger which used to seize him . . . ' (See Russian Texts, No. 39) The opposition continues with Kasatsky's hero-worship of Nicholas I contrasting with the theatrical play made by the emperor with his cadets' loyalty. Now there is an ironic shift of point of view as the emperor's reported speech is undermined by his own clichés: 'But when the graduating cadets were presented to him he no longer mentioned this but said, *as he always did*, that they must feel free *to turn straight to him*, that they should *serve him and their fatherland faithfully* and he would *always remain their foremost friend. Everyone was very moved as always . . . ' ((See Russian Texts, No. 40) The very mixing of three types of utterance in one sentence of reported speech—(a) granting permission (*mogut*) (b) exacting an oath of loyalty (*chtoby sluzhili*) and (c) making a promise (*on vsegda ostanetsya*)—unmistakably subverts the emperor's sincerity.

The surface message is more seriously subverted stylistically in the account of Kasatsky's ambitious path through his academic, social and military education. Within two paragraphs the verbs *dostigat'* and *dobit'sya* (to achieve) occur eleven times and the syntax takes on a sort of cataphoric urgency with gerunds preceding

main verbs and compound conjunctions constantly pointing forward like the
hero's over-weening ambition

Having achieved one thing he would set to succeed in something else.

Succeeded so well that . . .

Apart from his general vocation for a life which consisted in serving his Tsar
and Fatherland, he always set himself some goal, and, *no matter how trivial it
might be*, would commit himself to it totally and live *for nothing else until* he had
achieved it. But *as soon as* he achieved his chosen goal, another would immediately spring up in his consciousness and take the place of the previous one.
This striving to excel, and, *in order to* excel, to achieve the goal he had set,
filled his whole life.
(See Russian Texts, No. 41)

The larger-than-life syntax and vocabulary here, as later in the accounts of
Kasatsky's spiritual striving in the monastery and hermitage (where the dominant register becomes that of religious exercise and contemplation, but the
sentence structures reflect the same urgency and inner conflict), do not jar on the
reader because they seem appropriate to the high degree of intensity at which
Kasatsky lives every stage of his life.

What does jar is the curious and apparently quite unmotivated intrusion of the
author's *persona* into the third person narrative text in the next section and on
two other occasions. Tolstoy adopts the stance of a sociologist to enumerate four
levels of the upper classes in Russia from which he considers conventional social
attitudes stem. An intrusion of this kind is not unexpected in Tolstoy if we are
used to the appearances of the social and military historian in *War and Peace* or of
the ethnographer in *The Cossacks*. The superficial objectivity is undercut by a
satirical play with the key words on which so much snobbery is built: 'court
circles' (*pridvornye*), 'upper layers' (*vysshiye krugi*), 'lower layers' (*nizkiye krugi*),
'insider' (*svoi*), 'outsider' (*chuzhoi*), and a shift to Kasatsky's own point of view
as he discovers this snobbery for himself shows Tolstoy at his ironic best: 'But he
quickly became aware that the circles in which he was moving were lower circles
and that there were upper circles and that in these upper court circles, although
he was certainly received, he was an outsider; people were polite to him but their
whole attitude indicated that there were insiders and that he was not one of
them. And Kasatsky wanted to be an insider.' (See Russian Texts, No. 42) Three
voices are sustained in this carefully controlled style: the quasi-objective voice of
the biographer and sociologist, the hierarchic voice of social convention with its
fine and meaningless discriminations, and the response to this of the ambitious
but clear-sighted Kasatsky. Why, then, does Tolstoy feel it necessary to inter-
pose his own voice (not that of his intermediary narrator, but an unambiguous
authorial 'I') at the beginning of this section?—'Higher society at that time
consisted and, *I think*, always and everywhere does consist, of four sorts of

people . . . ' A page later, while generalizing about sexual attitudes, Tolstoy comments, again with an explicit authorial 'I think' and a comparison with present-day attitudes: 'In this view [idealizing feminine chastity] there was a great deal that was untrue and harmful due to the debauchery that the men allowed in their own case, yet as far as women were concerned such a view, so different from the view of young men *today* who see in every girl a female of the species on the look-out for themselves,—such a view was, *I think*, useful.' Since Tolstoy's narrator has already shown himself perfectly capable of expressing an opinion on these as on other matters, either directly or through the mind of Kasatsky, the sudden switch to a first person opinion seems curiously careless. Different in tone, and more ambiguous in its function, is the present tense on which the story ends: 'In Siberia he settled down as a hired hand for a rich peasant and *lives there now*. He works in his boss's kitchen garden and gives the children lessons and nurses the sick.' (See Russian Texts, No. 43)

A folksy ending perhaps? Yet one which hardly matches the sophistication of plot and style which has led to this, unless we are to read it as mimetic of the utter simplicity and renunciation of self which Kasatsky finally achieves. (We should note that the time switch here is *within the diegesis*; it is treated as part of the *histoire*, not, as with the many temporal shifts in *The Man on Sentry-Duty*, a deliberate switch to the *discours*.)

The narrative structure of *Father Sergius* is as starkly, perhaps naively, simple as the *vita* of a saint or one of those 'fools in Christ' so popular in the folklore of Christian Russia. There are no flashbacks, and any complexities in the causal motivation are due to paradoxes in the complex character of the hero rather than to any deliberate play with plot on the author's part. Each of the five phases of Kasatsky's spiritual quest is described to us in detail both from the conventional viewpoint of contemporary society and from within the hero's mind; indeed, a major sub-theme of this quest is the tension between the irreconcilable demands of social convention and individual integrity. Each phase ends in a key dramatic scene which brings alive this tension, epitomizes the problems confronting the hero in that phase, and brings about a change of heart and life-style. Each scene is an encounter with a woman and involves a specific sexual conflict, so that we are in no doubt about the place of lust among the sins Kasatsky has to conquer. In addition to this schematic structure of scenes as the test and turning-point of each phase, three of the women have variants of the same name: his fiancée is *Mary* (in its English form, beloved of the cosmopolitan upper class), the merchant's daughter who conquers his celibacy is *Mar'ya* (in its standard Russian form), while the daughter of the humble Praskov'ya Mikhailovna is *Masha* (in its familiar form); we would not be surprised to learn that the society lady who whispers about him in French to her friend Lise in the monastery church was *Marie*, or that the merry widow Makovkina who tries to seduce him in the hermitage was another Mary.

If the role of these women in the plot and some small features they have in common seem schematic or contrived, they come alive, however, as individuals in the encounters Kasatsky has with each of them. Here Tolstoy sustains a nice ambiguity between the dramatic and the ironic, since some of the time the vision seems to be that of Kasatsky himself, yet this is ironically subverted by the author's parody of the conventions of each scene. Mary, the Countess Korotkova, is a conventional society beauty—as conventional as Kasatsky's ambition to marry her in order to rise at court—and the scene between them has as conventional a setting as any proposal scene in a cheap romance: a hot May day on a garden bench in the shade of a lime tree, with nightingales and a light breeze waiting in the wings to sing and rustle the leaves at the appropriate signal for 'noises off'. That Tolstoy is deliberately making this scene a cliché becomes quite clear from the stress on 'angelic' or 'heavenly' or 'divine' purity of this 'goddess' in the white muslin dress. And this degree of naive conventionality, sentimentality even, in Kasatsky's perception is a necessary preparation for the shock he is to experience when he learns that she has been the mistress of his beloved Tsar. The economy of the dialogue between them is brilliant, with a reliance on elliptical and unfinished sentences, facial expression, gesture and movement as the subtlest vehicles of mood and interpersonal tension and of the irony of his avowed ambition to come closer to the Tsar through his relationship with her. Even the play with the singular and plural second person pronoun forms, *ty* and *vy*, signalling respectively intimacy and formality,[40] marks the shifting tensions perfectly—that is, until Tolstoy feels it necessary to tell us explicitly what he is doing

> He pulled himself up to his full height and stood in front of her with both hands resting on the hilt of his sabre.
>
> —I have only now discovered all that happiness that a man can feel. And it is you *[vy]*, it is you *[ty]*,—he said with a shy smile,—that have given me it!
>
> He was at that stage when he had still not grown accustomed to using *ty*, and as he looked up to her morally, he felt frightened of saying *ty* to this angel.
>
> —I have come to know myself thanks to . . . *ty*, have come to see myself as better than I thought.
>
> —I have known that for a long time. That is why I fell in love with you *[vy]*.
>
> A nightingale began to sing nearby and the young leaves rustled in a slight breeze.
>
> (See Russian Texts, No. 44)

We may forgive Tolstoy the stilted dialogue, the nightingale, and the breeze, since the irony over Kasatsky's naivety is a necessary prelude to the violence of his reaction when he learns of her unangelic past, but for a Russian readership, aware of the *vy/ty* opposition, the authorial explanation is superfluous and spoils the directness of the reader's perception of the drama underlying the rather simple words uttered. In any case, her consistent use of the formal *vy* form and his reverting from *ty* to *vy* as he learns the truth about his 'angel' make the significance of the opposition perfectly clear.

Tolstoy makes the same opposition of pronouns with great subtlety, and without needing to comment on the fact, in Kasatsky's long conversation with the humble and unattractive Praskov'ya Mikhailovna, in the last of his crucial encounters with women. As a poor cousin and friend of his youth who had always been despised by Kasatsky's set, and as someone who had married badly and been widowed and now had to support a worthless hypochondriac son-in-law and his family, she would most naturally be addressed as *ty* by the rich and well-born Kasatsky who had achieved almost sainthood through his monastic career, and she would naturally call him *vy*. But the dynamics of their dialogue is built on a complex interweaving of social and personal levels: their being related, their age, their presumed class difference, their presumed relationship as priest and worshipper, as guest and hostess, her humility and his new-found respect for her. There is a static matrix of fixed categories requiring particular forms of address—as well as many other stylistic features of their conversation—against which moves a kind of shifting veil of personal feelings and moods. This is one of Tolstoy's great dramatic dialogues, depending for its subtlety and power so much on the earlier course of the story and on its own context that it eludes adequate commentary. All the more pity, then, that the author feels it necessary to interpret it for us in the thoughts of Kasatsky as he sets out on his wandering. The curate's dog barking at him as he recedes from Praskov'ya's view would have been ironic enough a comment. But we find

> So that is what my dream meant. Pashenka is precisely what I should have been and was not. I lived for people, using God as an excuse, she lives for God, imagining that she is living for people. Yes, one good deed, a cup of water given without thought of reward, is worth all the blessings I am supposed to have achieved for people. And yet there was surely a speck of sincere desire to serve God?—he asked himself, and the answer was: Yes, but all that was sullied and over-grown with worldly fame. Yes, there is no God for one who has lived as I have done, for worldly fame. I will seek him.

We are not questioning here the sincerity of either Kasatsky or his author in their search for godliness through renunciation of the world, or the rightness of building a story around such an explicitly moral theme. It is precisely because every event, thought, and relationship in the story has pointed towards this conclusion and because the scene with Pashenka has focussed these tendencies into a single dramatic interaction that we resent Tolstoy's interpolation at this point.

The first of Kasatsky's 'temptations', which led him to reject the worldly atmosphere of a monastery near a city and seek spiritual peace in a hermitage, requires little comment except to point out that the decision is initiated by his overhearing a snatch of a conversation about himself in French (as Uspensky has shown with reference to *War and Peace*,[41] we can usually expect some irony underlying the use of French by Tolstoy's characters; French conversation between *Russians* is a sure symptom of convention and hypocrisy): '—*Lise, regardez à droite, c'est lui,*—said a feminine voice within his hearing.—*Où, où? Il n'est pas tellement beau.*' The point of view remains in Kasatsky's thoughts as he makes his way to meet his abbot and a distinguished guest at the altar, and at first sight his decision to leave the monastery seems to be motivated by his disgust with the worldliness of the abbot. But Tolstoy has subtly given us the key interchange in French between the two society ladies and we must infer that he really decides to go because his vanity has been wounded, and this is borne out by the ensuing correspondence about his sin of pride with his elder.

We need not read too much into this slight scene, however. The second of Kasatsky's 'temptations' is a richer scene in every sense. This is the attempt, made for a bet, by the widow Makovkina, to seduce Kasatsky the hermit, now known as Father Sergius, in his cave retreat. Of all the scenes in the story this one comes alive most vividly. Apart from the intrinsic excitement of a seduction scene and the sacrilegious thrill of the victim being a monk, sworn to celibacy yet afflicted constantly by lust, this vividness is due to the carefully controlled alternation of points of view between Sergius and Makovkina. Up to this point in the story the point of view has been predominantly Sergius-Kasatsky's, interspersed with omniscient narration—and occasional, usually gratuitous, intrusions by an authorial voice. This scene, however, opens once the narrator has 'placed' her in time and place and appropriate company, with the thoughts of Makovkina

> ... the lawyer and the officer sitting opposite were telling some sort of tall stories to the girl beside Makovkina, while she, wrapping her fur-coat tightly around her, sat motionless and thought: 'Always the same old thing, and always disgusting: red, shiny faces smelling of wine and tobacco, the same old conversations, the same old thoughts, and everything revolves around filth. And they are all contented and convinced that this is how things have to be and capable of going on living like this until they die. I can't. I'm fed up. I need something or other to upset all this and turn it all upside down. Maybe something like those people, in Saratov I think it was, who went off and froze to death. So what would our crowd have done? How would they have behaved? Vilely, I suppose. Every man for himself. And I'd have behaved vilely too. But at least I'm good-looking. And they know it. And what about that monk? Surely he's not got beyond appreciating that? Impossible. That's the one thing they appreciate. Like with that cadet in the autumn. And what a fool he was...'
> Ivan Nikolaich!—she said.
> —At your service.
> —How old is he then?
> —Who?

—Kasatsky, of course.

—Over forty, I think.

—And does he admit everyone, then?

—Everyone, yes, but not all the time.

—Cover up my legs. Not like that. You're so clumsy! Go on, a bit more, and some more, that's right. And there's no need to squeeze my legs.

In this way they got to the forest where the cell was.

Makovkina's 'stream-of-consciousness', with its shifts and half-articulated allusions, reveals a richly paradoxical nature, prone to self-doubt as well as to self-satisfaction, a worthy opponent for Father Sergius. And once he has been 'placed', physically and spiritually, by the narrator, we have an immediate switch to his thoughts where the shifting moods are conveyed by fractured syntax and spasmodic rhythms in much the same way as Makovkina's

> —Oh God! God!—he thought.—Wherefore dost Thou not grant me faith. Yes, lust, yes, that's what St. Anthony and the others fought against, but faith. They had that, but I have minutes, hours and days without it. What is the point of the world, all its delight, if it is sinful and one has to renounce it? But isn't it a temptation that I want to go away from all the joys of the world and cook up something where there's nothing, perhaps.—He said to himself and was horrified and disgusted at himself.—Filthy beast! Beast! You want to be a saint!—he began to scold himself. And stood up to pray. But as soon as he started to pray he had a vivid recollection of how he used to be in the monastery: in hood and cloak, looking magnificent. And he shook his head. 'No, that's not it. That's deception. But I deceive other people, not myself, and not God. I'm not a magnificent man, but pathetic and comic.' And he flung back the flaps of his tunic and looked at his pathetic legs in their shorts. And smiled.

The self-disgust, dissatisfaction, pride, and vanity compete as they do in Makovkina's thoughts. And the parallelism of the 'legs as sexual objects' with which each soliloquy ends is deliberate, for only a short soliloquy further and his thought becomes flesh: Makovkina knocks at his door.

The first phase of their encounter, when he looks at her through the window, struggles with her arguments and his own feelings, and lets her in to shelter while he goes into his inner sanctum to pray, is all conveyed from his point of view; but in order to sharpen the inner conflict and the mounting excitement, Tolstoy exploits the brilliant device of shifting from the visual (the most 'intellectual' and controlled of the senses) to the aural

> ... he wanted to go on reading the psalm, but he didn't read but involuntarily strained to hear. He wanted to hear. It was very quiet. The drops were still falling from the roof into the tin standing in the corner. Outside all was darkness, mist, and the biting snow. It was as quiet as could be. And suddenly there was a rustle by the window and quite clearly the voice—that same

gentle, timid voice, the sort of voice that could only belong to an attractive woman, murmured:

—Let me in, for Christ's sake . . .

All the blood seemed to rush to his heart and stop there. He couldn't draw breath. 'May God arise and his enemies be cast asunder . . . '

—But I'm not the devil . . . —and he could tell that the lips saying this were smiling.—I'm not the devil, I'm just a sinful woman who has gone astray [*zabludilas'*]—not metaphorically but in fact (she laughed), I'm frozen stiff and asking for shelter . . .

Perhaps the pun is overdone[42]; certainly when Tolstoy tells us that 'their eyes met and they recognized each other' in the next paragraph, we have no need of the laborious explanation: 'It wasn't that they had ever seen each other: they never had, but in the glance that they exchanged they (especially he) felt that they knew one another. There was no doubting after this glance that this was the devil and not a simple, good, kind, timid woman.' Once again, the writer is so keen to drive home the message that he will not listen to the stage director who knows that economy of words, of gestures, of expressions, and of explanations is what heightens the drama. Fortunately, the stage director in Tolstoy prevails for most of this scene.

When Makovkina gets inside the cell the viewpoint shifts to her and the corresponding shift in the language to simple colloquialism and diminutive forms throws a new and feminine light on the harsh furnishings of the monk's cell. But Tolstoy does not trivialize her and, for all her flippant coquettishness, she is aware of the enormity of what she is doing, and the chiasmatic arrangement of the conflicting adjectives at the end of the sentence shows: 'Her wet feet, especially the one, were bothering her and she hurriedly began to take her boots off, smiling all the while, pleased not so much at having achieved her goal as at having seen what had been troubling her so—this *charming,/ alarming,// strange,/ attractive man,* (*etogo prelestnogo, porazitel'nogo, strannogo, privlekatel'nogo muzhchinu*). The dramatist turns cinematographer in the crucial 'striptease' scene which follows, since he runs through it twice, first from her point of view, then Sergius's. And yet film is not the right analogy, since only writing can convey a scene first through the sense of *touch* of the stripper and then through the *hearing* of the 'voyeur' (the pleasure of voyeurism, after all, depends as much on the obstacles—having to imagine what you cannot see—as on what is seen). Moreover, Tolstoy makes sure that we know Sergius is aware of what is happening even though we only perceive it from his point of view later

—You won't come in, will you?—she asked, smiling. Because I've got to get undressed to dry off.

He did not answer, but went on reciting prayers the other side of the wall in a steady voice.

'Now there's a man'—she thought, tugging at her oozing boot. She tugged and couldn't get it off, and this made her laugh. And she laughed scarcely audibly, but knowing that he could hear her laugh and that this would have the effect she desired on him, she laughed louder, and this cheerful, natural, good-hearted laughter did affect him, and just as she had wanted.

Appropriately, the stress is on the sensuousness of the experience of undressing for Makovkina

'...Yes, he desires me'—she said, getting her outer boot and inner boot off at last and moving on to her stockings. To get them off, these long stockings with elastic tops, she had to lift her skirt up. She felt shy and muttered:
　　—Don't come in.
　　But there was no answer from behind the wall. The steady mumbling went on and there were sounds of movement as well. He must be bowing down to the ground,—she thought.—But he won't get over it by bowing,—she said. —He's thinking about me. Just as I am about him. He's thinking with the same feeling about these legs,—she said, pulling down her wet stockings and stepping with her bare feet on the palliasse and folding them under her. She sat like this for a short while, with her arms round her knees and gazing thoughtfully before her. 'Yes, this deserted spot, this silence. And no-one would ever know...'

Meanwhile, what Makovkina thinks through her sense of touch Sergius is seeing with his ears

Having recited all the vespers, he now stood stock still, staring at the end of his nose, and praying mentally, repeating over and over: 'Lord Jesus Christ, Son of God, have mercy upon me.'
　　But he heard everything. He could hear her rustling the silk material as she took off her dress, treading with bare feet on the floor; he could hear her rubbing her legs with her hand.

As Sergius decides that his only salvation lies in the self-torture of mutilation, Tolstoy, with the sure touch of genius, switches *his* viewpoint at the crucial moment to the sense of touch

He held his finger out over the flame and frowned, preparing himself for the pain, but for quite a long time he did not seem to feel anything, but suddenly —he couldn't decide at once whether it was painful and how painful it was— he winced and pulled away his finger, shaking it.
　　...he groped for the axe and felt for the chopping-block
　　—Now,—he said, and taking the axe in his right hand, laid his left index finger on the chopping-block, swung the axe and struck it below the second joint. The finger jumped away more easily than a piece of wood of the same thickness, spun round, and plopped onto the edge of the block and then onto the floor.

He heard the plopping sound before he felt any pain. But he scarcely had time to be surprised at the lack of pain when he felt a scorching pain and the warmth of flowing blood.

The sensuous quality of this experience is recalled later in the story, just before the entry to his cell, by now in another hermitage, of the merchant's daughter he is supposed to be going to heal: 'He remembered his prayers at the beginning of his solitary life when he would pray to be granted purity, humility and love, and how he had thought that God had heard his prayer, he was pure and had cut off his finger, and he raised the stump of his finger with its wrinkled folds of skin and kissed it . . . ' Given this mastery in conveying the direct sensuous experience with its instant connection to man's innermost soul, it may seem curious that Tolstoy devotes so little attention to the crucial turning-point in the story, this scene where the merchant's fat, ugly and sickly daughter succeeds in seducing Father Sergius, especially since he has spent several pages preparing us for the scene. We can hardly suspect him of puritanical coyness after the Makovkina scene which must be one of the sexiest in all Russian literature. No, the restraint is not moralistic, but artistic: the act must come as as much of a shock to the reader as it does to Sergius in order to provide a motivation for his final rapid renunciation of the image that his monastic life has imposed on him.

The renunciation is anticipated—if only we have been alert enough to notice it —by a very marked shift of style in the narrative. Tolstoy devotes several pages to describing Sergius' rational response to what is happening to him in the hermit- age as his fame spreads, and the style is ratiocinative and argumentative, with long complex sentences and strong adversative conjunctions. At the same time the sense of outside pressures on the monk is not only made explicit ('was he doing the right thing in succumbing to the situation into which he had not so much got of his own accord as he had been put by the archimandrite and abbot?'), but is conveyed in the urgent accumulation of paired comparative adverbs

the more and more time went on, the more and more strictly he regulated his life . . .

with visitors who grew more and more numerous . . .

More and more visitors came to see him . . .

Father Sergius' fame went on spreading further and further . . .

He thought about his being a burning candle and the more he felt that, the more he felt God's light of eternal truth weakening and growing dimmer . . . (See Russian Texts, No. 45)

The warring tensions are carried especially vividly in the syntax of one sentence with its insistent reported conditional clauses and its focus (in pronouns and passive verb forms) on Sergius, the sentient centre, as the passive object of an ineluctable process

> *If* they told *him that* people needed *him*, that *if* he *was to* fulfil Christ's law of love *he could not* refuse people's demand to see *him*, that it would be cruel to distance *himself* from these people, *he could not help* agreeing, and yet the more *he submitted* to this life, the more he felt the inward changing to the outward, felt the spring of living water *drying up in him*, felt that what he was doing was done more and more for people and not for God.
>
> (See Russian Texts, No. 46)

Suddenly there is a paragraph of decision and action on Sergius' part: the verbs become active and transitive with a future focus, the sentences are short, and relations between and within them are paratactic (in contrast to the complex hypotactic subordination of the preceding paragraphs)

> There was even a time when he decided to go away and hide. He even thought out in detail how to do so. He made himself a peasant shirt and trousers, a kaftan and cap. He explained that he needed these to give to people begging for clothes. He kept this outfit in his cell and thought about how he would dress up in it, cut his hair and go away. First he would go off on the train, travel three hundred versts, get off and walk from village to village. He asked an old soldier about the wandering life, about getting alms and lodging.
>
> (See Russian Texts, No. 47)

This of course is what Sergius does finally do, but first we have a partial return to the complex ratiocinative style and the comparative adverbs. At the same time, the theme of sexual temptation revives with the memory of the Makovkina incident and with a description of nature which echoes ironically the 'betrothal' scene which had initiated his monastic career

> The monk left and he remained alone on a bench under an elm tree.
>
> It was a glorious May evening, the leaves had only just burst from their buds on the birches, aspens, elms, cherry trees and oaks. The bird-cherry bushes behind the elm were in full flower and their petals had not yet begun to fall. Nightingales, one quite near and another two or three in the bushes down by the river, were chirping and bursting into song.

The scene is set, then, for the crucial turning-point in Sergius' life and in the story. The predicament in which he finds himself due to his growing fame can only be resolved by his escape, but it will take a shock to make him take the plunge, and the mechanism for that shock will be the last of the 'seduction' scenes. As we have said, however, the scene itself is underplayed, the description of the girl is sketchy, and their dialogue brief and unsubtle. The build-up of reactions and thoughts and plans in Sergius' mind ensures that this sudden and unexpected triumph of the flesh achieves its maximum surprise effect—on both the victim and us. In many ways it is Sergius' encounter with the merchant that seems more significant to the text of the story than that with his daughter. Here too there is a crucial switch of style. When he is shouting at the crowd to leave Sergius alone the merchant's language is vulgar and slangy

> The merchant, once he had helped Father Sergius to the bench under the elm tree, took it upon himself to act as a policeman and set about driving the people away in a most determined manner. He spoke quietly, it is true, so that Sergius could not hear him, but in a determined and angry voice:
> —Clear off, clear off! You've had your blessing, so what else d'you want, eh? Buzz off, or I swear I'll break someone's neck. Well, go on! Hey, you, you old bag, with the dirty leg-wraps, get weaving, go on. And where d'you think you're going? You heard, scram. God'll grant what he likes tomorrow, but now clear off, the lot of you!
> —Please, mister, let's just get a peep at his lovely face—said an old woman.
> —I'll give you peeps! Where are you creeping to?
> (See Russian Texts, No. 48)

But how the merchant's tone changes when he himself begs Father Sergius to heal his daughter! His speech is all archaic Church Slavonicisms

> So when the merchant had chased everyone away he came up to Father Sergius, without further ado kneeled down, and said in a loud voice:
> —*Holy father, pour your blessings* on my *ailing daughter* and *cure her of the pain of her sickness. I have dared to come nigh to your holy footsteps.*—And he folded his hands one upon the other. And he did and said all this as though he was doing something quite obvious and firmly established by law and custom, as if it was precisely in this way and in no other that one should, that one had to ask for one's daughter to be cured. He did it all with such certitude that Father Sergius himself began to think that that was how it all had to be said and done. But all the same he bade him stand up and tell him what was the matter.
> (See Russian Texts, No. 49)

Tolstoy now plays with the varieties of point of view made available by the juxtaposition of free indirect and direct speech, which highlights the bogus conventionality of the merchant's speech even further

> The merchant told him that his daughter, a maiden of twenty two, had fallen sick two years ago after the untimely death of her mother, had 'croaked', as he put it, and gone from bad to worse. And so he had brought her fourteen hundred versts and she was waiting at the inn until such time as Father Sergius might summon her to be brought hither. She wouldn't get up in the daytime as she was afraid of the light and could come out only after sunset.
> —Is she very weak, then?—said Father Sergius.
> —No, she has no particular corporeal weakness, but she's a *neorasthenic*

[deliberately mis-spelt in Russian to mean "won't grow", Trans.], as the doctor used to say. If thou wouldst bid her to be brought hither, Father Sergius, my spirit would soar. Holy father, bring alive a parent's heart, restore his kindred—save with your prayers his ailing daughter.
(See Russian Texts, No. 50)

The merchant's speeches have become almost pure play with speech conventions and the hypocrisy of his behaviour serves to epitomize for Sergius the social and religious hypocrisy that he has encountered at every stage of his life. Ultimately, Sergius-Kasatsky's conflict is not with lust, not with pride, and not with ambition, but with convention. He has had to suffer to discover the paradox that the more one strives to stand out as an individual, the more one is absorbed by conventions of education, of social class, of the religious life, while by merging in with the mass of humanity one finds one's integrity.

Such a didactic theme will of necessity require some artifice in the narrative structure and some allegorical pairing or contrasting of characters. But we can tolerate these artifices if the point of view is handled convincingly. D.H. Lawrence voiced a worry that many of Tolstoy's critics have felt vaguely but have been unable to pin down when he wrote: 'When the novelist puts his thumb in the scale to pull down the balance to his own predilections, that is immorality'. [43]

Now fixing the scale in advance is something that most novelists do and that most readers know novelists are doing, so it is doubtful whether D.H. Lawrence —of all people—had this in mind when he referred to Tolstoy's 'immorality'. The immorality he was surely referring to was the only one that matters to a creative writer—the betrayal of his own art—and this, as Lawrence's metaphor shows quite accurately, is a matter of small-scale manipulations in the weighing process. As far as the reader is concerned, it is not the inescapable moralistic intent which the critic deduces from 'a reading' of a work by Tolstoy, but rather the unfair ways he exploits his power to play with point of view within particular scenes, and often even within particular sentences, that, as Joyce Cary puts it, 'cause us so much uneasiness in the actual reading'. [44]

Perhaps Tolstoy mistrusted his own power as a dramatist. Few novelists have even approached him in the subtlety and economy with which he conveyed the tensions and dynamics of the way people interact. The telling entrance or departure, the way characters stand and move in relation to each other, every body movement or gesture, every flicker of an eyebrow or lip, every incomplete and ambiguous phrase uttered, keep us suspended between two or more points of view, totally convinced about the authenticity of this fragment of human drama. The significance of the respective viewpoints is always perfectly clear in relation to the characters of the participants in the scene and to the broader message of the work. And yet Tolstoy has an irresistible urge to cross all the t's and dot all the i's on our behalf as if we were peasant children enrolled in his elementary school at Yasnaya Polyana.

Father Sergius ends with a scene which seems to epitomize Tolstoy's strengths and weaknesses in the use of point of view

> If he sometimes managed to help people with a bit of advice or reading things for the illiterate or talking people out of a quarrel, he would walk away before they could thank him. And gradually the presence of God revealed itself in him.
>
> One day he was walking along the road with two old women and a soldier. They were stopped by a gentleman and lady in a gig and a man and woman on horseback. The lady's husband and daughter were riding, while the lady rode in the gig with someone who seemed to be a French traveller.
>
> They stopped to show him '*les pélérins*' who, according to a peculiar Russian folk superstition, travel on foot around the countryside instead of working.
>
> They spoke in French thinking they wouldn't understand.
>
> —*Demandez leur,*—said the Frenchman,—*s'ils sont bien sûrs de ce que leur pélérinage est agréable à Dieu.*
>
> They asked them. One old woman answered:
>
> —As God sees fit. If we've pleased God with our feet, we may please him with our hearts too.
>
> They asked the soldier. He said that he was all on his own and had nowhere to go.
>
> They asked Kasatsky who he was.
>
> —God's servant.
>
> —*Qu'est ce qu'il dit? Il ne répond pas.*
>
> —*Il dit qu'il est un serviteur de Dieu.*
>
> —*Celà doit être un fils de prêtre. Il a de la race. Avez vous de la petite monnaie?*
>
> The Frenchman found some change. And he gave them each twenty kopeks.
>
> —*Mais dîtes leur que ce n'est pas pour les cierges que je leur donne, mais pour qu'ils se régalent de thé; tea, tea*—smiling,—for you, old chap,—he said, patting Kasatsky on the shoulder with his gloved hand.
>
> —Christ save you,—answered Kasatsky, keeping his hat off and bowing his bald head forward.
>
> And this encounter was a source of great joy for Kasatsky, because he had despised the opinion of society folk and had accomplished the easiest and most trivial thing—he had humbly accepted twenty kopeks and given them to his companion, a blind beggar. The less the opinion of society mattered to him, the more strongly he felt God in him.
>
> (See Russian Texts, No. 51)

Now this apparently casual conversation by the roadside is rich in tensions, unspoken implications, and irony for the reader who has followed Kasatsky on his long moral and spiritual pilgrimage through the story. He had abandoned the rich, ambitious, status-seeking class into which he was born to become a monk because he could not stand the social and sexual hypocrisy and the patronizing arrogance epitomized by his fiancée when he discovered she had been the Tsar's mistress. As we saw earlier, we can usually expect some irony underlying the use of French by Tolstoy's characters. Here the reference, in French and in quotation marks, to '*les pélerins*' is underscored by the explanation, quite superfluous for Russian readers, presumably given by the lady or her husband in narrated discourse, about the 'peculiar' Russian folk custom of giving alms to wandering pilgrims, and by the patronizing arrogance toward the pilgrims of the subsequent exchanges in French between the Frenchman and his wealthy hosts, all of which Kasatsky, alone among the pilgrims, fully understands. Our knowing that Kasatsky understands gives especial piquancy, then, to the Frenchman's arrogant demand to know whether they were sure that their pilgrim's life was pleasing to God (in the light of Kasatsky's twenty years of doubt and moral and spiritual torment), and to his earnest attempt to persaude Kasatsky to spend his twenty kopeks of alms on '*tea*' (his one word of Russian, and even through the translation we can hear his broken accent) rather than squandering the money on candles in church (we, of course, know how disillusioned Kasatsky has become through twenty years of ritual worship in monasteries and hermitages as 'Father Sergius'), as he pats the Russian aristocrat-turned-pilgrim on the shoulder (taking care not to risk removing his glove). When Russians speak French, their speech is liable to be refracted through a verbal as well as dramatic irony: Kasatsky's simple and authentically humble Russian answer, 'God's servant', sounds altogether more pretentious when interpreted into French (behind the alternative semantics lies the opposition of two theologies); and we have been well prepared for the Russian lady's recognition, again in French, of his good breeding (though she cannot conceive of him as coming from higher than a village priest's family).

The brevity of Kasatsky's two only speeches in this encounter and our awareness of his silence in contrast to what he might have said makes his final 'Christ save you' to the Frenchman as double-edged a blessing as one could conceive in this context. (We will recall two earlier blessings he had given as a holy man, both equally ambiguous denials of his own holy status: when Makovkina, having failed in her attempt to seduce him in his mountainside retreat, begs him to forgive her and give her his blessing: '—In the name of the Father, the Son and the Holy Ghost,—she heard from behind the screen,—Go away.' (See Russian Texts, No. 52) On the other hand, when the humble and pathetic Pashenka asks for his blessing as he leaves her home, he answers: '—God will bless you. Forgive me for Christ's sake.' (See Russian Texts, No. 53) Even the speech and implied character of Kasatsky's companions allows a perfectly relevant but understated contrast to the rich people's arrogance: on the one hand, the pious peasant woman with her response in the form of a proverb; on the other, the pure lack of any meaning in the wandering of the soldier, who simply has nowhere else to go.

The richness of the implications behind the extreme economy and restraint of this whole dialogue shows Tolstoy at his most artistic. He has no need to spell them out, since we have lived through every spiritual and moral crisis that has brought Kasatsky from the brilliance and ambition of his youth to this dumb humility of his middle age. And yet Tolstoy does spell them out. He puts his thumb in the scale. Before this scene takes place we need to know how Kasatsky lives after renouncing his monastic life, and the acts of kindness enumerated in the first paragraph we quoted tell us this adequately enough. But we hardly need to be told (beginning with the 'And . . . ' of Gospel narrative): 'And gradually the presence of God revealed itself in him.' Still less does the novelist need to construe for us the scene itself with unctuous phrases about his hero finding joy in humility, and feeling God's presence in him increasing in proportion to his scorn for social opinion; that has been one of the major themes of the whole story. Still less again do we need the gratuitous touch about Kasatsky handing the twenty kopeks over to his companion, who—of course, though we only learn it now—turns out to be a blind beggar! The thumb slips into the scale, then, when Tolstoy decides he must drive home his message through the telling mode, even when it is more than clear from the dramatic episode.

Our analysis of the working of point of view in Tolstoy suggests that far from being a matter of the overall structure of the narrator's position vis-à-vis the people and events he describes, what count are the shifts at paragraph and sentence level and even within the contextual meaning of an individual word or phrase; within each scene the interplay between narrative, internal monologue, dialogue and reported or free indirect speech is highly significant. And yet the significance of point of view is not merely stylistic; it is bound up with the larger structures of narrative form, with the relationship between one character and another, one setting and another (even at opposite ends of the story), between the central reversal and the other dramatic scenes.

I have suggested that, for all the artistry with which Tolstoy constructs this story, he ultimately mistrusts his art and 'puts his thumb in the scale to pull down the balance to his own predilections'. According to D.H. Lawrence that is 'immorality', and if undermining one's own art is immoral, we must agree. But even Tolstoy himself maintains that it is inappropriate. To give our author the last word, even when he is being most didactic about art, in the essay 'What is Art?', he insists: 'The business of art is precisely to make understood and felt that which in the form of an argument might be incomprehensible and inaccessible.'

NOTES TO CHAPTER 3

1. Wayne C. Booth, *The Rhetoric of Fiction* (Chicago, 1961); Boris Uspensky, *Poetika kompozitsii* (Moscow, 1970); English translation, *A Poetics of Composition*, by Valentina Zavarin and Susan

Wittig (Berkeley, 1973); Gérard Genette, *Discours du récit* (*Figures III*, Paris, 1972, pp.67-282); English translation, *Narrative Discourse*, by Jane E. Lewin (Oxford, 1980).

2. Roland Barthes, 'An introduction to the structural analysis of narrative' (*New Literary History*, 6:2, 1974, pp.237-72); the French original of this important article was published in *Communications*, 8 (Paris, 1966, pp.1-27).

3. See also the analysis of Chekhov's *The Student* in L.M. O'Toole, 'Structure and style in the short story: Chekhov's *Student*' (*The Slavonic and East European Review*, XLVIII, 114, 1971, pp.45-67).

4. Barthes, *op. cit.* and Tsvetan Todorov, 'Les catégories du récit littéraire' (*Communications*, 8, 1966, pp.125-51).

5. See especially M.A.K. Halliday, 'Linguistic function and literary style' in Seymour Chatman (ed.) *Literary Style: A Symposium* (Oxford, 1971, pp.330-65); reprinted in M.A.K. Halliday, *Explorations in the Functions of Language* (London, 1973, pp.103-43). The relevance of this linguistic model to the study of the relationship between narrative structure and point of view is examined in L.M. O'Toole, 'Linguistic functions and the study of literary style' (*Melbourne Slavonic Studies*, 5-6, 1971, pp.106-23).

6. M.M. Bakhtin, *Problemy poetiki Dostoevskogo* (Moscow, 1929 and 1963); English translation, *Problems of Dostoevsky's Poetics*, by R.W. Rotsel (Ann Arbor, 1973); see also Julia Kristeva's penetrating discussion of Bakhtin's book: 'Bakhtine, le mot, le dialogue et le roman' (*Critique*, 239, 1967, pp.438-65).

7. All references and quotations from the text are from: F.M. Dostoevskii, *Sobraniye sochinnii*, x (Moscow, 1958, pp.378-419; author's translations).

8. See Eric Rhode's excellent article, 'Dostoevsky and Bresson' (*Sight and Sound*, Spring 1970, pp.82-3).

9. Booth, *op. cit.*, p.138.

10. Robert Louis Jackson, *Dostoevsky's Quest for Form* (New Haven 1966, p.1).

11. *Ibid.* p.58.

12. NB. *obraz* in Russian means both 'image' and 'icon'.

13. *Golos*, 2 Oct. 1876, No. 272.

14. Quoted by L. Grossman in his notes to the story, in this edition, see Note 7.

15. Dostoevsky, *Dnevnik pisatelya*, Jan. 1881.

16. Jackson, *op. cit.*, p.x.

17. Bakhtin, *op. cit.*, p.272.

18. On the connections with Goethe's *Faust* in the story, see below.

19. Booth, *op. cit.*, p.233.

20. V.V. Vinogradov, 'Stil' Peterburgskoi poemy *Dvoinik*', *Mysl'* (Petrograd, 1922).

21. Barthes, *op. cit.*, p.21; second ref. p.8.

22. He transfers the notion to the Gil Blas reference: 'The girl's vivid appreciation of this masterful scene must bear witness to her sensitive cultural and artistic understanding'.

23. Quotations are from Goethe, *Faust*, Part I, translated by Philip Wayne (Harmondsworth, 1949).

24. Roman Jakobson, 'Linguistics and Poetics', in T.A. Sebeok (ed.) *Style in Language* (Cambridge, Mass., 1960, p.355).

25. Bakhtin, *op. cit.*, pp.246-7.

26. *Ibid.* p.70.

27. Vinogradov, *op. cit.*

28. Yurii Tynyanov, 'Dostoevskii i Gogol': K teorii parodii' (Petrograd, Izd. OPOYAZ, 1921); reprinted in *Brown University Slavic Reprint*, IV, 1966.

29. P.M. Bitsilli, 'K voprosu o vnutrennei forme romana Dostoevskogo' (Sofia Universitet, Istoriko-filologicheski fakul'tet. *Godisnik*, XLII, 1945/46 pp.1-71); reprinted in *Brown University Slavic Reprint*, IV, 1966.

30. Bakhtin, *op. cit.*, p.222.

31. Quoted by L. Grossman in notes to the story, *op. cit.*, p.519.
32. The significance of the technical grammatical terms we refer to may be clarified by reference to the table (2) at the end of Halliday's article: 'Linguistic function and literary style', *op. cit.*, Note 5.
33. Bakhtin, *op. cit.*, p.12.
34. We have preserved the Old Church Slavonic forms here, following Bakhtin, since they express both the religiosity and the contrast between the intimate and alienating second person forms of address.
35. Quotations and references are from the 90-volume edition of Tolstoy's works: L.N. Tolstoy, *Polnoye sobraniye sochinenii*, 1-90 (Moscow, 1928-1958, 31, pp.5-46; author's translations).
36. A misnomer if we use the term in contrast to first person narration, since first person narration is through the voice of an 'I' figure, while third person narration is *about* third persons but through a depersonalized voice.
37. By 'hero' in this context we mean, of course, the 'sentient centre' or 'centre of conscious-ness' of the story who, in terms of the *action* of the story might be an anti-hero or even a villain.
38. Gerard Genette, *Le discours du récit* (*Figures III*, Paris 1972, p.187).
39. See L.M. O'Toole, *op. cit.* Note 3, p.66.
40. For a full discussion of this question historically, socially and in nineteenth-century literature see Paul Friedrich, 'Structural implications of Russian pronominal usage' in William Bright (ed.) *Sociolinguistics* (The Hague, 1966, pp.128-64).
41. Boris Uspensky, *op. cit.*, Chapter 2.
42. In Russian *zabludit'sya* means 'to go astray' in both the physical and moral sense, cf. the same root in *bludnyi syn*—the Prodigal Son.
43. D.H. Lawrence, quoted by Henry Gifford in 'Anna, Lawrence and "The Law" ' (*Critical Quarterly*, 1, No. 3, 1959).
44. Joyce Cary, *Art and Reality* (New York, 1958, pp.161-2).

4

FABLE

Korolenko: *Makar's Dream*
Pushkin: *The Post-Stage Master*

I

So FAR we have mainly examined the refraction of short stories through the large-scale lenses the writer has selected for projecting a total, syncretic image of his chosen theme. Narrative structure and point of view, as we have seen, operate indexically, that is, they involve choices by the writer which will have implications for the whole work. Even quite small-scale choices at the micro-level of style, such as Gogol's hyperbole and alogism, or Tolstoy's play with French and Russian speech or formal and informal pronouns of address, seem to be a direct consequence of the author's most fundamental decisions about the shape of his story. As far as the reader and critic is concerned, we may say that his perception of these choices comes from a 'reading' of the story, an overall interpretation of its meaning which he can only attempt after he has reached the end.

'Reading', however, takes place through time and as we first read a piece of narrative fiction we only gradually piece together the discrete pieces of information we are given into something resembling a story. The syntagmatic structures which enable us to do this operate on two main dimensions—those of time and causality. We structure the world of the fiction as we structure the world we live in on the assumption that temporal chains and the sequence of cause and effect have some objective reality, and however anarchic the order in which we learn of events, however arbitrary the causal relationships with which the writer intrigues us, we cannot help recreating a 'real' temporal and causal sequence out of the story as we read it.

This distinction between the recreatable 'dispositional' world underlying the fiction and the 'expositional' world in the form in which the writer presents it to us is crucial to the insistence of the Russian Formalists on discriminating between *fabula* (fable) and *syuzhet* (usually translated as 'plot'); to quote Tomashevsky who frequently summed up Formalist theory most cogently: '...the *fabula* is the totality of motifs in their logical causal-temporal chain, while the *syuzhet* is the totality of the same motifs in that sequence and connectivity in which they are presented in the work.'[1] Now it will be noted that this definition presupposes that the totality of motifs which we discover behind 'the sequence and connectivity in which they are presented in the work' (the 'dispositional' order, as Petrovsky termed it, behind the 'compositional' order) forms a single, 'logical', causal-temporal chain. It assumes an identity between the causal and the temporal. This seems to be an unnecessary and unhelpful conflation of the temporal and causal which is not bound by any over-riding 'logic'. The Formalist theorists of narrative—Shklovsky, Eikhenbaum, Tomashevsky, Petrovsky—deserve every credit for their insistence on analyzing the actual texts of novels and stories and juxtaposing the textual sequence of motifs with the original sequence which could be recovered from the text. (This was not a new idea: after all, a whole rhetoric of narrative in the seventeenth and eighteenth centuries had been built on the Homeric model of opening the narration *in medias res* before filling in necessary historical and biographical information in the form of a flashback; what was new was the rigour with which the Formalists incorporated this distinction into their method.)

The separation of the temporal and the causal in the 'original' order of events can be justified on two main counts. In the first place, the psychological processes involved are almost certainly different. Our reconstruction of *time* sequences from narrative texts is a fairly mechanical procedure whereby such superficial elements in the text as stated dates and times, adverbial phrases of time, its sequentiality and extent, verb tense and temporal deixis are sorted and rearranged —usually without much conscious effort on the reader's part—to form a convincing temporal sequence for the events narrated. We are able to process the text in this way because we are automatically processing *language* in this way every day of our lives. *Causality*, in narrative and in life, is surely a very different matter. Many sequences of cause and effect are routine and can be objectively verified, but most of the ones that are of interest in literature are unique to a particular situation and have to be interpreted subjectively according to our knowledge of human motivation and individual and group responses. We make predictions about how a particular person or character will act in a given set of circumstances or how a particular social group will react to a given act of God or man according to what we like to call the 'laws' of human nature or social culture. But we turn out to be wrong in life too often for comfort, and novelists seek to discomfort us by upsetting our fondest predictions. In other words, our data for deciding about causality is only to a small extent language data (and we are used to seeing through lies, bombast, miscalculation and misinterpretation) and is mainly our knowledge of *life*, human relationships and human meaning. It would seem appropriate, therefore, to keep separate our analysis and reconstruction of time and causality on psychological grounds.

In the second place, there seem to be good reasons for doing so on specifically literary grounds. Some narrative genres play with time sequence without this raising any serious problems about causes and effects. The 'time-machine' variety of science fiction does this. On the other hand, mystery stories intrigue the reader and make his imagination work hard to establish patterns of causality without necessarily involving a marked disruption of the time sequence. Detective stories sometimes require the accurate reconstruction of a time sequence in order to establish a causal pattern, although the readers' and detectives' search for motives often means that mere temporal clues have to be discounted. Utopian novels and the more moralistic or philosophical type of science fiction tend to require us to transfer our preconceptions about individual and social motivation to a new time dimension so that we have to re-examine those preconceptions.

Time, then, poses its own set of problems for the novelist, the reader and the literary critic and needs to be treated separately. Our account of 'fable' in this chapter will therefore focus on temporal relationships, while we will devote the next chapter, and two further analyses, to an examination of causal relationships under the heading of 'plot'.

Our method will be to start by reconstructing the fable, comparing the time patterning we thus discover with the temporal composition of the actual text in terms of sequence, duration and focus, then considering the implications of the time structuring for the other dimensions through which the theme is refracted and for our interpretation of the story's meaning. As we have stressed through-out this book, none of the levels of analysis can be isolated ultimately from the other levels. At the analytical stage we can and must handle one type of pattern-ing at a time, but at the synthesizing stage the patterns that emerge on separate levels will relate to each other and create other kinds of patterning which we must attempt to describe. Thus aspects of the temporal patterning will relate to narrative structure, point of view, character, setting—and, indeed, plot.

The Russian stories I have chosen to illustrate the potentialities of time-play in narrative contrast in many ways. Korolenko's story *Makar's Dream* uses a third person omniscient narrator to tell a rather naive and simple story apparently in direct chronological sequence. However, the first third of the story unfolds in the 'real' world of the Yakut village where Makar lives, while the remainder takes place in a dream-world where Makar believes he has died. The contrasts in pace are important, but so too are the elements of flashback to earlier stages in Makar's life which influence the outcome of his trial in heaven and which, perhaps, influence our judgement about the shape of the narrative structure. Pushkin's *The Post-Stage Master*, on the other hand, is a deliberate and sophisti-cated exercise in restructuring time with partial narratives by a first person narrator and the hero which involve a variety of framing techniques. The whole story could be viewed as an interplay between a dynamic story line and a series of static verbal genre paintings.

Three of the best modern critical works on time in narrative literature are A.A. Mendilow's *Time and the Novel*,[2] W.J.M. Bronzwaer's *Tense in the Novel*[3] and Gérard Genette's *Discours du récit: essai de méthode*.[4] All criticism on this prob-lem has been foreshadowed, and largely overshadowed, by Laurence Sterne's *Tristram Shandy* (1760-68) and Marcel Proust's *A la recherche du temps perdu* (1913-1927).

II   Korolenko: *Makar's Dream*, 1885; (*Son Makara*)[5]

As we pointed out in Chapter 1, the imposition of any model on the text of a work of art involves the unavoidable risk of artificiality and arbitrariness, and nowhere is this more true than when we reconstruct an original chronological sequence out of the events as they are presented in the narrative text. For one thing, this *fable* is of rather doubtful validity, since the writer is unlikely to have thought up the facts of his story in strict chronology and then rearranged them in the order in which they occur in the story. The story itself *is* the world the writer has given us and we are not so much reconstructing as *construing* a neatly chronological world behind his text; we are refracting his reality, not reflecting it. Nevertheless, most scientific and humane disciplines employ techniques of analysis (for instance, spectroscopy, slow-motion photography, or statistical sampling) which appear to do violence to the object studied and yet provide a great deal of otherwise unattainable information. What counts is the use that can be made of the information. The fable we can construct for *Makar's Dream* or *The Post-Stage Master* is of very little interest in itself, but throws light on the actual composition of the stories when we see it in relation to the other levels we are analyzing and attempt to interpret the stories' themes.

Makar's Russian ancestors had fought to cultivate a tiny area of manageable land in the vast and impenetrable forests of the Yakut province of Eastern Siberia and had gradually built the small township of Chalgan to the point where this collection of wooden huts and skin yourts boasted a Christian church, a Yakut regional administrator (Toyon) and a saloon bar run by Tartars. In the process the Russians had intermarried with Yakuts and had adopted many of their ways of dressing, eating and even talking. Makar was born, clear-eyed and innocent, into this community; he married and had children and worked hard as a wood-cutter and trapper, but hardship, the harsh climate and constant demands for money from the civil authorities and the church had beaten him down. His children had either died in infancy or had left home to fight hardship on their own, his eldest son had been taken off to the army and was probably dead. Even when his first wife was ill he had to be out woodcutting instead of nursing her. One old man had simply left his wife in Chalgan to find peace and salvation in a mountain retreat. Makar sought solace more and more in drinking the watered-down vodka fortified with nicotine which the Tartars sold and escaped the reproaches of his second wife, who was much stronger physically and morally than he was, down at the saloon bar. Six years before the story opens he had been cheated out of a horse by a Tartar who died a year later, and four years previously had lost his drinking companion, Ivan the village priest, who fell into the fire while drunk.

He no longer went to church, but would boost his pocket and his self-esteem from time to time by chatting with some educated Russians, probably political exiles, who lived at one end of the village. One Christmas Eve he went out to earn a rouble by delivering firewood to them and then went to the saloon to get drunk. When he and a Yakut were thrown out of the saloon into the snow he made his way home to bed and fell asleep and dreamed that he found a superb fox in the traps laid by his neighbour and rival Alyoshka. When Alyoshka catches him stealing the fox, they fight, the fox escapes and Makar dreams that he dies lying in the snow.

He is aroused by a kick from the village priest Ivan who has come to conduct him to the Last Judgement by the Grand Toyon, a folksy combination of the Christian God and a Yakut governor. As they journey eastwards through forests, mountains, ravines and over a high plateau, they meet the Tartar who had cheated Makar over the horse; he is galloping to Judgement but still making slower progress than Makar and Ivan on foot. They then meet the old man who had left home in search of salvation, but had been sent back by the Grand Toyon to fetch his wife whom he had to carry on his back. They pass thieves laden with stolen goods, fat Yakut toyons on high saddles with their tall hats scraping the clouds, poor working people scuttling along on foot and a murderer striving vainly to wipe the blood off himself in the snow. The sight of flocks of the innocent souls of children, who had died through poor food and the dirt, smoky fires and draughts endemic among yourt-dwellers, brings him to the threshold of the hut-palace where the Last Judgement is to take place.

Ivan is interrogated about Makar, and the special scales which are reserved for Chalgan people, with an extra-large pan for the sins and a pit beneath it, are prepared. Makar, cunning to the last, checks the scales to be sure he is not being cheated and wishes he could use the steel yard he is used to and from which he usually gains some extra profit. The Grand Toyon enters, the dove of the Holy Spirit flies in and settles on his knee and the Judgement begins. The positive score for hard work that Makar claims—the thousands of poles cut, and hundreds of loads of firewood delivered and bushels of corn sown—are checked by Ivan in Makar's records and found to be exaggerated, but still the gold pan of the scales sinks to mark his virtue. Unfortunately, the extra-large wooden pan for his sins sinks rapidly under the weight of the 21,933 times he has cheated people and the 400 bottles of vodka he has drunk. He tries to check the sinking pan with his foot, but this is only further evidence that he is a trickster, a lazybones and a drunkard and he is sentenced to carry the church verger and the police super-intendent around on his back like a horse.

At this point the Son of the Grand Toyon enters and sits at his Father's right hand. He expresses understanding and sympathy for Makar's fate and Makar, previously barely articulate, is filled with the gift of speech. With mounting eloquence he tells them of all his hardship and suffering and persecution, the loss of his elder son, his ailing first wife and all his children. When the Grand Toyon says that he prefers the clean in body and pure in spirit, Makar protests that he too was born clean and pure, but life's burden has spoiled and sullied him. His anger turns to tears of self-pity as the Grand Toyon tells him he will find truth in heaven and they all weep as the wooden pan of the scales rises higher and higher.

The first thing we note about this time structure is that the action of the story in 'real world' terms lasts only three or four hours, while we are given information about a whole lifetime. This is made possible, of course, by the dream technique which allows for a very flexible play with time and is made necessary by the Last Judgement episode which is the culmination of both dream and story. Secondly, practically all that we learn of Makar's personal past comes in the last three pages of the story; in some respects the story works backwards from his present to his past. Yet this is not merely a matter of temporal structure, since the four main phases of the story correspond to five distinct points of view which are very precisely graded. *Makar's Dream* opens with a frankly ethnographic account of the history of Chalgan and the mores of the three main ethnic groups who live there: Yakuts, Russians and Tartars. Makar's present life and relations with other inhabitants of Chalgan, as typified by his celebration of Christmas Eve, are observed by a narrator who seems to be torn between his role as folklorist and ethnographer and his need to get inside his hero's mind. He only really succeeds in doing so when Makar has collapsed into bed in a drunken stupor and dream logic takes over. Now, in the episode of the fight over the traps with Alyoshka we get a vivid insight into the anxieties and tensions which currently trouble Makar. These gain in authenticity as he journeys after death to the Grand Toyon in the company of his dead friend and drinking companion, the old priest Ivan. Their close understanding allows for a degree of frankness between them (quite absent in the scene between Makar and his wife, for instance) which permits Makar to re-examine in emotional and moral terms some episodes from his former life, such as the quarrel with the Tartar over the stolen horse and the departure from Chalgan of the old man who was seeking solitary salvation. Ivan acts as a kind of sounding-board for Makar's half-articulated thoughts and even, as emissary for the Grand Toyon, is able to express Makar's hidden motives. Finally, in the Last Judgement episode we are given both a supposedly objective report of the pluses and minuses of Makar's whole life and Makar's own subjective justification for his life which gains him redemption. In other words, as we peel away the layers of the onion, we come closer to the real Makar—and the tears flow faster.

Two folk images in the story epitomize both the difference between the Makar we meet at the beginning and the Makar who emerges at the end and the change in point of view which has accompanied the change. In the first sentence of the story the narrator refers to 'poor Makar' as 'that same Makar on whom, as everyone knows, all the pine cones fall': the folk saying sums up the combination of stupidity and bad luck that makes him one of life's victims, but at the same time holds him at arm's length, like the proverbial Irishman or Armenian. Just before the end of the story Makar uses another forest image to describe his second wife and himself growing old and weak together in their hard world: 'They stood as solitary as two orphan fir trees stand out on the steppe, battered on every side by cruel snowstorms'. This time, however, the image is Makar's own, not 'as everyone knows', and it is the culmination of his most eloquent plea for mercy before the Grand Toyon: from being a timeless figure of fun, Makar has become a real and poignant person for whom time has run out.

As we have indicated already, Korolenko is not equally successful in his hand-ling of the narrative voice in the five phases of the story, and this is almost certainly a reflection of some confusion in his aims. While he is setting Makar in his geographic and social context, the author-as-ethnographer maintains an objective informative style which nevertheless allows for occasional excursions into Makar's own mind. Comparing himself with the native Yakuts of Chalgan: 'He was very proud of his roots and would sometimes run down the other ''pagan Yakuts'', although to tell the truth, he was himself no different from the Yakuts in either customs or way of life.' Characteristically for the development of the story as a whole, the narrator penetrates further into Makar's mind and style when the latter is drunk, although we should note that the amount of direct quotation is again minimal; rather, as Bakhtin put it, 'the alien voice permeates the narrative utterance' [6]

> He *worked terribly hard,/lived in poverty* and suffered *hunger and cold. Did he have any thoughts* besides the endless worries about wheaten pancakes and tea?
> *Yes, he did.*
> When he got drunk he used to cry. 'What a life we have,—he would say, —Oh Lord God!' Apart from this he would sometimes say he wished he could chuck up everything and go off to the 'mountain'. There he *wouldn't plough/or sow, wouldn't cut/and carry firewood*, wouldn't even grind corn in his hand grinder. He would just be saved. What sort of mountain this was, or where it was, he didn't know exactly; *he only knew that there was such a moun-tain, firstly,// and secondly that it was somewhere far off*,—so far away that *not even* the Toyon governor *himself* would be able to get him from there . . . *And he wouldn't pay any taxes* either, of course.
> (See Russian Texts, No. 54)

Apart from the brief quotation, Makar's own colloquial style, indeed his linguis-tic inadequacy, comes across in the brevity and balance of the phrasing: 'worked terribly hard/lived in poverty' (*rabotal strashno/zhil bedno*); 'suffered hunger and cold' (*terpel golod i kholod*); 'wouldn't plough/or sow, wouldn't cut/and carry firewood' (*ne budet ni pakhat'/ni seyat', ne budet rubit'/i vozit' drova*) and the chiasmus of 'he only knew that there was such a mountain, firstly,//and secondly that it was somewhere far off' (*znal tot'ko, chto gora eta yest', vo-pervykh, //a vo vtorykh, chto ona gde-to daleko*). The vocabulary is the simplest possible and faintly biblical: 'hunger and cold' (*golod i kholod*), 'neither plough nor sow' (*ni pakhat ni seyat'*) and the feeling is conveyed by the bravado of 'himself' (*samomu*) or the thematization in the reversed word order of the last sentence. Even the naively didactic rhetorical question and answer: 'Did he have any thoughts . . . ? —Yes, he did' (*Byli li u nego kakiye-nibud' mysli . . . ?—Da, byli*) fits in quite well with the shift to Makar's own consciousness.

There is a marked change in the style and tone of the narration in the second phase of the story, the launching of the story proper. The ethnographer in

Korolenko still provides us with background information about the educated Russians from whom Makar earns his rouble for a Christmas Eve drink, and about the Tartar landlords who sell him their diluted vodka. He gives us the Yakut names for common objects, with a translation where necessary: 'He got up and put on his tattered *sona* (fur coat)'; 'he caught his old pinto mare in the *alas*', presumably to heighten the authenticity of Makar's Yakutized Russian. The narrator's main aim here seems, indeed, to be to get inside his peasant hero's thought processes and perceptions of the real world.

Since the story is subtitled 'A Christmas Story', we may accept the folksy opening 'It was Christmas Eve' (*Delo bylo v kanun rozhdestva*) and the colloquial 'they were out of bread' (*khleb byl v iskhode*) as essential tone-setting devices. Even the sentimental tone that pervades this part of the story—the idealization of the Russian intellectuals, the anthropomorphism of Makar's horse who regards his behaviour with a kind of sardonic resignation, the Christmas-card picturesqueness of the description of the Russians' yourt on the edge of the village— may be justified in a 'Christmas Story', although the combination in this latter scene of dimunitives, doubled adverbs and the personification of nature seems overplayed: 'On the very edge of the village stood a *tiny little* yourt. From its roof, as from the other yourts, rose *high into the air* the smoke from *the hearth*, clouding over the cold stars and bright moon with its white *billowing* pall. The firelight *danced*, reflecting through the dull ice blocks. All was still outside.' (See Russian Texts, No. 55) If we assume that Korolenko's main aim in this part of the story is to provide insights into Makar's mind through his encounters with the few characters who people his world—his wife, the Russian intellectuals, drunken Yakuts, cheating Tartar innkeepers and his horse—then we may be bothered by the inconsistency between the direct representation of that mind, through his words and reproduced thoughts, and the authorial gloss on that representation which frequently becomes a rather laboured irony. For instance, his wife scarcely warrants the 'stepped' syntax and ironic 'wonderfully' of: 'His wife, a powerful, sinewy, wonderfully strong and just as wonderfully ugly woman . . . ' (see Russian Texts, No. 56) or the irony of the 'caress' in: 'He gave her such a hard thump on the shoulder that she staggered, and winked at her cunningly. A woman's heart was like that: she knew that Makar was bound to pull a fast one on her, but gave in to the charm of a husband's caress.' (See Russian Texts, No. 57) This tongue-in-cheek pseudo-Gogolian manner of describing every encounter between Makar and his wife is carried even further when he reels home drunk: 'The first chime of the church bell had rung out in the frosty air when Makar went into his hut. His first words to his old lady were to inform her that a fox had got caught in their trap. He had totally forgotten that the old lady had not been drinking vodka with him and was gravely startled when, in spite of this joyful news, she immediately delivered a savage kick just below his spine. Then, as he slumped onto the bed she managed to get him in the neck with her fist.' (See Russian Texts, No. 58) Does the archness of the euphemisms here really help to convey the savagery of Makar's relations with his wife, or, conversely, does it really attenuate the savagery and make it more entertaining? Similarly, the Tartar landlord's brutal handling of Makar is made no more bearable by the humour of his supposedly preferential treatment: 'He went up to the Yakut and, seizing him by the scruff of the neck, flung him headlong out of the saloon. Then he went up to Makar. As he was a local resident, the Tartar showed him more respect: opening the doors wide, he served the poor chap such a kick from behind that Makar flew out of the hut and landed nose-first in the snow-drift.' At this stage in the story Korolenko has already established that he is not writing satire or farce and the mismatch in the style seems to point to a difficulty he is having in getting to grips with his characters of low class and low intelligence. The slapstick humour and rather heavy irony seem to keep us, and him, from identifying fully with the hero: the narrator is unwilling, or perhaps unable to give himself fully to the alien point of view represented by Makar and the others. It is as if a framework of *narodnik* paternalism prevents us from entering fully the world of Chalgan. During his imprisonment and exile in northern Russia and Siberia Korolenko had met many of the revolutionaries who sought a new future for Russia through the 'people' and had himself been attracted by the *narodnik* programme. However, his close contact with the common people while he was in Siberia ('at the state's expense', as he put it) left him finally critical of *narodnik* naivety. He was disinclined to 'pay homage to the wisdom of the common people' and in a letter written a few years after he wrote *Makar's Dream* he said quite frankly: 'It is time we stopped feeding the people all this intellectual chaff of lisping namby-pamby morality, fables about good and wicked peasants, the destructiveness of the city and the advantages of life in the countryside even when people are dying of famine there.' [7] Now *Makar's Dream* is very far from the lisping namby-pamby morality of the *narodnik* authors Korolenko was criticizing, but there does seem to be an uncertainty of tone in these 'real life' episodes of the story. [8]

Curiously, this uncertainty does not extend to the dream sequences. It is as if the dream logic had released him from a pre-occupation with verisimilitude and allowed his imagination to take wing. Against the regular accompaniment of the Christmas church bells which are the link between the real world of Chalgan and the dream world of the fight over the traps in the forest and the journey to the Grand Toyon, Makar's unconscious thoughts move along in short, rhythmic sentences linked paratactically. There is an urgency without time; paradoxically, the sentences conveying Makar's frantic actions in the dream are hardly at all marked by time adverbs, whereas the longer, more leisurely descriptions of the landscape lit up by the Aurora Borealis have strong temporal marking. Compare

He was lying on the bed. His head was burning. A fire seemed to be scorching him inside. Through his veins spread the strong mixture of vodka and tobacco liquor. Down his face flowed the cold rivulets of melted snow; the same rivulets were also flowing down his back.

with

> *Meanwhile* the moon had gone down and up above, in the very zenith, there was a whitish cloud which started shining with a shimmering phosphorescent glow. *Then* it seemed to break apart, expand and turn to spray, and from it streams of multicoloured fire *quickly* stretched out in different directions, *while* the semicircular dark cloud to the north grew even dimmer. It turned black, blacker than the forest which Makar was approaching.

This 'purple passage', clearly a product of the educated narrator's mind rather than Makar's, does not interrupt the flow of the dream sequence; rather, it provides a dynamic backcloth, supposedly in 'real time', to the time-free peregrinations of Makar. The two time-scales fuse in the later passage just before he 'dies'

> He had been walking *for a long time*. According to his calculations he should have *long since* come out of the Yamalakh forest and should have spotted the church tower, but he was *still* going round in circles in the forest. The thickets seemed to be bewitched, clutching him in their embrace. *From far away* the same triumphant ringing *still* carried to him. Makar thought he was moving towards it, but the ringing *got* farther away and *as* the peals came quieter and quieter a dull despair overtook Makar's heart.
>
> He was weary. He was crushed. His legs kept giving way under him. His battered body ached with a dull pain. His hands and feet were numb. His bare head felt as if it was being crushed by red hot iron hoops.
> (See Russian Texts, No. 59)

The short, staccato sentences in the last paragraph convey, like convulsions, the motor reactions of his despair. The longer, measured periods of the preceding paragraph combine the calm unconcerned rhythm of nature with a stress on the passing of time: 'for a long time, long since, still . . . still . . . as . . . further' (*uzhe dolgo, davno, vse . . . vse . . . po mere togo, kak . . . vse . . .*). Yet time seems to merge into space, Makar measures his time of walking by his distance from the bells. In the surrealist landscape of the dream, as in a Salvador Dali landscape, the clocks have melted, perspective is no longer to be trusted for a sense of spatial relationships and the observer is trapped in a scene of fearful clarity without the reassuring human measures of time and space.

The interplay between light and darkness and between the high and low signalled in the previous passage about the Northern Lights becomes crucial not only to the setting for Makar's journey over moonlit plain and through dense forest, through deep gorges and along the high plateau, but to the theme itself. The lights of Chalgan amid the dark Siberian forest prefigure the brightly lit hut of the Grand Toyon, just as the church bells on high and the falling blade of the fox traps prefigure the gold and wooden pans of the scales in which Makar's virtues and sins are to be weighed.

As Makar and the priest Ivan advance on their journey to the Last Judgement, the shifting of dimensions becomes quite explicit: time comes to be measured in spatial terms, but now space, too, shifts to a relationship between low and high, which is itself the product of the darkness/light opposition

> But they had evidently been walking for a long time. True, Makar had not yet seen the dawn, but to judge from the expanse around he thought they had been walking for a whole week at least: they had left behind them so many gullies and crags, rivers and lakes, had passed through so many forests and over so many plains. Whenever Makar looked over his shoulder it seemed as if the dark Taiga forest was itself running backwards away from them, while the high snowy mountains seemed to be melting in the nocturnal gloom and quickly disappearing over the horizon.
>
> They seemed to be climbing higher and higher. The stars were becoming bigger and brighter all the time. Then from behind the crest of the mountain they had climbed to appeared the edge of the moon which had set long since. It seemed to be hurrying to get away but Makar and the priest chased it. At last it once more began to rise above the horizon. They set off across a flat very high plateau.
>
> Now it had grown light, much lighter than when night fell. This happened, of course, due to their being much closer to the stars. The stars, each as big as an apple were really brilliant, and the moon, like the bottom of a big gold barrel, shone as bright as the sun, lighting up the whole plateau from end to end.

The abstractness of the landscape—and the abstractness of the ideas being expressed—are perfectly offset by the concrete simplicity of the folk simile at the end.

This Homeric switch from the lofty to the folksy is beautifully handled in each of Makar's encounters after death with those he had known during his life. On the one hand, the little priest Ivan (modelled on a real priest in Amga where Korolenko lived in exile) is Makar's guide and mentor on his journey to the Last Judgement; on the other hand he is the subject of a ribald folk anecdote about being so drunk that he leaned too far into the fireplace to light his pipe, fell into the fire and was burned up, all except for his legs which were given a proper funeral service. In a similar vein, the Tartar who had stolen Makar's piebald horse has a magical air as he gallops over the plain throwing up 'clouds of snow dust which glittered with the multi-coloured gleams of the stars' rays'. Like everything else on the dream journey, the horse's speed is outside time, so that Makar easily overtakes it on foot. Makar's response to this vision, however, is to accuse the Tartar of cheating even in death so that he won't even spare him a leaf

of tobacco for his pipe. He is aggrieved when Ivan tells him that this meanness
will cost him a hundred sins before the Grand Toyon

—So why didn't you tell me before?—snapped Makar.
—Well, it's a bit late to teach you now. You should have learned about that
from your priests while you were alive.
Makar lost his temper. He never had got any sense out of priests. They would
accept their tithe, but couldn't even teach you when you had to give a Tartar a
leaf of tobacco to get your sins absolved. A hundred sins was no joke . . . and
all for one little leaf! . . . It must be worth something!
—Hang on,—he said,—One leaf will do for us and I'll give the other four to
the Tartar right now. That'll make four hundred sins off.

Makar's naivety and incurably mortal ethics are delightful and wholly unsenti-
mentalized.

In the third of Makar's encounters, with the old man who had sought salvation on his own but had been ordered to go back to carry his wife to the Grand
Toyon on his back, the Last Judgement scene towards which Makar is moving is
anticipated and the selfishness of solitary salvation duly punished, but the scene
ends in an entirely down-to-earth manner

Makar felt even more sorry for the old man and was heartily glad that he
hadn't managed to go off to the 'hills'. His old lady was a tall, massive old
woman and he would have found it even harder to carry her. And if she'd
made things worse by prodding him with her foot like an ox she would probably have ridden him to his second death.

Out of sympathy he was about to take the old woman by the feet to help his
pal, but he'd scarcely gone two or three steps when he quickly had to let go of
the old woman's feet in case they came off in his hands.

The rather surrealist, or 'sick', joke which rounds off this meeting is perfectly in
harmony with the dream logic of the episode and brings back the dream motif of
detached feet: Makar 'awakens' to the after-life by a shove from Ivan's foot—
that same priest Ivan whose only relic after dying in the fire was his feet; later
Makar is to attempt to stop the wooden pan of the scale full of his sins from
sinking further with the 'accidental' interference of his foot.

We have seen time disappearing in *Makar's Dream* into the semantic poles of
light and darkness or height and depth, but a crucial opposition we have neglected so far is that of silence and sound. The prevailing state in Chalgan, in the
forest, in the dream landscape through which Makar travels and even at the hut
of the Grand Toyon, is silence. The silence is an essential element in the lives of
people—natives and exiles—living in the dense forests of the Siberian taiga or
travelling over the snowy expanse of the Altai plateau. When the silence is
broken human life is asserting itself, things happen: a fragile contact is made

between Makar and his wife or Makar and the Russian exiles; a croaking song breaks from the lips of a Yakut or Makar as the Tartar liquor does its work, and always the contrast with the prevailing silence is pointed up

> He sang that he had drunk up five loads of firewood and that his wife would thrash him. The sounds which tore themselves from his throat, croaked and groaned so mournfully and pathetically in the evening air that an exiled stranger, who had climbed onto the roof of his yourt at that moment to close off his chimney, felt an even deeper sadness in his soul at the sound of Makar's song;

church bells ring for Christmas Day; a slight rustle in the woods is a fox running among the trees; a dull thud is the trap blade falling to kill the fox. After Makar dies, there is no reference to sound, except for the conversations he has with Ivan the priest, the Tartar horse thief and the old man, until they reach the hut of the Grand Toyon where they are greeted by 'a wonderful yet somehow familiar' song of dawn.

The sound which gives us the key to the story's structure and theme, then, seems to be music. The song of dawn has a framing role at the end of the story precisely opposite that of Makar's croaking drunken song at the beginning and the two are linked by bells. The dumb misery of Makar's wretched life in Chalgan and angry relations with its inhabitants culminates in his incoherent singing as he staggers home from the saloon. This episode also marks the transition between the real world and the world of Makar's dream: it is the opening frame for his journey. The closing frame is the song of dawn which marks the transition to the heavenly palace-hut of the Grand Toyon where that wretched life is weighed in the balance. In contrast to the passage we have just quoted where Makar's singing induces such melancholy, the very description of the dawn out of which the triumphant song emerges takes the form of a hymn or orthodox chant, with lines separated typographically; simple archaic anaphora which also form a framing pattern of two (And + noun) openings around a series of (And + adverbial) openings, as shown by the linking lines in the quotation below; a distinct rhythm; and an end cadence to each line. (See Russian Texts, No. 60 for this complex structural, metric, syntactic patterning which cannot, of course, be translated.)

> Makar had not noticed before that it seemed to
> be growing lighter on the plain ...
> And the stars had gone out, and the moon had
> gone down. And the snowy plain had grown dark.
> Then above it the mists lifted and stood around
> the plain like a guard of honour.
> And at one point, in the East, the mists had
> grown brighter, like warriors dressed in gold.

And then the mists wavered, the golden warriors
bowed down.
    And from behind them emerged the sun and stood
on their golden crests and surveyed the plain.
    And the plain shone all over with an unbelievable
dazzling light.
    And the mists rose triumphantly in a massive
chorale, broke apart in the West, and, wavering,
were carried aloft.
    And Makar thought he heard a wonderful song.

Quite apart from the formal syntactic, metric and phonic qualities of this passage,
it represents a number of key semantic transitions: darkness turns to light, the
invisible becomes visible, the gaze moves upwards, the earthly shifts to heavenly,
the fortress with its guard of honour becomes a cathedral with choir. Is this, then
the peripeteia of the story? We have neglected to discuss the narrative structure
of *Makar's Dream* so far, and, for all the significance of the fable, we must reassert
that the interpretation of the theme comes from our reading of the narrative
structure.

    'Stories for Christmas Eve' (*svyatochnye rasskazy*), to recall the story's subtitle,
are traditionally narrative interpretations or allegories on some aspect of the life
of Christ. When Makar comes before the Grand Toyon he sees his whole life
with piercing clarity and can calculate every positive deed and every sin almost
without the 'visual-aid' of the heavenly scales. The early part of the Last Judgement really tells Makar, and us, things we already knew about him. The peripeteia comes with the entry of the Grand Toyon's Son, Jesus, of course. His
intercession on Makar's behalf does not automatically tip the scales the other
way, however. Its effect is to make Makar articulate—and this is what makes the
difference

> Then something amazing happened. Makar, that same Makar who had never
> in his life been able to string more than ten words together, suddenly felt in
> him the gift of speech. He began to speak and was amazed at himself. There
> seemed to be two Makars: one speaking, the other listening in astonishment.
> He couldn't believe his ears. His speech flowed forth smoothly and
> passionately, the words came tumbling out one after the other and then
> formed themselves into long elegant strings. He was not shy. If he happened
> to stumble, he corrected himself at once and shouted twice as loud. But the
> main thing was, he felt he was speaking convincingly.

Many motifs in the story come together now: as the exiled Russian intellectuals
in their yourt in Chalgan had been the audience to Makar's stumbling 'pidgin'
Russian, now the divinities at the court of the Grand Toyon listen and marvel as
Makar eloquently presents his case (we will not insist on the analogy with the

sense of mission which inspired so many populist exiles from the intelligentsia who found themselves, like Korolenko, in the outposts of Siberia!); as the church bells had rung out over a semi-pagan Yakut village to give the inhabitants a hint of hope of redemption, had provided the continuity between Makar's drunken return home, his 'death' in a snowdrift, so the dawn hymn we have been analyzing is a kind of overture to the last act of the story where Christ himself brings redemption; the priest Ivan who had represented Christianity for Makar in Chalgan yet had been weak and sinful enough himself to make real contact with him, confirms by the end the possibility of redemption through understanding; the semantic oppositions have been fully realized as the scales make concrete the low/high movement, as the clouds part and replace the darkness with light and enlightenment, as silence turns not merely to sound, not merely to song, but to the eloquence of a new-found gift of tongues. Korolenko's 'Christmas Eve story' reworks that thread of the Christian message which has always been so strong in Russian Orthodox teaching since Metropolitan Ilarion of Kiev explored it in his *Sermon on Law and Grace* in the middle of the eleventh century: 'Judaism had meant the domination of Law over Man; Christ, having freed Man from subservience to the Law, established the dominion of Grace; the moon was replaced by the sun, darkness by light, the night's coolness by the day's warmth, the bondswoman Agar by the free Sarah; now slavery to the law turns to a filial attitude to God and hopelessness changed into hope of eternal life.'[9] Does the fact that the main elements of the narrative structure are concentrated in the last eight pages then mean that the story is unbalanced or, more seriously for us, that our preoccupation with the time structure was misplaced? Surely not, since the whole of the scene before the Grand Toyon, and especially the speech Makar is able to make in his own defence once the Son of the Toyon has appeared, depend for their impact on our knowing his humble hero both from the outside—in the ethnographic and narrative accounts of his real life in Chalgan—and from the inside—in his dream fight with Alyoshka and the dream journey after death. The movement of the story is inwards to the essence of Makar, from the facts as seen by an alien observer to the reality as experienced, from the inarticulate burbling of a Yakutized peasant Russian to the eloquent presentation of his case for grace. But this movement requires a movement from Makar's present into his past. As we saw in reconstructing the fable, the 'real life' description of Makar yields only some broad ethnographic data about his ancestors; the dream journey provides some episodic insights into some typical moments of his past with the priest Ivan and the Tartar horse thief; but the Last Judgement takes us back to the facts—so many faggot cuts or furrows ploughed—and to the justifications of poverty, hunger and toil, isolation, loss of family and alienation of self. The time reversal in the story is essential to its theme.

III   Pushkin: *The Post-Stage Master*, 1831; (*Stantsionnyi smotritel'*) [10]

Superficially, Pushkin seems to have chosen the same broad theme for his story as Korolenko: the case for the defence of the 'little man', but on every level he handles this theme quite differently. Whereas *Makar's Dream* purports to be a Christmas folk story which grows out of the ethnographic portrait, *The Post-Stage Master* purports to be a sentimental tale growing out of the thematic journal essay. Separated by some fifty years, both writers are responding to two prevailing genres of their day, playing with them structurally and thematically and relating them to each other in a quite distinctive way. In each case the play with time and the nature of the mismatch between the dispositional sequence and the expositional sequence is an important element in our refraction of the genre conventions and has implications for the narrative structure, point of view, character and setting which affect our interpretation of the story.

Both writers, by their choice of genres and theme, have been faced with the problem of combining the points of view of an educated sympathetic narrator and an uneducated and inarticulate central character. Korolenko, as I have tried to show, was less successful in solving this problem in the real-life scenes than in the dream sequences. Pushkin makes the task doubly difficult by making his sympathetic observer the first person narrator. This involves not only two points of view, but two time sequences for both the events narrated and the acts of narrating them. In order to see how Pushkin set about combining these, and to gauge how successful he was, let us start by retelling separately the fables of both the narrator and the post-stage master.

For some twenty years A.G.N., a titular councillor, has travelled all over Russia on government business, stopping at virtually every post-stage to change his horses, have a meal and rest. This has enabled him to get to know post-stage masters well, to share their resentment at the arrogance of senior officials and to see them as people and not mere dictatorial officials. In May 1816 he was travelling in a junior capacity when he was caught in a sudden downpour of rain and soaked to the skin. At the nearest post-stage he changed his clothes and then ordered tea. The post-stage master summoned his fourteen-year-old daughter, Dunya, and sent her to fetch the cream. While he filled out the order for horses, the narrator looked round the room, at the series of pictures depicting the parable of the Prodigal Son, at the neat and colourful simple furnishings and at his host. When Dunya returns with the samovar he chats with her, then gives her tea and the father a glass of punch. After a long conversation he takes his leave and, being seen off to his post chaise by Dunya, asks her for a kiss in the hall.

Returning to the same station several years later, he approaches with foreboding and finds that, indeed, both the cottage and its owner have changed for the worse: the house looks neglected and Samson Vyrin, the post-stage master has aged and looks ill and unkempt: Dunya has left and he seems not to care where she is. The titular councillor plies him with punch and learns how she had run off

to St Petersburg three years previously with a young hussar who would not send
her home to her father or even let him see her. Long after leaving the station the
narrator remembered the old post-stage master's story and tears.

Quite recently, presumably nearly ten years later, the narrator had been travelling through the same area and on learning that the station had been closed
down, drove over to see if the post-stage master was still alive. On a grey autumn
evening he learned from the brewer's wife who now lived in the cottage that
Samson had died of drinking about a year previously. Her boy leads him to the
cemetery where Samson is buried and tells him how the village boys loved him.
He learns that in the summer a beautiful lady in black with her three small children had wept to hear of his death and had visited the cemetery and lain on his
grave, giving the priest some money before she left. The titular councillor gives
the boy five kopecks and is glad he spent the extra money coming to find out
about his old friend.

The fable of the post-stage master himself is rather different in orientation.
Samson Vyrin had lost his wife and lived alone with his daughter Dunya, in
charge of the post-stage. While he filled out the official forms, Dunya, pretty and
lively like her mother, would charm every passing traveller, no matter how
impatient or bad-tempered, and many would stay to supper just to be in her
company. She was a perfect housekeeper and was adored by her father.

One winter evening about a year after the narrator's first visit and three years
before his second, a fine young hussar had arrived, lost his temper on hearing
there were no horses and been pacified by Dunya. After supper horses were available, but when the post-stage master returned from harnessing them he found
the hussar had taken ill and was unable to travel. He let him have his own bed
and next day sent for the doctor. Dunya nursed and fed him. The doctor
prescribed two days' peace and quiet, the hussar paid him twenty-five roubles
and they ate a good meal together. Two days later the hussar was quite recovered
and in fine spirits and, as it was a Sunday, agreed—at her father's insistence—to
take Dunya to the church at the far end of the village. As time passed Samson
grew anxious and went to look for his daughter at the church; as she had not
been there, she must have ridden on with the hussar to the next station, but
when the coachman came back drunk that evening he reported that the couple
had gone on further. The post-stage master fell ill with fever and was treated by
the same doctor, who admitted that the hussar had only feigned illness. When he
was better he asked for two months' leave and set off on foot to find Dunya, first
in Smolensk and then in St Petersburg where he stayed with an old army
comrade. He found the inn where the hussar Minsky was staying and begged
him to let him have Dunya back. The hussar asked for his forgiveness, but
refused to let her go and swore she would be happy with him. He then pushed
some banknotes into his cuff and hustled him out. Seeing the money, Samson
threw it down angrily and when he turned to pick it up again it had been
pounced on by a well-dressed young man who rushed for a cab.

Two days later he tried to see Minsky again, but was turned away. By chance he ran across his cab that same evening, followed it to a house and, on the pretext of delivering a note to Dunya, gained entrance. Through an open doorway he caught sight of his daughter, dressed in high fashion, caressing Minsky's head, obviously happy. When she looked up and caught sight of him, Dunya fainted and Minsky angrily sent him packing. It was pointless to lodge an official complaint, so he left the city two days later and returned home. He had heard nothing from Dunya for three years and did not know if she was alive or dead. He assumed she must have gone down in the world, like the Prodigal Son. He lived on, drowning his sorrows in drink, until they closed the post-stage, made friends with the village children, and died several years later.

It may be objected that these summaries of the story's two fables consist of nothing but bare events and reduce the story to a mere synopsis by omitting all the rich texture of description, dialogue, narratorial comment and emotional response which make Pushkin's original such a delight to read, and at times by reversing, moreover, the order of events by which the author chooses to intrigue us. And this is precisely the point: boring though the fable may be to read 'neat', it nonetheless offers a chain of reference for the real pleasures of the text.

The first thing to note is the degree to which the first of these fables, the titular councillor's, focuses on the behaviour of the post-stage master, while the latter's fable focuses on his daughter Dunya. This is due in part to the interweaving of genres: the narrator's tale owes most to the conventions of the eighteenth-century polemical essay in the style of Karamzin, Radischev and Novikov, or Addison and Steele, and is an answer to the epigraph from Vyazemsky about post-stage masters being dictators; the story of 'poor Dunya', on the other hand, uses the situations and language of the sentimental romance typified by Karamzin's *Poor Liza* (1792) where an innocent peasant girl's love is abused by a frivolous army officer. We will consider later the ways in which Pushkin produces a pastiche of both these genres in *The Post-Stage Master*; for the moment we will analyze the way the distinct frameworks they offer are interwoven to structure the temporal exposition of the events and the influence this has on narrative structure, point of view and characterization.

The diagram by Shukman (1977)[11] in Figure 6 demonstrates very vividly the distinct time planes of the essay and sentimental story genres. The story starts in the essay writer's present from which he surveys his twenty years of travelling around the post-stages of Russia and then 'homes in', as the essay writer should, on a particular post-stage master who will exemplify his theme. Since Pushkin has camouflaged the origins of the essay, we cannot, of course, tell how many years ago his ironically precise date of 'May 1816' actually was: although Pushkin wrote the story in 1830, it purports to have been found among the papers of 'the late Ivan Petrovich Belkin', a landowner, who had written down the story, at an unspecified date, from the account of the titular councillor

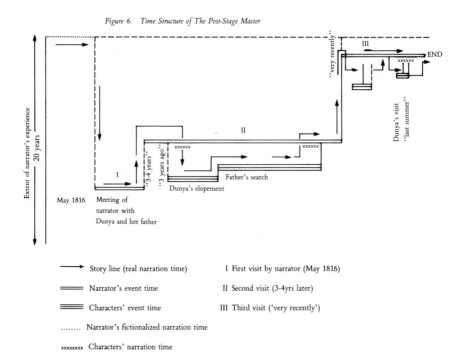

Figure 6.   Time Structure of The Post-Stage Master

→ Story line (real narration time)	I First visit by narrator (May 1816)
═ Narrator's event time	II Second visit (3-4yrs later)
═ Characters' event time	III Third visit ('very recently')
.... Narrator's fictionalized narration time	
xxxxxxx Characters' narration time	

A.G.N. The first meeting the narrator has with Dunya and her father, with its description of the room and his farewell kiss with Dunya is well within the style of the essay episode, and even his return three to four years later, continues this style. The foreboding he senses, however, leads not merely to a description of the changed appearance of the room and the behaviour of the post-stage master, but opens the way, with the aid of a glass of punch, for the telling of the self-contained narrative of Samson Vyrin (who, significantly, is at last named, although subsequently he is referred to, by function, as 'the post-stage master', 'the poor post-stage master', 'the poor father', 'the old man', etcetera). The event-time of the characters in this 'sentimental tale' ('three years ago') now takes over with the father's narrative refracted, but without interruption, through the third person narration of the titular councillor. This encompasses the hussar's illness and stay at the post-stage, his elopement with Dunya; the father's illness and search for the couple in St Petersburg; his interview with Minsky (also named now) and the fateful moment when he glimpses the couple together, obviously happy; his return home and sadly resigned mood. All of these events follow a very precise time scale: 'the next morning', 'by dinner time', 'in two days' time', 'a further day passed', 'the third morning', 'It was Sunday', 'not half an hour had passed', 'that evening', 'two months' leave', 'early the next morning', 'before eleven o'clock', 'that very evening', 'two days later', 'And now it's more than two years that I've been living on my own without Dunya'. This accurately plotted sequence is suspended, as it were, in the timeless world of the essay, which we rejoin for the narrator's third visit to the post-stage: 'Not very long ago', 'in the autumn', 'around sunset', 'about a year back', 'in the summer'. This framing of the precise, perfective aspect of the post-stage master's narrative within the vaguely delimited imperfective aspect of the narrator's essay is an extension of the grammatical opposition of verbal aspects which, as Uspensky has shown, is a common device in narrative: '...the fixation of time through the use of the imperfective aspect of the verb (*verba dicendi*) may serve as a framing device for the narrative. The same device of compositional framing may be adopted in order to isolate a part of the narrative and turn it into a relatively independent text.' [12] Elsewhere in his important book *A Poetics of Composition* Uspensky distinguishes two narrative positions we have discovered in Pushkin's story: 'In general, the temporal and spatial position of the synchronic narrator has an immediate connection with the time and space of the events which he describes, while the "panchronic" narrator is removed to a broader and more abstract plane.' [13] In *The Post-Stage Master*, as we have seen, the 'synchronic' narration is the old man's 'sentimental tale' projected on the 'panchronic' backcloth provided by the titular councillor's essay.

Not that the two genres which make up the story are to be distinguished only in terms of their temporal structure. Stylistically, too, they contrast sharply. The long opening paragraph is a classic example (or pastiche, for with Pushkin we can never be quite sure) of the rhetoric of the polemical essay. It is composed of two major sections: A. Generalization, B. Particularization, each of which has four stylistically quite distinct, though parallel, sub-divisions:

A.   I   Challenge to readers: rhetorical questions (with negative and imperfect); triple phrasing; abstraction.

     II   Appeal to readers' understanding: hortative; triple phrasing.

     III   Definition: rhetorical question-answer; quasi-precision; hyperbole.

     IV   Culmination: climax—anti-climax; marked syntactic and intonational patterning with opposition.

B.   I   Typical encounters: dynamic present-tense verbs; conditionals; exclamations; heavy patterning for routines: 'On entering his poor dwelling...' (*Vkhodya v bednoye yego zhilische...*)

II   Appeal to readers' sympathies: hortative, sentimentalism: (Let's get to the heart of the matter... —*Vniknem vo vse eto khoroshenko...*)

III Author's own experience: exaggeration; colloquialism with archaism; didacticism: (a few words more... —*yesche neskol'ko slov...*)

IV   Culminating paradox: (As for me, I confess... —*Chto kasayetsya menya, to priznayus'...*).

I have merely indicated the opening of each sub-division in the B section above. Let us look in more detail at the style and rhetoric of A (the lines are numbered for ease of reference):

I   1 Who has not cursed post-stage masters. Who has not wrangled
     2 with them? Who, in a moment of anger has not demanded the fateful
     3 book from them, therein to inscribe their useless complaint about
     4 persecution, rudeness and inaccuracy. Who does not consider them
     5 monsters in human form, equal to scriveners' ghosts or at least the
     6 highway men of Murom?

II   7 However, let us be fair and try to put ourselves in their place and
     8 perhaps we will begin to judge them far more leniently. What is a
III 9 post-stage master? A real martyr of the fourteenth grade protected
    10 by no more than his rank from a thrashing, and then not always (I
    11 invoke my readers' consciences). What is the employment of this
    12 dictator, as Prince Vyazemsky jokingly calls him? Is it not a veritable
    13 penal servitude? No peace, day or night.

IV 14   All that wrath which has accumulated throughout a boring journey
    15 the traveller vents on the post-stage master. Let the weather be foul,
    16 the road filthy, the coachman stubborn, the horses not pulling—the
    17 fault is the post-stage master's.
        (See Russian Texts, No. 61)

We have noted the negative rhetorical questions in I; these combine with the imperfect verbs to generalize the behaviour of travellers in the same way as an adjective with the present tense generalizes in IV. The questions are tripled ('Who has not... who has not... who has not...'—*Kto ne... Kto ne... Kto ne...*) just as the points of comparison in lines 5-6, the hortatives in 7-8 and the noun-adjective combinations in IV are tripled, yet Pushkin is too good a poet to make the tripling perfect, so he either interrupts the pattern (2, 5, 8), or extends it with a subordinate clause (3-4) involving a further tripling of nouns, or adds another non-matching main clause (16-17). These devices in prose are analogous to a natural poetic rhythm breaking against a strict metrical pattern in poetry: the pattern is simultaneously reaffirmed and denied. The asides (7, 8, 11, 12) serve to modify both the regular syntactic patterning and the dogmatic tone of the argument. The hyperbole and classical reference of 'the fateful book' (*rokovoi knigi*) (2) and the grandiose or bureaucratic archaism of *daby, onuyu* (3) *tokmo*

in section B, *sii stol'... sut', koimi* are similarly modified
[...]racticality in their contexts. For the focal point of this
[...]ches from the grandiloquence of complex syntax, lofty
[...]es of intonation to define his victim-figure with an oxy-
[...]listic and social: 'a real martyr of the fourteenth grade'
[...]*dtsatogo klassa*). For his climax, as we have seen, he
[...]syntactic figures, noun-copula-adjective, triples it (16),
[...] (17), and then reverses it (17). Even the adjectives used
[...]he time dimension, since the long attributives denote
permanent characteristics ('Whenever X is foul, Y are filthy and Z is stubborn'),
while the short predicative adjective 'at fault' (*vinovat*) denotes temporary state
('Each time S is at fault').

As a transition from the high-flown rhetoric of his essay opening to the
simplicity of the post-stage master's narrative the narrator uses the emotional,
euphemistic, apostrophic style of the 'sentimental traveller' (Sterne, Radischev,
Karamzin): 'As may easily be guessed, I have friends from the honourable profession of post-stage master. Indeed, the memory of one of these is precious to me.
Circumstances brought us together, and it is about him that I now propose to
chat with my gentle readers.' (See Russian Texts, No. 62) Recalling his power-
lessness as a young junior official, the sentimental traveller continues his essay in
a heavily antithetic style

> Consequently post-stage masters treated me quite unceremoniously and I
> often had to take by force what, in my opinion, was mine by right. Being
> young and hot-tempered I used to rail at the baseness and pusillanimity of the
> post-stage master when he handed over the team of horses prepared for me to
> the barouche of some titled official. I took just as long to become accustomed to a
> discriminating servant passing me by with some dish at a governor's dinner.
> Nowadays both actions seem to me to be in the order of things. Indeed, what
> would become of us if in place of the ever-convenient rule 'rank must respect
> rank' another came into use such as 'intelligence must respect intelligence'?
> (See Russian Texts, No. 63)

With the account of his arrival at the post-stage where he meets Dunya and her
father, the narrator switches to Pushkin's usual brisk, economical, dynamic
narrative style so well described by Lezhnev and others.[14] The short sentences
powered by perfective verbs soon come to a halt, however, as the narrator stops
to examine closely the series of pictures on the wall depicting the key scenes from
the parable of the Prodigal Son. Here time stands still as he describes in the
present tense, with a wealth of fixed Homeric epithets, the action in each of the
four scenes: the movie camera has stopped running and we are presented with
four stills. The timing of this interlude is important in two senses: it draws attention to itself by its static quality and it occurs at the key moment before the
narrator has his tea with the father and his flirtation with Dunya. It then recurs,

of course, when the titular councillor returns to the post-stage to hear Samson Vyrin's tale of woe when the first thing he notices is the series of pictures. As Gershenzon and Bayley have shown,[15] the Prodigal Son pictures are not mere picturesque décor, nor are they merely a framing device, although their function as a frame is an important structural feature of the story: they are thematic, or perhaps we should say 'antithematic', since they really subvert the theme

> Pushkin's tale not only implies an ironic comment on its predecessor *Poor Liza* by Karamzin but supplies solicitude of a more discriminating kind.
>
> It also contains a more elaborate element of parody. As earlier readers must have spotted, and Gershenzon convincingly demonstrated, it reverses the Parable of The Prodigal Son, texts and pictures from which adorn the walls of the station-master's little house. And when Dunya goes off with the hussar her father persists in interpreting the event in the light of the parable. He will search for his 'lost lamb', forgive her and bring her home. When he traces the hussar to Petersburg the trail of the unexpected begins. He begs his daughter to be restored, even though her honour is lost, but the ashamed and yet exasperated young man assures him that Dunya is very well off . . . The final irony is that it is the old man and not his child who goes to the bad. He dies of drink, grieving over the fall of his prodigal daughter, who is bringing up a family in happiness and security . . . The old station-master cannot grasp that events in real life do not follow the traditional pattern of the moral law and the scriptures.[16]

Pushkin satirizes the old man's limitations, then, just as he satirizes impatient officials at post-stages, arrogant young hussars, German doctors, titular councillors with literary pretensions, and, for that matter, all writers of polemical essays and sentimental tales. But he satirizes him gently, with tact. For *The Post-Stage Master* is not a direct reversal of the Prodigal Son story: in the parable the home scenes with which it begins and ends give equal attention to the father and the sons, while the scenes of prodigality and its aftermath focus exclusively on the son. In Pushkin's version, however, we only glimpse Dunya three times: once when the narrator first meets her, secondly when her father glimpses her through the open doorway in Minsky's St Petersburg apartment, and thirdly as the beautiful lady who came to visit the post-stage master's grave, as reported by the red-headed, cross-eyed urchin who guides the narrator on his last visit. And not only is our view of her each time refracted through the viewpoint and language of an avowedly biassed witness—an impressionable young official who fancies kissing her, a distraught father who had expected to find her feeding swine, and a village lad who is hoping for a tip for his services—but it is further refracted by being presented iconically, as a visual cliché. As Bocharov has shown,[17] it is not only the explicit description of the Prodigal Son pictures that has three simultaneous functions: to halt the action of the story, to frame a significant scene, and to promote expectations which are contradicted by the story.

Each of our views of Dunya turns into a kind of *tableau vivant*, or genre painting, fixing it in the viewer's, and our, memory for future recall and reference. The surreptitious kiss in the hallway of the post-stage station is described minimally: 'In the hall I stopped and asked for her permission to kiss her; Dunya complied . . . ' But this pretty scene is at once transfixed with a line of remarkably prosaic verse set in a sentence of remarkably florid prose

Many are the kisses I can count to my score.

'Since I have been doing that,'

but not one of them has left me with such a long-lasting, such a pleasant memory.'
(See Russian Texts, No. 64)

(A very ornate frame for such a dull picture!) The scene of Dunya visiting her father's grave the summer before the narrator's last visit is similarly distanced and made aesthetic. Physically, the boy watches her 'from afar' (*izdali*) but his vision of the 'fine lady' who: 'rode in a six-horse carriage with three little lords, and with a nurse-maid, and with a black lap dog' (see Russian Texts, No. 65) is also a genre-painting or, with its disjunct itemizing of what the boy had seen, 'a glittering display of toys'.[18]

The central and most elaborate genre painting is glimpsed at the central turning point of Samson Vyrin's own story: 'In the room, which was furnished superbly, sat Minsky, wrapped in thought. Dunya, dressed in all the luxury of high fashion, was sitting on the arm of his chair, like a horsewoman on her English saddle. She was gazing at Minsky, twining his black locks on her glittering fingers.' The physical limitations of the post-stage master's viewpoint are nicely conveyed here by the post-modification of the noun phrases, which allow each detail to be taken in in turn, and by the inexplicit reference to her jewellery in the metonymy of 'her glittering fingers'. But the rather forced poses of the lovers belong in a world that he could not recognize: a late eighteenth-century genre painting of a salon scene—or perhaps a scene in a French novel of the period—while the vision of Dunya as a horsewoman on her English saddle is beyond the ken not only of her father, but of the titular councillor as well. This artificial exotic touch makes the scene more vivid for each level of perceiver—the old man, the narrator and the reader. But it also keeps it remarkably inexplicit. Dunya's pose is conventional; her reaction to the key moment of drama as she catches sight of her father is equally conventional: ' "Who's there?"—she asked without raising her head. He still did not speak. Getting no reply, Dunya raised her head . . . and with a cry fell to the carpet.' Minsky plays an active role in this moment of drama, as earlier when confronted by the post-stage master; we know enough of the old man's grief and hopes by now to infer his reactions; but all that we need to know about Dunya—how she feels about Minsky now she lives with him, her feelings about her father, how a simple country girl fits into St

Petersburg high society—is encapsulated in the conventions of a genre painting and those three dots.

The account of Dunya's seduction and abduction by the hussar has led us to expect a reworking of the *Poor Liza* theme. Character, attitudes, relationships, behaviour, setting and language all predispose us to expect, if not death, then 'a fate worse than death' for Dunya. Karamzin's gay and pretty heroine lives in rustic simplicity with her widowed mother (the switch of parents in Pushkin's version might be a device for camouflage or pastiche, were it not for the haunting image of the father of the Prodigal Son which is so firmly engraved on our memory); she conceals from her mother the extent of her commitment to the handsome but devious young officer, Erast, who enjoys his country idyll and then returns to Moscow to marry a society bride, deceiving Liza into thinking he has been posted far away in the army; he even tries to 'pay her off'—the final betrayal which leads her to suicide (Minsky, though, pays off the father who then drinks himself to death); the sentimental tone is sustained to the end with the visits of the officer, now married, to the grave of his poor Liza by the lake in the woods where they had loved. The three dots imply all these possibilities, but the enigma of Dunya's real situation, feelings and attitudes has to be sustained to the end when her visit, in obvious prosperity and happiness, to her father's grave reveals the extent to which the sentimental myth has been subverted. Liza, for all the independence of young love, is a prisoner of her mother's conservative social and emotional assumptions: the first priority is marriage, and you marry within your class. Dunya is the radical answer to her father's imprisonment within the fourteenth rank of the civil service and the ethics of the Parable of the Prodigal Son.

At the centre of the story, then, are three dots whose content can only be filled in indexically by the end of the story. Not only by the end, though, since that content depends on its function, syntagmatically, in relation to the post-stage master's expectations, and those of his intermediary, the titular councillor, and those were 'inscribed' in the earlier genre paintings of the Prodigal Son story and the kiss scene. One static visual image is framed by three other static visual images. But it is also enclosed—and refracted—by other kinds of framing device, spatial, temporal, phraseological and ideological, to borrow Uspensky's terms.[19] The post-stage master's view of the scene is most immediately framed by the open doorway. We are made ready for a full view of his daughter by having her fully named: until now she has been merely Dunya, his name for her, but in his conversation with the maid at the door she becomes 'Avdotya Samsonovna' (just as previously we only have Samson Vyrin and Minsky named at the point where they are about to figure as human beings rather than as bearers of functions). The episode is framed by an altercation with Minsky and, beyond that, by the post-stage master's arrival in and departure from St Petersburg. The story of his loss and search is retold largely in the language of the titular councillor, but this is framed by the verbatim report of the post-stage master's own words, heavily

folksy-colloquial, full of proverbs, parallelism, archaisms and rhetorical questions. Indeed, it would not be too far-fetched to see Vyrin's opening speech as
echoing, though with an appropriate change of key, the peroration with which
the story opens

> So you knew my Dunya?—he began.—But then, who didn't know her! Oh,
> Dunya, Dunya! What a girl she was. No matter who used to come by,
> everyone would praise her, no one would condemn her. The ladies would give
> her presents, one a kerchief, another ear-rings. The gentlemen travellers used
> to stop off as if to have dinner or a bite of supper, but really just to get a longer
> look at her. You'd get some lord, no matter how angry he was, calming down
> when she was there and having a gracious conversation with me. Believe me,
> sir: couriers, state messengers would get chatting with her for half an hour at a
> time. The house was run by her: whatever needed tidying or cooking, she'd
> find time for. And I, old fool that I am, could never see her and enjoy her
> being there enough; didn't I love my Dunya, then, didn't I nurse my baby;
> didn't she have a good life? Oh well, you can't keep away evil by swearing,
> what is fated can't be dodged.
> (See Russian Texts, No. 66)

The question inevitably arises why Pushkin does not convey the whole of the
post-stage master's story in his own words. Apart from the narrative conventions prevailing in his time, it is clear from this short piece of monologue that the
recital would be so slow and repetitive and weighed down with particles, colloquial syntax and proverbs that it would make interminable reading. In any case,
as Kozhevnikova has made quite clear,[20] even the most authentic sounding colloquial speech in literature depends on a judicious selection and placing of key
features which people think of as being colloquial, rather than on authentic
verbatim reporting. There are enough traces of Samson Vyrin's speech style in
the narrator's retelling to remind us of the source of facts and emotions: 'A
batman cleaning a boot on a boot-tree announced that the master was taking a
nap . . . ' (*Voyennyi lakei, chistya sapog na kolodke, ob'yavil, chto barin pochivayet . . .*),
'What could one do! the post-stage master gave up his own bed to him' (*Kakkb
byt'! smotritel' ustupil yemu svoyu krovat' . . .*), 'From the order for horses he knew
that Captain of the Cavalry Minsky was en route from Smolensk to St
Petersburg' (*Iz podorozhnoi znal on, chto rotmister Minskii yekhal iz Smolenska v
Peterburg*) and so on.[21]

The colloquial frame to the post-stage master's narrative is resumed at the end
with the same stylistic features

> So here I am,—he concluded, for three years already living without Dunya
> and not hearing sight nor sound of her. God knows whether she's alive or
> dead. Anything can happen. She's not the first, and she won't be the last girl
> to be lured by some passing rake, kept for a bit and then cast aside. There's any

number of them in Petersburg. Silly little fools, dressed up in satin and velvet today, and tomorrow there they are sweeping the streets with the riff-raff from the taverns. You can't help wondering from time to time whether Dunya's gone on that downhill path, and you can't help having sinful thoughts and wishing her quiet in her grave . . .
(See Russian Texts, No. 67)

As well as matching the colloquial frame at the start of his narrative, this piece recapitulates the important latent themes (*podtekst*) of the *Poor Liza* and *Prodigal Son* stories. The 'sentimental tale' is framed by the narrator's arrival and departure, which are framed by the intervals of several years between his visits, which are framed by the 'outer' visits where the focus is mainly on Dunya, and the whole complex is framed by the polemical essay on post-stage masters.

This is not the end of the framing, however, since the titular councillor's 'true' story is narrated and taken down by the landowner Ivan Petrovich Belkin; but since he is dead, all the Belkin stories are handed over to a further fictional frame, Pushkin's 'editor'.[22] *The Post-Stage Master* is a perfect semiotic object: an empty sign of three dots is framed an almost infinite number of times and it is the relationship between the frames, temporal, spatial, thematic, generic and stylistic which create its significance. Pushkin achieves the reverse of what Gogol and Dostoevsky were to do in the stories which we have analyzed. While they allowed the story to be overwhelmed by a single act of discourse, he has given us a complex and many-layered interplay of discourses out of which we must create the true story.

In both *Makar's Dream* and *The Post-Stage Master* the underlying temporal sequence has been considerably restructured, and, despite the more or less precise time clues, it has taken us some effort to reconstruct the fable. The ultimate effect is to destroy time, through dream logic in the case of *Makar's Dream*, and through the workings of memory in *The Post-Stage Master*. It has been claimed that one of the fundamental aims of all art is the destruction of time. Perhaps, less sweepingly, we may claim that in these short stories time has been projected onto space: for Korolenko memory creates a dream space out of the facts of a peasant's life in the endless forests and plains of Siberia; for Pushkin memory creates a mythic space out of the hopes and fears of a petty official in the village of * * *. For the reader, time is one dimension of a semiotic space from which meanings are to be refracted.

NOTES TO CHAPTER 4

1. Boris V. Tomashevsky, *Teoriya literatury. Poetika* (Theory of literature. Poetics.) (Moscow-Leningrad, 1930, p.137); for a translation of these and other related concepts, see 'A contextual

Glossary of Formalist Terminology' in L.M. O'Toole and Ann Shukman (eds.) *Russian Poetics in Translation* (Essex, 1977, No. 4, pp.13-48).

2. A.A. Mendilow, *Time and the Novel* (London, 1952).
3. W.J.M. Bronzwaer, *Tense in the Novel: An Investigation of Some Potentialities of Linguistic Criticism* (Gröningen, 1970).
4. Gérard Genette, *Discours du récit: essai de méthode* (*Figures, III*, Paris, 1972, pp.67-273); English translation, *Narrative Discourse* by Jane E. Lewin (Oxford, 1980).
5. All quotations from the text of *Makar's Dream* are taken from V.G. Korolenko, *Sobranie sochinenii v10 tomakh'* I (Moscow, 1953-56, pp.103-30; author's translations.)
6. M.M. Bakhtin, *Problemy poetiki Dostoevskogo* (Moscow, 1929 and 1963, p.270).
7. V.G. Korolenko, *Sobranie sochinenii v10 tomakh*, 10 (Moscow, 1953-56, p.173).
8. This uncertainty in the fictional mode is particularly intriguing, since we can compare it with Korolenko's description of Zakhar Tsykunov and his Yakut wife (on whom Makar and his wife were modelled) in his autobiography, *The History of My Contemporary*. In this factual work, one of the classics of Russian memoir-writing, Korolenko describes the couple, from whom he rented a room while he was exiled in the Yakut village of Amga, objectively and with humour, but with none of the forced irony we find in the story. We may perhaps ascribe Korolenko's heavy-handedness in this part of *Makar's Dream* to immaturity, the pressure of short-story form to dramatize relationships and to the supposed demands of a metropolitan audience. See V.G. Korolenko, *Istoriya moego sovremennika* (Moscow, 1965, pp.763-4).
9. See Dmitrij Cizevskij, *History of Russian Literature from the Eleventh Century to the End of the Baroque* (The Hague, 1960, pp.36-8).
10. All quotations from the text of *The Post-Stage Master* are taken from A.S. Pushkin, *Polnoe sobranie sochinenii*, 8 (Complete Collected Works) in 16 vols., pp.95-106; author's translations).
11. Ann Shukman, 'Ten Russian short stories: theory, analysis, interpretation' (*Essays in Poetics* 2, 2, Keele, 1977, p.50; reproduced with the permission of the author).
12. Boris Uspensky, *Poetika kompozitsii* (Moscow, 1970); English translation by Valentina Zavarin and Susan Wittig: *A Poetics of Composition*, Berkeley, 1973, p.151).
13. *Ibid*, p.113.
14. A. Lezhnev, *Proza Pushkina* (Pushkin's Prose) (Moscow, 1937 and 1966); see also V.V. Vinogradov, *Stil' Pushkina* (Moscow, 1941); A. Slonimsky, *Masterstvo Pushkina* (Moscow, 1959 and 1963); and D.D. Blagoi, *Masterstvo Pushkina* (Moscow, 1955).
15. M.O. Gershenzon, *Mudrost' Pushkina* (Pushkin's Wisdom) (Petrograd, 1918); John Bayley, *Pushkin: A Comparative Commentary* (Cambridge, 1971, pp.310-12).
16. Bayley, *op. cit.*, pp.311-12.
17. S.G. Bocharov, *Poetika Pushkina* (Moscow, 1974, pp.163-74).
18. N. Ya. Berkovsky's phrase, from *Stat'i o literature*, pp.287-8, quoted by Bocharov, *op. cit.*, p.172. Pushkin was not unique, of course, in freezing the action into a *tableau vivant*. The device is common in the theatre of many cultures and periods, and, as Andrew Wright has shown, was a favourite trick of Fielding's. What may be special about Pushkin's use of the device is the complex relationship between his tableaux and the many layers of framing he plays with, as in the central Dunya scene. See Andrew Wright, *Henry Fielding: Mask and Feast* (London, 1965).
19. Uspensky, *op. cit.*, has a detailed chapter on each of these levels, with excellent examples from literature of many genres, as well as chapters on the interaction between various levels and the analogies between framing and other aspects of point of view in literature and in the visual arts.
20. Kveta Kozhevnikova, *Ustnaya spontannaya rech' v epicheskoi proze* (Spontaneous spoken speech

in narrative prose) (*Acta Universitatis Carolinae Philologica Monographia XXXII*, Prague, 1970).

21   These examples are given by Vinogradov and Bocharov, *op. cit.*

22.   The complexities of Pushkin's 'Editor's Foreword' to the *Tales of Belkin* are well discussed by Jan M. Meijer in 'The Sixth Tale of Belkin' in Jan van der Eng, A.G.F. van Holk, Jan M. Meijer (eds.) *The Tales of Belkin by A.S. Pushkin* (Paris, 1968, pp. 110-34).

5

PLOT

Pushkin: *The Pistol Shot*
Gorky: *Twenty-Six Men and a Girl*

I

WE HAVE already discussed, in Section I of the last chapter, our reasons for departing from Formalist theory and separating the study of causal relations in narrative (plot) from the study of temporal relations (fable). What we have not attempted consistently in any of the analyses so far is to study the episodic structure of a story, that is, the ways in which each episode, each 'chunk' of the action, relates to the ones that come before it and after it, to other episodes elsewhere in the story, and to the story as a whole. Inevitably in studying narrative structure we were bound to point to certain episodes as having greater significance for the trajectory of the stories, and in studying point of view and fable we drew attention to patterns of parallelism, situation rhyme and framing between disjunct episodes. The time has now come to acknowledge one of the simplest truisms about narrative—that it consists of episodes arranged and linked in a sequence. We perceive the action in more or less discrete 'chunks' which can usually be given rough-and-ready labels ('temptation to desert', 'trial', 'punishment', 'acquisition of coat', 'loss of coat', 'appeal to authority', etcetera), and our expectation that these will be connected by some causal link, however disturbed the temporal order may be ('arrival' —'memories of earlier visit'—'hospitality'—'flashback narration of intervening action' — 'departure'), is normally fulfilled. When a writer deliberately suppresses the causal links, puts effects before their causes, or subverts the whole concept of causality in some other way, he is still playing with our assumptions regarding cause and effect: a negative case is still a case.

One of the major problems is to define the size of unit we are going to take as an episode. Sometimes our ready-made labels are helpful: 'theft of coat' is a brief, well defined element fitting appropriately between 'celebration of acquisition of coat' and 'grief at loss of coat', but of these two episodes the first involves a string of actions or sub-episodes such as 'arrival', 'disrobing', 'greeting', 'toast', 'eating and drinking', 'card-playing', etcetera, while what we earlier labelled 'acquisition of coat' occupies the first third of the story and involves 'perception of need', 'first visit to tailor', 'reaction', 'second visit to tailor', 'saving up', etcetera, to say nothing of the wealth of descriptions, digressions, flashbacks and so on which comprise the main text of Gogol's story. There is the problem of comparability of units, then, since a consistent method of analysis and description requires us to be consistent in cutting up what we are analyzing, and there is the problem of divisibility of units, since one unit, say, 'arrival' might in one context be realized merely as 'he arrived' and in another consist of a string of sub-routines. These problems are not peculiar to narrative structure, however; they are as acute in life and language. The social psychologist has to postulate 'frames'[1] and 'routines' as units for the description of social interaction, knowing that these will vary in scale and significance in different social contexts, while the linguist will cut up his data into sentences, clauses, phrases, words and morphemes, or tone groups, feet, syllables and phonemes, depending on which aspects of their relationship he wishes to concentrate on. The episodic units, like social 'frames' and linguistic units, are the product of our complex and flexible ways of classifying the world and, like those units, can only be specified in functional terms.

The first full-scale attempt to produce a grammar of narrative functions was Vladimir Propp's *Morphology of the Folk Tale*, first published in 1928.[2] Propp had felt intuitively that the magic folk-tale was a genre with a remarkably consistent and unified structure. By a close and consistent analysis of a hundred tales he isolated the thirty-one 'most abstract and constant elements of plot structure' and called these 'functions'. He defined the 'function' as 'the act of a character in a fairy tale distinguished by its significance for the action as a whole'.[3] Thus every unit is defined not by its external and largely accidental characteristics, as had been the case in earlier classifications of folk-tales, but by its role in relation to the totality of units to which it belongs.

Viktor Shklovsky[4] and Boris Tomashevsky[5] were using the concept of narrative function in a similar way in their discussions of more modern written literary genres. When the work of the Formalists was 'rediscovered' in the early 1960s, Propp's contribution inspired the most active debate and imitation, particularly among French structuralists. We have already invoked Roland Barthes' distinction between distributional (syntagmatic) and integrative (paradigmatic) relations in a text and it will be appropriate at this point to summarize in more detail that section of his seminal article on the structural analysis of narrative in which he elaborates this distinction.[6] Propp's functions were distributional in character, marking stages in the sequence of the narrative. The integrative role that certain of the key functions play, correlating with more diffuse concepts such as character or value or mood, had to be appended, almost as an afterthought, to his analysis. Barthes argued that our recreation of the story from the text requires a basic distinction from the start between those units (*functions*) whose sanction is always 'further on' (syntactic), and those (*indices*) whose sanction is 'higher up' (semantic). He thus combines Propp's notion of functional units with the linguistic distinction, propounded by de Saussure and Jakobson,[7] between the syntagmatic and paradigmatic axes of language. Barthes introduces a further important subdivision of his units into two sub-classes. Functions may be of two types: *cardinal functions* (or 'nuclei'), and *catalyses*; indices may be either *indices proper* or *informants*.

The relevance of these four categories to our analysis of plot may be clarified if we try to summarize Barthes' brilliant and closely reasoned argument[8] in diagrammatic form and then illustrate it with a simple example:

Figure 7. Barthes' Classes of Narrative Units

UNITS

FUNCTIONS   INDICES

distributional—refer to *operations*; correlate with units on the same level of meaning—a complementary and consequent act; form *syntagmatic*, horizontal relations; imply *metonymic* relata: functionality of *doing*.	*integrative*—refer to *concepts*; completed by reference to *another level*—a more or less diffuse concept which is still essential for the meaning of the story; form *paradigmatic*, vertical relations; imply *metaphoric* relata: functionality of *being*.

Cardinal functions (nuclei)	*Catalyses*	*Indices Proper*	*Informants*
involve *change*— have *consequences*; chronological + *logical* consecutive *consequential*; important through their 'risk'; to alter nucleus = to alter *story*	one-sided parasitic functionality; *merely* chronological and consecutive; fill in the 'safety zones'; constant phatic function; to alter catalysis = to alter *discourse*	*refer to* character, feeling, atmosphere; have implicit *connotations*; imply *decoding*; have *strong* functionality; function on level of *story*	*identify situation* in time and space; *pure data*, meaningful; carry ready-processed information; have *weak* functionality (increase authenticity, etcetera); function on level of *discourse*

Barthes makes two important qualifications about this schema: 'First of all, a unit can at the same time belong to two different classes ... certain units can be mixed units.'[9] This will be apparent even in the simple piece of narrative which follows, where a + sign in our notation indicates dual functioning.

The text is from an English children's version of *Rumpelstiltskin*:

At sunrise/the King arrived.   *Informant*: identifies situation in time/
                                        Catalyst: consecutive action

He was astonished and more than delighted to see so much gold.	*Index:* 'greed', connotations of character.
Yet he was not satisfied.	*Cardinal function:* fraught with consequence.
The sight of the gold only made him more greedy	*Index + Cardinal function:* 'greed' and its consequences consolidated.
He took the miller's daughter/ to a second room,/ much larger than the first one.	*Catalyst:* consecutive action/ *Informant:* place / *Index* (+ *Cardinal*): increase in size (has consequences).
It too was full of straw.	*Informant:* pure data.

Barthes' second qualification is also illustrated in this text, which only contains one cardinal function or nucleus: 'the King dissatisfied'. Barthes' linguistic parallel is instructive

> In the second place, it should be noticed that the four classes just mentioned are subject to another distribution—closer to the linguistic model, incidentally. Catalyses, indices, and informants indeed have one characteristic in common: they are *expansions* in their relation to the nuclei. Nuclei . . . form finite sets consisting of very few terms; they are logically controlled, at once necessary and sufficient. Once this framework has been constituted, the other units fill it in according to a mode of proliferation which has no theoretical limits. As everyone knows, that is what happens to the sentence, which is made up of simple propositions, yet keeps sprouting any number of duplications, paddings, convolutions, and so forth. Like the sentence, narrative can give forth any number of catalyses.[10]

At this point Barthes reasserts rather than replaces Propp's basic argument that it is a finite set of functions ('cardinal functions', in Barthes' terminology) which create the dynamics of the narrative and that other elements pertaining to the description of character, time, place and so on are auxiliary and not confined in number. We might take the linguistic analogy further: if the two main dimensions of *sentence* structure, as Fillmore proposes,[11] are 'propositions' (a tenseless set of process-participant relations involving verbs and nouns) and 'modality' (which includes such modifications of the basic proposition as negation, tense, mood and aspect), then these are analogous, at an abstract level, to the two main dimensions of *narrative* in our model: 'narrative structure' and 'point of view'. The central peripeteia of a story is then the focal moment of transitivity, the 'process' whereby the 'participants' change from one state (of fortune, danger, relationships, mind, etcetera) to another. In Propp's scheme this gives priority to the central functions of the conflict and victory of the hero over the villain, or, depending on one's interpretation of magic folk tales, the solving of the task (or problem, etcetera) and receipt of the magic means by the hero.

This is not to deny the validity of the other (cardinal) functions in both Propp's and Barthes' narrative grammars. Each episode has a cardinal function or nucleus which produces a partial, temporary or provisional change of fortune, etcetera for the central participants, just as a paragraph should contain a central advance in the argument (an idea, event, action, opinion) to which the other sentences relate, or a sentence has a main clause containing the central proposition, to which any number of subordinate clauses, each with its own nucleic proposition may relate. (There are constraints, of course, on the way various types of subordinate clause relate to the main one in a well-formed sentence, just as there are constraints on the way the episodes relate to the peripeteia in a well-formed narrative.) To complete the analogy, the 'catalyses' of sentence structure will be co-ordinate main clauses and subordinate clauses of time, purpose and cause; the 'indices' will be adjectives, adjectival clauses and phrases, etcetera; while the 'informants' will include adverbs and adverbial phrases and clauses of time and place.

Hopefully, then, Barthes' categories of narrative unit offer us a consistent set of terms for classifying the units of plot according to their function in the narrative as a whole. Most importantly for us, they enable us to relate these plot 'functions' to narrative structure, point of view, character and setting. We will start by analyzing the broad episodic structure of each story in terms of which of the four functions is predominant in each episode; then we will consider the implications of this structure for the story's other dimensions; finally, we will attempt a more 'delicate' analysis[12] of the functionality of the sub-episodes of which the episodes are composed for a more detailed view of the causal sequences and stylistic choices involved.

II   Pushkin: *The Pistol Shot*, 1831; (*Vystrel*)[13]

Although this story shares with *The Post-Stage Master* the distinction, among the five *Tales of Belkin*, of using a first person narrator and making the story's resolution depend on the connection of two internal flashback narratives related by other characters (the dénouement is a 'renouement', the unknotting a reknotting), *The Pistol Shot* has a far stronger stylistic unity. This is due mainly to the less complex character of the narrator and the greater coherence of the episodic structure.

As many commentators have pointed out,[14] the two-stage duel as narrated by each of the protagonists involves a great deal of parallel structuring of the two sections of the story. Our listing of the episodes in two columns (with letters indicating their sequence) will highlight the parallels:

SECTION I	*SECTION II*
A. Life in a provincial army post.	K. Life on a poor country estate.

B. Tedium relieved by one lively and exceptional individual, Silvio.

L. Tedium relieved by rich Countess and her husband.

C. His behaviour (tense, mysterious).

P. Count's behaviour (friendly, open, casual).

D. Description of Silvio's room: his shooting prowess.

O. Description of Count's room. Narrator's and Count's shooting prowess.

E. The card-cheating incident: no duel.

F. Narrator's embarrassment, but special relation with Silvio.

N. Narrator's reaction to Count and Count.

Q. Entry of Countess: Narrator's embarrassment.

G. Arrival of mail: Silvio's decision.

M. Arrival of rich neighbour.

H. Silvio's farewell party.

I. Narrator & Silvio: Silvio shows French cap, shot through.

R. Narrator & Count: Narrator notices Swiss picture, shot through.
Recognition: 'X' Silvio
'rake' Count.
Challenge

Flashback to 6 years ago:
1. social setting and challenge to duel.
2. characterization of self and opponent.
3. reputations of self and opponent.
4. duel scene:
   a) waiting
   b) attitude of Count
   c) (lots drawn), 12 paces

   d) shot 1 to Silvio, but cedes to Count
   e) Count shoots cap
   f) Count: no fear (cherries)
   g) Silvio: anger—sarcasm—threat
   h) Silvio refuses shot

Flashback to 5 years ago:
1. social setting and honeymoon.
2. recognition of Silvio.

3. duel scene:
   a) delay
   d) Masha's entry and reaction
   b) 12 paces—start again—draw lots
   c) shot 1 to Count

   d) Count shoots picture
   f) Count's fear
   g) anger—sarcasm—threat

   h) Silvio renounces shot. Exits, firing at picture.

J. Plans: Silvio to Moscow—departure.

S. Silvio departs.

T. Epilogue: Silvio's death.

The parallel descriptions, A and K, which open each section of the story are primarily indices of setting and narratorial tone with the army officer, Lieutenant Colonel I.L.P., later retired and turned landowner, characterizing himself implicitly through his language and attitudes. The next episodes, B and L, function differently at different levels of the story: the introduction of Silvio in Part I and the Count in Part II is merely catalytic for the protagonists themselves, but for the narrator it has consequences, it is a cardinal function. The descriptions of the behaviour and the rooms of Silvio and the Count, C-P and D-O, are strongly indicial of the contrasts in their characters and way of life. Although Pushkin has deliberately avoided an exactly parallel sequence here, these episodes clearly function similarly to predispose the narrator to interpret the stories he is told in a particular way. Episodes E-F and N-Q seem as if they should be cardinal functions. The first involves a highly dramatic scene and the second depicts a high degree of tension in the narrator: we expect them to have significant consequences, but they turn out to be merely sequential, as catalyses merely clearing the way for the next cardinal functions, the arrival of Silvio's letter and the discovery of the mutual acquaintance with Silvio. They are, however, key indices of character and feeling. Pushkin uses almost exactly parallel phrasing to introduce the main cardinal functions of each episode: the break in army routine when the mail is delivered paves the way for the important news for Silvio that his rival has been traced (G), while the break in a landowner's routine when a new neighbour moves in paves the way for the discovery by the narrator and the Count that they both know Silvio—now he too has been 'traced' (M-R2).

These cardinal functions of 'recognition' are significant for both the narrator and the protagonist; they establish the essential bond which motivates the contained narrative, told in flashback by Silvio and the Count respectively. Although flashbacks may on occasion be indicial in character, they normally contain at least one nucleus and frequently contain the whole sequence of nuclei which comprise the narrative structure. Neither I nor R does this, however. Pushkin, in fact, is playing with our expectations about the conventions of framed narrative in the short story. In a story of only ten pages a frame narrative nearly four pages long describing the narrator's meeting with the hero and providing the motivation for the hero to confide in the narrator might be expected to lead to a single flashback narrative incorporating the central action. Following this convention, the frame would then be completed by a short epilogue at the story's end describing the parting of hero and narrator and the hero's subsequent fate. The central narrative in *The Pistol Shot*, however, concerns an uncompleted duel which ends in frustration for one of the principals. The structure of Pushkin's story is mimetic of the split in the duel (according to the conventions a unitary transaction) and the reader's 'frustration' and search for 'satisfaction' mimes that of Silvio.

As our table of episodes shows, the parallel behaviour expected of the parties to a duel emerges as an almost complete parallelism in the episodic structure of the flashback narratives: *histoire* has become *discours* once again. Each revelation is sparked off by the sight of an artifact with exotic foreign associations—a French military cap, a picture of a Swiss landscape—which has a bullet-hole through it. These are thus both cardinal functions and indices. In the duel scenes themselves the ritual performances of measuring twelve paces and drawing lots are catalytic and, therefore, fully parallel, but it is the contrast between the other parallel elements in the duel scenes that proves most significant. (As Jan van der Eng says in his article on the Belkin Tales, 'Parallelism is a means of comparing not only similarities, but differences, contradictions and paradoxes'. [15]) In the first duel scene (I 4.a)) it is the Count who keeps Silvio waiting; in the second (R 3.a)) Silvio delays. In the first encounter the Count's casual attitude is a distraction; in the second, it is the entry of his wife—the very reason why he can no longer be casual—that distracts the duellists. When Silvio draws the straw for the first shot he is too excited and cedes it to the Count; he then accuses the latter of being 'devilishly lucky' when he wins the first shot in the second duel. The French-style cap and the Swiss picture acquire their function as the target for the wasted shot by the Count in each duel. This is where the laconic ambiguity of the story's title takes on its full force: syntagmatically, as a cardinal function, the shot that *is* fired in each duel provides a motivation for the telling of the story of that duel; and yet it is the indexical power of the shot that is *not* fired, operating paradigmatically throughout the whole story—in the second epigraph, in the duel that failed to take place over the cards, in the right to his shot that Silvio retained and in his final wasted bullet fired on top of the Count's shot in the picture—that gives the story so much of its meaning. Perhaps the enigma of the non-shot is only resolved with the bullet that kills Silvio in the Battle of Skulyani; or was he killed by a sabre?

The important point, of course, is that the actual shots (through the cap and the picture) signify primarily on the discourse level; they allow for the spontaneous introduction of the next piece of enclosed narrative in flashback, although, like the Count's cherry stones, they have some iconic function as a memory trace. The non-shot, on the other hand, signifies on the story level: it is the main motivating force for all of Silvio's actions, speech, behaviour and, indeed, appearance—it provides a focus on the psychological plane. But it is also a focus on the plane of social conventions: is a duel a valid transaction if it is split in two with six years between? It is a moral focus: can the dubious morality of the duel as a way of settling social, usually sexual, disputes be sustained if it is thus split and its arbitrariness revealed? It ultimately becomes a focus for the metaphysical despair of the Romantic hero who can find no point in a life where the superiority for which he has had to strive is usurped by someone with the natural superiority of the Count.

The peripeteia is a psychological one, as explained in the dénouement by Silvio: 'I am satisfied, I have seen your alarm, your timidity; I have forced you to fire at me, that is all I want. You will remember me. I leave you to your conscience.' The turning-point is the Count's show of alarm. At last he seems to be taking Silvio seriously. At their first duel his response to the threat of a bullet from Silvio was to spit out cherry pips in his direction. When Masha bursts in on their second duel he explains

'My dear, . . . can't you see that we are joking? There was no need to get so frightened! Go and drink a glass of water and come back to us; I want to introduce an old friend and comrade-in-arms to you'. Masha still couldn't believe it. 'Tell me, is my husband telling the truth?', she said, turning to the fierce Silvio,—'Is it true that you are both joking?'—'He is always joking, Countess',—replied Silvio,—'Once he gave me a slap in the face as a joke, shot through this cap here as a joke, has jokingly just missed me; now I've got an urge to do a bit of joking . . . '

As we pointed out in Chapter 3, Silvio shares with the equally touchy hero of *A Gentle Spirit* a horror of not being taken seriously. That hero's crisis was not resolved by the suicide of the heroine. It is not certain, despite the interpretation of the narrator and some commentators, that Silvio's crisis is resolved by the Count's response. Certainly he replies 'in a frenzy', but his actual words express dignity and a continuing concern for honour and not the alarm that Silvio reads into them: 'With these words he took aim at me . . . in front of her! Masha threw herself at his feet. "Get up, Masha, for shame!—I shouted in a frenzy,—And you, sir, will you stop making fun of a poor woman? Are you going to shoot or not?"' (See Russian Texts, No. 68) A careful reading of this speech suggests that the Count's 'frenzy' is a response to his wife's timidity and not at all an expression of his own. To Silvio he insists on honourable behaviour and is impatient for the shot to be fired. This is what makes Silvio's next empty gesture necessary: he is a brilliant shot and the only way he can show his superiority to the Count is to 'cap' his shot in the Swiss picture without seeming to take aim. As with *Mozart and Salieri* (written at precisely the same time as *The Tales of Belkin*) mere technical proficiency, whether as a composer or marksman, is trivial beside the genius of those chosen by the gods. Mozart's closing speech seems to echo Silvio's description of his adversary

We chosen ones are few, the careful children of fortune
Who despise and scorn mere usefulness,
Priests of the cult of beauty only. [16]

Silvio: I have never in my life met such a brilliant child of fortune! Imagine youth, intelligence, beauty, the wildest gaiety, the most carefree bravery, a famous name, money he hadn't even counted and which he never had to have transferred, and you can imagine what effect he must have had among us. My primacy was shaken.
(See Russian Texts, No. 69)

It is not jealousy or the threat of another's superior abilities that cuts deepest, however. It is the sheer indifference of Mozart towards his art that astonishes Salieri: 'You were on your way to me with such [great inspiration]/And still could stop by the inn/And listen to the blind violinist! [ruining your music]—Oh God!/Mozart you are not worthy of yourself.' And it is the Count's indifference to his fate that Silvio cannot bear

> At last his life was in my hands; I stared at him avidly, trying to catch just some shadow of anxiety . . . He stood, covered by my pistol, picking ripe cherries out of the cap and spitting out the pips which flew as far as me. His indifference enraged me. What was the use, I thought, of depriving him of life when he himself placed no value on it whatsoever?
> (See Russian Texts, No. 70)

Silvio's parting gesture, then, is to waste the precious shot which he has lived and prepared for for the past six years. Whether or not Silvio's death as narrated in the closing sentence of the story constitutes a similar empty gesture must be a matter of interpretation. J. Thomas Shaw[17] summarizes the debate around whether this was the only possible end for a 'superfluous man' or 'a serious, heroic desire for the independence of the Greeks' (a contemporary political issue about which Pushkin himself felt quite strongly), and himself suggests a third possibility: that 'Silvio's only real *métier* was military service . . . ' and that the epilogue offers 'an adequate application—in battle—for the quality of valor, emphasizing the incompleteness of valor as an ideal in other contexts'. The cryptic epilogue, presented as an unsubstantiated rumour (*Skazyvayut, chto . . .*), and following a most cryptic resolution of the problem of the unfired shot that leaves one wondering whether the story has a peripeteia at all, need not, perhaps be definitively interpreted one way or the other; all three interpretations remain valid. Despite his intense and obsessive preparation for the final shot, Silvio has still not succeeded in making the Count experience fear or value his life more than his honour: his 'superfluousness', so amply illustrated, psychologically, morally and socially, could only lead to a kind of suicide. On the other hand, the Ypsilanti uprising provided an appropriate test for both his military valor and his despair. Thirdly, however, the story is a kind of proof that the kind of valor which is appropriate in real battles is absurdly inappropriate when transposed into the unreal ritual of the duel.

The unreality of the conventions involved in the duel and the expectations they arouse in society are spotlighted in the three 'duels' in *The Pistol Shot*, for none of them is actually a real duel at all. The first 'non-duel', after the recently arrived officer had cheated at cards, although it is eagerly anticipated by the narrator and his comrades, never gets beyond the insult stage: the expected challenge is never made. The focus, in fact, falls on the reaction of the other officers and the narrator to the non-event. Similarly, although Silvio depicts the scene and negotiations of the second duel very vividly, the main tension for the narrator and the reader is in his reactions to the half-completed engagement. As we have seen, the third duel which ends with two bullets lodged one on top of the other in a Swiss mountain scene is as abortive, duellistically speaking, as the first two. The tension is in the subsequent state of mind of Silvio as he departs and of the Count as he relives the experience in narrating it. In other words, our main interest is not the action itself, but the psychological motivation for, and reaction to, the action. The 'excitement curves', as our Figure 8 shows, do not coincide; the psychological interest heightens as the action reaches its *anti-climax*:

Figure 8

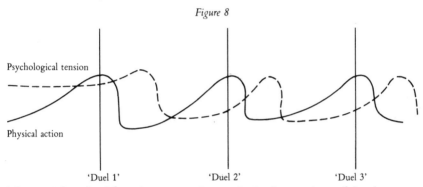

Psychological tension

Physical action

'Duel 1'   'Duel 2'   'Duel 3'

The crucial cardinal functions seem, then, to be in the reactions of the characters, not in their actions: perhaps, we are merely giving a definition of a 'psychological story'. As Eikhenbaum points out,[18] in spite of the rapid drama of the duel scenes, the story as a whole is anything but fast-moving. Pushkin subtly holds back the progress of the story and makes one feel every step. A basically very simple fable turns into an ingeniously complex plot structure through the intercession of a narrator whose personality and change of life-style motivates the division of the story into two parts and the slowing down of the section between them; this plot is then complicated further by being refracted through the consciousness and speech of three radically different narrators.

When he comes to look more closely at the opening to the story, Eikhenbaum senses a rhythmic tendency due to Pushkin's talents as a writer of verse: of the opening clauses all vary between six and fourteen syllables, but most are of seven, eight or nine, with longer phrases being followed and balanced by shorter ones (12-7, 14-6, etcetera). He sees this as an echo of the 8-9 syllable iambic tetrameter line with three or four stresses. This is ingenious and persuasive, but downgrades, I think, Pushkin's genuine narrative competence in characterizing his narrators and characters by their speech. At least as significant in the opening lines of the story is the brisk style of the army officer's report. The time-tabling of the day into three provides a triptych of laconic matching pairs, each linked by a different conjunction: 'In the morning study, riding training; dinner at the regimental commander's house or in some Yid's inn; in the evening punch and

cards.' (See Russian Texts, No. 71) The laconic quality of the syntax continues
in Episode B which is ostensibly a description of Silvio's personality, but also
succeeds in telling us a great deal about the narrator. Lieutenant Colonel I.L.P.
favours co-ordinate structures linked by colons and semi-colons: since there are
virtually no subordinate clauses, the logic of his description is carried through the
intonation. This dynamic quality is increased by the predominance of transitive
verbs and the small proportion of adjectives. Silvio is not described statically, but
in terms of his behavior and the effect that behaviour has on the young officers.
The oppositions between their military status and his civilian status, their youth
and his seniority (at thirty-five), their inexperience and his experience, their naive
simplicity and his gloomy sarcasm and brusqueness, their openness and his air of
mystery, their Russianness and his foreignness, are developed in terms of the
transactions between the group and the individual, rather than in the antithetical
structures we find in the essay style with which *The Post-Stage Master* opens

> Only one man belonged to our company without being a soldier. He was
> about thirty-five and we therefore considered him old. His air of experience
> gave him many advantages in our eyes; in any case his normal gloominess,
> sharp manner and sarcastic tongue had a powerful effect on our young minds.
> A sort of mystery surrounded his life; he seemed to be a Russian, but bore a
> foreign name.
> (See Russian Texts, No. 72)

Silvio's enigmatic quality grows out of a series of paradoxes: he is a Russian but
has a foreign name; he is an officer but is in forced retirement; although living in
a provincial backwater he has broader horizons; his apparent poverty and asceticism are offset by his extravagance, and so on. His personality seems to be the
unstable product of a set of transactions, an index already of the incomplete transaction underlying the whole story. Silvio's very existence is the result of a narratorial transaction: 'Silvio (as I shall call him) . . . ' The hero fades into the story
rather as we saw him fading out in the epilogue. For all the precise information
about the Ypsilanti campaign, it is only a rumour that that is where he died:
'They say . . . ' (*Skazyvayut, chto* . . .).

The first actual transaction which provides a test for the group of the quality of
this mysterious individual is the challenge to his authority over cards. Like most
episodes which are cardinal functions, this has its own structure of nuclei and
other units. It opens with an informant which sets the scene in time and space. A
framing sequence of actions which are characteristically in the imperfective
aspect[19] provides the indices of mood and character before the perfective verb
which embodies the first cardinal function which we might label 'adversary's
error'

(INFORMANT)   One evening ten or so of our officers were dining in
(INDICES)   Silvio's quarters. We were drinking in our usual style,

> That is, a great deal; after dinner we tried to persuade our host to be banker for a round of cards ... It was Silvio's custom to preserve total silence while playing, he would never argue or enter into explanations. If a punter should happen to miscount, he would immediately either pay up what was due or note down the excess. We knew this and let him run things his own way; but among us there was one officer who had been transferred to us quite recently.

(CARDINAL FUNCTION)

> In playing he *absent-mindedly drew one card too many*.
> (See Russian Texts, No. 73)

The cardinal functions now develop in a flurry of perfective verbs: 'correction' is followed by 'argument', 'counter-correction', 'counter-counter-correction', 'taking offence', 'act of aggression', 'act of evasion' and 'dismissal'. The place of this moment of drama is natural as perfective verb follows perfective verb. There is a contrast in the syntax of the officer's actions and those of Silvio, however, which gives these cardinal functions an indicial role: every one of the officer's acts involves a qualifying clause with a gerund or participle, as if his uncertainty or anger make him hesitate, while all of Silvio's acts are conveyed in brisk, unhesitating perfectives (only the qualifying clauses are italicized)

> ... there was one officer *who had been transferred to us quite recently. In playing* he *absentmindedly* drew one card too many. Silvio picked up the chalk and amended the score in his usual way. The officer, *thinking that he had made a mistake*, started to argue. Silvio silently went on dealing. The officer, *losing patience*, took the rubber and rubbed out what he thought should not have been written down. Silvio took the chalk and wrote it down once more. The officer, *inflamed by the wine, the gambling and his comrades' laughter*, considered himself cruelly insulted, and *seizing in a fury a copper candlestick from the table*, hurled it at Silvio who barely had time to dodge the blow.
> (See Russian Texts, No. 74)

Only in the final cardinal function of this sequence, when Silvio, too, has lost his temper, is his action delayed by a qualifying clause: 'Silvio stood up, [having turned] *white with anger*, and with glittering eyes said: "Sir, be so kind as to leave, and you may thank God that this has happened in my house."' To the surprise of the officers, Silvio does not challenge the officer to a duel but contents himself with the symbolic act of firing bullet after bullet into an ace of cards pinned to the gates of his courtyard. This cardinal function which so affects the narrator's attitude to the hero sets the tone for the later duels not only by being a non-event, but because it epitomizes the shift from the action plane to the symbolic plane. Later, equally symbolically, the Count shoots Silvio not through the head but through the cap and 'fires' cherry pips at him while waiting to be shot, and they both fire shots at a picture in the final scene: perhaps we are to understand Silvio's parting shot as a sign that he is reconciled to fighting the Count according to the latter's rules.

Silvio's 'failure' to engage the officer in a duel affects the narrator more strongly than the other officers and the point of view is now firmly singular. The early part of the story shows a progressive narrowing of focus: 'the regiment' narrows down to Silvio, 'the officers' narrows down to 'one officer', and 'we' narrows down to 'I'. In describing his own reactions to Silvio's behaviour the narrator modifies the brisk, matter-of-fact, soldierly tone of the earlier part of the story and indulges what he calls his 'romantic imagination'. The syntax becomes more convoluted, with longer sentences and more complex subordination, archaic phrasing and inversions creep into his style and metaphors and similes are used more freely

> Possessing from nature a romantic imagination, I had up to now been more attached than anyone to a man whose life was an enigma and who appeared to me as the hero of some mysterious tale. He liked me; or at least it was only with me that he would abandon his usual sharp sarcasm and chat about various things in a simple-hearted and extraordinarily pleasant way. But after that unfortunate evening the thought that his honour had been sullied and not wiped clean due to his own fault, this thought never left me and prevented me from behaving with him as I had done before.
>
> (See Russian Texts, No. 75)

The narrator's change of style prepares the way for the almost melodramatically Romantic image of Silvio he presents after receiving the fateful letter. The farewell party is hyperbolically, almost hysterically, cheerful, with one of Pushkin's characteristic 'party pieces' with 'corks popping *every minute*, glasses foaming and fizzing *without cease* and us *with the utmost* enthusiasm wishing the departing one bon voyage and *every possible* good fortune'. But as Silvio takes the narrator aside to confide in him, the image belongs more to the worlds of Byron or Walter Scott, or the Gothic novel: 'The guests had left; we two remained and sat down opposite each other and silently lit our pipes. Silvio was troubled; there wasn't a sign of his manic gaiety. A gloomy pallor, glittering eyes and the thick smoke coming out of his mouth gave him the appearance of a real devil.' Silvio himself affects a somewhat self-conscious aphoristic style of speaking which verges at times on parody of Romantic attitudes: 'I have not got the right to expose myself to death.' Who, one asks oneself, has ordained this right in Silvio's case? This becomes clearer in the indicial section where he describes his own character and background. Here the aphoristic pattern involves a repeated motif of a general situation which he claims to epitomize. This shows a ruthless intellectual honesty and ability to handle general issues—and word etymologies —which is beyond the narrator: 'In our day rowdyism was in fashion: I was the champion rowdy in the army. We used to boast about drunkenness: I outdrank the famous Burtsov celebrated by Denis Davydov. There were duels taking place every other minute in our regiment: I was at all of them either as a witness or as one of the principals.' Our final vision of Silvio through the narrator's own eyes reverts to the melodramatic image

> —You can guess,—said Silvio,—who that *certain person* was. I am going to Moscow. Let's see whether he will accept death as calmly before his marriage as he once awaited it over a breakfast of cherries!
>
> As he uttered these words Silvio stood up, flung his cap onto the floor and started walking up and down the room like a tiger in its cage. I listened to him without stirring; I felt strange and contradictory feelings disturbing me.

Fortunately, Pushkin senses the need to refract the melodramatic cliché of the caged tiger through the naive and portentous reactions of his Lieutenant Colonel I.L.P.

The role of the narrator is crucial to the plot structure of *The Pistol Shot*. As we have seen, the real events in the story are the internal, framed narratives of Silvio and the Count. But their meetings with the narrator only happen by chance and only chance circumstances lead to their telling him their stories. One story relates events six years prior to their telling, the other five years, and yet a temporal 'joint' is achieved by the beginning of the second internal narrative following shortly on the end of the narrator's first piece of narration: presumably a very short time elapses between Silvio's departure from the regiment and his arrival at the Count's estate, since he is on his honeymoon. The two duel sequences occur in widely distant locations and one is out of doors, in a spring dawn, the other indoors, at twilight. They only come together through the chance appearance of a 'third dimension' who is not even a witness. He only knows the protagonists' *character* at first hand; his knowledge of the *events* is refracted through their attitudes, emotions and language. He is, in fact, only a frame, and we never penetrate the mystery of either Silvio's or the Count's motivation. Bocharov puts it well

> In narrating their stories to a third person both participants can achieve objectivity. Hence their stories, as if turning to face each other and penetrating each other, are also turned towards a third neutral outsider whom they cannot do without. They rise above their petty internal quarrel and gain a new objective reality in Pushkin's narration: the ends get tied in the third dimension which objectively becomes the culmination for the two others. [20]

Apart from his technical narrative function, however, Lieutenant Colonel I.L.P. represents society. He characterizes himself quite fully through his language and attitudes and his is clearly the conventional social norm to which the eccentric transactions of the protagonists have to be related. In an age and society where a man's honour is tested through gambling at cards and duelling, cheating at cards and personal assault are expected to meet with retribution, the firing of the first shot in a duel is expected to be followed by the second. We, with the narrator, seek for an explanation first in Silvio's character and later in the Count's story. But you are not expected to spit cherry pips at your opponent or deliberately fire at a painting instead of at him in a duel. We are intrigued by the unconventional behaviour of both the participants in a social transaction which has clear and explicit rules. No less are we intrigued by the turns in the plot of this short story, a narrative genre where we expect to have all the loose ends of cause and effect tied up for us by the end, but where we find we have had to refract for ourselves two sets of motivation into a coherent causal sequence.

III Gorky: *Twenty-Six Men and a Girl. A poem*, 1899; *(Dvadtsat' shest' i odna, Poema)* [21]

Apart from the key role they played in the cultural life of their time, it would be hard to find two Russian writers whose lives and works contrasted more sharply than those of Pushkin and Gorky. It is intriguing, therefore, to discover in Gorky's *Twenty-Six Men and a Girl* a plot structure which is almost exactly parallel to the plot structure of each half of *The Pistol Shot*, written nearly seventy years earlier. We might schematize the sequence of functions as shown in Figure 9.

It might be objected that this is a fairly standard sequence: many narratives have a *challenge-test-outcome* as their central complex of cardinal functions or nuclei and for these to engage our involvement and sympathy the protagonists of this triad have to be characterized and contrasted and placed in some kind of setting. The key element relating the three narratives in question, however, is the relationship between their protagonists and the group to which they stand in contrast and which reacts to their central conflict. Significantly, we do not observe the conflict directly, but only as it is refracted through the report of it to the narrator by one of the principals (first Silvio, then the Count) or through the restricted viewpoint of the group themselves (the twenty-six). It is this refraction of the central action through the onlookers' point of view—or perhaps we should say this displacement of the action to the periphery by the point of view which takes over the centre of the narrative—that is such a striking and distinctive feature of both of these stories.

The parallelism in the plot serves to highlight the differences between Gorky's story and Pushkin's as well as the resemblances, however. Syntagmatically, the plots contribute to quite different narrative structures; paradigmatically, the indicial content of the functions comprising each plot is entirely different.

Each of the duel scenes in *The Pistol Shot* represents a separate narrative structure, as we have seen, with the resolution suppressed or held in abeyance. The story's resolution depends on the narrator's, and the reader's, success in combining the two halves: the nature of the peripeteia depends on our interpretation of Silvio's final shot and on our interpretation of *his* interpretation of the Count's

Figure 9

	INDEX	NUCLEUS (INDEX)	NUCLEUS (INDEX)	NUCLEUS	INDEX	NUCLEUS
	Tedious routine of an isolated group →	Appearance of a vivid relief figure →	Challenge to relief figure →	Test and victory of challenger →	Reaction of group →	Outcome
PS (1)	army officers	Silvio	Count	'duel' 1	passively	two narratives
PS (2)	land owners	Count	Silvio	'duel' 2	hear report	
26 & 1	pretzel makers	Tanya	soldier	seduction	respond actively	a moment of life

N.B. PS = *The Pistol Shot*
26 & 1 = *Twenty-Six Men and a Girl*

change in attitude. Many readers take Silvio at his word when he says he is content to have made the Count afraid of him and see his bullet, casually aimed at the Count's in the corner of the picture, as a token of his moral victory. Our reading found Silvio as sceptical as we were of the Count's change of heart, so that his bullet is a mere gesture of frustration, on target technically but not morally, and his suicidal involvement at Skulyani the only resolution.

Gorky's story only encompasses a single sequence of plot functions, yet we have some difficulty in pinning down a single peripeteia due to the shift from the real action—the soldier's 'conquest' of Tanya—to the psychological drama which is taking place in the minds of their twenty-six watchers. Although the actual lovemaking takes place 'off-stage' in a cellar, the seduction scene is very precisely and symmetrically structured to produce a kind of extended chiasmus. First Tanya crosses the yard and disappears behind the cellar door, then the soldier . . . then the soldier emerges, and then Tanya. Even the details of their manner and appearance form a mirror image in each case: first Tanya's way of walking, then the expression on her face . . . then the changed expression on her face, then her changed way of walking; first the soldier's twitching moustache, then his hands thrust in his pockets . . . then his hands in pockets, then the twitching moustache. Even the intervening landscape shares this chiasmic pattern: rain—dreariness—roofs—snow—mud-splashes—snow—roofs—dreariness—rain. (Although Gorky had a propensity for both euphemism and symbol, this landscape is not to be dismissed as merely one of those symbolic euphemisms —the waves pounding on the rocks, fireworks bursting in the sky—with which the romantic novel and Hollywood and the Soviet cinema drew a discreet veil over what was going on in the bedroom. The mudstains on the snow and the frowning puddles are, or course, symbolic, and the paragraph does cover the interval during which the couple are in the cellar, but the focus is on the slowly passing minutes for *the watchers* and the dreary rain symbolizes *their* dampened spirits. The refraction of the seduction through their impoverished imagination makes this scene both necessary and apt.) The whole scene, like the landscape paragraph, is symmetrically framed by three pause dots

We did not wait long . . . Soon with hurrying steps and thoughtful face, Tanya crossed the yard, skipping over the puddles of melted snow and mud. She disappeared behind the door into the cellar. Then, unhurried and whistling, the soldier strolled across to the same spot. His hands were thrust into his pockets and his moustache twitched . . .

It was raining and we watched the raindrops falling in the puddles and the puddles frowning beneath their blows. The day was damp and grey—a very dreary day. On the roofs there was still a layer of snow and on the ground dark patches of mud had already appeared. And the snow on the roofs was also covered with a brownish muddy tinge. The rain fell slowly, it spattered mournfully. We felt cold and miserable with waiting . . .

The first to emerge from the cellar was the soldier; he strolled slowly across the yard, twitching his moustache, thrusting his hands in his pockets,—just as he always was.

Then Tanya came out too. Her eyes . . . her eyes were shining with joy and happiness, and her lips—were smiling. And she walked as if she were asleep, staggering a little, with unsure steps . . .

We could not bear this calmly.
(See Russian Texts, No. 76)

This is certainly a climax of a kind. The change in Tanya is quite evident, and even the syntax describing the soldier has shifted slightly. Before he went in the verb forms were passive: 'his hands were thrust into his "pockets" (*zasunuty*) and his moustache "twitched" (*shevelilis'*).' When he comes out these verbs have become active and transitive: 'twitching his moustache' (*shevelya usami*) and 'thrusting his hands in his pockets' (*zasunuv*). The most dramatic change comes over the twenty-six watchers as they burst out of the door and whistle and whoop their rage at the astonished helpless girl. The symmetrical framing of the central scene was not to highlight it as a turning-point in the story, but as a deliberate visual, even cinematic, device to limit the visual field of those watching and to retard the action for them as well as for the reader. For they are not, of course, simply spectators, they are *voyeurs*. It is a kind of orgasm as they burst through the doors and into the yard to ejaculate their scorn and insults. And as their hatred explodes in the tripled verbs and adverbs

we *leaped out* into the yard and *whistled* and *yelled* at her *malevolently, loudly, wildly*

We *laughed, roared, bellowed;*
(See Russian Texts, No. 77)

we realize we are witnessing a kind of verbal gang rape. But the girl is no helpless victim; she understands well enough the frustration that has brought them to this as she calmly and with dignity sums up their predicament: 'Suddenly her eyes flashed; she unhurriedly raised her hands to her head and, straightening her hair, loudly but calmly said straight in our faces:—Oh you miserable convicts!' Tanya recognizes that it is not just sex that they must experience vicariously, but life itself. The desecration of their idol had started on a psychological plane long before the seduction, for they themselves had set the seduction in motion by challenging the soldier. The key conversation in the story takes place when the soldier comes into the pretzel bakery tipsy and shows off about two of the girls from the gold embroiderers' workshop upstairs fighting over him and about his success with women in general. The baker is provoked by his vulgar self-satisfaction to taunt him cryptically

—It doesn't take much strength to fell baby fir-trees, but try felling a pine . . .

—You mean—is it me you're talking to?—asked the soldier.
—Who else . . .
—What are you on about?
—Never mind . . . let it pass!
—No, you hang on! What d'you mean? What pine tree?

The exchange is then interrupted by a piece of philosophizing (to which we will return) and then resumes: '—No, you tell me—who?
—Shall I tell you?—suddenly the baker turned to face him.
—Well?
—D'you know Tanya?' The sacred name has been uttered, the challenge is specific and this must be the central cardinal function, the peripeteia, of the story. Overt individual acts, however, have deep causes in the psychology of the group in Gorky's story. After their previous conversation with the soldier, the pretzel-makers had discussed his potential conquests among the gold embroiderers. The bright innocent tones of the diminutives describing them are already sullied by the men's vulgar conversation

> . . . And we kept on talking about him and about his future successes among the gold-embroiderers who when they met us outside would either, compressing their lips disapprovingly, pass us by to one side, or would bear down on us as if we were not even there in their way. But we always just admired them both out in the yard and when they walked past our windows—in winter dressed in some sort of special little fur caps and coat, in summer wearing little bonnets with flowers and holding little multicoloured parasols. And yet among ourselves we would talk about these girls in such a manner that if they had heard us they would have been in a frenzy of shame and hurt.
> (See Russian Texts, No. 78)

The collective admiration of the pretty seamstresses turns to dirty jokes about them and the way is paved for one individual—again the baker—to utter the unutterable: '—All the same what if he went and spoiled our little Tanya!—the baker suddenly said in a worried tone.' Gorky's account of the group's reaction is magnificently ambivalent. Their impulse is to protect and warn Tanya, but the seed of the idea of sacrifice has been sown, and the bulky figure of the soldier now stands figuratively between her and them as it is to stand physically before and after the seduction scene

> We all fell silent under the impact of these words. We had somehow forgotten about Tanya: the soldier had blocked her from our view, as it were, with his solid, handsome figure. Then a loud argument started up: some said that Tanya wouldn't let herself go that far, others insisted that she wouldn't be able to resist the soldier, finally a third group proposed if the soldier started bothering Tanya—to break his ribs for him. And in the end we all decided to keep an eye on the soldier and Tanya and warn the girl to be wary of him . . . This stopped the arguing.

The most noteworthy thing about their reaction to the taboo topic is that in their excitement they cease to be a single monolithic group: three parties to the argument emerge. Up to now Gorky has stressed the unity and indivisibility of the twenty-six men in their misery and poverty. The long opening description of the story stresses their collective wretchedness; even a song, started by a single voice and taken up by two or three more voices, only serves to reunite them and reaffirm their anguish; in the face of Tanya or the soldier they seem to become an inert, inseparable mass. Yet here, aroused by the prospect—even promise—of danger to their idol, they can be variously motivated. Perhaps Gorky's greatest *tour de force* in this superbly structured story is his control of the interplay between group and individual psychology. He has come near to writing an entirely first person *plural* narrative. There are two elements that prevent him from doing so, one a matter of point of view, the other of plot. On the one hand, the narrator who represents the group to us is bound to be more intelligent and perceptive and articulate than his fellows, however fully he claims to be part of the group consciousness. The physical point of view can be genuinely collective as the twenty-six gaze up enraptured at Tanya four steps above them (another cinematic 'shot') or with curiosity up at the new employee in the bakery, the soldier, as he stands in a cloud of frost-smoke on the same plinth of a threshold, or with vicarious lust as they spy on the couple crossing the courtyard to the cellar. But the psychological point of view of these dumb, browbeaten illiterates has to be refracted through the discourse of an articulate, intelligent and perceptive narrator.

The narrator's distinctive role is to perceive, narrate and philosophize. The baker turns out to have the distinctive role of activating the cardinal functions of the plot; he acts on behalf of the group when some initiative is needed. Before we even recognize him as an individual the sound of his shovel stands out 'quickly and malevolently scraping against the floor of the oven, tossing the slippery pieces of boiled dough onto the hot bricks' and there seems to be something demonic about him in the red glow of the stove. He is the one who tosses into Tanya's apron the freshest and nicest pretzels straight from the oven; he invites the soldier to stop and chat when he first visits them; he is the one who has the idea that the soldier might want to 'spoil' Tanya; and, as we have seen, he is the one who issues and specifies the challenge to the soldier. He plays the key role in the final conversation with and about Tanya before the seduction: she has come to the door, as gay as ever, but is met by a threatening silence instead of the usual eager response of the twenty-six

> She was obviously surprised at the unaccustomed greeting,—and suddenly we saw her turn white, grow anxious, begin to fidget and she asked in a choking voice:
> —Why are you . . . like that?
> —What about you?—the baker flung at her gloomily, not taking his eyes off her.

—What about—me?

—Never mind . . .

—Well, give us the pretzels quick . . . She'd never rushed us before . . .

—You'll make it in time!—said the baker, not moving and still staring at her face.

Then she turned suddenly and disappeared out of the door.

The baker picked up his shovel and muttered calmly as he turned back to the stove:

—So—it's all fixed! . . . Oh, soldier boy! . . . The swine! . . .

The rest of us, like a herd of rams, bumping each other, went over to the table, sat down without speaking and sluggishly began to work. Before long someone said:

—And yet, you never know . . .

—Oh sure! Tell us another one!—snarled the baker.

We all knew that he was a clever chap, cleverer than us. And we understood his snapping back as a certainty of the soldier's victory. We felt sad and anxious . . .

We have noted the significance of three-dot pauses elsewhere in this story as well as in Pushkin and Dostoevsky. If there is one stylistic fault in this beautifully elliptic dialogue and narrator's commentary, it is that Gorky has overplayed his three-dot pauses. The implicit meanings are quite clear without being underscored so often in this way.

The baker, then, plays an active role in tempting fate on behalf of the other twenty-five, a sort of devil's advocate who represents that element in their minds that has to test their goddess and longs for the act of sacrilege. It is significant that the conversation we have quoted is his last 'solo appearance'. During and after the seduction scene he has disappeared back into the group consciousness from which he emerged, his plot role accomplished.

Any other signs of individuality are quickly squashed by the group. If anyone should ask Tanya to do him a special favour or suggest that they were fussing too much over her he would be jeered at. We should not, perhaps, be surprised that the story tends to be passed over in silence by Soviet critics. Although Gorky makes it clear from the start that their living and working conditions and lack of hope are a direct result of their exploitation by a capitalist baker, the story stands as a terrible revelation of the power for evil of the collective mind and the group hysteria at the end is as powerful as any of the mob lynching scenes in classic Westerns like *The Ox-Bow Incident*.

It is genuine individuality that is beautiful in *Twenty-Six Men and a Girl*, not group consciousness. Tanya, a sixteen-year-old servant girl and the out-of-work soldier are ordinary enough people by most standards, but by the debased standards of the pretzel-makers, they are gods. The three key indicial episodes in the plot are the long opening description of the collective misery in the bakehouse and the two individual portraits of Tanya and the soldier. In both these cases the physical charm of clear blue eyes, pink skin, strong white teeth and long thick hair are stressed. The angelic vision of Tanya is deliberately juxtaposed with the appearance of the twenty-six: 'We loved to see her nose pressed against the glass and the fine white teeth gleaming behind the pink lips which were parted in a smile . . . A long thick plait of chestnut hair fell across her shoulder and lay on her breast. We, dirty, ignorant, ugly people would look up at her from below . . .' The soldier appears, also above them, in a cloud of frosty air worthy of a visitation from Olympus: 'The frosty air, bursting in through the door in a thick smoky cloud, swirled at his feet and he stood on the step looking down at us from above, and from beneath his blonde, neatly twirled moustache gleamed strong yellow teeth.' The smile in each case is a kind of assertion of a life-force. The only physiognomy that warrants a description at the beginning of the story in the hellish cave where the twenty-six work is that of the demonic baker's oven

> The huge stove looked like the ugly head of a fairy-tale monster,—it seemed to rear up from under the floor, open its gaping maw full of bright fire, breathe on us with its hot breath and watch our unending toil with the two black cavities of the air-vents above its forehead. These two deep cavities were like eyes—the pitiless and passionless eyes of a monster: they always gazed with the same dark stare as if they had grown weary of watching slaves, and, expecting nothing human from them, despised them with the cold scorn of wisdom.

For all the differences in the images presented in these passages of the dainty Tanya, the forceful soldier and the monstrous stove, the structure of the presentation is remarkably parallel: the mouth as a source of light, the eyes viewing the pretzel-makers and their work from an objective and uncaring stance.

The monster-stove is only one of the personified inanimate forces that threaten and rule the twenty-six 'living machines' in their ill-lit, ill-ventilated and barred-up cellar: windows gaze out at the pit, the sunlight is unable to push through to them through the glass, the boiling water purrs in the cauldron, the baker's shovel scrapes malevolently, the glow from the fire trembles on the wall, laughing silently. The whole of the first two pages of indicial description are built on an opposition between the life of these oppressive forces outside—of which the only human one is the bakery owner—and the lifelessness of the pretzel-makers who have to rock as they knead the dough in order not to turn to wood (*chtob ne oderevenet'*), whose movements have become totally mechanical (*my v prodolzhen-iye dlinnykh chasov mekhanicheski dvigali rukami i pal'tsami*), and whose senses are so numbed that they can no longer even abuse one another (a fine rhythmical stepped series of conditional clauses here): 'But we rarely even abused each other —how can a man be to blame for anything if he is half-dead, < if he is like a wooden idol, < if all his feelings have been crushed by the burden of toil?' (See Russian Texts, No. 79) The 'pathetic fallacy' in Gorky's romantic allegory, then, is a Marxist one: it is not the forces of nature that are anthropomorphized, but the artefacts of a man-made industrialized world, threatening the last spark of humanity in its victims.

It is not only the metaphors, however, that justify Gorky in subtitling his story 'a poem'. There are numerous examples on many levels of structure in the opening section of the 'poetic function' of language which, according to Roman Jakobson's famous dictim, 'projects the principle of equivalence from the axis of selection into the axis of combination'.[22] On the syntactic level the most obvious of these is the selection of passive forms to express the plight of the entirely passive 'living machines': the nominative pronoun 'we' (*my*) only occurs with verbs of getting up and sleeping, kneading, mechanically moving, growing accustomed and remaining silent, in other words, in contexts stressing the routine and mechanical and lifeless; otherwise the narrator always refers to them as 'us' (*nas, nam, nami*), the objects of someone else's activity. The very first word of the story sets out the pattern

> There were twenty-six *of us*
> Our boss called *us* rogues and gave *us* for dinner . . .
> It was stuffy and cramped *for us* . . .
> It was hard and nauseating *for us* . . .
> It [the stove] breathed on *us* with its hot breath . . .
> (See Russian Texts, No. 80)

Passive participles, referring to either the twenty-six or their prison, form long chains

> living machines, *locked up* in a damp cellar . . .
> at the pit *dug out* facing us and *lined* with bricks . . .
> the frames *were barred* . . .
> the panes, *covered* with flour dust . . .
> beneath the heavy ceiling *covered* in soot and spiders' webs . . .
> between the thick walls *decorated* with stains of mud and mould . . .
> (See Russian Texts, No. 81)

These same passive qualifying clauses frequently incorporate a prepositional phrase suggesting containment, restriction, suppression: *in, between, beneath,* etcetera. The last two quoted also exemplify one of the dominant patterns of selection in the 'poem'—partly syntactic, partly intonational, partly phonetic— of paired nominals or adverbials

> It was stuffy and cramped for us living in the stone box beneath a low heavy ceiling covered with soot and spiders' webs . . .
> It was hard and nauseating between those thick walls decorated with stains of mud and mould . . .
> (See Russian Texts, No. 82)

The matching pairs are most directly mimetic of the repetitious routine they are the slaves of in the time adverbials and the adverbial phrases indicating mutual position

And all day from morning until ten at night . . .
And all day . . .
From morn till night . . .
Day in, day out . . .
nine against nine . . .
(See Russian Texts, No. 83)

The patterning is more specifically phonetic, appropriately enough, in the onomatopoeic descriptions of the sounds in their life. For instance, the play on the vowel 'y', and the liquid and sibilant consonants shifting to velar and dental stops: 'the boiling water in the cauldron purred meditatively and mournfully;' (see Russian Texts, No. 84) or the hard back vowels 'o' and 'a' and the reverse shift in the consonants from labial, dental and velar stops to liquids and sibilants to match the meaning of: 'the baker's shovel malevolently and quickly scraped along the bottom of the oven, tossing the slippery pieces of boiled dough onto the hot bricks.' (See Russian Texts, No. 85) All these devices are perhaps necessary to express the 'anti-lyricism' of this song from the lower depths. They are not sufficient to make it a poem. They are all brought together most meaningfully, and most movingly, in the description of the singing that brings the men together and releases them from their bondage. Anyone familiar with Russian folk singing will recognize the pattern of growth from a quiet solo, through the poignant harmonies of two or three voices, to the stirring polyphony of a full choir. It has rarely been so well described in words (with all the patterns of syntax, sense and sound coming together) or been invested with such a deep poetic significance. This is the one moment in the story where an individual act leads to collective harmony and where the collective consciousness is a power for good

. . . Sometimes we would sing and our song would start like this: in the middle of working someone would suddenly sigh the heavy sigh of a weary horse and start to sing, ever so quietly, one of those drawn out songs whose plaintive-caressing tune always lightens the burden in the soul of the singer. One of us would sing and at first we would listen to his solitary song in silence, and it would fade and be muffled beneath the heavy cellar ceiling, like the tiny glow of a bonfire in the steppe on a damp autumn night when the grey sky hangs over the earth like a leaden roof. Then the singer would be joined by another, and now two voices quietly and yearningly floated through the fug of our crowded pit. And suddenly several voices at once would take up the refrain,—it would surge up like a wave, grow stronger and louder and seem to part asunder the damp heavy walls of our stone prison . . .

All twenty-six would sing; the loud, long since sung-out voices would fill the workshop; the song would feel trapped there: it would beat against the stone of the walls, groan and weep and revive the heart with a quiet tickling pain, irritate the old wounds in it and awaken a yearning . . . The singers sigh heavily; one might suddenly break off from singing and listen for a long time to his comrades singing, and then merge his voice into the common tide once more. One, with a poignant cry of 'Ekh!' would sing with his eyes shut and perhaps the dense, broad wave of sounds would appear to him as a road stretching away into the distance, lit by a bright sun,—a broad highway, and he would see himself walking along it . . .
(See Russian Texts, No. 86)

The only Russian critic (apart, apparently, from Gorky himself and Lenin) to have expressed real appreciation for *Twenty-Six Men and a Girl* was D.S. Mirsky. Yet even he is unable to find any virtue in Gorky's style

> . . . Gorky's Russian is 'neutral', the words are mere signs and have no individual life. If it were not for certain catchwords, they might have been a translation from any language. The only one of Gorky's early stories that makes one forget all his shortcomings (except the mediocrity of his style) is the one that may be considered as closing the early period, *Twenty-Six Men and a Girl* (1899) . . . The story is cruelly realistic. But it is traversed by such a powerful current of poetry, by such a convincing faith in beauty and freedom and in the essential nobility of man, and at the same time it is told with such precision and necessity, that it can hardly be refused the name of a masterpiece. It places Gorky—the young Gorky—among the true classics of our literature.[23]

An English critic must be diffident about disagreeing with a Russian native critic as perceptive as Mirsky, but over the question of Gorky's style in this story we must disagree. The description of the birth of the singing in the long passage we have quoted is surely anything but 'neutral' and could surely not have been a translation from any language (certainly it defies translation *from* the original Russian into an English which is adequate to the rich interplay of sound and syntax and imagery). Moreover, it is hard to see how a story 'told with precision and necessity' could exemplify Gorky's 'mediocrity of style'.

On the contrary, while sharing Mirsky's enthusiasm for the elegant structure of the story and the poetry of its theme, we would insist that these depend on the rich contrasts in style. The rather flat tone of the plot narrative—those cardinal functions which grow out of the baker's individual initiatives—is the necessary 'proletarian base', stylistically speaking, against which we can appreciate the elliptical sparseness of the dramatic dialogues, the lyric freshness of the portraits of Tanya and the soldier, and the powerful orchestration of the 'purple passages' in which the conditions of life of the twenty-six and their mute response are described. The style has a paradoxical role to play in relation to the plot. It is at its most vivid and varied when the living death of the twenty-six is being described; as soon as the 'living machines' begin to come alive through the vicarious drama they have set in motion between the soldier and the girl, the style becomes more neutral. This is a reflection of the psychological paradox underlying the story: the twenty-six actually wallow in their communal debasement. The vividness of their dream of 'a road stretching away into the distance, lit by a bright sun' as they respond to the song depends on the sunless monotony of their daily lives. The collective excitement they experience as their idol is tested depends on the grey uniformity of their collective plight. Ultimately, they cannot stand the bright light of a real life experience; the most they can stand is a symbolic experience, and that not for long: the fragile bubble of a dream aroused by a song soon bursts, and the tenuous ideals they have entrusted to the unknowing Tanya have to be punctured, because such ideals might enable them, or force them, to come to terms with being individuals.

We saw that the crucial conversation where the baker taunts the soldier about his sexual prowess was split into two. There is a significant paragraph of philosophizing by the narrator between the mention of the 'pine tree to be felled' and its being named as Tanya. Ostensibly the paragraph is about the soldier

> He could not have had anything to respect apart from his ability to debauch women; perhaps, apart from this ability there was nothing alive in him and that was all that allowed him to feel like a living person.
>
> For there are people for whom the most valuable and the best thing in life is some kind of disease of their mind or body. They carry it around with them throughout their life and are only alive through it; as they suffer from it they feed on it, they complain of it to others and use it to draw attention to themselves. For this they extract sympathy for themselves from people and apart from this they have nothing. Rob them of this disease, cure them, and they will be wretched because they will be being deprived of their only means of living,—they will become hollow. Sometimes a man's life is so impoverished that in spite of himself he is forced to value his vice and live by it; and you might say that often people are vicious out of boredom.

This seems to be an authentic piece of authorial philosophizing about the main character in the limelight, the soldier. But its key position in the narrative structure of the story makes it point both ways. In fact, this theme of coming alive through some vice is made explicit a page later when the narrator shows the response of the twenty-six to the Faustian challenge: 'From that day we began to live a sort of special life full of nervous tension,—we had never lived so fully before. For days on end we would have arguments, we seemed to become cleverer, we began to talk more and better. We felt we were gambling with the devil and our stake was—Tanya.' The soldier might seem to come alive through his debauchery, but at least it was a manifestation of his own life and health and vitality; the twenty-six have no life or health or vitality. Their living is vicarious, at one remove.

The story is a brilliant and pessimistic revelation of the death in life of the collective consciousness and a reassertion of the life force in the individuals, Tanya and the soldier. Perhaps the sex they enjoy is cynical and unromantic, but it is their sex and they do enjoy it. The idol has asserted her right to be human, above idolatry and leaves the stage of the courtyard *humanitas intacta*: 'And walked away, erect, beautiful and proud.' For the twenty-six bakehouse prisoners the 'poem' comes full cycle

> And we were left in the middle of the yard, in the mud, under the rain and the grey sunless sky . . .
> Then we too walked silently away, back to our damp stone pit. As before, the sun never peeped in at our windows and Tanya never called again! . . .
> (See Russian Texts, No. 87)

NOTES TO CHAPTER 5

1.   Erving Goffman, *Frame Analysis. An Essay on the Organization of Experience* (New York, 1974).
2.   V. Ya. Propp, *Morfologiya skazki*. Voprosy poetiki, XII (Leningrad, 1928); republished in Moscow, 1969; English translation, *The Morphology of the Folk Tale* (Bloomington, Indiana, 1958).
3.   *Ibid.* p.10.
4.   Viktor Shklovsky, 'Novella tain' (The mystery story) in *O teorii prozy* (On the Theory of Prose) (Moscow, 1926, pp.125-40).
5.   Boris Tomashevsky, *Teoriya literatury (Poetika)*, Moscow-Leningrad, 1925; English translation: Part 1 in L. Lemon and M. Reis (eds.) *Russian Formalist Criticism: Four Essays* (Lincoln, Nebraska, 1965); Part 2 in L.M. O'Toole and A. Shukman, *Russian Poetics in Translation*, 5 (Essex, 1978).
6.   Roland Barthes, 'Introduction à l'analyse structurale des récits', *Communications*, 8 (Paris 1966, pp.1-27); English translation by Lionel Duisit in *New Literary History*, 2, 1975, pp.237-72.
7.   See Roman Jakobson, 'Two aspects of language and two types of linguistic disturbances', in Roman Jakobson and Morris Halle, *Fundamentals of Language* (The Hague, Mouton, 1956); an interesting recent treatment of the metaphor/metonymy contrast is David Lodge's *The Modes of Modern Writing* (London, 1977).
8.   Barthes, *op. cit.*, pp.246-56.
9.   *Ibid.*, p.250 (the author has slightly amended the translation).
10. *Ibid.*, p.248.
11. Charles Fillmore, 'The Case for Case', in A. Harms and E. Bach (eds.) *Universals of Linguistic Theory* (New York, 1968, pp.1-40).
12. The scale of 'delicacy' is a technical term used by Halliday and other systemic linguists to denote depth of detail in the analysis of language. Halliday describes it as 'a cline running from a fixed point at one end (least delicate, or "primary") to that undefined but theoretically crucial point (probably statistically definable) where distinctions are so fine that they

cease to be distinctions at all, like a river followed up from the mouth, each of whose tributaries ends in a moorland bog' (M.A.K. Halliday, 'Categories of the theory of grammar', *Word*, 17. 3, 1961; republished in Gunther Kress (ed.) *Halliday: System and Function in Language* (Oxford, 1976, p.62). The degree of delicacy used depends on the purpose for which the analysis is being made. Here we wish to penetrate to some of the more delicate stylistic realizations of Barthes' structural units.

13.   Quotations and references are from the 17 volume edition: *Pushkin, Polnoye sobranie sochinenii* 8 (Moscow, 1937-59, pp.65-74; author's translations).

14.   For example: D. Blagoy, *Masterstvo Pushkina* (Moscow, 1955, pp.223-40); A. Slonimsky, *Masterstvo Pushkina* (Moscow, 1959, pp.224-40); S. Bocharov, *Poetika Pushkina* (Moscow, 1974, pp.174-82); J. Thomas Shaw, 'Pushkin's 'The Shot' ', *Indiana Slavic Studies*, III, (The Hague, 1963, pp.113-29); Jan van der Eng, A.G.F. van Holk, Jan M. Meijer, *The Tales of Belkin by A.S. Pushkin* (The Hague, 1968, pp.61-85).

15.   Jan van der Eng, *op. cit.*

16.   Pushkin, *Mozart and Salieri*, in *Sochineniya*, 2 (Moscow, 1954, p.372).

17.   *Op. cit.*, Note 13, pp.122-4.

18.   B. Eikhenbaum, 'Problemy poetiki Pushkina', in the collection A.L. Volynsky (ed.) *Pushkin-Dostoevsky* (Petrograd, 1921).

19.   See B. Uspensky, *op. cit.*, in our Note 12, Chapter 4.

20.   S.G. Bocharov, *op. cit.*, p.180.

21.   Quotations and references are from M. Gorky, *Sobranie sochinenii v 30 tomakh* 4 (Moscow, 1950, pp.279-93; author's translations).

22.   Roman Jakobson, 'Closing statement: Linguistics and poetics', Thomas A. Sebeok (ed) *Style in Language* (Cambridge, Mass., 1960, p.358).

23.   D.S. Mirsky, *A History of Russian Literature* (London, 1949, p.382).

6

CHARACTER

Turgenev: *Asya*
Chekhov: *The Black Monk*

I

'CHARACTER' is the area of literary criticism where everyone has some contribution to make. The earliest stages of explicit analysis of fiction and drama in the secondary school involve the recognition, classification and summarizing of character traits. Even in the nursery school, even before he can read, as he lies in bed listening to fairy tales and other exciting or improving fictions, the child learns to distinguish deliciously between the heroes and the villains;[1] as he watches Punch and Judy shows—or 'Sesame Street'—he learns to appreciate some ambiguity of moral character and cheers Mr Punch and hisses the Policeman or their modern equivalents. But while recognizing what the characters represent—their content, as it were—he soon comes to learn how their roles relate to the plot and to each other,—their function.

In general, the analysis of character becomes more subtle and sophisticated as it moves from particular features and emotional reaction to generalized types and intellectual abstraction. The scale of sophistication might be seen as ranging through the following eight questions:

1. Who do you like or dislike?
2. What human characteristics do you recognize?
3. What social types do the characters represent?
4. What psychological types or states to they exemplify?
5. What philosophical positions do they represent?
6. How do they relate to each other (major/minor, foreground/background, dynamic/static, etcetera)?
7. What are their functional roles in the plot?
8. In the total *Gestalt* of the literary form what structural relations do the character roles enter into via all the levels? That is, apart from the abstract configurations of characters *per se*, how does character relate to narrative structure, to point of view, to fable and plot and setting?

A fully structuralist approach does not, of course, exclude the humane awareness of character manifested by the earlier questions. In fact, *pace* the naive structuralists who only recognize a structure if it is formulated algebraically, and the no less naive opponents of structuralism who brand any attempt at systematic analysis and terminological clarity as 'reductionist', it is at the level of character that the dialogue between analysis and intuitive insights that we have already emphasized must take place.

One of the commonplaces of fiction criticism holds that the short story differs from the novel in its inability to present character comprehensively or convincingly; the brevity of the form encourages a schematic representation of character and the paucity or narrow range of events allows for very little development of character. This view is argued strongly by Sean O'Faolain

> Characterization is something that can be no more than assumed in a short story. If one looks for a detailed characterization one finds only puppets; one does not therefore look for it—another tacit agreement between author and reader. Instead we are given further hieroglyphics. We may, for example, be given situation, which always exposes some temperament or character; or conversation, which, if bright enough, reveals it; or gestures which express it, by which I do not mean that people make gestures—they are gestures, that and no more . . .
>
> The instrument of characterization may be composed of no more than a couple of strings; it is the virtuosity of the writer to play subtle tunes upon this simple instrument. [2]

O'Faolain, of course, is referring to the *short* short-story of perhaps a dozen pages, of which he is an acknowledged master, and we may have cheated by selecting stories by Turgenev and Chekhov which are nearer *novella* length. I do want to claim, however, as careful a choice of stories to illustrate the depiction and functioning of character as that I have made for exploring the other levels of short story structure. Far from merely offering some 'given situation which always exposes some temperament or character', I will claim that the raison d'être of these stories is character, indeed, that the crucial events comprising the narrative structure are characterological events and that the other levels are to some degree subservient to the revelation of character; in short, character is their theme.

The relation between characters and events in narrative may be seen as analogous to—even as an extension of—the relations between participants and processes in sentence structure. Just as many verbs presuppose particular semantic features in their subjects and/or objects ('to feel', 'to trust'—*animate*; 'to manage', 'to murder'—*human*; 'to laze'—*male*; 'to nag'—*female*; 'to ricochet'—*inanimate, ballistic*, etcetera), many actions (or *functions*, to use Propp's term[3]) presuppose more or less defined characters who perform them or are subject to them. This is most easily illustrated in a highly conventionalized genre such as the fairy-tale where 'departure from home', 'quest' and 'victory in conflict' are typical *hero* actions; 'testing' and 'aiding with magic means' are *donor* actions; while 'abduction', 'pursuit' and 'defeat in conflict' define the *villain's* sphere of action. Conversely, as with case grammar,[4] the verbs are defined by the presence or absence of the semantic features marking their typical subjects, direct and indirect objects, associated conditions, etcetera, and narrative events are at least partially determined by the characters of their protagonists, victims, and attendant circumstances. As we shall see, this grammatical schematism is by no means peculiar to fairy tales, but accounts for some of our ability to 'process' quite complex works of literary art. This argument for the interdependence of character and event has been most cogently put by Marvin Mudrick

> We may define a fictional event as the representation in language of any psychic or psycho-physical phenomenon which is observed as a process rather than as an entity. To start with an event, as the writer of fiction does, is to accept the obligation to observe as processes even those phenomena we ordinarily observe as entities, i.e. persons and things. It is in the nature of fiction, then, to emphasize change and development: not, as in philosophy, in terms of principle; not, as in poetry, through the ideogrammatic summations of aphorism and metaphor, but change and development caught continuously in the act. It follows that ideally, in fiction, characters and events are indistinguishable; that characters observed as entities or as principles or as ideograms impede the fictional action; that events do not illustrate character, they are the media in which processes are observed in the act of individuating those continuously changing phenomena we call persons and things. All of which is not to say that characters may not be abstractly considered, or that they may not in some special way transcend the events that constitute them.[5]

It is, of course, the critic's job to consider characters abstractly and to make them, for a time, 'transcend the events that constitute them'. Before we analyze in detail the features and functions of the characters in *Asya* and *The Black Monk*, let us consider some of the devices for the creation and development of character exploited in the other stories we have examined.

A character's *name* may signify something to us even before we see him or her in action. It may be *allegorical*, as with Father Sergius (a hermit monk in search of purity and spirituality) or Samson Vyrin (Biblical strength containing the seeds of its own downfall). It may be less specifically *allusive*, as with Silvio (exotic foreigner, with the romance of Italy), or Miller (unmilitary liberalism, with German connections), or Postnikov (the self-abnegation of one fasting). It may even be *onomatopoeic*, as we saw with Akakiy Akakievich. But the *lack of a name* may be as significant as the connotations of a name: Akakiy's 'opposite number' in *The Overcoat* is all title—a Person of Consequence; the twenty-five workers (other than the chief baker) in Gorky's bakery are an anonymous inert mass; and both the narrator and the heroine of *A Gentle Spirit* are so far the epitome of abstract qualities that mere names would have been a serious distraction from their conflict (although all the minor characters in the story, inseparable from the 'real' world, have names). Here we must take issue with those theorists of the *nouveau roman* like Alain Robbe-Grillet and Roland Barthes who insist that the reader-centred bourgeois novel of Balzac and the rest of the nineteenth century made a cult of the named hero or heroine who 'possessed' their name as their families possessed property, whereas the modern novel escapes into a 'writerly' world of pure relationships and processes involving agents but no names.[6]

Naming is by no means the rule in the stories discussed in this book (all written in the nineteenth century for largely middle-class readership), and I think I have shown to what extent their narrative and philosophical interest depends on purely abstract semiotic relations and processes—as claimed for the *nouveau roman*.

Another means for the creation of character which the 'age of Realism' might have been expected to favour is detailed *physical description*. But of the writers represented here only Turgenev, Tolstoy and Chekhov offer us more than the sketchiest details. All the authors are much keener to offer explicit moral and psychological description from the point of view of either the narrator about himself (*A Gentle Spirit, Asya*) or of an omniscient narrator about his hero (*Father Sergius, Makar's Dream*). Most often the economy of the short story is best served by a focus on the telling gesture or mannerism or physical characteristic that typifies the psychology or moral stance of the character: the post-stage master sighing over his glass of punch; Silvio firing shots and the Count flicking cherry stones; Akakiy pursing his lips to make a letter or a decision; Asya scrambling around like a high-spirited mountain goat and Gagin posturing in his artist's hat; Tanya and the soldier radiating light and laughter in the doorway of the bake-house; Father Sergius sensually and self-absorbedly stroking the stump of his amputated finger; and the gentle spirit smiling, complete and impregnable, as she sews.

Details of the *setting* may be an illustration of character (Silvio's bullet-scarred room or the post-stage master's woodcuts of the Prodigal Son story), or an extension of character (the cramped quarters of Akakiy and the hero of *A Gentle Spirit* as opposed to the vast and terrifying expanse of St Petersburg squares; Father Sergius' cell versus the open road; Makar's hut in the *taiga* versus the open plateaus of Siberia.

In a sense, though, all these devices of naming, physical or psychological detail and setting are merely illustrative of character which is established by the speech and actions of the characters themselves, the comments and reactions of other characters and explicit flashback, biography or commentary of the narrator, that is, all that constitutes the *events* of the narrative. It is normal, as Marvin Mudrick says, that 'events do not illustrate character, they are the media in which processes are observed in the act of individuating those continuously changing phenomena we call persons and things'.

If the main characters in the short story are 'dynamic' precisely because they 'develop with the story', that is, they change through the events or, conversely, the changes in their character actually constitute those events, we should note that it is the static nature of the minor characters that accentuates this dynamism. The 'flat' characters, as E.M. Forster calls them, emphasize the depth of those seen 'in the round'.[7] They are a necessary part of the furniture of the world within which the protagonists move, like 'extras' in films or 'walk-on parts' in the theatre, but they have to be perceived as 'ideogrammatic summations' and any observation of them as entities (Makar's neighbour, perhaps, or the priest Ivan) or as principles (Father Sergius' cousin Pashenka) or as ideograms (the Metropolitan in *The Man on Sentry Duty*) 'impedes the fictional action'.[8]

To return briefly to the question of comparative length and the delineation of character raised by Sean O'Faolain, this problem too is well argued by Mudrick

> Narratives of short-story or novella length are likely to approach the conditions of poetry for the reason of length alone: the shorter the work of fiction, the more likely are its characters to be simply functions and typical manifestations of a precise and inevitable sequence of events . . .
>
> Most great fiction generates interest through those of its events which establish a community of complex individual lives . . . There are no Emma Bovarys or Elizabeth Bennets in short fiction: to establish a community in which such characters can be conceived to exist requires the time and space, and the uncertainty, of a novel. The partisans of poetry point out, quite correctly, that novels have nothing like the inevitability of poems. 'Anything can happen in a novel.' Character, in fiction as in life, is fate, but it is also potentiality.[9]

Characters in the short story have the inevitability we discussed at the beginning of this chapter of agents or patients related by verbal process, or event. For grammatical, or narratological, purposes we may agree with Tzvetan Todorov's formulation in his *Grammaire du Décameron*

> The meaning of 'person' is so general and unavoidable that we do not see it as such. This absence of meaning makes the proper noun perfect for fulfilling its function of agent. The agent is a person; yet at the same time it is nobody [*personne*]. In fact the structure of the sentence shows us that the agent cannot be seen as any property; it is, rather, an empty form that various predicates (verbs or attributes) come to fill out.[10]

To that extent, then, character and event are indivisible. And yet in the process of reading we do not only perceive characters as agents of events, we tend to 'process' them into entities with a semantic content of their own, for only in this way can we assess them as a whole, remember them and talk about them. What we so arrogantly termed the 'most sophisticated' criticism of character, the awareness of its structural role in a complex *Gestalt*, cannot finally be abstracted from the 'most naive' which involves the personality of the reader reaching out to grasp and to greet the personality of the sympathetic character. We have to analyze characters on the three levels proposed by Greimas,[11] those of actor, role and 'actant' in order to do justice to the proper concerns of all the eight modes of criticism we mentioned

> We must distinguish between actor, role and actant, corresponding to a progressive abstraction of the functions of the characters, ranging from a mere

individual appearance in the text (THE ACTOR) to a superindividual behaviour common to several actors (THE ROLE) and to the purely epic function,
invariable in any form of narration (THE ACTANT). [12]

This distinction will provide a starting-point for our analysis of the characters in
Asya and *The Black Monk*.

II   Turgenev: *Asya*, 1858 [13]

The charm of Asya, the girl and the story, is in their enigmatic quality. As *actress*,
the heroine confronts the narrator and, following him, the reader with a series of
riddles: the reasons for her erratic behaviour, the nature of her relationship to
Gagin, the nature of her response to the narrator himself. The plot consists
almost wholly of the gradual answering of these riddles: with actual physical
movement reduced to a kind of shuttle ferry service across the Rhine between
the twin spas where the narrator and his new Russian friends live; the 'events'
are various kinds of meeting which turn out to be occasions for the transmission
of new information which either clarifies the dominant enigma or deepens
it. The scenes are a kind of repertoire of the *topoi* for encounters: a chance
meeting at a country festival, hospitality in the vineyards, conversation in a
ruined castle, coquetry from an upstairs window, accidental eavesdropping on a
love scene in the arbour, unburdening of secrets beside the river under the
madonna statue's protection, first signs of tenderness beneath the Lorelei rock,
a boat drifting in the current, intimacy in the artist's studio, a tryst in the ruins,
notes via a messenger boy, secret meeting at the house of a simple old woman,
frantic search through the town at night, revelation in the deserted house,
meditation by the river: Turgenev might have ransacked the libretti of all the
Romantic operas from Mozart to Puccini to find such a trite string of common-
places.

   And yet the story does move—in both senses: it follows a very distinct progression of these 'information-events', and it succeeds in engaging the reader's
sympathy and involvement. This is because the focus is on character rather than
event. As Robert Liddell reports, 'Henry James, for whom the starting-point in
the creation of his novels was generally a fragment of plot, gives an interesting
account of the completely opposite method used by his friend Turgenev

   The germ of a story, with him, was never an affair of plot—that was the last
   thing he thought of: it was the representation of certain persons. The first
   form in which a tale appeared to him was as the figure of an individual, or a
   collection of individuals, whom he wished to see in action, being sure that
   such people must do something very special and interesting. They stood
   before him, definite, vivid, and he wished to know, and to show as much as
   possible of their nature. The first thing was to make clear to himself what he
   did know to begin with; and to this end he wrote out a sort of biography of

each of his characters, and everything they had done and that had happened to them up to the opening of the story.' [14]

As the narrator of *Asya*, N.N., says in the second paragraph: 'It was only and exclusively people that interested me'—though he gives the lie to this claim with an exquisitely detailed sketch of the little spa of Z. where he was staying, the first of many memorable landscapes in the story. However, the landscapes are set-pieces, like the author's *Poems in Prose*, and can hardly be said to have the dynamic potential of his characters (though we will have to return to some of the symbolic aspects of the setting which clearly do relate to the characters).

The first hint we have of Asya's existence (apart from the title) is her name being spoken: '—Asya, had enough?—a man's voice suddenly said behind me in Russian.—Let's wait a little longer,—replied another, woman's voice in the same language.' (See Russian Texts, No. 88) The affectionate diminutive form of 'Anna' and the intimate *ty* pronoun and colloquial phrase already suggest a relationship before we perceive either of the speakers as individuals and it is significant that here, as later, N.N.'s awareness of the heroine is both *via* Gagin and governed by their relationship—one might even say, subject to his will and initiative. The narrator turns, and his view of the girl is masked: 'My gaze fell on a handsome young man in a peaked cap and a broad jacket; he was holding the arm of a not very tall girl in a straw hat which covered the whole of the upper part of her face.' Once he comes to describe their physical appearance, we again see the young man, Gagin, first, clearly outlined and unambiguously attractive, while every observation of Asya is qualified in some way

> ... I liked Gagin at once. There are happy faces around of the sort that every-one gets pleasure in looking at, as if they warmed or caressed you. Gagin had just this sort of face, kind and gentle, with big soft eyes and soft curly hair. He spoke in such a way that, even without seeing his face, you could tell just from the sound of his voice that he was smiling.
>
> The girl he called his sister, seemed at first glance to be very attractive. There was something distinctive and special in the shape of her rather dark round face, with tiny slender nose, little cheeks almost like a child's and bright black eyes. She had a graceful figure, but somehow not yet fully developed. She did not resemble her brother at all.
> (See Russian Texts, No. 89)

Everything is dubious about her: she was *called* his sister, *seemed at first glance* [but?], *rather* dark, *almost* like a child's, *somehow not yet fully, not at all*. The point is, of course, that both characters are refractions of the narrator's perception and we already know a good deal about his character and mood.

N.N. recalls being twenty-five, healthy, cheerful, comfortably off and with-out a care, travelling through Europe to 'complete his education'. He has no set itinerary, prefers people to tourist attractions, is responsive to nature but is happiest in a crowd of people, 'studying them with a kind of joyful and insatiable curiosity'. He has just been jilted by a flighty young widow after an affair in one of the Rhineland spas and feels rather lonely, with sharpened responses to the sights, sounds and smells of the little town of Z. where he is staying. His first encounter with Gagin and Asya seems to grow out of his awareness of all the young people at the student festival expressing love freely and lightheartedly

> It cheered me to look at the students' faces; their embraces, exclamations, youth's innocent flirting, burning glances, laughter without cause—the best laughter in the world—all this joyous bubbling of fresh young life, this surg-ing forward—never mind where to, as long as it's forward,—this cheerful expansiveness moved me and kindled something in me. 'What about joining in?'—I wondered . . .
> —Asya, have you had enough?

N.N. is the true Romantic outsider: vividly aware of others' spontaneous feel-ings and self-expression, but unable to join in; young in years, but old in his reasoning; his own aspirations undercut by self-doubt. Friedland [15] and others have pointed out that precisely when he was writing *Asya* Turgenev was working on his famous article 'Hamlet and Don Quixote' whom he saw as 'milestones in the evolution of human nature, the extreme expressions of two tendencies, two distinctive approaches by man to his ideal'. Turgenev was exploring the whole problem of the 'superfluous man' whom he saw as a crucial representative of Russian public life. His aristocratic superfluous men represent the Hamlet features which Turgenev referred to as 'the expression of the centri-petal egotistical forces of nature' (what psychologists a century later were to call 'introversion'). Hamlet shares with Turgenev's heroes 'a tendency to analysis above all and egoism . . . he is a sceptic and constantly worrying and tormenting himself. His most vulnerable trait is his indecisiveness'. Don Quixote, on the other hand, represents 'the centrifugal force of nature ("extrovert"), whereby everything that exists exists only for others. He represents the heroic lofty prin-ciple of self-sacrifice'.

If the *actor* N.N. has been thrust into a *role* by this association with the Russian 'superfluous man' modelled on Hamlet, however, we must remember that both actor and role are refracted through the narrator's awareness of himself twenty years later. For the man of forty-five telling the story is not at all the same person as the twenty-five-year-old living the experiences. His language reveals this from the very first paragraph. He has a marked taste for aphorism which often leads him to digress

> It did not even occur to me at that time that man is not a plant and that he cannot bloom for long. Youth feeds on gilded honeycakes and thinks they are their daily bread; but there comes a time when you'll be begging for a mere

crust. But there's no point in talking about that.
(See Russian Texts, No. 90)

He often lapses into cliché: and if aphorism is a kind of conventional worldly wisdom, cliché is mere verbosity with the thought conventionalized right out of it. N.N. opens the story with a string of clichés

> At that time I was about twenty-five,—began N.N.—the deeds of yesteryear, as you see. I had only just broken out to freedom and had gone abroad not in order to 'round off my education', as they used to say in those days, but I simply wanted to take a look at God's own world.
> (See Russian Texts, No. 91)

If the narrative is to be controlled by such a cliché-monger, the reader may well say to himself, what credence can we give to his interpretation of events and characters. And indeed, the affair with the flighty widow, the consolation of travel in a pretty and exotic landscape and the reflection 'I considered it my duty to give myself up for a while to sadness and solitude' do not greatly raise our hopes. And yet Asya is so fresh and spontaneous and beautiful and mysterious that she enchants both the narrator and us instantly. Her vitality and charm burst through the elaborate frames of the point of view: even though she is always perceived by the grace of Gagin and in terms of her ill-defined relationship with him, and they are both perceived by a young man with an inclination to posture, and they are all perceived by the young man's later incarnation with his tendency to cliché and aphorism, the figure of Asya always eludes categorization and retains her integrity and individuality.

This requires a considerable degree of determination because she is always having roles thrust upon her. The reader's perception of Asya is constantly being framed by some social or literary role. Before the narrator even knows of her existence he spends long hours seated on a stone seat under a massive ash tree beside the Rhine; the nearby ferry across the Rhine is, as it were, the gateway from N.N.'s real world in Z. to the enchanted kingdom where Asya and her brother are staying, the twin spa of L. Under this ash we find 'A little statue of the madonna, with the face almost of a child and a red heart on her breast pierced by swords, sadly gazed from out of its branches'. Already we have presaged for us Asya's purity, femininity, childish innocence, sadness and potential martyrdom, with perhaps a suggestion of her being under the shadow of the (masculine) ash tree. The madonna reappears at a significant moment in Chapter 8 when the narrator is forgiven for his abrupt departure to the mountains by Gagin and Asya. Asya actually seeks contact with him for the first time in the story: 'In the hallway Asya suddenly came up to me and held out her hand; I squeezed her fingers lightly and made a slight bow to her.' Gagin crosses the Rhine with him on his way home and they sit on the bench beside the madonna to admire the view, whereupon Gagin clears up the mystery of their relationship and tells him

the story of her life. This releases her from the roles of sister claimed earlier by
Gagin and lover as suspected by N.N. especially after the 'love scene' he overhears in the garden. It does not, however, completely disambiguate the relationship since there are incestuous overtones (i.e. *combining* the earlier roles) about
many of Gagin's references to her, both earlier in Russia and now on their
travels. We do not so crudely assume actual incest between them, but the
reader's imagination is gently tickled with the possibility of such a relationship,
rather as there are overtones of homosexuality in N.N.'s boundless admiration
for Gagin. However, *autre temps, autre moeurs*. The madonna symbol recurs at the
end of the story to round it off.

More fleetingly episodic roles into which N.N. or Gagin or the reader fit Asya
include the exotic Spanish beauty with whom the poet wants to elope in the
Pushkin song that Gagin sings to wake N.N.: 'Dost thou sleep? With my guitar
I will arouse thee . . . ' or, more specifically, the sea-nymph Galatea in Raphael's
painting: ' . . . and once again thought of that "capricious little girl with the
strained laugh . . ." "She's moulded like Raphael's little Galatea in the Farnesi
chapel,—I whispered,—and she's no sister of his." ' While the motivation for
this role is primarily erotic, the water-nymph role is carried over to the Lorelei
motif first mentioned by Asya herself in her first long conversation with N.N. in
Chapter 9. This mention falls curiously between the mention of the two older
authority-figures in her life, her father and Frau Louise. Asya feels free to
mention her father once N.N. has heard the story of her life from Gagin, yet
changes the subject when N.N. asks if she loved him

> —Did you love your father?—I said and suddenly to my great chagrin, felt
> myself blushing.
> She did not answer and also blushed. We both fell silent. Far off along the
> Rhine a steamer was racing and puffing smoke. We both fell to gazing at it.
> —Why don't you tell me [about your hike]?—whispered Asya.
> —Why did you laugh today the moment you saw me?—I asked.
> —I don't know myself. Sometimes I want to cry, but I laugh. You mustn't
> judge me . . . by what I do. Oh, by the way, what's that fairy tale about
> Lorelei? That must be *her* rock we can see over there. They say that at first she
> drowned everyone, but as soon as she fell in love, threw herself in the water. I
> like that story. Frau Louise tells me all sorts of fairy tales. Frau Louise has a
> black cat with yellow eyes.

Framed between the figures of a totally benevolent father and the potentially
malevolent witch-like Frau Louise, the Lorelei story is pregnant with meaning for N.N.—is he to be one of the fishermen who will be lured by her singing
to destruction on the rocks? Or, when she has declared her love for him,
will she throw herself into the Rhine? The thought certainly occurs to him
when she disappears and, failing to find her with Frau Louise, he rushes to the
river

'Where could she have gone, what has she done to herself?'—I exclaimed in
the anguish of impotent desperation ... Something white suddenly flashed on
the very bank of the river. I knew the spot; there, above the grave of a man
who had drowned some seventy years back, stood a stone cross with an
ancient inscription which had half grown into the ground ... My heart sank
... I ran up to the cross: the white figure disappeared. I shouted: 'Asya!' My
wild voice even frightened me—but no-one responded ...

Another role involving first love aroused but not responded to is Asya's mention
of Pushkin's heroine Tat'yana. But she appears to misquote Pushkin deliberately
in order to associate the name with her mother, another simple dark-haired
Tat'yana from the Russian countryside

'Where's now a cross and the branches shade
Above my poor mother!'—she said in a murmur.
—That's not how it is in Pushkin,—I commented.
I'd like to be Tat'yana,—she went on just as thoughtfully.
(See Russian Texts, No. 92)

The change of words from 'nurse' to 'mother' seems trivial, but the vision N.N.
sees next is radiant: 'I gazed at her all bathed in the bright sun's rays, all comfor-
ted and meek. Everything shone joyously around us, below and above—the sky,
the earth and the waters; the very air seemed charged with radiance.' A suitable
setting indeed for the madonna figure N.N. has fallen for; the Tat'yana connection relates to both Asya's mother and Asya herself.
   The dialogue which follows is intriguing

—Look how beautiful it is!—I said, involuntarily lowering my voice.
—Yes, it is beautiful!—she replied just as softly, without looking at me.—If
you and I were birds,—how we would soar, how we'd fly ... We'd simply
drown in that blue sky ... But we're not birds.
—But we might grow wings,—I objected.
—How so?
—Live a little and you'll learn. There are feelings that lift us off the ground.
Don't worry, you'll have wings.
—Have you had them?
—How can I put it ... I don't think I've flown yet.
Asya grew pensive again. I bent towards her slightly.
—Do you know how to waltz?—she asked suddenly.

Superficially, N.N.'s sententious pronouncements are about love and Asya's
questions are about whether he has been in love, specifically, perhaps, with the
young widow she has heard about. But Asya does not need to live a little to find
out, she doesn't need lectures about feelings, or reassurances that she will fly.
And she senses intuitively that N.N. cannot fly, or love: all she can do is invite

him to a conventional surrogate for flying, the waltz—as played by her brother's fiddle.

Roles, literary and symbolic, seem to pin Asya down. So why does she herself play so many roles? Every view we have of her in the first half of the story finds her playing a different part—the shy, demure maiden, the dignified, stylish society beauty, the capricious faun, the Russian peasant girl, the earnest student, the domesticated Dorothea (after N.N. had been reading aloud from Goethe's *Hermann and Dorothea*), the wilfully mysterious tease, the meek submissive saint. All, of course, are attractive roles and may be seen primarily as refractions of N.N.'s vision of her as he gradually falls in love. And yet she is clearly choosing the roles and he is led to remark 'What a chameleon that girl is!' Perhaps skilfully switching roles to play on his curiosity and lead him on, like the Lorelei. Certainly the reader is intrigued and enraptured by turns by her many guises. And yet her very role-playing manifests her real freedom: she does not have to be bound by the social conventions of types of occasion (like the cliché encounters we enumerated) or the expectations of literary or artistic stereotypes others try to capture her with. While playing the roles game, she chooses hers arbitrarily and escapes classification.

This brings us to the third level of character analysis we have discussed, that of 'actant'. In a sense, this is the most abstract level of character, a kind of generalization that puts the character on a par with all the characters from other works that have been agents, patients, helpers, etcetera in a narrative process and, hence, it abstracts out all the individual traits which make the character 'live' for us. And yet since characters in books only 'live' through their function in the narrative, we may find the ultimate Asya via the story's narrative structure.

At the most abstract actantial level the story appears to be a quest, with N.N. as Seeker, Asya as Sought Object, and Gagin as Mediator. This relationship is developed on many dimensions:

1. N.N. as stereotype Romantic traveller in search of new experience, Asya as that exotic experience, Gagin as gatekeeper to the experience;

2. N.N. as seeker of treasure, Asya as treasure beyond price, Gagin as guardian of treasure;

3. N.N. as suitor, Asya as ward, Gagin as father-figure/guardian;

4. N.N. as lover, Asya as beloved, Gagin as rival/confidant;

5. N.N. as lover of the elemental (in landscape and humanity), Asya as the elemental ('gunpowder', says Gagin; 'an untamed wild animal or fermenting wine', says the narrator), Gagin as Pandora;

6. N.N. as Romantic seeker of Nature, Asya as natural beauty and freedom, Gagin as artist-medium who thinks he has 'succeeded in catching nature by the tail' (Chapter 11);

7. N.N. as art connoisseur, Asya as artist's model, Gagin as cliché artist in a Van Dyck hat and blouse;

8. N.N. as seeker of information, Asya as new information (mystery), Gagin as provider and controller of information;

9. N.N. as educated man of reason, Asya as untamed mind, Gagin as guardian-educator and artist;

10. N.N. as pure ratiocination and loss of feeling, Asya as intuition, imagination and immediacy, Gagin as artist mediator, giving rational form to the irrational;

11. N.N. as ruled by social and moral convention, Asya as spontaneity constantly threatening convention, Gagin as controlled unconventionality (family background, travel, art).

This list of homologies (which, given space, we might have written as N.N. : Asya : Gagin—Seeker : Sought Object : Mediator—suitor : ward : guardian, etcetera) is too schematic, of course. It pins down too rigidly personality traits and role features which in the literary text are in constant interplay, and, even looking at the list, we can see how the roles subsumed under each actantial function overlap: for instance, the artist, however stereotyped, is simultaneously a guardian, mediator and educator of the intuitive. Thus, in the roles they play in each scene and in the very style of behaviour and language they adopt, the three main characters constantly shift position and reveal different facets of their personalities. Moreover, their actantial roles shift as the story progresses, and this is the crucial point: the story starts with N.N. in search of Asya's identity and ends with him in search of his own identity. If the question posed by the beginning is 'Asya?', by the end it has become '*A ya?*' ('And I?')—not only 'what is to become of me now?', but 'Who am I, then?' The Hamlet-like figure of N.N. has discovered the existential question: 'To be, or not to be?' The vital catalyst for this change in the direction of the search is Asya herself.

The Romantic personality cannot stand too much reality. While Asya is still a mystery—whether in her relationship with Gagin or in her chameleon-like shifting of roles—, the *prospect* of a liaison with her is enchanting; once he has lost her, the narrator's retrospective nostalgia for her feeds his sentimental brooding. But faced with her physical reality, offered unconditionally, and her total surrender of self, N.N. starts inventing conditions: her strange, fiery nature, her unpredictability, her social class and upbringing (note the shift even here from personality traits to conventional social status and role). N.N. may have unconsciously anticipated some aspects of Asya—and imposed others—in the complex conventional (institutionalized, Christian) symbol of the little madonna statue, but Asya has more simply and intuitively anticipated N.N.'s fateful behaviour in the form of a folk superstition, also on the Rhine: the first words she ever addresses directly to

him are as the ferryman rows him back across the river after their first parting:
'—You've rowed into a column of moonlight and broken it.' The column of
moonlight is both Asya's ineffable magic which he breaks and, as he sees it, 'a
golden bridge across the river', the possibility of a love which will span the
distance between the twin spas of Z. (N.N.'s world) and L. (Asya's). The Rhine
is constantly referred to as a line of transition in this sense and the landscape is
almost too neatly symmetrical a setting for the constant meetings and partings of
such opposite 'actants'. But the minor actantial role of the Charon-like ferryman
links the river with the death motif in the madonna, the Lorelei and the dead
man's cross, so that for both Asya and N.N. in their respective ways, their brief
love is a kind of death.

Frau Louise is a minor character with an important actantial role in the narrative structure. Combining the functions of confidante and chaperone, custodian
of the lovers' trysting-place and informant, she moves from a thoroughly down-
to-earth role (widow of the town's burgomeister) to a supernatural role of fairy-
godmother or witch (depending on N.N.'s mood). In fact, her shift from the real
to the mysterious is inversely parallel to Asya's evolution from a mischievous,
unpredictable faun to a young woman who understands her own heart and sees
through N.N.'s ambivalence with a wisdom beyond her years.

It was Chernyshevsky (a critic much-maligned in the West for his supposed
obsession with social issues in literature, but actually extremely sensitive to a
text's aesthetic qualities) who first pinpointed the significance of the interview at
Frau Louise's

> N.N. at first seems worthy of Asya: his behaviour is irreproachable, his heart
> open to all lofty feelings, his honour unshakable, his mind absorbed with all
> that our age of noble aspirations could think ... Asya believes that he can
> answer the tormenting question: 'How should one live?' ('What must I
> do? I'll do everything you tell me ... '). Love brings maturity of mind to
> Asya: she 'grows wings'. It is N.N. who is overcome by dualistic, contra-
> dictory feelings: alongside the intoxicating sense of happiness being near, an
> irrational anxiety and fear creeps in, fear over the unavoidability of a rapid,
> almost instantaneous, decision. This is no 'forgivable' clash of love versus
> duty: N.N. knows that he can marry Asya without hindrance, he knows he's
> loved; until this moment Asya's love seems an unattainable happiness ... yet
> she herself terrifies him. The interview at Frau Louise's exposes him more
> than her.

Chernyshevsky's article was called 'Russian man at the rendezvous',[17] and characteristically saw Turgenev's hero as once more typifying the 'aristocratic intelligentsia' and 'the fatal weakness of gentry liberalism'. But he was surely not
wrong to insist that the story be related back to its Russian context. One
Russian writer after another throughout the nineteenth century had only to set
foot outside his native land to evoke its landscape and people most poignantly

and to engage with its problems most cogently: Pushkin and Lermontov in the Causasus, Gogol in Italy, Herzen in London, Dostoevsky in Germany, Chekhov in Sakhalin and Turgenev in Germany, Italy, France and England.

Asya achieves stability of character when the Russian in her takes over from her other shifting roles; it is then that N.N. knows that he has met his match, for there is an integrity and striving for truth in the Russian woman which frightens him far more than any misgivings about her social origins or impetuous nature. References to Russian *men* are quite uncomplimentary: Gagin comments soon after they meet that Russians at a festival would have smashed the windows and broken the chairs (Chapter 2), and later (Chapter 3) that his painting is poor and immature: 'I haven't studied as I should, and that damned Slavonic casualness gets the upper hand. While you're dreaming of work you soar like an eagle: you feel you could shift the earth from its orbit—yet in executing it you grow weak and tired at once.' N.N. characterizes Gagin in terms of both positive and negative Russian traits

> The more I got to know him the more strongly I was drawn to him. I soon understood him. He was a purely Russian soul, truthful, honest and simple-hearted, but unfortunately a trifle flabby, lacking in tenacity and inner fire. Youth did not bubble in him like a spring; it glimmered with a quiet light. He was very kind and intelligent, but I could not envisage what would become of him as he matured. (Chapter 4)

On the other hand, the same chapter ends with a chance scent of hemp sending a wave of nostalgia for Russia over the narrator that seems to resolve his vacillating mood

> I remember I was walking home not thinking of anything but with a strange burden in my heart when suddenly I caught a scent which was strong and familiar but quite rare in Germany. I stopped and saw beside the road a small bunch of hemp. Its smell of the steppes instantly reminded me of my native land and aroused a passionate nostalgia in me. I longed to breathe Russian air and walk on Russian soil. 'What am I doing here, why am I trailing round foreign places among alien people?'—I exclaimed, and the dead weight which I had felt on my heart suddenly resolved itself into a bitter and burning excitement.

Soon he begins to think about Asya and admits that when he goes back to L. the next day this nostalgia may have affected his view of Asya

> I found them both in the sitting-room and, strange to relate!—whether or no it was because I had been thinking a lot about Russia overnight and that morning—Asya appeared to me as a totally Russian girl, and a simple one at that, almost a maidservant. She was wearing an old dress, had brushed her hair back behind her ears and was sitting quite still by the window and sewing in an embroidery frame, modestly and quietly as if all her life she had never been

doing anything else. She hardly said anything, placidly glanced now and then at her work and her features took on such an insignificant and everyday expression that I couldn't help remembering our homegrown Katyas and Mashas. To round off the similarity she began to hum quietly 'Oh mother, my dear'. I looked at her little yellow faded face, remembered yesterday's dreams and felt a tinge of regret.

For the first time we get a direct view of Asya and it is Gagin who is seen second, posing as the artist seeking inspiration. Asya's role may seem to have been assigned to her by N.N.'s imagination, but she has the same simplicity and directness and honesty when they have their fateful rendezvous at Frau Louise's house in Chapter 16. She hardly needs to speak

> She slowly raised her eyes to look at me...O, glance of a woman in love—who can describe you? They begged, those eyes, they trusted, beseeched, surrendered...I could not resist their magic. A fine fire ran through me like burning needles; I bent and put my lips to her hand...
>
> I heard a tremulous sound like a spasmodic sigh and felt on my hair the touch of a trembling hand, fragile as a leaf. I raised my head and saw her face. How it had changed! The fearful expression had disappeared and the gaze went far away and drew me after it, the lips were slightly parted, the forehead was as pale as marble and the curls were swept back as if the wind was blowing them. I forgot everything and drew her to me—her hand relented submissively, her whole body was drawn after her hand, the shawl fell from her shoulders and her head lay quietly on my breast, lay beneath my burning lips...

But the erotic magic is in prospect (for N.N. as a young man) and in retrospect (for N.N. as narrator), and never to be realized in the present (Asya's only tense), for she only has to whisper 'I'm yours...' and his arm slip around her waist, when...

> But suddenly the memory of Gagin blazed through me like lightening.
> —What are we doing!...I shrieked and jerked back convulsively. —Your brother...but he knows everything...He knows I am seeing you.

The shadow of Gagin and the fear of Asya's questionable past and uncertain future fall again between Asya and N.N., and our eloquent hero—who could do no more than repeat his beloved's name as she sat waiting to give herself to him: 'Anna Nikolaevna...Anna Nikolaevna...Asya...' (he cannot even make up his mind whether to address her formally or intimately)—now falls to babbling accusations about whose fault it is that Gagin knows of their tryst, the same Gagin who has already told N.N. that he would welcome him as a brother-in-law. N.N., the Romantic individualist, no longer has any personal, individual priorities—either his own or Asya's; he is obsessed only with the social imperative: '—Your brother knows everything. I had to tell him everything.—Had to?—she murmured inaudibly. Apparently she couldn't come to and hadn't understood me properly.' (See Russian Texts, No.93) He rationalizes to the end: we know that Asya's barely audible question is the ultimate challenge to N.N.'s absurd social conventionality. He has to explain it away—until her total disappearance from the spa brings home to him his personal loss. After this scene, despite the physical search for Asya through the town, by the river, and later in Cologne and all the way to London, the focus of the narration shifts from her to N.N. His is the character that needs to be explored and explained.

Chernyshevsky's subtle insight was that the Russian man's 'rendezvous' was with himself. Asya is as much a catalyst for the narrator's self-exploration as Dostoevsky's heroine in *A Gentle Spirit*. Hopefully it will be clear, in spite of the similarities in character between the protagonists of that story and those of Asya, that their narrative structure poses a quite different kind of challenge: the gentle spirit challenges the obsessively conventional narrator by her death, with which the story begins and ends; Asya challenges with her vitality, integrity and will to live which shifts the narrative focus on to him after the rendezvous.

And, of course, the atmosphere is totally different. It was another social-minded contemporary critic—but this time a poet, Nekrasov, who wrote to congratulate Turgenev when *Asya* was published: 'I embrace you for your story, for its delightful goodness. It pervades spiritual youthfulness and it is all the pure gold of poetry. This beautiful setting suits the poetic storyline without any strain, and something beautiful and pure for us has emerged.'[18] Whatever our doubts about N.N.'s—or Turgenev's—decisiveness as a lover and a man of action, our admiration for his—or Turgenev's—incisiveness as an artist must be unreserved. His landscapes, setting the mood—N.N.'s and ours—for the presentation of character are pure prose poems

> I loved wandering through the town at that hour; the moon seemed to stare down at it fixedly from out of a pure sky; and the town sensed this gaze and stood, responsive and submissive, totally bathed in its light, in that light which was serene yet at the same time quietly roused the spirit. (Chapter 2) (See Russian Texts, No.94)

No, this is not a 'pure' prose poem and is not merely a setting for character: the interplay of moonlight (feminine, elemental) and town (masculine, man-made) presages the interplay between Asya and N.N. for the whole story. But he continues

> The cock on the high Gothic belfry shone like pale gold; shot with the same gold were the streaks of current over the black gloss of the river; tiny thin candles (the Germans are thrifty!) modestly glowed in narrow windows beneath slate roofs; vine tendrils mysteriously poked their twirled moustachios from behind stone walls; something would run across in the shadow by the ancient well on the triangular town square, a sleepy whistle from the

nightwatchman would suddenly ring out, a kindly dog growl quietly, and the air simply nestled against one's face and the lime trees smelt so sweet that your breast involuntarily breathed in deeper and deeper and the word: 'Gretchen' —not quite an exclamation, not quite a question came to one's lips of its own accord.

Once again, the gentle arousal and yearning for love at the end anticipate later developments in the story; but we cannot ignore the sensuousness of the sights, sounds, smell and touch of the night scene, nor the predominantly male (and, indeed, phallic) potentiality of steeples, candles and vine tendrils. Critics, by and large, are restrained—either by prudishness or mistrust of the 'pathetic fallacy' (phallusy?)—from noting erotic elements in landscapes. And yet in a Romantic landscape in what is, after all, a love story we may well find the closest integration of natural scene and character. We would argue that the male quality of the narrator's townscape seems to be matched by the predominantly female anatomy of the country scene in which we find the ruined castle where Asya leaps and scrambles

> The path to the ruins wound up the slope of a narrow wooded valley; at the bottom of it ran a brook, noisily winding its way across the stones, as if in a hurry to merge with the mighty river shining calmly beyond the dark edge of the sharply clefted mountain ridges ... (Chapter 4)[19]

The sexual opposition is more subtly conveyed by the play of light: N.N. seems most responsive to darkness and shade and every tone of sunset, while Asya is perceived in bright sunlight or sitting by a window. Much of the lyrical quality of the narration is in the radiance with which she seems to light up every scene.

The final 'poem in prose' we will quote is the shortest chapter, 10, which brings together Asya and Gagin in their mutual roles, N.N. at his most alert and sensitive, the symbolic ferryman across the Rhine and all the forces of Nature conspiring to reflect N.N.'s mood through all his senses. But the medium is *language* and it is the binary rhythm of the sentences (miming the rocking of the drifting boat and the beating of his heart) and the play of sibilants (the wavelets slapping) the nasal and liquid consonants (the heart's meditation) that carry the message

> The whole of that day passed perfectly. We were as merry as children. Asya was very sweet and simple. Gagin was filled with joy looking at her. I left late. When we got to the middle of the Rhine I asked the ferryman to let the boat drift downstream. The old man raised his oars—and the majestic river carried us along. Gazing around, listening and remembering, I suddenly felt a secret anxiety in my heart ... I lifted my eyes to the sky—but even there there was no peace: sprinkled with stars, it went on shimmering, moving and trembling; I bent down towards the river ... but there too, even in those dark, cold depths, the stars wavered and trembled; I sensed an anxious animation everywhere—and the anxiety grew in me too. I leaned on the edge of the

boat . . . The whisper of the wind in my ears, the quiet gurgling of the water astern irritated me, and the fresh breath of the wave did not cool me; a nightingale sang out on the bank and infected me with the sweet poison of his sounds. The tears welled up in my eyes, but they were not tears of an objectless joy. What I felt was not that dim but recently experienced sense of all-embracing desire, when the spirit expands and sings, when it feels that it understands all and loves all . . . No! there kindled in me a thirst for happiness. I still dared not give it a name,—but happiness, happiness to repletion—that's what I wanted and yearned for . . . And the boat was still drifting and the old ferryman sat and dozed, bent over his oars.

(See Russian Texts, No.95)

This chapter is placed almost exactly at the centre of the story, in terms of chapters and even of pages, and, quite obliquely, marks the key transitions of the story. The Rhine, as we have seen, is the boundary line that N.N. constantly has to cross between the static, conventional, male-bachelor world of Z. and the dynamic, unconventional, female-erotic world of L. Transported by the Charon-like oarsman, he is once again leaving the territory that has represented a renewal of life and significance and returning temporarily to a lonely, lifeless existence which is inspired only by memories and aspirations. His life, that of the Romantic dreamer, has only past and future: he must seek a meaningful present in the company of Asya, for whom the present is the only tense. The day he has spent with her and her brother has been full of simple child-like joy focussed on Asya, joy of which she was the spontaneous agent. Now darkness has fallen, N.N. has left the radiance of her presence and, like the boat with oars raised and passive oarsman, can only drift in the current of life. By the stage of transition represented by this prose poem all the riddles about Asya's character and relationships seem to have been cleared up, yet N.N. is still full of anxiety and foreboding. The story's focus now shifts, as we have seen, from an exploration of Asya's nature to an exploration of the nature of the Romantic hero: just as he now gazes into the water from the gently rocking boat and sees the trembling reflection of the stars in the night sky, in the second half of the story he will gaze into the firmly cradling and gently caressing character of the mature young Russian woman and see—his own timorous self reflected.

The story has started with the narrator's perception and discourse as a vehicle for the portrayal of an enigmatic and childlike Asya, but as the heroine's mystery is gradually resolved (not too bluntly and rationally, for she remains a movingly poetic creation) and she matures, the narrator regresses to an infantile dependence on convention, on Gagin and Frau Louise, on Asya herself and gradually her reactions become the vehicle for the portrayal of Turgenev's Hamlet-like narrator-hero.

We spoke at the beginning of this chapter of the relation between character and events. But in Turgenev's story the characters are the events and the story moves with the reflection of tiny shafts of character and mood in the natural world outside man.

III Chekhov: *The Black Monk*, 1894; *(Chernyi monakh)* [20]

The schematic landscape in *Asya*—with the key transition-line of the Rhine running between the twin spas on its opposite slopes, the crossing-point on N.N.'s side being marked by the statue of a child-like madonna beneath the shade of an ash and on Asya's side by the grave of a drowned man—is more than mere neutral setting: it is, as we have seen, symbolic of the characters and their relationship. Chekhov's *The Black Monk* uses a different, but no less geometric pattern to convey a number of important themes which are also embodied in the characters.

Seven of the nine sections of this story have as their setting the estate of the Pesotskys where the hero, Kovrin, comes to relax and recuperate. Topographic-ally, the estate consists of a series of concentric circles, each involving a different type of cultivation and each the stage for a different type of dramatic interaction between the characters. Moreover, each of the three protagonists is defined to some extent by the sphere in which he operates best, and his influence on the events of the story (grammatically, his 'ergativity', as it were) is measured by the trajectory of his movement between the spheres. A diagram may help to clarify this scheme:

Figure 10

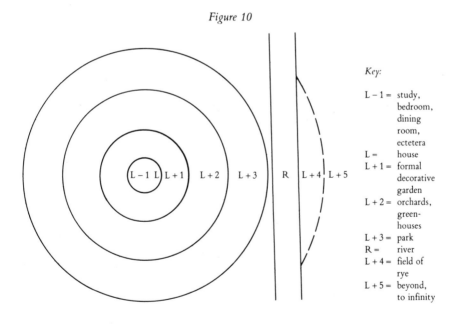

Key:

L − 1 = study, bedroom, dining room, ectetera
L = house
L + 1 = formal decorative garden
L + 2 = orchards, green-houses
L + 3 = park
R = river
L + 4 = field of rye
L + 5 = beyond, to infinity

Egor Semyonych operates best—is most true to himself—in the (L + 2) sphere. As a dedicated horticulturalist, he is committed to the balanced and efficient running of the orchards and greenhouses whose products—fruit, saplings, graft-ings—are famous for their quality throughout European Russia and bring in a handsome income. Refined techniques of cultivation are constantly at risk from the spheres beyond (L + 2), however: a frost threatens the fragile blossoms; an ignorant (i.e. uncultivated) peasant hangs his coat on a branch or ties up his horse to a trunk and the fruit-tree is ruined; competition for labour between the orchard and the field crops (L + 4) threatens the prompt harvesting of peaches and plums; no-one from the world outside could be trusted to run the orchards with love and efficiency, and unless Pesotsky's daughter marries and produces a grandson who can carry on the cultivation with the same skill and devotion, the same fate at the hands of the philistine property-developers awaits Borisovka as was to overcome the cherry orchard in Chekhov's play, ten years later.

There is an extremity, and even perversion, in Pesotsky's love of his orchards that becomes clear when he moves to the inner spheres. In the decorative garden nearer the house, at (L + 1), his gardening skill seems bent on deforming nature. At the beginning of the story, as Kovrin travels to the estate, his thoughts about it are conveyed in two paragraphs of soliloquy. The first consists purely of his childhood memories and the enchantment of all the brilliant flowers: 'Such astonishing roses, lilies and camelias, such tulips of every possible colour starting from bright white and going all the way to soot-black, such a wealth of blooms as Pesotsky had, in fact, Kovrin had never encountered anywhere else.'

In the next paragraph, however, the apple of childhood memory turns out to have a worm in it: Pesotsky's own scorn of this type of fancy gardening is mentioned and the fairy-tale atmosphere is threatened by ogres

> That which was the ornamental part of the garden and which Pesotsky himself scornfully referred to as fancy nonsense had made a fairy-tale impression on Kovrin at one time in his childhood. Here there was every kind of caprice, recherché deformity and mockery of nature! Here there were fruit tree espaliers, pear-trees shaped like Lombardy poplars, spherical oaks and limes, an umbrella-shaped apple tree, arches, monograms, chandeliers and even the date 1862 made out of plum-trees, the year when Pesotsky first took up horticulture.

The impression of a fairy-tale is now anchored firmly in Kovrin's childhood; the tenor of this description is adult in both its technicality and its scepticism. The further the account of the 'mockery of nature' goes on the more it is domesticated. With its candelabras and monograms and date, the garden has been turned into a parody of a drawing-room or study, (L-1). And of course it is in this sphere that the unattractive and perverted side of Pesotsky's monomania becomes more evident. Whereas his work in the orchard seems to be wholly creative, achieving a moral status through the successful realization of nature's potential, in the study it turns destructive, deforming not just Pesotsky's creative energies, but the science to which he believes he is making a contribution as well

> Left alone, Kovrin lay down as comfortably as possible and set to to read the articles. One had the title: 'On intermediate cultivation', another: 'A few words on Mr. Z.'s comments concerning the redigging of soil for a new

garden', a third: 'Once more on grafting with a dormant eye'—and all along the same lines. But what a restless uneven tone, what a nervy, almost morbid fervour! Here was an article apparently quite peaceful in its title and objective in its contents: it was about the Russian Antonov apple-tree. But Yegor Semyonych had begun it with '*audiatur altera pars*' [now let the other side be heard] and ended it with '*sapienti sat*' [enough for a man of any intelligence], and between these dicta a whole fountain of poisonous words directed at the 'scholarly ignorance of messieurs our patent horticulturalists who observe nature from their lofty seats of learning', or M. Gochet 'whose success has been created by ignoramuses and dilettantes', and along with it an inappropriately forced and insincere regret that peasants stealing fruit and breaking the trees in the process could no longer be flogged.

(See Russian Texts, No. 96)

To Kovrin reading these articles the triviality of the concerns, the aggressively controversial tone and the pseudoacademic mannerisms signal the 'caprices and recherché deformities' of a creative genius out of its element, a megalomania gone sour.

Now *The Black Monk* is frequently interpreted as a study in megalomania, mainly because Chekhov referred to the story in these terms in a contemporary letter.[21] But the key victim of megalomania is the young scholar, Kovrin. His sphere in the schema is, of course, the study, at (L-1); here he is relaxed, hard-working and inspired and here he realizes his true nature just as Pesotsky realizes his at $(L + 2)$. For the most part, he is uneasy and out of his depth at $(L + 1)$ and $(L + 2)$, while $(L + 3)$, the expanse of park, he uses as a transition to the river and the rye-field beyond, $(L + 4)$, where he encounters the vision of the black monk. His megalomania runs in the opposite direction to Pesotsky's, for, of course, as characters they are foils for each other. Whereas Pesotsky's genius gets distorted as he moves towards the centre, Kovrin's gets distorted as he moves towards the periphery: the metaphorical monsters of his mind, the pine-trees with bared roots like shaggy paws on the steep river-bank are his equivalent of the monsters created by the hands of Pesotsky in the ornamental garden, and his hallucination of the black monk matches the scientific straw-men with whom Pesotsky quarrels on paper. It was not, perhaps, a chance etymology that inspired Chekhov to base the outdoor hero's surname on the word-root meaning 'sand' (*pesok*) and his indoor hero's on the root meaning 'carpet' (*kovyor*)—with the added connotations of magic carpets whisking him off to exotic dimensions of the imagination.

As with most of Chekhov's heroes living on country estates, the park represents a kind of intermediate territory, sufficiently uncultivated to contain elements of wild nature, yet available as an extension of the country house itself for social interaction. The bench in the park with its views to the horizon where Kovrin sits and chats with his vision is a kind of extension of the terrace where Tanya serves tea.

Tanya is most truly herself at (L), in the house. If she ventures out into the garden and orchard it is as her father's assistant and kin and in her first conversation with Kovrin she admits that, for all her personal loyalty to her father, his is an alien world for her

>—Thank you for coming, Andryusha. Our friends, the few we have, are quite uninteresting. We have nothing but orchard, orchard, orchard. Stem, half-stem,—she laughed,—Oporto, Rennet and Borovinka apples, grafting and pollinating . . . Our whole life has gone into the orchard, I don't even dream of anything else ever but apple and pear trees. Of course, it's good and useful, but sometimes you want something else for a change. I remember, when you used to come and see us for the holidays or whatever, the house would become somehow fresher and brighter as if the dust-covers had been taken off the chandeliers and furniture. I was just a little girl then but I still understood.
>(See Russian Texts, No. 97)

Chekhov is sometimes unjustly dismissed as a stylist, notably by Mirsky, [22] and he certainly avoids ornate stylistic effects, but if style includes the expression of character through accurate choice of words then he must be considered a master. We have barely begun our analysis, yet three quotations have included lists of words, phrases or titles that were highly significant of the attitudes to the garden of those uttering them: for Kovrin the ornamental garden was a collection of trees masquerading as man-made objects which became progressively more domestic as the list went on; for Pesotsky horticulture was perverted into a progressively more aggressive and pettifogging list of pseudo-academic articles; for Tanya it is a list of technicalities which contrasts with the cosy domesticity of her real aspirations.

Tanya only moves outwards into the $(L + 2)$ sphere once, and this symbolizes her re-orientation—or perhaps *dis*-orientation—when Kovrin proposes to her

>—No, let's talk seriously!—he said.—I'll take you with me, Tanya. All right? Will you come with me? Do you want to be mine?
>—Well!—said Tanya and tried to laugh again, but no laugh came and red blotches came out on her face.
>She started to breath fast and walked off quite quickly, *but not towards the house, but further off into the park.*
>—I have never thought about it . . . I never thought!—she said clenching her hands as if in desperation. [author's italics]

Chekhov, with the trained and practised eye of a doctor, notices the psychosomatic symptoms—the laughter that doesn't come, the red blotches on the face, the faster breathing—which signal her state of disturbance far more clearly than her few and almost meaningless words.

Kovrin's proposal is the only genuine expansion of Tanya's horizons; the wedding and all the preparations for it are naturally based on the house and although she goes to live in the city with him afterwards (L + 5), she is immediately reintroduced as 'poor Tanya' and has retreated to bed (L − 2) with a headache: 'Poor Tanya, who used to get a headache in the evenings from the unaccustomed life in the city, had already been asleep for a long time and occasionally murmured deliriously some kind of incoherent phrases.' Tanya's response to stress is always to move inwards: she locks herself in her bedroom for a whole day after quarrelling with her father, and only after Kovrin has reassured her and healed the breach is she able to resume normal relations with Pesotsky in the garden (L + 1), the neutral ground between his territory (L + 2) and hers (L): 'When Kovrin went out into the garden a little later, Yegor Semyonych and Tanya were strolling side by side along the avenue as if nothing had happened, both eating rye bread and salt since they were both hungry.' The severely practical explanation in a throwaway manner which ends this paragraph and the chapter is another typical trait of Chekhov's style: what they are eating is the most basic Russian symbol of simple, direct conviviality—rye bread and salt; it even links symbolically the extremes of the topographical schema around which the story is structured: salt, the household (L) product par excellence, and rye, the product of (L + 4). But the writer has provided all the clues we need for reading this symbol and he refuses to spell it out.

The clues are very carefully placed throughout the structure of the story. At least three other clues to Tanya's need for enclosure occur: the first physical description of her, through Kovrin's eyes, draws attention to the raised collar of her coat which prevents her from moving her head freely (surely an anticipation of *The Man in the Case*, written four years later); after Kovrin's proposal, she seems to hunch up and turn in on herself (note the concentration of *so*-prefixes): 'She was stunned, stooped over, hunched up and seemed to age ten years in an instant . . . ' (See Russian Texts, No. 98) Even the motherly Varvara Nikolaevna, who replaces Tanya when Kovrin's illness becomes more serious, is in bed asleep during his final, and fatal, conversation with the black monk.

The one major 'character' whom we have not yet placed in the topographical schema of the story is the black monk. As a vision arising out of some Middle-Eastern legend of a thousand years ago, he originates at infinity, as it were, and only takes human shape as he sweeps up to Kovrin from the field of rye, at (L + 4). On this occasion he only gazes at Kovrin, but the next time they meet and have a long conversation he has already come right into the park. As he penetrates Kovrin's psyche, he simultaneously penetrates to (L), by the window in the dining-room, where he listens to Kovrin's conversation, and then to the bedroom (L − 1), first at the estate and later in the hotel in Sevastopol. Thus, the black monk moves centripetally through the schema in proportion to Kovrin's centrifugal process. This reciprocal movement charts the course of the hero's megalomania.

We have, however, been oversimplifying in suggesting that the spatial dimension is the only significant scale on which we have to operate. The concentric

circles of Pesotsky's estate, although so significant for the functioning of each of
the characters, are only one dimension of the semiotic space of the story.[23]
'Space' in this sense includes the purely *spatial* relations we have been investigat-
ing which represent one of the most clearly structured and recognizable dimensions of meaning in any story text, a semiotic system that models the world of
the narrative. But it also has the more general sense of the field created by complex networks of relationships as used by mathematicians ('topological space'),
optics-physicists ('chromatic space') and electrical engineers ('phase space'). The
term 'dimension' also involves a pun, including both the notion of *cross-section*,
which assumes that our narrative—or any art work—can be 'cut' at many different levels and angles and that many of these 'cuts' will reveal meaningful and
semiotically determined sets of relations, and also the notion of *measurable proportions*, insofar as these dimensions can be shown to share points and edges and faces
with each other—which is a geometrical way of saying that they are related
semiotically.

A dimension that is clearly important for our interpretation of Kovrin's
megalomania, and hence of the story, is that of relative degrees of health and sick-
ness. Not only Kovrin, but each of the other two protagonists undergoes some
kind of physical or psychic breakdown at key points in the plot (using the word
in our technical sense of causal relations, as in Chapter 5). Taking the notional
norm of uninteresting good health we share with Chekhov as 'H', we can
construct a scale along the following lines, see Figure 11.

As we have seen, Pesotsky functions best in his own sphere, so that laying
smoke to protect the fruit trees or getting in the peach and plum harvest he
works with heightened energy and enthusiasm; if the work pressure gets too
intense, however, $(H + 2)$ is perverted to $(H - 1)$ or $(H - 2)$ and he explodes in
scientific anger and sarcasm against his 'distinguished' colleagues, or in an
owner's anger against the lazy and incompetent peasants, or in a personal quarrel
with his daughter; when this marriage he has spent his life cultivating between
his daughter and his ward, and in which all his hopes for the future are invested,
fails and he overhears Kovrin putting the blame on him for arranging the whole
thing, he weeps, lets things go and in the end dies. Just as Tanya's spatial range is
relatively limited, her health ranges from her slightly nervy norm upwards to her
heightened excitement, $(H + 1)$, when Kovrin proposes (but with the unhealthy
symptoms we have noted) and during the wedding preparations, and down-
wards to personal anger in the quarrel, nerves, headaches, and delirium as the
marriage fails $(H - 2)$ and to hatred and cursing to damnation in her final letter to
Kovrin, $(H - 3)$. Kovrin, as the central character, covers every possible state of
health. A change of scene, life among friends, good food and fresh air give him
heightened energy and keenness; progressively as he works and thinks more
intensely, he sees the vision of the black monk which induces a state of exaltation
in which the 'eternal truth' of the world is within his grasp. But as we have seen
with the other characters, Dr Chekhov knows that any state of health only too

Figure 11

                                                                (H + 3)
                                                                vision
                                                                exaltation
                                                    (H + 2)
                                                    intense work
                                                    and thought
                                        (H + 1)
                                        heightened
                                        energy
                            (H)
                            (H – 1)
                            scientific anger
                            overwork
                            pallor, nerviness
                (H – 2)
                personal anger
                headaches, fevers
                insomnia
                hallucinations
                'the cure'
        (H – 3)
        schizophrenia
        megalomania
        TB
        hatred
(H – 4)
death

easily becomes its opposite: visions may be hallucinations and symptoms of megalomania, overwork and heightened nervous energy lead to insomnia and consumption, and the 'eternal truth' hovering at (H + 4) may turn out to be death, at (H – 4).

There are clearly many points at which this dimension of the characters' state of health, individually and vis-à-vis each other, interacts with the spatial dimension. The geometry of the story—which is already too multidimensional to represent other than algebraically, i.e. in symbols, is further enriched by the dimension of time. The present for all of the protagonists is composed of a past (T – 2) (Tanya's childhood, Kovrin's youth, the ambitions of Pesotsky's maturity) and a near future (the immediate outcome of the harvest, the wedding or Kovrin's intellection). For Kovrin it extends back a couple of thousand years to the ancient Greeks or a thousand years to the origins of the black monk and, once he is inspired by that, (T – 3), forward to the future for humanity (T + 3) and immortality $(T + \infty)$. Clearly the dimension of time relates quite significantly to the 'space' and 'health' dimensions of each of the characters.

Before we examine in detail the fourth and most important dimension of the story, which is built on the opposition culture/nature, and which, as we have hinted already, impinges on all the other dimensions, we should pause to consider the ways in which we learn about the characters. As we pointed out in the first section of this chapter, our perception (or refraction) of the personal characteristics and role of each protagonist evolves as we read the text from a multiplicity of clues: some information is given directly by the narrator; some is conveyed through the point of view of one of the other characters, either through their direct speech or through their thoughts and soliloquies. In a psychological study like *The Black Monk* a considerable amount of essential information about the characters is likely to be transmitted through their own speech and thoughts. Thus we have a scale of possible points of view from external narrator to internal character, and the proportion of the knowledge of the character conveyed by each of these points of view will help to define the genre of narrative we are analyzing. At the same time, of course, we refract a great deal of knowledge of the characters from their actions, i.e. character and event define each other. To return to our initial distinction between character and role and *actant*, it is likely that character and role are mainly conveyed through the various external and internal points of view we have enumerated, while the *actant*, almost by definition, is determined by actions and events.

As a writer who is most interested in showing his characters from the inside, Chekhov resorts very sparingly to the direct narratorial delineation of character. Strictly speaking, it is only in the first two paragraphs that he provides one or two clues about Kovrin and Pesotsky from an authorial point of view before entering the consciousness of his central character. It is noteworthy that these clues concern social role rather than character and are cryptic to the point of ambiguity

> Andrei Vasil'ich Kovrin, *M.Phil.*, had worn himself out and reached a state of nervous exhaustion. He didn't take any treatment but more or less in passing, had a chat with a doctor-friend over a bottle of wine, and he advised him to spend the spring and summer in the country. As luck would have it he got a long letter from Tanya Pesotskaya inviting him to come and stay with them in Borisovka. And he decided that he really ought to go away for a while.
> ... then ... he set out by coach to see *his former guardian and tutor* Pesotsky, *a horticulturalist renowned throughout Russia.*
> (See Russian Texts, No. 99)

The words and phrases with broken underlining in the Russian text already indicate the working of Kovrin's own consciousness: the familiarity of the names (his own patronymic as pronounced, not as written; the familiar name for Tanya; and the plain surname for his guardian) and the mildly colloquial phrases take us inside his mind at once. However, the italicized words and phrases are not information that Kovrin would need to rehearse for himself. And yet the information they convey to the reader is so partial that he is left wondering about it for the rest of the story. Kovrin's social role is to be an academic philosopher, and this is clearly relevant; but 'magistr' can also mean the head of a knightly or monastic order (potentially very significant for his later visions and delusions of grandeur) or, alternatively, could have the ironically colloquial overtones of 'maestro', as it might be uttered by Pesotsky. We do need to know Pesotsky's relationship to Kovrin (in the italics at the end of this passage), but how important for the story is his fame throughout Russia? And is there some implicit connection between his 'cultivation' of his ward and his horticulture?

The physical appearance of Tanya and Pesotsky is described from Kovrin's point of view soon after his arrival: Kovrin is amused by how knowledgeable she is about protecting the orchard from frost: 'He laughed and took her by the arm. Her wide, very serious, frozen face with fine black brows, the raised coat collar which prevented her from moving her head freely, her whole presence, thin and finely moulded, with her dress tucked up to avoid the dew, he found very touching.' This view of Tanya, clearly reflecting Kovrin's approval of her is juxtaposed significantly with his words describing how she looked five years previously: 'you were still just a child. You were so skinny and leggy and tousle-haired in your little short dress and I called you "heron" to tease you!... What a difference time makes!' For all his appreciation of the grown-up Tanya, there is still a trace of the 'kid sister' in his attitude to her which colours his behaviour throughout most of the story. Indeed he seems to be infected by the *idea* of loving her more than by love itself

> She talked long and enthusiastically. For some reason it suddenly occurred to him that in the course of the summer he could get attached to this little, fragile, talkative creature, get carried away and fall in love,—the position of both of them made it so possible and natural! This notion touched and amused him; he bent down to that sweet anxious face and sang quietly:
> 'Onegin, I shall not conceal that I love Tat'yana madly...'
> (See Russian Texts, No. 100)

The degree to which his love is self-induced, a matter of intellect rather than passion, is highlighted by his using a neuter noun 'being' (*suschestvo*) to describe her and then launching into the most clichéd aria from Tchaikovsky's opera, a sort of Russian equivalent to 'Your tiny hand is frozen'!

Pesotsky only makes any comments about his daughter once, and typically he is talking to Kovrin about the future of the estate. In a way, the opinions expressed and the nervous staccato colloquial style contribute more to our knowledge of *him* than of Tanya

> And when I die who's going to look after it? Who's going to work? The head gardener, the workmen? Well? Well, I'll tell you what, old chap: the

main enemy in this business of ours is not the hare or the may-bug or even frost, but the stranger.

—What about Tanya?—asked Kovrin, laughing.—She couldn't possibly be worse than a hare. She loves and understands the work.

—Yes, she does love and understand it. If she gets the orchard after my death and runs it, of course, that would be the best thing possible. But what if, heaven prevent, she gets married, whispered Yegor Semyonych and looked at Kovrin in terror.

—That's the thing! She'll marry, kids'll come along and there'll be no time to think about the orchard. What I'm most afraid of is that she'll marry some fine fellow who'll get greedy and rent out the orchard to tradesmen and everything'll go to the dogs in the very first year! In our line wenches are God's scourge!

(See Russian Texts, No. 101)

It is characteristic of Pesotsky's megalomania that he categorizes people according to role and does not notice them as personalities. Tanya, as a woman, might endanger the orchard, so potentially she is as much of a threat as the hare and may-bug.

Our first view of Pesotsky's character is via his setting. Chekhov's country houses are always eloquent about their owners: the author himself so energetically imposed the stamp of his own personality and enthusiasms on every house he lived in, that it seemed natural to him to depict houses and estates as reflections of their owners.[24] Pesotsky's vast house has a kind of neo-Classical grandeur with columns and lions, but the potential decline the owner so much fears is already evident in the peeling stucco. The lackey in tails by the entrance seems to represent the extreme of artificial domestic culture which imposes itself on the park, divided up 'in the English manner', which is described as gloomy and stern (*strogiy*) implying both the formal rigour and the harshness of Pesotsky in his darker moods. Later there is a stress on the strict regimentation of the trees in the orchard (another manifestation of Pesotsky's harsh will, though once again the description is modified by an ambiguity, since the narrator points out that the military precision pays off in income from the fruit trees).

Pesotsky's physical appearance is described from Kovrin's point of view immediately after the first meeting with Tanya in a fairly neutral tone, but his constant haste and preoccupied air are conveyed in a style very like Pesotsky's own style of speech: 'He looked extremely preoccupied and was always hurrying somewhere with an expression as if to say you only have to be one minute late and everything's ruined!' (See Russian Texts, No. 102) The sense of precise measurement and hyperbole [author's italics in the Russian text] and the tension of the colloquial imperative-conditional [broken underlining] are echoed in the character's first two speeches

it's frosty, as you see, but you only have to lift up a thermometer on a stick sixteen feet or so above the ground and it's warm . . .

However capacious your mind is, you'll never pack everything into it.
(See Russian Texts, No. 103)

It is, in fact, Pesotsky's style of speaking and the relationship between his speech and his other behaviour that offers the main clues to his character. He closes this first conversation with Kovrin with a calm, if ambiguous, hope

> You're still going on with that philosophy, I suppose?
> —Yes. I'm reading psychology now, but I'm mainly studying philosophy.
> —And you don't get bored?
> —Quite the contrary, it's what I live for.
> —Well, God grant you . . . —muttered Yegor Semyonych, stroking his greying side-whiskers thoughtfully.—God grant you . . . I'm really pleased for you . . . really pleased, old boy . . .

If Yegor Semyonych finds it hard to put his affection and admiration into words when he is talking to Kovrin, he is instantly articulate when it comes to a threat to his orchard

> —Who's gone and tied their horse to an apple-tree?—his despairing heart-rending cry could be heard.—Who's the swine and rabble that's dared to tie a horse to an apple-tree? Oh my God, oh my God! They've ruined everything, sullied everything, mucked up everything, turned everything to filth! The orchard's done for! It's ruined! Oh my God!
> (See Russian Texts, No. 104)

The repetitive violence of the questions, the swear words, the ejaculations and the hyperbolic prefix *pere-* are the most direct expression of Pesotsky's forceful megalomaniac character, and we are surprised when he calms down and repeats his blessing to Kovrin: '—Well, God grant you . . . God grant you . . . —he muttered.—I'm very glad you've come.'

Chekhov is a master of the framing device in narrative. This vignette of the real Pesotsky framed by the contrasting tone of the murmured blessing has the same structure as the important description of Tanya's moods before the wedding in the sixth section of the story. As we have seen, Pesotsky's character is fully realized in the orchard, (L + 2), so that scene is framed by the (L − 2) world of Kovrin; now, by contrast, Tanya's domestic world of dowries and wedding preparations, (L), is framed by the bustle and incipient violence of life in the orchard, (L + 2)

> In the glasshouses the peaches and plums were already ripe; the packing and dispatch to Moscow of this delicate and tricky cargo took a lot of attention and hard work and fuss. Due to the summer being very hot and dry, every tree had to be watered which took a great deal of time and manpower, and masses of caterpillars appeared which the workmen and even Yegor Semyonych and Tanya, to Kovrin's utter disgust, squashed just with their fingers.

This background is mentioned a page later after the account of Tanya's feelings: 'These new sensations took possession of her completely, she helped her father mechanically and noticed neither the peaches, nor the caterpillars, nor the workers, nor how quickly the time was rushing past.' Like a picture frame or a bridge passage in a piece of music, however, the purpose of the frame is to highlight the subject framed. Here the subject is the hectic preparation for the wedding, with the scorching smell of hot irons taking over from the smouldering leaves in the orchard and a rushed and nervy seamstress taking over from Yegor Semyonych. The switch to this indoor bustle of Tanya's physical world enables us to enter her mental world for the only time in the story. Though reported by the narrator, the style is that of her own inner speech

> Tanya felt as if love and happiness had taken her by surprise even though ever since she was fourteen she had been convinced for some reason that it was her that Kovrin would marry. She was amazed and bewildered and lost all confidence . . . One minute she would be overwhelmed by a wave of such joy that she felt like soaring up through the clouds and worshipping God, then she would suddenly recall that come August she would have to leave the nest and her father, or else, God alone knows where, she'd get the idea that she was worthless and shallow and unworthy of such a great man as Kovrin,—and she would go off to her room, lock herself in and weep bitterly for several hours on end. When guests were at the house she would suddenly find Kovrin extraordinarily handsome and believe all the women were in love with him and envied her and her heart would fill with rapture and pride as if she had conquered the whole world, but he only had to smile graciously at some young lady and she would be trembling with jealousy, would go off to her room again—and again there would be tears.
> (See Russian Texts, No. 105).

This is the only context in the story where we penetrate to Tanya's innermost being and it brings together her depth of feminine emotion and sensitivity (offsetting the wilful male worlds of her father and fiancé), her humility (offsetting their megalomania) and her *childishness*, This is where Tanya's character and role and actantial function come together: her response to stress—whether a quarrel with her father, the 'threat' of marriage, or the alienation of her husband—is to lock herself up, weeping, an infantile retreat to the womb (L − 3?). Before the marriage and the emergence of Kovrin's hallucinations she plays the child's role and makes of him a second parent; afterwards, when he is undergoing the cure, she inflicts the child's role on him and tries to mother him back to normality. Actantially in the narrative structure, her charming childishness and emotionality are the catalysts that induce Kovrin to forsake his monastic cell of a study and marry her, creating a tension between new domestic pressures on the hero and his search for sublime truth through his visions. Tanya has one more important catalytic function in the story: she frequently entertains a group of young people from neighbouring estates to music in the drawing-room, and the serenade they sing about a girl who in a delirium hears a divine harmony in the garden induces in Kovrin the mood for his own visions of the black monk and his yearning for eternal truth and beauty.

The black monk, in so far as he can be regarded as a genuine character in the story, is described in terms of his physical appearance three times. His features represent the stereotype of Kovrin's image of a holy man from the Arab world of a thousand years ago: grey hair, black brows, pale, emaciated face; dressed in a dark robe but with head and feet bare; his hands crossed on his breast: a Byzantine icon almost. We are struck less by the obvious similarities between the three descriptions than by the variations Chekhov weaves with the verbal material they provide. The first appearance naturally makes the most dramatic impact on Kovrin

> A monk dressed in black, with grey hair and black brows, his hands crossed on his breast, came rushing past . . . His bare feet did not touch the ground. After rushing on a dozen or so paces, he glanced round at Kovrin, nodded his head and smiled at him affectionately and yet at the same time cunningly. But what a pale, horribly pale and emaciated face!
> (See Russian Texts, No. 106)

Here the stress is on movement, with rapid semelfactive verbs. When they next meet in the park the emphasis shifts to verbs of perception and recognition, descriptive adjectives and nouns, and the more leisurely pace of longer sentences

> . . . from behind a pine-tree just opposite him there emerged, silently and without the slightest rustle, a man of medium height with his grey head uncovered, all in dark clothing and bare-footed, looking like a beggar, and black brows stood out sharply on his pale, seemingly dead, face. Nodding his head in greeting, this beggar or mendicant noiselessly came up to the bench and sat down and Kovrin recognized the black monk. For a minute they both regarded one another—Kovrin in astonishment, the monk affectionately and, as before, slightly cunningly, with a knowing look.
> (See Russian Texts, No. 107)

The sound texture produced by the play with sibilants (mainly hushed fricatives, *sh* and *sch*), here shifts to a brisker repetition of clear *s* sounds in the monk's last appearance which happens in a swirl of verbs of movement as the first time

> A tall black column like a whirlwind or tornado appeared on the far shore of the bay. With terrifying speed it was moving across the bay in the direction of the hotel, all the time getting smaller and darker, and Kovrin barely had time to step aside to make way for it . . . The monk with grey head uncovered and black brows, barefooted, his hands crossed on his chest, rushed past and stopped in the middle of the room.

—Why didn't you trust me?—he asked reproachfully, gazing affectionately at Kovrin.

(See Russian Texts, No. 108)

As we have suggested, these three passages relate to each other almost like musical variations with enough parallelism in the choice of vocabulary (notes) to establish their similarity, but enough difference in the dynamism (tempo) and sound texture to point up the contrasts appropriate to their different contexts (as in a musical theme and variations). This is just one of the structural patterns in Chekhov's narrative that have led several commentators to compare his short stories to musical composition. The framing of episodes (like musical themes or subjects) in passages of modulation which we have already noted is another such pattern. Even on the scale of the whole story we may note a contrast, as between 'movements', between the *allegro* of Kovrin's stay on the Pesotsky estate as far as the turning-point of his marriage to Tanya and the *adagio* of the winter night in the city and his long slow cure the following year. Finally, the last chapter, with its rapid survey of intervening events, the summary of Kovrin's life in a turbulent soliloquy and the sudden drama of the collapse of his relationship with Tanya through her letter and the final vision of the monk and tragic dénouement of his death produces a *scherzo* and *coda* to round off the work, a kind of concerto for Kovrin and orchestra.

Since the central point of view throughout the story is Kovrin's—whether via his actual thoughts or the narratorial interpretation of them—we never learn about his physical appearance. Only an oblique hint is given as to how he once *had* looked in the penultimate section of the story. This is done through a negation of what had been and the observers are not human participants in the drama but the mysterious pine-trees on the steep river bank above the field of rye

> The gloomy pine-trees with shaggy roots which last year had seen him here so young and confident and full of joy, now were not whispering, but stood motionless and dumb as if they did not recognize him. And indeed his head was shaved, he no longer had his fine long hair, and his face, compared with last summer, had grown fatter and paler.

This Russian Samson has been shorn of his mystical strength by the ministrations of his Delilah and, characteristically, Chekhov echoes his enervation in the land-scape: 'Where the previous year there had been rye, now reaped oats lay in rows.'

The views we gain of Kovrin from the speech of others are always in terms of his *role*, and one of his tragedies—as so often with Chekhov's heroes—is that he is always having roles thrust upon him and cannot escape them. For all his 'magisterial' qualities, he has to respond to Tanya's admiration for his interesting, independent and impressive life by committing himself to the restricting life and values of the country estate—and thereby losing his interest and independence;

Pesotsky's love and admiration for him (or, rather for his role), also first conveyed by Tanya, also has a 'binding clause': 'I mean, you know my father worships you. Sometimes I think he loves you more than me. He's proud of you. You're a scholar, an extraordinary man, you've made a brilliant career for yourself and he's convinced that you've turned out this way because he brought you up.' The third section of the story opens with a resounding 'but' which is full of implications: 'After supper when the guests had left he went off to his own room and lay down on the settee: he wanted to think about the monk. *But* after a minute Tanya came in.' Kovrin's relations with Tanya have been wholly cordial—his childhood friendship and present affection which will grow into love (though, as we have seen, he is smitten by the *idea* of love rather than a consuming passion). And yet this 'but' begins to lay bare the tension between his true character and aspirations and the roles and plans they are imposing on him. Tanya is seeking his confirmation of her own father-worship; Pesotsky seeks the scholarly opinion of a 'fellow scientist' about his writings, but these concerns have become trivial since he glimpsed his vision of the black monk and the pretentiousness of the horticulturalist's papers only irritates him. However, Pesotsky's business is cultivation and Kovrin is his most favoured plant: the $(L+2)$ man is not going to allow his favourite sapling to grow wild out in the $(L+4)$ spaces of the rye-field beyond the pine-trees. He must be pruned to a world of dimensions that he, Pesotsky, can comprehend, grafted to a world of (L), his other dearest tree, Tanya. Distraught at the idea of the orchard being neglected or sold when he dies, he conceives the ideal solution: Kovrin should marry Tanya. He starts hesitantly, but is soon utterly blunt

> I'll tell you straight: you're the one and only fellow I wouldn't be afraid of giving my daughter's hand. You're an intelligent man and you've got heart and you wouldn't let my beloved business go to rack and ruin. But the main thing is, I love you like a son . . . and I'm proud of you. If somehow or other a romance developed between you and Tanya—well! I'd be very pleased and even overjoyed. I'm saying this straight, without any false flattery, as an honest man.

Pesotsky's honesty is so naively patent that he cannot help giving away his real reason for match-making. And in the next breath the old gardener is envisaging cross-fertilization, whose fruit will further the same cause: '—If you and Tanya should have a son, I'd make a real gardener out of him,—he said after a moment's thought. Still, 'tis but an idle dream . . . ' Dream or no, it is Pesotsky's row with his daughter and the charm of her vulnerability in the following section that prompt Kovrin's proposal.

This shift from the stereotype of Kovrin's social role (as perceived by Tanya and Pesotsky) to his actantial role, suspended between his attachment to them and his search for ultimate truth and beauty (via scholarship and mystical visions), highlights the dimensions of the opposition between nature and culture which is one of the deepest and most pervasive themes of the story. Pesotsky's horticulture has tamed nature: this has positive results both scientifically and commercially, and, as we know from Dr Astrov in *Uncle Vanya* and from *The Wood-Demon*, the ecological theme of responsible cultivation of nature's potential was an essentially positive message in Chekhov's art and a virtual obsession in his life, whether at Melikhovo or in Yalta. But Pesotsky's enthusiasm verges on megalomania and this results negatively in the ornamental garden, in the distortion of natural shapes almost beyond recognition. There ought to be a happy mean between these extremes, but it would need a man of greater moderation than Pesotsky to find it. As for his daughter, Tanya, she has cultivated all spontaneity out of herself with her blind dedication to her father and the orchard.

If horticultural genius can only lead to dangerous extremes, is there any hope for philosophical genius? This is the enigma that Chekhov embodies in the character and fate of the hero. The academic researcher in Kovrin tames his natural speculativeness in night-long poring over books in his study (L − 1); the disciplines of philosophy and psychology and language study, reinforced by the stimulants of tea, coffee, tobacco and conversation, induce a hot-house culture which may mirror the phantasmagoria of the ornamental garden and Pesotsky's overheated scientific disputes. Only the black monk, sweeping towards him across the rye-fields, (L + 4), from infinite time and infinite space, offers a hope of natural wisdom. The monk tells him that he is one of God's chosen ones who serve eternal truth, destined for immortality, and that genius must live beyond the simple everyday cares for health and comfort of ordinary men: 'Heightened awareness, stimulation, ecstasy—everything that distinguishes prophets and poets and martyrs for an idea from ordinary folk, is alien to man's animal nature, that is, physical health. I repeat: if you want to be healthy and normal, go and join the herd.' Yet when Kovrin asks him what he means by eternal truth, the black monk fades away like Alice's Cheshire Cat and he is left with his aspirations of realizing his great potential and with his memories. These are phrased with a terrible tragic irony: 'Across his memory flashed his past—pure, chaste and filled with hard work.' (See Russian Texts, No. 109)—because it anticipates the link that Pesotsky brings out a few pages later between Kovrin and his mother

—Say what you like, but blood counts for a lot. His mother was an amazing woman, most noble and intelligent. It was a pleasure to look at her good, clear, pure face, just like an angel's. She could draw beautifully, she used to write poetry, could speak five foreign languages and sing . . . Poor thing, may she rest in heaven, she died of consumption.

The unreal Yegor Semyonych sighed and, after a moment's silence, went on:

—When he was a boy growing up in my home he had just the same face of an angel, clear and good. He had the same way of looking and moving and talking, just as gentle and elegant as his mother's. And what a mind. He used

always to amaze us with his mind. So it's no wonder he's a magister! No wonder at all! And you just wait and see, Ivan Karlych, what he'll be in ten years' time! You won't be able to get near him!
(See Russian Texts, No. 110)

The obvious irony here is that they wouldn't get near him in ten years' time because within three years he would be dead, and *that* because of the deeper irony of his similarity to his mother—in looks, in intelligence and charm, in physical weakness. For the terrible 'eternal truth' that the black monk would not tell Kovrin may have been what every doctor knows: that you can't escape from your genes. Dr Chekhov may be suggesting that Kovrin's path to 'higher aware-ness' and 'eternal beauty' might lie outside the study in the infinity of the sky beyond the rye-field, but would lead to a pool of blood in a hotel room beside the eternal sea; for Kovrin the escape from an artificial culture, whether intellectual or domestic, led back to his own nature and there were sown the seeds of death.

The black monk is a paradoxical figure in an exquisitely paradoxical story

—But you're a mirage,—muttered Kovrin.—Why are you here sitting with me in the same spot? This doesn't tie in with the legend.
—It makes no difference,—replied the monk after a pause, in a quiet voice, turning to face him.—The legend, the mirage and I are all the product of your stimulated imagination. I am a ghost.

His triple nature is made explicit: as a legend he is a cultural symbol, a response to the music and story of the feverish girl in the serenade, a reaction against the drawing room culture of the people singing it; as a mirage he is a scientific phenomenon, a response to the worlds of psychology and horticulture, yet eluding explanation by either; as a ghostly vision he is an individual experience, at once a projection outwards to eternal truth, independence and immortality and a projection inwards to the contingent truth of Kovrin's dependence and mortality. He addresses Kovrin with one of his own philosopher's syllogisms: '—I exist in your imagination, but your imagination is a part of nature, therefore I exist in nature too.' (See Russian Texts, No. 111) This is a beautiful piece of mimesis with the form perfectly mirroring the argument. Kovrin himself almost recognizes the black monk's contingency at the end of their conversation: 'It's strange, you keep repeating what often occurs to me too,—said Kovrin.—It's as if you had been spying and eavesdropping on my secret thoughts.' As we have seen, the monk had got beyond even his secret thoughts, even his unconscious fear of intellectual culture, to his very genetic chemistry. No wonder that Kovrin and the reader find the monk's smile, affectionate yet cunning, which is mentioned each time he appears, so eerie.

The monk looks at him affectionately once more when he appears to him in Yalta. In his cunning he makes Kovrin utter a dying cry to Tanya and fills his soul with the infinite joy of dying, of returning to nature, while the serenade and the mediocrities of human culture play on in the room below.

NOTES TO CHAPTER 6

1. See Bruno Bettelheim's wise and perceptive treatment of the child's response to narrative in *The Uses of Enchantment* (New York, 1975).
2. Sean O'Faolain, *The Short Story* (Cork, 1972).
3. V. Ya. Propp, *Morfologiya skazki, op. cit.,* Note 2, Chapter 5.
4. Charles Fillmore, 'The Case for Case', *op. cit.,* Note 11, Chapter 5.
5. Marvin Mudrick, 'Character and event in fiction' (*Yale Review*, 1960, L, pp.202-18).
6. This aspect of *nouveau roman* theory is very lucidly discussed by Ann Jefferson in *The Nouveau Roman and the Poetics of Fiction* (Cambridge, 1980, Chapter 2).
7. E.M. Forster, *Aspects of the Novel* (London, 1927).
8. Mudrick, *op. cit.,* p.211.
9. Mudrick, *op. cit.,* p.215.
10. Tzvetan Todorov, *Grammaire du Décaméron* (The Hague, 1969, pp.28-9).
11. A.J. Greimas, 'La structure des actants du récit' (*Word*, 23, 1967, pp.221-38).
12. Sorin Alexandrescu, 'Semantic analysis of Faulkner's characters' (*Semiotica*, 4, 1971, pp.37-51).
13. All references and quotations from the text are from I.S. Turgenev, *Sobraniye sochinenii v 10 tomakh*, 6 (Moscow, 1962, pp.164-200; author's translations).
14. Henry James, *Partial Portraits* (London, 1888, p.314) quoted by Robert Liddell, *A Treatise on the Novel* (London, 1947, p.90).
15. V. Friedland, Notes to *Asya* in I.S. Turgenev, *op. cit.,* 6, p.262.
16. *Ibid.* The quotations from 'Hamlet and Don Quixote' are taken from Friedland's article.
17. N.G. Chernyshevsky, *Polnoye sobraniye sochinenii* (Complete Works) 5 (Moscow, 1960, p.159). The Russian title is *'Russkii chelovek na rendez-vous!'*
18. N.A. Nekrasov, *Polnoye sobraniye sochinenii i pisem* (Complete Works and Letters) 10 (Moscow, 1952, p.374).
19. A discreet veil is usually drawn by critics over the equally erotic female landscape in the second section of Coleridge's 'Kubla Khan'.
20. All references and quotations from the text are from A.P. Chekhov, *Sobraniye sochinenii v 12 tomakh*, 7 (Moscow 1962, pp.288-321; author's translations).
21. He called it a 'medical' tale of a young man suffering from megalomania'.
22. 'No writer excels him in conveying the mutual unsurpassable isolation of human beings and the impossibility of understanding each other. This idea forms the core of almost every one of his stories, but, in spite of this, Chekhov's characters are singularly lacking in individual personality. Personality is absent from his stories. His characters all speak (within class limits and apart from the little tricks of catchwords he lends them from time to time) the same language, which is Chekhov's own . . . Another shortcoming is Chekhov's Russian. It is colourless and lacks individuality. He had no feeling for words. No Russian writer of anything like his significance used a language so devoid of all raciness and nerve.' (D.S. Mirsky, *A History of Russian Literature*, New York, 1949.) Our evidence here and later in our analysis suggests that Mirsky, for all his undoubted sensitivity, was more alert to the colour of words in themselves than to the subtly significant relationships between words.
23. For a full discussion and illustration of the problem of 'semiotic space' see L.M. O'Toole,

'Dimensions of semiotic space in narrative' (*Poetics Today*, 4, 1981); also, for the mathematical basis of the theory, R.H. Atkin, *Multi-dimensional Man* (Harmondsworth, 1981).

24.   Donald Rayfield highlights this trait in his interesting book, *Chekhov: the Evolution of his Art* (New York, 1975). Speaking of the period leading up to the writing of *The Black Monk*, he writes: 'Chekhov's way of life in Melikhovo seems dissociated from his writing. His time, especially in 1893, when he wrote very little fiction, was almost entirely given to farming and horticulture . . . Chekhov would not delegate: he surveyed ground, costed buildings, ordered timber and dug out ponds. This manic enthusiasm is reflected only in parody: the hero of *The Black Monk* (1894) has a father-in-law obsessed with an orchard, terrified of frost ruining the blossom' (p.134). Perhaps the more serious implication of the writer's ironic self-portrait is that every positive productive act contains the seeds of its own negation and destruction: as we shall see, this offers a convincing thematic link between the heroes.

7

SETTING

Turgenev: *Bezhin Meadow*
Chekhov: *The Peasants*

I

A CURIOUS FEATURE of modern literary scholarship is the almost universal neglect of setting in the study of narrative prose. Narrative structure, plot, point of view and character are the subjects of elaborate theorizing, close analysis and comparison, and comprehensive literary history, but setting often gets no more than a passing reference. This may be partly a reaction against the priority accorded by the nineteenth century to descriptive writing in criticism, against the cult of nature in poetry and prose, and the ease with which the 'pathetic fallacy' was both exploited by writers and noticed by critics.

This reaction was expressed most forcibly by Robert Liddell in his *A Treatise on the Novel* (1947): 'The aesthetics of descriptive writing have not yet received sufficient attention—it is commonly held in too great esteem, particularly when it occurs in works of fiction. Painting or music that has a strong literary element is now severely criticized. It is time for an attack to be made on the pictorial element in literature.'[1] Liddell himself argues for a very limited function for background description, praising Jane Austen as a model of tightly controlled description,[2] and taking Dickens and Hardy to task for allowing their landscapes to become obtrusively symbolic[3]

> Fiction is the delineation of character in action, and the landscape in the background is merely incidental . . . In fiction that is a representation of characters in action, the background will probably serve a negative rather than a positive purpose. It will be there less for the sake of being what it is, for example, an English country village, as for the sake of not being anywhere else. Its function is limitative, to keep the characters still, and to allow us to concentrate upon them and upon the happenings. When we can see the characters and the action clearly, then the background may fade out of focus.[4]

The argument is provocative, but disastrously over-prescriptive; it would reduce the short story to a painfully narrow genre, let alone the novel. Of course, to ground characters and events in an authentic background is a major function of setting, but even at this level some finer discrimination is required: will the same features of the setting simultaneously fix the individual personality of a character, his social role, and his narrative functions (as distinguished in our last chapter)? Must we not differentiate between setting in *time* and setting in *place*, or are there types of description (times of day, climatic conditions) where they are fused?

Surely even between background and characters there are many possible relationships. And the effect of background descriptions on the reader—our refraction of
the setting—may vary considerably according to the context.

We will be considering all these aspects of the problem in some detail in this
chapter, but we cannot, with Liddell, afford to neglect—or despise—the metaphorical and symbolic functions of setting. One critic who has attempted to
focus on this relationship between the practical and symbolic functions of background description is D.S. Bland, who summarizes an admirably balanced article
on the subject as follows

> The nature of the novel, in its beginnings, was such that a greater degree of
> localization of the characters was required than in the older literary forms,
> because these characters were less universal, more closely related to their own
> day and age. This localization was achieved by setting them in a solidly
> constructed environment. But it is not long before description is being used
> more widely, to reveal, first, general characteristics, and then particular
> moods . . . In drama participation in the moods of the characters is achieved
> through the direct contact between actor and audience, and is embodied in
> action, in pauses and tones of voice, and so forth. But participation in the
> novel is much less direct (we read it all in our own internal tone of voice, for
> example) and one way to make the connection is through the evocative power
> of descriptive passages. Here . . . the novelist was able to learn something from
> the development of landscape painting at this time.
>   Next description can rise to the level of symbol, and so stand for more than
> the writer expresses directly, or else express in succinct form what otherwise
> might have been more laborious.[5]

These four stages in the evolution and functioning of background description—
localization, characterization, mood and symbol—provide a much firmer
starting-point for the analysis of setting than Liddell's exclusive prescription,
but they are still quite broad categories which obscure some further distinctions
we might wish to make. As we have said, localization may be achieved differently depending on whether the focus is on the character's individuality, his
social typicality or his narrative function; there may be a distinction between
social specification and social comment; some characters may actually be part of
the background description, like static figures in a painting or extras in a film;
the setting may be used dynamically to reflect contrasts between the characters,
or contrasts between their moods or their reactions to events as well as to reflect
the personality and mood of a single character; we may want to distinguish
between mood, which is within the characters, and 'atmosphere' which involves
a multidimensional play between the moods of several characters, the narrative
voice and the reader; symbols may be of local, episodic significance or may
synthesize the theme of the whole work.

Structuralist approaches to the problem of setting have also been few and have tended to be over-schematic. Claude Levi-Strauss never fails to take account of the setting for the heroes' actions in folk myths, but maps only the deepest binary oppositions like above/below, mountain/valley, sky/earth, land/water, East/West, etcetera which relate primarily to abstract narrative functions—parallel or contrasting moments in plot structure—or to mythical categories such as heaven/the underworld or scarcity/plenty. To be fair, in his most subtle and elaborate analysis of *The Story of Asdiwal*[6] Levi-Strauss succeeds in relating these actantial and mythical functions to geographical, economic and social features of the communities that have produced the mythic tale, but we never have a sense of Asdiwal's individuality. This would be in line with the great anthropologist's conception of myth as a form of collective thinking—and no doubt he would dismiss our preoccupation with personality as somewhat low-level, even 'bourgeois'—, but nonetheless a hero who simultaneously takes an earthly and a heavenly bride, quarrels with his in-laws, or who can talk walruses into transporting him home under the sea has some claims on the reader's, or listener's, attention as an individual.

Roland Barthes in his 'Introduction to the structural analysis of stories', to which we have often referred, makes a basic distinction between the distributional units of narrative ('functions'), which refer to operations, and the integrative units ('indices'), which refer to concepts. Clearly most elements of setting will belong to the second category, where he then distinguishes between 'indices proper'—which have a strong functionality, referring to character, feeling, atmosphere, etcetera and have implicit connotations, that is, require to be decoded—and 'informants' which merely identify a situation in time and place, consist of pure data which is immediately meaningful, and have the weak function of creating or increasing authenticity. There are two problems here: firstly, despite its elegance and theoretical validity, it is not clear what one can do with this distinction, apart from merely classifying units as they appear in a text;[7] secondly, the sharp binary cut actually reduces and over-schematizes Bland's four-fold functions of background description with a consequential gain in explanatory power, but a loss in descriptive usefulness. In other words, the model is too powerful for most kinds of literary criticism. Moreover, as Barthes' own examples make clear (James Bond's telephones, or whisky drunk in an airport lounge), the interesting cases are those where what appear to be mere informants, providing ready-processed information, actually provoke the reader into decoding further possible connotations (e.g. 'instant multiple communicative power', 'expensive relaxation between bursts of rapid mobility'). Thus the clear division breaks down—although the insights gained in the process are not to be sniffed at.

In his famous analysis of Balzac's *Sarrasine*[8] Barthes seems to have given up looking for 'pure informants' and tries to account for elements of the setting within three of his five 'codes': the code of Semes or Signifiers, which uses hints or 'flickers of meaning' to produce connotations; the Cultural Code, collective, anonymous and authoritative, which speaks for and about what it seeks to establish as 'accepted' knowledge or wisdom; and the Symbolic Code, whereby recognizable groupings in various modes within the narrative ultimately generate the dominant 'figure in the carpet'. Despite the sophistication and brilliance of Barthes own analysis by means of these codes, it is still not clear how distinct they are, either conceptually or in their textual realizations.

The topological model I have used to explore character in Chapter 6 involved the sorting out and grading of the elements of setting in place and time and relating them systematically to characters, plot episodes, and so on. In principle, it provides a genuinely structural method for mapping the groupings and connotations that Barthes is talking about, particularly if we enrich the 'back-cloth geometry' of the text with the notion of 'traffic' produced by the reader's involvement in the connotative process.[9] However, while the multiple concentricities of Chekhov's *The Black Monk* lend themselves to such a mathematically structured approach, and the almost obtrusive symmetry of the landscape in Turgenev's *Asya* seems to beg for an analysis in terms of mythical oppositions, we will try to focus here more exclusively on the characteristics and functions of setting itself.

Among twentieth-century literary theories perhaps only Northrop Frye's *Anatomy of Criticism*[10] comes near to integrating the many typical features and functions of setting into an overall typology of modes and genres, characters and plots. For Frye the essential communicative medium—the 'language'—of literature is the image. This language must be studied both anagogically ('in terms of the total order of words comprising a literary work') and analogically ('in terms of its references to social, biographical, psychological and cultural patterns in the world surrounding the work and in other literary works')

> If we do not accept the archetypal or conventional element in the imagery that links one poem with another, it is impossible to get any systematic mental training out of the reading of literature alone. But if we add to our desire to know literature a desire to know how we know it, we shall find that expanding images into conventional archetypes of literature is a process that takes place unconsciously in all our reading. A symbol like the sea or the heath cannot remain within Conrad or Hardy: it is bound to expand over many works into an archetypal symbol of literature as a whole.[11]

Frye's stress on archetypal imagery, developed out of Frazer and Jung, reminds one of Levi-Strauss' mythical oppositions. For him, however, the binary structures which can be observed in recurrent images are not merely patterns to be culled from a text, nor analogues of broader cultural, economic or social structures. They bear a complex multidimensional relationship to Frye's five literary modes classified according to the hero's power of action: myth, romance, high mimetic, low mimetic and ironic. Hence they are crucial to the syntagmatic structure of particular works, i.e. to the plot, the action in which the hero's power is made manifest. Thus, while it is possible for background description only to function statically, as a mere locus for an episode, or a social definition of a character, it is likely to have a dynamic function as well, marking the progression from episode to episode—or halting or changing the rhythm of that progression—, or else reflecting or making possible the development of a character. Although Frye does not isolate background description for special treatment, this offers a far richer theory of setting in narrative fiction than the other proposals we have seen, and I will be referring to it in the proposals which follow; my debt to Frye's classification of archetypes will be clearly evident in the analysis in this chapter.

Before attempting our own classification of the functions of setting and the ways in which they are realized in texts, let us briefly survey the stories already analyzed in earlier chapters and attempt some generalizations.

In both of the stories by Pushkin the background details are sparse and with a strong function in motivating plot and character. The setting is usually man-made and reflects social categories. In *The Pistol Shot* the enigmatic persona of Silvio is set against a background of life in a provincial army post, while the immediate setting is an unusually poor hut distinguished only by a rich collection of pistols and walls riddled with bullet holes. By contrast, the Count's mansion is characterized by conventional formal luxury, its only remarkable feature being a Swiss landscape painting shot through with two bullets. The events all happen in early summer and the only mention of natural background is in the timing: cards are played in the evening, the first (flashback) duel took place, naturally, at dawn, while the second (later flashback) took place in the early evening. Enough has been said of the parallels in this story for it to be clear that, apart from the minimal social and personal details, the main function of setting is structural in the most geometric sense, contrasting and framing the two equally unresolved episodes. The Count's picture is a typical piece of Pushkinian semiotic irony: a natural landscape has been captured in paint and framed, yet what catches the eye is not the Swiss view, but the bullet holes which have punctured the illusion.

Conversely, in *The Post-Stage Master* a central scene, that of Dunya and Minsky in Minsky's apartment, is turned into a genre-painting and framed by successive layers of schematized plot, the whole story forming an ironic commentary on the reader's presuppositions about the Prodigal Son pictures. In this story, however, there is some use of natural background, but always governed by plot structure: a rainstorm in May motivates the narrator's first halt at the post-stage; winter weather provided an excuse for Minsky falling ill and then covered his tracks; autumn provides a desolate scene and a desolate mood for the narrator's discovery of the post-stage master's decline and death. Pushkin pays a kind of minimal lip-service to the seasonal archetypes described by Northrop Frye: the romantic myth of spring, the ironic myth of winter, and the elegaic myth of autumn; but, as with his other structural devices, we feel that he is deliberately teasing our genre expectations in a constant pastiche.

Any humour in Leskov's use of setting, on the other hand, is slanted towards satire. The apparently neutral storm that sets the action in motion is described in terms of the ritual calendar ('around Epiphany time'), a specific historical time and place (the Winter Palace in St Petersburg in 1839, i.e. the most repressive period of Nicholas I's reign) and, stylistically, in terms of the reactions of the populace. This socialization of the natural world leads on without strain to the social settings which are to be satirized according to their reactions to Postnikov's misdemeanour: the officers' quarters, the regiment, the police station, the office of the chief of police and the Metropolitan's study. Always the sparsely described setting is a backcloth for the conventional official reactions to a humane act.

Tolstoy's more extensive use of setting is also strongly social in meaning, but less clear-cut in its function than that of Leskov. Spring and winter are used in their archetypal meanings: spring for the 'comedy' of Kasatsky's proposal scene in May—where, as we have seen, the comic 'stage properties' of nightingales and rustling leaves seem to be overplayed deliberately; winter for the multiple irony of the widow's assault on his virtue, and spring again for the parallel 'comedy' of the monk's loss of celibacy. In the latter two scenes, where the hero is 'Father Sergius' and not 'Kasatsky', the setting is ritualized both in its calendar—Shrove Tuesday and the Feast of the Assumption—and in the physical details of the hermit's cell: asceticism, gravity and security versus luxury, frivolity and risk: two conflicting versions of Life and Death. There is plenty of overt sociological commentary, but the satire is not pointed at external manifestations of hypocrisy or corruption, as with Leskov, but rather internalized in the conflicts experienced by the hero—a subtler form of satire with which we become far more deeply involved.

Korolenko, too, indulges in overt ethnography and sociology while making the internal drama of Makar's dream of Judgement Day the main vehicle for his social criticism and satire. More than any other writer we have been considering, he gives us a detailed ethnographic description of the Yakut township and its inhabitants; the interrelationship between Yakuts, Russo-Yakuts, Tartars and Russian exiles are presented in comic vignettes during both the waking life and the dream of Makar, and the anthropological detail extends to fox-trapping, horse-thieving and drunkenness. But these scenes experienced and dreamed by Makar are comic because their symbolic value is overplayed: the fox-trapping scene in the snowy moonlit forest becomes an apocalyptic vision, the Tartar who stole his horse and the old man struggling to carry his wife on his back are figures out of purgatory, and the Tartar booze-hut is a glimpse of hell. As we have seen, all these visions have as a dominant key the overarching symbolism of Christmas Eve and the action scenes are both framed and modulated by the sound of church bells, the fires of heaven (moon, stars and aurora borealis) and the mythic oppositions up/down, silence/sound, warmth/cold. And we analyzed in detail the most deliberate piece of scene-setting—purple prose for its own sake—in the highly rhythmic and schematic paean of praise as Makar draws near the gates to heaven.

Much of the charm of Gorky's story depends on a similar tension between the starkly realistic socio-economic plight of the twenty-six bakers and the symbolism of their setting. Every detail of their cavern, from the mildewed bricks to the voracious maw of the stove-monster, is pure demonic imagery. And yet three elements in their lives lift these damned souls towards the only apocalypse they can conceive of: the power of song in unison, and the bright aura of sun and fresh air surrounding the visions, above them, of Tanya and the soldier. When their angel falls, however, through their own collective will, the setting reverts—perhaps too obviously—to the elegaic rain and mud and puddles of the only too real world of their prison-yard.

With Dostoevsky and Gogol we find very little use of setting, or rather, we encounter a deliberate denial of the value of realistic background for their purposes. Realism for Dostoevsky, here even more than in his novels, is psychological realism, so every 'property' of the hero's mind is constantly on display and it is these that form the backcloth for the transactions which constitute the plot. Even the 'scene-setting' of the opening page is, as we have seen, a short-cut to the questions which are obsessing him. Later, apart from the claustrophobic topography of his pawnbroker's office and 'den', which plays such an explicit role in his relationship with his 'gentle spirit', all the background detail is sociological, not physical: we learn just enough of the institutions of pawnbroking, newspaper advertising, regimental life, challenge to duels, marriages and dowries, retirement to the Crimea, etcetera to comprehend the reactions of this archetypal 'outsider' to their conventions. The atmosphere of the story is dark and wintry because, in Northrop Frye's terms, the myth of winter underlies this most ironic of genres, the Menippean satire, or 'anatomy'.

Winter is the one realistic element—well, partly realistic—in that other 'anatomy' in our collection, Gogol's The Overcoat. The 'powerful foe' that sets the story in motion by making Akakiy need a new coat is the northern frost; the vast snow-covered squares of St Petersburg become the pitiless arenas where the hero loses himself and his new coat; a cold whirlwind kills Akakiy; and finally a gust of wind steals the coat of the Person of Consequence. There is a realistic enough contrast between the labyrinth of dark, narrow, winding streets in which Akakiy lives and the broad, well-lit thoroughfares of the more prosperous parts of St Petersburg to which he ventures in his new overcoat, but the details are pure fantasy. The fantasy is either his own—the shop window with the painting of a beautiful lady with her leg bared and a moustachioed gent peeping from behind a door; the lady who flashes past Akakiy in the street—or, more subversively, the fantasy of the narrator. For Gogol is deliberately subverting the setting conventions of realist prose through two grotesque devices. Either he is deliberately vague about time and place, doubting the accuracy of his memory and supplying approximate times and locations

Akakiy was born in the night, if my memory does not deceive me, before the 23rd March . . . When and at what time he entered the department and who instated him no-one could rightly remember.

Where exactly the official lived who had issued the invitation we can't say, unfortunately; our memory has started deceiving us badly and everything there is in St Petersburg, all the streets and houses, have mingled and got so muddled up in our head that it's downright difficult extracting anything from there in any sort of order.

This conforms, of course, to the colloquial unreliability of the *skaz* technique, but is very unsettling for the realist in us that expects narrators to be reliable sources of basic information. However, we are in a grotesque world where nothing is what it seems and all the facts and events in the story grow out of mere verbiage; the St Petersburg atmosphere is highly convincing without being grounded in real times and places.

Gogol's other main device for overturning our expectations about setting is to present a particular scene as a common occurrence, in the imperfect, and make the landscape more active than the hero: 'Besides, he had a peculiar knack as he went along the street of arriving under a window just as all kinds of rubbish was being hurled out of it, so that he was for ever bearing off on his hat the rinds of water melons and canteloupes and that kind of nonsense.' Or else a horse's muzzle appears from nowhere, rests on his shoulder and blows a gale at his cheek, or he gets showered with lime or brushed against by a chimney-sweep. The trivia of a demonically active, menacing setting impinge constantly on the passive hero—and yet, in a sense, it is his fault, his 'knack', to be so accident-prone. The setting in *The Overcoat*, like Akakiy and the Person of Consequence, like the turns in the plot, comes into existence accidentally, either through some trivial passive event or through some quirk of linguistic patterning.

All the functions of setting are most fully realized in the stories by Turgenev and Chekhov, so we may use the two stories analyzed in the last chapter to construct a kind of check-list of these functions before we go on to analyze the working of setting in detail in their stories *Bezhin Meadow* and *The Peasants*. Before listing the possibilities under different heads, however, we must stress that any one element of setting in a story may well be fulfilling two or more functions. As we have seen with Northrop Fry's archetypes, a courtyard or village street in the rain, with puddles and a cloudy sky, may be simultaneously: (1) necessary information as to the time and place of events; (2) a narratorial comment about the desirability of the events; (3) an element of structure, such as a frame, a mark of the dénouement, or a concluding cadence; (4) a symbol of the elegaic theme of a hero or group doomed to failure, i.e. the mark of the tragic myth. These, then, will be our four provisional categories of the functions of setting: the Informative, the Commentative, the Structural and the Symbolic.

A. Setting can be used *informatively* in the following ways:

1. A location is established: the narrator of *Asya* is abroad, travelling in the Rhine valley; Kovrin goes to stay on the country estate of his guardian Pesotsky. Liddell claims that 'it will be there less for the sake of being what it is . . . than for the sake of not being anywhere else'. This is witty, but simplistic, since this information may well have social or symbolic value as well: the Russian intellectual travelling abroad or convalescing amid a whirl of horticultural activity are of thematic significance. And if such information is lacking, as with Dostoevsky, or unreliable, as with Gogol, we feel the lack acutely—we sense a deviation from the norm.

2. A time is established: *Asya*'s narrator was twenty and getting over an unhappy love affair; Kovrin arrives in April to spend the summer at Borisovka.

3. The setting creates authenticity: the twin Rhineland towns are set among vineyard-covered hills, dotted with ruined castles, with higher mountains in the background; the estate is naturally divided into a recreation area (the formal garden), working areas (the orchards and greenhouses) and uncultivated areas (the park and beyond).

4. The setting fixes a social framework: young Russian intellectuals from landed gentry families meet abroad amid German student festivities; Pesotsky's house is grand, with columns and stone lions.

5. The setting makes a social comment: Asya, of whose peasant stock we only learn later, seeks out unconventional or wild settings; the stucco on Pesotsky's house is peeling, and the market garden and its owner are feeling new economic, social and scientific pressures.

6. The setting helps to define a character's individual personality: Asya scrambles daringly and provocatively up the ruined chapel walls; Tanya belongs in the comfortable cultured world of the drawing-room.

7. It defines a character's social role: Gagin poses elegantly in his painter's studio; Kovrin burns the midnight oil in his philosopher's study.

8. It helps establish a character's narrative function: the arbour where the narrator overhears the enigmatic conversation between Asya and Gagin establishes Asya as the focus of the narrator's enigma, about her and about himself; each of the characters in *The Black Monk* has a 'proper' sphere of activity, as we saw in Chapter 6, and any departure to other spheres (Pesotsky to the study, Kovrin to the river bank, Tanya out into the park) creates the tension which motivates their subsequent actions (search for an heir, for universal truth, for marriage).

At this stage we ought to say a word about *topoi*, or the 'commonplaces' of the fiction of a particular genre, or period, or culture, since these offer a kind of 'shorthand' for whole sets of connotations and predispose us to expect certain kinds of action. In the Russian world glimpsed in our chosen stories the most typical *topoi* (roughly in order of frequency, and indicating the most typical states or actions they imply) are:

(a) the *kabak*, usually translated as 'tavern', but whereas the English word, like Turgenev's German *biergarten* normally has connotations of cheerful relaxation

and conviviality, in the nineteenth-century Russian context it spells misery (Korolenko, Chekhov, Pushkin), exploitation (Korolenko's rich Tartars, Chekhov's ruthless peasant types) and lonely alienation and search for oblivion;
(b) the barracks: a military world of fixed rules (Leskov, Tolstoy), all-male society and codes of honour protected by duelling (Pushkin, Dostoevsky);
(c) the drawing-room: a focus of (mainly feminine) culture, comfort and convivial conversation (Pushkin, Tolstoy, Chekhov); verandahs play a similar role (Chekhov);
(d) the church, usually viewed from afar: a haven of positive moral, social and aesthetic values (Korolenko, Tolstoy, Chekhov);
(e) the garden: a place for romantic encounters, proposals and confidences (Turgenev, Tolstoy, Chekhov);
(f) the meadow: a contact between the 'civilized', though often corrupt, world of man and the innocent though controllable world of nature (Turgenev, Chekhov—both stories);
(g) the bonfire: the focal point in a meadow at night-time; a circle of comfort and conviviality, warmth and illumination in a dark, alien, threatening world; tends to stimulate story-telling of a kind that links the wild and the domestic, the risky and the safe (Turgenev, Chekhov);
(h) courtyard and stairs: highly schematic, ritualized turning-points (Gogol, Dostoevsky);
(i) the road: naturally, a means of transfer (Korolenko, Chekhov), but also loss (Pushkin, Turgenev);
(j) the river: a means of transition, especially symbolizing a change of psychological or mental state (Turgenev, Tolstoy, Chekhov);
(k) the forest: the wildest, most alien and threateningly demonic setting (Korolenko, Chekhov), though *in extremis* it may be a place of retreat (Tolstoy).
As will be clear from many of these examples, an advantage of the *topos* is that along with its 'prepackaged' information it usually includes some predetermination of related action and of symbolic significance.

B. These *topoi* also assist in our next general category of the function of setting, the Commentative:
1. A particular background may serve not merely to 'fix' a character socially, but to incorporate the author's or narrator's implied comment on the prevailing social relations: apart from its many symbolic functions, the Rhine is a clear barrier between Asya's world, the town of L., and the narrator's world, the town of Z., which he crosses at his peril, and of course it transpires that his main reason for refusing her love ultimately is his fear of their social inequality; the town is an alien element to Tanya, the daughter of a country landowner, and it is revealing both that she falls into a state of depression as soon as Kovrin moves her to his town apartment and that she has to be replaced by a townswoman when the consumptive hero ends up in his seaside hotel.

2. The other kind of comment that may be implied by a particular setting is a *moral* one: the waitress from the *biergarten* (a background-figure, like the madonna statue) has accepted the love that was offered to her by her rather ordinary young man, while the narrator is aware of his own moral cowardice in refusing the challenge presented by Asya's love; the bare roots of the pine trees sticking out of the clay river-bank are the only perceptive witnesses of Kovrin's moral surrender under the ministrations of Tanya and her father.

C. The functions of setting in relation to the structure of narrative are at least as significant as the way they reflect content. Setting must, in Northrop Frye's terms, be viewed anagogically as well as analogically. In fact, in its dual functioning we might well regard setting as proof of the inextricable bond between form and content in art.

1. Setting functions to change the scene. This apparent tautology is an important basic function: if the *mimesis*, the representation of 'real' events, is conveyed by bursts of action or conversation, the shifts in their background are an important part of the *diegesis*, whether from town to country, inland to seaside, interior to exterior, home to abroad. A conversation between the narrator and Asya is quite different in Frau Louise's dark room and on a steep hill-path past a vineyard; when Kovrin talks to Pesotsky in the orchard, the old man is master of the situation, but the roles are completely reversed in Kovrin's study.

2. Even Robert Liddell's quip that the background helps to keep the characters still is quite important: once Asya has left the Rhineland town for Cologne and London, everything changes; and once Kovrin is stuck in his seaside hotel he can never revive the magic mood of the orchard, the park and the rye-field or his former relations with Tanya and her father.

3. Setting may certainly reflect the development of a character: the Rhine looks quite different when the narrator fears that he may have lost Asya from how it appeared when he was filled with curiosity and hopes about her; when Kovrin returns to the river-bank shorn of his power he sees not a rye-field but a field of mown oats.

4. Related to this, parallel settings may reflect some parallelism of plot or character: the male aspect of the roofscape of the town of Z. contrasts with the female landscape through which Asya leads the narrator; as we saw under C.1., the status of Pesotsky and Kovrin is reversed when they move into each other's spheres, and, more crucially for the plot, Pesotsky's 'domesticating' of Kovrin back to health on the verandah is far more threatening than his attempts to cultivate in him the idea of marriage in the orchard.

5. Some characters are simply part of the setting and this defines their structural role vis-à-vis the main characters: Ganchen, the ferryman and the carousing students in *Asya*; the estate foreman, the dressmaker and the irresponsible peasants in *The Black Monk*.

6. In still more purely structural terms, setting may frame episodes or

conversations: the Rhine as N.N. arrives to see Asya and her brother—the Rhine as he departs; the orchard filled with wraithes of smoke before and after Tanya's first conversation with Kovrin.

7. It may offer a change of scale which has an important effect on the reader's perception of the story: N.N.'s eavesdropping in the enclosed garden versus his walking-trip to the mountains; the black monk whirling up to Kovrin's cramped hotel room across a bay from the sea.

8. It may offer a change of rhythm. Robert Liddell saw it as a positive disadvantage of background description that it distracts from the activities of the characters and the pace of the action.[12] And yet from the reader's point of view such a shift in rhythm, in dramatic intensity and in emotional charge may be extremely productive, enabling him to recover from the preceding action and get it into perspective before the next burst of action. This is certainly true of the narrator's contemplation of the Rhine in the moonlight after making the acquaintance of Gagin and before he begins to observe Asya more closely over supper; perhaps, too, the nocturnal description of the bay at Sevastopol is a necessary *rallentando* before the critical scherzo of the black monk's last fateful appearance to Kovrin.

D. The Symbolic functions of setting are less readily classified. It may be possible to distinguish between a local, episodic symbol reflecting the current mood of one of the characters and one of those overarching symbols that synthesize the whole theme of a story, but it is in the nature of symbols that their meaning continues to reverberate beyond their immediate context, so such a distinction will be somewhat forced. The narrator's boat cutting through the shaft of moonlight on the Rhine is interpreted as an ill-omen by Asya in her first words to N.N. as he leaves them after the first encounter; and when he reaches the other side he is reassured to see the moonbeam like a golden bridge linking the two banks. But the omen and her superstitious fear and his complacency have implications for the characters and the plot throughout the story, as much, in a way, as the more obvious symbol of the statuette of the madonna with the child-like face and the bleeding heart which recurs with more pervasive symbolic intent throughout the narrative. Similarly, the deformities that Pesotsky inflicts on the trees and shrubs in his formal garden immediately reflect Kovrin's present state of tension and his memory of childish terrors; yet, as we have seen, the deformation of the natural, whether in nature or in his human 'saplings', is the ruling urge of Pesotsky's life.

One of the main symbolic functions of setting that is, perhaps, taken too much for granted by critics is the alternative world it offers to that of the petty deeds and aspirations and fears of the human characters. This alternative world may be spiritual or moral or both, but it often produces an antiphonal effect as a seemingly aware natural world 'comments' tacitly on the human action. This may have originated in the commentary and rival strife conducted by Homer's gods on Mount Olympus and in the relation between the chorus and the protagonists in Greek tragedy. By the nineteenth century it had clearly become an essential aspect of the 'pathetic fallacy' which was so central to the thought and poetic practice of Wordsworth and his successors. This is discussed in much detail and with great insight by Joseph Warren Beach in *The Concept of Nature in Nineteenth-Century English Poetry*. According to Beach, this personification of Nature in the eighteenth and nineteenth centuries is to be ascribed to: 'the poet's desire to associate the "beauteous forms" of the out-of-doors world with the laws and order of the universe, reinforcing the aesthetic pleasure derivable from these beauteous forms with the philosophical notion of order and unity, and vice versa.'[13] This tendency is of historical and philosophical significance since its represents: 'a philosophical bridge from faith to unfaith . . . It made possible the passage without too great emotional strain from mediaeval Christian faith to the scientific positivism which tends to dominate cultivated minds today.'[14] His argument is summarized best near the end of the book, and it contains many of the points about the spiritual and moral values invested in the natural setting that we will be looking out for in *Bezhin Meadow* and *The Peasants*

> In the poetry of Wordsworth, the pleasure taken in the forms of the natural world, especially in rural scenes, is almost invariably associated, more or less consciously, with the thought of universal nature conceived as an orderly system . . . scientists and theologians share the conviction that nature, in the whole and in every detail, is the result of providential design. The order of nature may be taken by men as a form of conduct. The wellbeing of men is provided for within the frame of nature. With men, as with the lower animals and vegetable organisms, natural impulses tend towards the well-being of the individual, and we are guided by the admonitions of pain and pleasure, especially the latter. Virtue is more natural to us than vice, providing us with greater and more lasting gratifications . . . Communion with nature in the country, where her forms have not been obscured by man's artificial inventions, is beneficial to man, leading him as it does to reflection of her benevolent dispositions and harmonies. Wordsworth's preference of country to town, like that of many eighteenth-century poets, is probably somewhat coloured by the romantic legend of the Golden Age, in which man's heart and manners were still natural, uncorrupted by institutions and ideas which had swerved from the simplicity of nature. Wordsworth's view of the child and the peasant as being particularly close to nature and sharing in her wisdom is analogous to the romantic view of the savage, or primitive man . . . [15]

I have quoted this passage at length because it contains many clues that will help us to interpret the function of setting, particularly for peasants and children—indeed, for peasant children—in the stories of Turgenev and Chekhov.

II Turgenev: *Bezhin Meadow,* 1851; (*Bezhin Lug*)[16]

On the face of it, the central setting of *Bezhin Meadow* is the perfect pastoral scene as it might have been conceived by Wordsworth: a broad pasture, enclosed by a bend in the river and a hill, and a group of children—peasant children too—sitting around a bonfire telling stories, observed by an urban narrator nostalgic for the simple and primitive pleasures of unspoilt Nature.

As Kenneth Clark reminds us in *Landscape into Art*, the enclosed garden or meadow has been a powerful *topos* in Western art since the Middle Ages

> The discovery of the garden: the enchanted garden—be it Eden, or the Hesperides, or Tirnanogue—is one of humanity's most constant, widespread and consoling myths . . . Paradise is the Persian for 'a walled enclosure', and it may well be that the peculiar value set on gardens in the later Middle Ages is a legacy of the Crusades . . . Dante begins his journey in a dark wood; he nears its end when the wood thins out, and he sees beyond a stream a lady singing and picking the flowers with which her whole path is embroidered. Forty years later the garden provides a refuge for Boccaccio's charming companions, who withdraw to 'a plot of ground like a meadow, the grass deep-spangled with a thousand different flowers' to tell their stories, while the plague festers outside the wall. [17]

But any positive force presupposes its opposite: Dante's meadow is the respite from Purgatory and Hell, Boccaccio's garden—a refuge from the living hell of the plague, and Turgenev's meadow is such a powerful image in the story because it allows a relief from the darker forces of a natural and supernatural world which constantly beset man with threats. In his first description of the pastoral scene Turgenev tells us explicitly: 'the gloom was fighting with the light', and this is expanded into a symbolic battle which becomes a recurrent motif throughout the story

> It was a wonderful scene: around the fires a reddish circular glow would tremble and seem to die down as it thrust out into the darkness; a flame, flaring up, would throw quick flickers from time to time beyond the circle's edge; a thin tongue of light would lick the bare willow twigs and then immediately disappear; long, angular shadows, bursting in for a moment, would take it in turns to run right up to flames: the gloom was fighting with the light. Occasionally the flame burned less strongly and the circle of light shrank, out of the advancing darkness a horse's head would suddenly poke up, bay-coloured with a crooked flash, or all white, would gaze at us closely and vacantly, hurriedly chewing the long grass, and, dropping once more, would disappear at once.
> (See Russian Texts, No.112)

The language here is as dynamic as the conflict it describes: the glow *trembles, dies down, thrusts out*, the flame *flares up, throws flickers*; a tongue of light *licks* the twigs and *disappears*; shadows *burst in* and *run up* to the fires; the circle of light *shrinks*. But this is not the anthropomorphism of the 'pathetic fallacy': the forces of nature are engaged in a mythic struggle where man is almost irrelevant; only the ghostly horses' heads provide a link between the primitive battle of natural forces and the human world.

We will have to return to the symbolic function of the interplay between light and darkness, and the role played by animals and birds as intermediaries between the alien worlds of nature-and-the-supernatural and the tenuously secure world of man. For the time being, let us test the categories of the functions of setting that we outlined in the first section and see how far they account for the back- · ground of Turgenev's story.

In terms of basic information we learn that the narrator loses his way home in a particular named area of Tula province, a favourite huntig area of mixed woodland and undulating open country to the south of Moscow. The month is July and the story spans one evening, night and sunrise. A sense of authenticity is first created by naming particular locations—'Parakhin Bushes', 'Sindeyev Plantation'—and then undermined when he finds he is wrong. We know from the *Sportsman's Sketches* as a whole that the narrator is a youngish member of the landed gentry who enjoys enriching his hunting expeditions by observing and talking to a variety of peasant types whom he encounters. The social background of the boy-horseherds is described explicitly in a paragraph that is worth quoting since it typifies Turgenev's tendency to move from a generalized static account to a vivid piece of particularized dynamic description

> I was mistaken in thinking that the people sitting around the fires were drovers. They were simply young peasant lads from the nearby village who were guarding the herd. In hot summer weather our folk drive the horses out into the fields at night to graze: in the daytime they would get no peace from flies. Driving the herd out early in the evening and bringing them back at sunrise is a great treat for the peasant boys. Astride the liveliest colts, hatless and in their old sheepskin jackets, they gallop around gaily whooping and shouting, waving their arms and legs about, springing high into the air and laughing loudly. The powdery dust rises like a yellow column and follows in their path; you hear the cheerful galloping from afar off, the horses run with their ears pricked; ahead of them all, with his tail trailing and constantly changing pace, gallops some shaggy chestnut with thistles in his tangled mane.

And, once again, it is a semi-wild horse that provides the link between the human world and nature.

The setting, then, helps to fix the social framework and provides a comment on it. Perhaps the only way in which it helps to define a character's individual personality is in the figure of Pavlusha, the most practical, down-to-earth and courageous of the boys, who constantly ventures out of the circle of firelight into the enveloping darkness and, ultimately, has the most real contact with the supernatural world of the boys's stories. Of course, the narrator himself is frequently defined by his reactions to the setting. The story opens with a detailed but very generalized description of a typical July day, which very curiously combines objective observation with a sense of incipient drama without actually mentioning the observer. The purely factual account of the changes in the sky from early morning to noon to sunset is given an emotional resonance by adjectives and adverbs of emotion and by the syntactic tension of adversative conjunctions like 'but' and 'unless' and a recurrent pattern of negative introduction, that is, features being first defined in terms of what they are *not* before we are told what they are. As a poetic device this is reminiscent of the negative-comparison presentation of the Russian oral epic poems (*byliny*) 'Tis not the bright falcon that swoops on geese and swans/And on the little grey ducks that migrate—It is the warrior of Holy Russia that swoops Down, down upon that Tartar army.'[18] (See Russian Texts, No.113) The 'morning' section of Turgenev's description will serve to illustrate these features (adversatives and introduction-through-negation are in italics in the Russian text, while broken underlining indicates these epithets and adverbs which seem to contain some emotional involvement of the unseen observer)

> From earliest morning the sky is clear; the morning light does not burn like a furnace: it suffuses the sky with a shy blush. The sun is not fiery, not white-hot as it is in the drought of a heat-wave, not a dull crimson as before a storm, but bright and radiant with its welcome—it floats up peacefully beneath a long narrow cloud, shines through freshly and plunges into its violet mists. The thin upper edge of the stretched-out cloud glitters with snaky whisps; their shine is like forged silver . . . But suddenly the dancing beams gush out, —and merrily and magnificently, as if soaring upwards, the mighty orb rises. (See Russian Texts, No.114)

Apart from the emotional involvement of the epithets marked, this passage exemplifies two important and pervasive features of Turgenev's prose style in general that were noted by Chicherin:[19] (1) the double epithet whose function is both musical and semantic, involving either a transition from one feature to another: 'not fiery, not white-hot' (*ne ognistoye, ne askalennoye*); 'bright and welcomingly radiant' (*svetloye i privetno-luchezarnoye*), or else the juxtaposition of two separate but mutually conditioning epithets: 'dull crimson' (*tusklo bagrovoye*); 'merrily and magnificently' (*veselo i velichavo*); (2) verbs, signifying qualities rather than actions, that bring to the surface the poetic essence of an object, particularly powerful in this passage as a result of the tension between the imagery of fire: 'burns like a furnace . . . fiery . . . white hot . . . forged' (*pylayet pozharom . . . ognistoye . . . raskalennoye . . . kovanogo*) and of water: 'is suffused . . . floats up . . . plunges . . . gush out' (*razlivayetsya . . . vsplyvayet . . . pogruzitsya . . . khlynuli*). Finally, the musicality of this piece of prose poetry is enhanced by the alliteration of the consonants and assonance of the vowels of the key word *svetilo* (/s/, /v/, /t/, and /l/; /e/, /i/, /o/) in the rising cadence of the penultimate phrase—**i veselo i velichavo slovno vzletaya**. The effect is to strengthen both the harmony and the power of the semantically crucial final word: the chord is resolved in a towering crescendo.

The point of our apparent digression into linguistic minutiae here is to stress the extent to which Turgenev engages the reader's involvement in what appears to be a purely factual description. The narrator is not evident as a personality yet, but his image is refracted for us through the semantic and musical qualities of the style, like a ghostly holograph constructed out of laser beams.

Even when the narrator has labelled himself as a hunter returning from grouse-shooting in Tula province, it is the setting and his reactions to it that define his personality: he is seeking the security and comfort of the familiar, but encounters only the discomfort and insecurity of an alien landscape

> With rapid strides I crossed the long 'plantation' of bushes. clambered up the hill and, instead of the expected familiar plain with its oak-grove to the right and the little low white church in the distance, saw quite different places that I did not know at all. At my feet stretched a narrow valley; directly ahead a dense aspen wood reared up like a sheer wall.

The cosily organized landscape painting, with its broad plain, its oak-grove to the right and its (diminutive) white church in the middle distance, has been blocked out by a natural world of constrictions and obstruction ('narrow... dense... sheer'). The narrator's response is to panic: 'I halted in bewilderment, and looked around me... "Aha!—I thought,—I've landed up in quite the wrong spot: I was tending too far over to the right"—and surprised at my own mistake, I rushed down the hill.' The stress here is on human error ('the wrong spot... too far... mistake'), but the scene acquires more sinister features

> I was immediately overwhelmed by an unpleasant, unmoving dampness, just as if I had gone down into a cellar; the dense high grass on the bottom of the valley was all wet and glowed whitely like a flat tablecloth; somehow I couldn't bear to walk on it... Bats were already skimming above the sleeping tops of the aspen trees, mysteriously wheeling and trembling on the dimly bright sky; a late hawk flew fast and straight in the upper air, hurrying to its nest.

The opposition between the lonely hunter-narrator seeking security and a mysteriously threatening nature is focussed in the hawk and the bats. The narrator tries to rationalize himself back from an unencompassable dream world (epithets and negatives in italics in Russian Texts) into a real world where places have names

> At last I made it to the corner of the wood, but there was no path there: some kind of uncleared low bushes spread out wide in front of me, while the deserted prairie could be seen far far away beyond them. I stopped again. 'What's going on?... Wherever am I, then?' I tried recalling how and where I had walked in the course of the day... 'Hey! but that's Parakhin

Bushes!—I exclaimed at last,—Precisely! And that must be Sindeyev Wood
. . . So how on earth did I get here! So far off beam . . . '
(See Russian Texts, No.115)

But place-names no longer help; night falls, nature in her most ominous aspect
becomes more and more the active agent, the narrator the passive victim (note
the distribution of active and passive verbs), and the hawk intent on home
becomes some disorientated and unidentifiable night bird—again a wild creature
as intermediary between the supernatural and human worlds

> Meanwhile night was approaching and growing like a storm cloud; darkness
> seemed to be rising all around with the evening mists and even pouring down
> from above. I came upon an untrodden, overgrown path and set off down it,
> carefully looking where I was going. All around me everything was turning
> black and going still, and only the quail called now and then. A small night
> bird rushing low and noiselessly on its soft wings almost crashed into me and
> wheeled aside in fright. I came out on the edge of the bushy area and picked
> my way along a boundary strip. I was already finding it difficult to pick out
> the more distant objects; the fields lay white and dim all round; and beyond
> them the gloomy darkness advanced with every moment in massive clouds.
> (See Russian Texts, No.116)

Another example of brilliant poetic mimesis at the end of this passage is where
the unconstricted cosonants /l/ and /n/, depicting the open expanse of fields,
give way to the highly constrictive consonant clusters (in heavy type): /zd/,
/mgn/, /dv/, /gr/, /dn/, /vzd/, /mr/ which, combining sonant and stop consonants articulated in different parts of the mouth, are as difficult to pronounce as
the darkness was to penetrate. [20]

When the narrator stumbles into a shallow dell with its standing white stones
gathered as if for a secret meeting, we have left far behind the comforting familiarity of villages with white churches and have entered a dark pagan world of
superstitious dread and nature worship. Virtually all the past verb forms and
adjectives are neuter now [italics in the Russian text], and again it requires an
animal's voice to express his fear and anxiety

> I was at once overcome by a strange feeling. This dell was shaped like an almost
> perfect cauldron with gently sloping sides; standing upright at the bottom were
> several large white stones,—it looked as if they had crawled together to hold a
> secret meeting there,—and it was so dumb and muffled down there, and the sky
> hung over it so flat and mournful, that my heart shrank. Some little wild creature
> gave a weak and pitiful squeak among the rocks.
> (See Russian Texts, No.117)

So far we have seen that in the first part of the story, which seems at first sight to
be purely a piece of landscape painting, the setting is used to establish the character and mood of one of the principal participants, the first person narrator. But

we must not exaggerate: the first few pages are a brilliant piece of literary landscape painting too; and for all his helplessness and superstition in the face of the alien forces of nature at nightfall, his account is saved from sentimentality by irony. The most alien and supernatural point in his journey is compared to that most familiar and domestic of objects, a cooking-pot or cauldron. And while his secret dread is being transmitted through the wheeling of night birds and the squeaking of animals, we still have his English setter, 'Dianka' (a Russianized diminutive of the mythological huntress), as an animal mediating with the world of civilization

> 'Now where can I be?'—I repeated again out loud, stopped for a third time and looked enquiringly at my yellow-spotted English setter Dianka, unmistakably the most intelligent of all four-footed creatures. But the most intelligent of four-footed creatures only waved her little tail, mournfully blinked her tired eyes and could give me no worthwhile advice at all.
> (See Russian Texts, No.118)

However helpless and unassertive the man and hunter at this moment of despair, in his role as *narrator* he preserves full initiative to switch the tone of his narrative.

We have shown that the setting in *Bezhin Meadow* plays a fairly decisive role in revealing the narrator's character: nature is an active force impinging on both his consciousness and his actions, and through his reactions we refract the essential traits of his character. Is the setting as important in the delineation of the boys' characters? It is, but in a much more subtly integrated way. Turgenev's sportsman is a fairly stock figure from the genres of the thematic essay and the sentimental journey, and we might regard this characterization as a device for emphasizing his sensitivity and increasing the value of his function as a frame for the central stories of the 'sketch', i.e. those of the boys. That is to say, the setting functions in two of the ways we outlined in the first section of this chapter: *informatively* and *structurally*.

But this dual function of the setting is even more significant in relation to the boys, and this highly original aspect of Turgenev's art seems to have received little attention from the commentators on *A Sportsman's Sketches*. The central section of the story opens with a pen portrait of each of the five boys in turn: the narrator first guesses their age, then focusses on their general appearance, their face, their hair, their expression, and their clothing. With brilliant economy he is able to convert a few minimal bits of information into a provisional assessment of their social background and individual personality (in the case of Kostya it is the very *lack* of physical description that marks the inwardness of his character). Equally brilliantly Turgenev then summarizes the portraits he has drawn in the briefest possible description of the boys' poses: Pavlusha, the practical one, kneeling to watch the potatoes cook; Fedya, the eldest and master-of-ceremonies, reclining in casual relaxation; Ilyusha wearing an anxious frown; Kostya, with head thrust forward, gazing somewhere into the distance; Vanya motionless beneath his *bast* mat. So, with the characterization over, we can get on with the stories? No, because the very

way the stories are told, their subject-matter, form, style and manner of telling are
not merely consistent with the image we have of their characters, but refract it further. Characterization is not our main theme for this chapter, and it would require a
whole separate chapter to map the intricacy of the interweaving of narrative manner and personality: Ilyusha's authority on the folklore of the supernatural, but his
tendency to give his ghost stories a realistic context; Kostya's nervy superstitious-
ness that needs the firm constraints of ritual story-telling to preserve some ration-
ality; Pavlusha's down-to-earth realism, which finds a cheerfully rational explanation for the most mysterious phenomena; Fedya's contribution in drawing out the
others to tell their stories; and Vanya's near-invisibility as he hides away from the
world of ghosts his older companions are invoking.

What of the setting? Does the natural background simply disappear once the
boys' narration section is launched? By no means: each of the nine internal narratives is framed by an observation about the scene by the bonfire or sounds from
the surrounding darkness. Structurally, then, the setting operates once more as a
framing device, but a complex and subtle one, since the natural feature described
usually has features in common with both the preceding and the following
stories; like a series of modulating chords relating two distinct keys in a sonata, it
provides both a separating frame and a linking transition. The splashing sound,
of perhaps a pike, links Ilyusha's story of the goblin at the water-mill with
Kostya's story of Gavrila and the water-nymph; a white dove flying into the
glow of the firelight links the story of Baba Ulyana foreseeing her own death (a
departing spirit) with Pavlusha's and Ilyusha's account of Trishka, the Antichrist
(a Holy Ghost). But informatively too these glimpses of setting tell us more
about the boys' personalities. There is a characteristic dialogue after the second
story, Kostya's account of Gavrila being summoned by a water-nymph: Fedya
comments 'But there must be water-nymphs around here too, mustn't there?',
eliciting further information or stories, to which Kostya replies, 'No, this is a
pure spot without any spirits', but adds with typical apprehension 'The only
thing is—the river's not far away.' We then have the narrator's own description
of the curious twanging sound (borrowed by Chekhov in *The Cherry Orchard*?),
at which Ilyusha characteristically whispers 'The power of the Cross be with
us!', whereas Pavlusha, ever practical and concerned with the needs of this
world, exclaims 'Hey, you wretched crows, what are you scared of? Look, the
spuds are done.' We will quote this whole passage to illustrate this remarkable
interplay of structural linkage/framing and informative characterization of four
different characters

   —Did your dad tell you all that himself?—went on Fedya.
   —He did. I was lying in the loft and heard everything.
   —It's weird! Why should he be so sad? . . . I mean, she must have taken a
liking to him to call him like that.
   —Oh, she did,—put in Ilyusha.—Oh yes. She wanted to tickle him to death,
that's what she wanted. That's what they do, those water-nymphs

—But there must be water-nymphs round here too, mustn't there?—commented Fedya.

—No,—answered Kostya—this is a pure spot without any spirits. The only thing is—the river's not far away.

They all fell silent. Suddenly from somewhere a long way off came a pro-longed, resonant, almost wailing sound, one of those inexplicable sounds of the night which sometimes break out in the deep silence, rise upon the air, linger and slowly fade at last as though dying away. You listen, and there seems to be nothing there, yet the resonance is still there. It's as though some-one had uttered a long drawn-out cry under the very vault of heaven, and someone else had responded in the woods with shrill, harsh laughter, and a faint hissing whistle soars along the river. The boys exchanged glances and shivered . . .

—The power of the Cross be with us!—whispered Ilyusha.

—Hey, you wretched crows!—shouted Pavel,—What are you scared of? Look, the spuds are done. (They all came up to the pot and began to eat the steaming potatoes; only Vanya did not stir.) What about you then?—said Pavel.

But he didn't creep out from under his mat. The pot was soon completely empty.

Not only the four active boys are characterized here; even Vanya's timid *inaction* is governed by the dynamic setting.

A similar interaction among the boys provides the final frame for the series of internal stories before they all settle down to sleep. While Pavel is away filling the pot with water from the river, Kostya tells the story of the boy, Vasya, who had drowned in this same river. His narration is in a vivid colloquial style and has the ritualized structure of the folk-hagiography: (1) the hero's sterling qualities in childhood; (2) his mother's foreboding; (3) her ritual invocation; (4) the crisis as he drowns; (5) the mourning lament. The dying cadence of this tale is inter-rupted by the appearance of Pavel—whose visit to the river was the motivation for its telling

—Here comes Pavlusha,—said Fedya.

Pavel came up to the fire carrying a full cooking pot.

—You know, lads—he began after a pause,—something awful's happened.

—Oh, what?—asked Kostya hurriedly

—I heard Vasya's voice.

They all shuddered.

—What, what d'you mean?—stammered Kostya.

—God's honour. I was just bending down towards the water and suddenly hear my name being called in Vasya's voice just as though it came from under the water: 'Pavlusha, hey, Pavlusha, come here.' I got away. But I managed to scoop some water.

—Oh, God have mercy on us, have mercy on us!—said the boys, crossing themselves.

—That was the water-spirit calling you, Pavel,—added Fedya . . . —And there we were just talking about Vasya.

—Ah, that's a bad omen,—said Ilyusha slowly.

—Well, never mind, let it be!—declared Pavel firmly and he sat down again,—There's no dodging your fate.

Again Fedya is the initiator of new topics here, Ilyusha the expert on superstition, Kostya the focus of nervous reactions, and Pavel the practical, no-nonsense boy. Each time the setting impinges on the boys in the course of their storytelling, whether in the form of mysterious noises or intrusions of wild birds and animals, Pavel either rallies them to practical tasks or has a rational explanation to calm their alarm: the dogs were merely barking at a wolf; a dove flying into the glow of the bonfire is looking for a perch for the night; a mysterious noise is a heron calling or, if it isn't the soul of Akim the woodcutter complaining, it is just frogs; and the last whistling they hear is just snipe migrating. Pavlusha is clearly the one who most consistently captures the narrator's attention with his courage and decisiveness: 'I couldn't help admiring Pavlusha. He was very attractive at that moment. His far from handsome face, animated by the swift ride, was flushed with bold adventurousness and unflinching determination. Without so much as a twig in his hand, at night, without a moment's hesitation, he had galloped off after a wolf . . . "What a fine lad!"—I thought as I gazed at him.'

Most Soviet commentators, along with their Slavophile predecessors in the nineteenth century, use passages like this to advance their thesis that *Bezhin Meadow*, like the other *Sportsman's Sketches*, was primarily an attempt by the liberal Turgenev to undermine the clichés about peasant fecklessness or clownishness that had typified Court and bourgeois Russian literature before him (rather like the image of the British working class or the American negro in films before the 1960s) and to show his positive traits of dignity (Fedya), sensitivity (Kostya), culture (Ilyusha), and courage and practicality (Pavel). This element is undoubtedly present in *Bezhin Meadow*—and it was certainly a major reason for the rapturous reception with which the stories were greeted as they appeared in the literary magazine *Sovremennik* between 1847 and 1851. But to focus exclusively on this element is to ignore the narrative structure of this story and, most importantly, the interaction of setting and character on which the story hinges.

So far we have analyzed in some detail the informative and structural functions of setting in the story and have discovered a commentative function, insofar as the boys' and the narrator's reactions to their surroundings reveal positive or negative traits of their characters and social background. The priority we give to this function will ultimately depend on our own political convictions and aesthetic taste. But we have barely begun to consider the symbolic function of setting, which is vital to an interpretation of this story. Symbols are devices for

focussing, on an instantly perceivable scale, the multiple strands of meaning in a
work of art: as lenses refract light-waves, symbols refract waves of meaning. The
last of the boys' dialogues, which we analyzed above, clearly provides us with
further information about their characters and clearly provides a structural transition (both a frame and a link) between the central section of nine narratives by
the boys and the narratorial frame of the sportsman's sleep, departure and reactions to the dawn. But one narrative moment in this dialogue is of crucial
symbolic significance to the whole story: it is Pavel who hears the voice of the
drowned Vasya summoning him. That is, the most practical and least superstitious of the boys is the only one who actually experiences the supernatural within
the time dimension of the story. The other boys, Ilyusha and Kostya, attest to
their own or others' eye-witness accounts of ghostly visions, but these have
already been transmuted into the prefabricated form of stories. Pavel typically
shrugs aside his fear with the curt boast: 'But I managed to scoop some water',
but the fact remains that he actually heard Vasya's ghostly voice at precisely the
time when the other boys, unbeknown to him, were talking about Vasya.

I would claim that Pavel's brief experience of the supernatural is symbolic for
the whole story and, indeed, constitutes a central peripeteia for *Bezhin Meadow*
which allows for a thematic integration by the reader of the four apparently distinct sections, which otherwise are held together by rather tenuous structural
links: the long opening section of the narrator losing his way and coming upon
the boys; the description of the boys and their stories; the narrator's departure
and homeward journey; and finally, the disturbingly laconic epilogue: 'Unfortunately I must add that in that same year Pavel met his end. He was not
drowned: he was killed when he fell from a horse. Such a shame, he was a splen-
did lad!' So Pavel did not 'dodge his fate'. But his death was not the one that
seemed to be ordained by the voice of the drowned Vasya or the watery setting of
most of the boys' stories: death came out of the darkness that surrounds our
waking, conscious, rational lives—like a horse's head or a dove swooping suddenly into the bonfire's glow—and snatched the peasant lad who perhaps had
most to contribute if the yoke of serfdom was ever lifted—as, of course, it was,
precisely ten years later. The horse as a means of death is a brilliant exploitation of
that element of the story's setting—animals and birds—which consistently acts
as intermediary between the security of the rational world of man and the risks
lurking in the supernatural.

The natural setting, then, is simultaneously all three elements: the safe manageable world of familiar woods, small white churches, papermills, bridges, hills
and fields; the threatening supernatural world of unknown dells, mysterious
convocations of stones, ghostly apparitions, goblins, wood-sprites and water-
nymphs, voices from the beyond, and the mystery of a fourteen-year-old's accidental death; and between these, the sound and sight of animals and birds,
bonfire sparks flying out into the darkness and shadows looming into the light,
and, perhaps, stories, anecdotes and folk superstitions, which at once give the

rational mind some sense of controlling the supernatural and bring that alien world alive with words. Turgenev is, I think, deliberately ambiguous in *Bezhin Meadow* about whether the boys' summoning up of the supernatural in their stories actually induced Pavel's death. His cool denial of Pavel's being drowned (had we really expected that?) leaves open that interpretation. What is quite unambiguous throughout the story is the dynamic role of the setting. Whether it is the sun bursting through clouds on a hot July day, or the last rays of light resisting the advancing gloom, or a brightly gilded church on a hill versus a sombre dell, or the bonfire light fighting the encroaching darkness, or the warmth of human conviviality against the cold of loneliness, or enlightenment hopefully triumphant over ignorance—everywhere the unifying symbol of *Bezhin Meadow* is 'the gloom was fighting with the light' (*mrak borolsya so svetom*).

III   Chekhov: *The Peasants*, 1897; (*Muzhiki*) [21]

We might have subtitled this chapter 'A tale of two meadows', since the meadow is a central element in the setting of both Turgenev's and Chekhov's stories. As so often with the *topoi*, or 'common-places', that we illustrated in the first section, the meadow fulfils several functions in both cases. It may be instructive to consider the similarities and the differences in the functioning of Bezhin meadow and the meadow below the village of Zhukovo in Chekhov's story.

In purely informative terms, we know that both meadows are low-lying with a river running through and they are both used for grazing, one for horses and the other for cattle and geese. They also serve as a place of recreation and conviviality: story-telling at night among five small boys around a bonfire, or singing and dancing and church-going for the brightly dressed girls of Zhukovo. But these resemblances have structural, commentative and symbolic implications which are very different in each story. Bezhin meadow lies low by contrast with the hilly, wooded and broken ground that the narrator first has to negotiate; it is a haven of comfort and human conviviality, protected by a bend in the river, and structurally it forms the arena for the major central section of the story. But the river is also a potent source of danger from the supernatural, recreated in the boys' stories, and the grazing horses, beside their socio-economic function, behave as a symbolic link between the 'real' world of the bonfire light and the mysterious enveloping darkness. As we have seen, the play of light and dark is also the play of the social and the natural worlds and, with growing symbolic intensity, of the natural and supernatural worlds.

Structurally, Chekhov's meadow is transitional rather than focal: the river is a boundary between two equally green, lush, grazed meadows; but while the one leads gently up to the trees round the manor-house and the five cupolas of the church of the peaceful and prosperous large village (*selo*) opposite, the other leads up a steep clay scarp-slope, broken by random paths and the litter of broken pottery, to the booze-hut (*kabak*) and the wretched huts of the small village (*derevnya*) of Zhukovo. Apart from this socio-economic transition, the meadow offers a kind of occasional respite, for Ol'ga and the reader, from the miseries of family and public life in Zhukovo, a pastoral symbol of the life that might have been in the Russian countryside, a pointer to a world where educated middle-class confidence and competence and Christian compassion might illuminate the dark, mean, selfish, cruel lives of the peasants.

Bearing in mind this central difference between the two stories—Turgenev bridging the real and the supernatural, Chekhov the real and the desirable—let us look more systematically at the functions of setting in *The Peasants*. As Thomas Bruford points out: 'It is characteristic that even the scene of the action is usually not given a name, or not a real one. It is simply in the country, or in a small or large town, and in the absence of other indications it is apparently to be taken as in the heart of Russia.' [22] Zhukovo might be anywhere in central Russia; as it happens, we know from Chekhov's biography that *The Peasants* is based on conditions he had observed only too closely while working for the previous five years among the peasants at Melikhovo, some fifty miles south of Moscow. The tension between country and town comes out forcefully in the characters, their relation with each other, and even their style of speech. Chekhov provides an explicit sociological account of the effects of urbanization on Russian village life since the Emancipation at the beginning of the third section, when the relatives visit the Chikil'deyev household on Sunday to hear news from Nikolai and Ol'ga

> All the Zhukovo lads who could read and write used to be taken off to Moscow and put only into waiters' and floor-porters' jobs (just as the ones from the big village over yonder only got jobs as bakers), and this had been the way it was for ages, even before the Emancipation of the Serfs when some Zhukovo peasant called Luka Ivanych, by now a legend, who was working as a buffet-waiter in one of the Moscow clubs, had got jobs in his line only for his own villagers, and they, once they had got on their feet, would send for their own relatives and get them jobs in inns and restaurants; and ever since then the village of Zhukovo had been known to the other inhabitants in the area as 'Loutsville' (*Khamskaya*) or 'Lackeyton' (*Kholuyevka*).

The implicit social comment is already here in the nicknames and in the different status of the jobs which the men from the manorial village can expect. But Chekhov builds this commentary right into the artistic structure of the story by making Nikolai and his wife and daughter behave like townspeople (their politeness and gentility, but also their self-pity), react as city-dwellers to rural crudity (their vision of the hut, of Kiryak's treatment of Marya, grandma's beatings), and, most remarkably, in their language. In the very first paragraph the narrator's neutral exposition of the situation—which Thomas Winner likens to a medical case study[23]—shifts into the mode of free indirect discourse which reflects Nikolai's way of thinking directly in the syntactic order, the choice of colloquialisms and evaluative words (italicized in the Russian text): 'Whatever money there had been of his own or his wife's he had spent on getting cures, there was nothing left to feed on, he got bored doing nothing, and so he decided that he really ought to go home to his own village. It'd be easier being poorly at home, and cheaper to live; it's true what they say: at home the walls support you.' (See Russian Texts, No. 119) Ol'ga, his wife, provides the central consciousness for the whole story and the touchstone for the crudity of rural life, and yet in her speech she epitomizes the most irritating habits of a peasant woman who has adapted to town ways: her vision of life and religion is built of stereotypes, and her language never deviates far from the cliché, whether of liturgy and scripture, folk proverb or chant, or terms of endearment

> —E-eh, deary,—she said, as she settled down to bed in the hay beside Marya, —You can't cure grief with crying! Just put up with things. In the scriptures it says: whosoever shall smite thee on thy right cheek, turn to him the other also . . . E-eh, deary!
> Then in a chanting undertone she told her about Moscow and her life there working as a chamber-maid in furnished rooms.
> —And in Moscow the houses are big and built of stone,—she said,—There are many many churches, forty times forty, deary, and in the houses they're all gentle folk, such beautiful, such refined people!
> (See Russian Texts, No. 120)

Ol'ga's sisters-in-law respond very differently to her refinement: for Marya, Ol'ga represents an unattainable but consoling dream; for Fekla, she embodies all that is most alien and artificial in city manners, and from the context of Section 6 it is clear that Chekhov values her crude country vitality above the effete bourgeois mannerisms of Ol'ga

> One morning,—it was already the beginning of September,—Fekla brought up two buckets of water; she was pink from the cold, healthy and beautiful; Marya and Ol'ga were sitting at the table and drinking tea.
> —Tea and sugar!—she said mockingly.—Quite the fancy ladies!—she added, putting down the buckets.—They've got in the habit of taking tea every day. Watch out you don't get all blown-up with the tea!—she went on, looking at Ol'ga with hatred.—You've really lived it up in Moscow with your puffy face, you fat bitch! She swung round her yoke and struck Ol'ga on the shoulder so that both sisters-in-law could only clap their hands and exclaim:
> —Oh, lordy!
> (See Russian Texts, No. 121)

(A note in Chekhov's diary for February 19th 1897, when he was writing the story, makes clear how close his attitude is to that of Fekla: 'Dinner at the "Continental" to commemorate the great reform [the Emancipation, in 1861].

Boring and irrelevant. To eat dinner, drink champagne, make a racket, and make
speeches about the self-awareness of the people and about their conscience and
freedom, and so forth, while all around the table slaves in tail-coats, those same
serfs, keep darting around and coachman wait outside in the frost—is to lie to the
Holy Spirit.')

As several of our quotations have shown already, the *time* in which the story is
set, Chekhov's 'present', thirty-six years after the Emancipation of the Serfs, is
important to the theme of the story. In the evening after Fekla's conversation
with Ol'ga and Marya the whole family are sitting in the hut, lit by a solitary
candle, winding silk for the local factory—enough to make, perhaps, twenty
kopecks a week. (Later, in the winter, they do tailoring and bootmaking jobs at
home and it is clear that the peasant economy is dependent on the exploitation
involved in this kind of cottage industry.) The topic of conversation is 'the good
old days', before Emancipation, which the old man recalls in a kind of naive
folksy chant

> —It was beter with the masters,—the old man was saying as he wound the
> silk.—You'd work, and eat, and sleep, everything in its proper order. You'd
> get cabbage soup and gruel for dinner, and more again for supper. Cucumbers
> and cabbage—as much as you liked: you'd eat voluntarily, to your heart's
> content. And there was more discipline. Everyone knew his place.
> (See Russian Texts, No. 12)

—not a very memorable diet, but better than dirty bread and tea smelling of fish-
heads! But Osip's memory, like the lamp, burns dimly and smokily, and when
someone's shadow blots it out, the bright moonlight takes over. Moonlight
nearly always represents the truth behind human self-deception in Chekhov, and
it becomes clear that Osip is idealizing the memory of those colourful days when
the peasants were used as beaters by the hunting landowners and were rewarded
with the essence of their demoralization—vodka—while all the fat game was
carted off to the groaning tables of Moscow (town versus country again).

Grandma's memories reveal that even the women of the gentry when she was
young were subordinated to the drunkenness and debauchery of their menfolk
(we may notice that the narratorial voice takes over here and the resulting free
indirect speech gives priority to accurate and lucid syntax over the odd colloquial
phrase)

> She told them about her mistress, a kindly, god-fearing woman, whose
> husband was a rake and a debaucher and all of whose daughters had got
> married the Lord knew how: one had married a drunkard, another a petty-
> bourgeois, while the third had been carried off secretly (Granny herself, still
> just a girl, had helped carry her off), and they'd all quickly died of grief just
> like their mother. And recalling all this, Granny even sobbed.
> (See Russian Texts, No. 123)

The 'town versus country' theme takes over again as the little, bald, gnome-like ex-chef of General Zhukov calls to stay the night and swaps cooks' yarns with Nikolai. The full comedy and pathos of today's derivative but grandiose French cuisine when juxtaposed with the rough but adventurous style of Russian cooking in the old days emerges neatly in their last exchange

> They talked about rissoles and cutlets, various soups and sauces, and the chef, who also remembered everything well, told them the names of dishes which were no longer made; for instance, there was a dish that was made out of the eyes of bulls and was known as 'morning awakening'
> —But did they make Cotelettes Maréchal?—asked Nikolai.
> —No.
> —Oh, what a poor lot of chefs you were!
> (See Russian Texts, No. 124)

Section 6 ends on the two most ironically ambiguous touches of the whole story. Marya gets up at dawn to milk the cow, and Nikolai climbs down from the stove, gets his tail-coat out of his case, puts it on and going over to the window, strokes the sleeves, grips the lapels—and smiles. Then he carefully takes it off, hides it away and lies down again. For Chekhov, as for all the great Russian 'realists', the truth is beyond speech,[24] and it is the actions of the least articulate characters that signify the most. After Nikolai's heart-rending attempt to recapture his identity, Marya comes back and kindles the stove, and it is she, the inarticulate butt of the drunken Kiryak's lust and beatings, the helpless slave of the household, the mindless child-bearer, the peasant most imprisoned by all the conditions of post-Emancipation Russia, who, half-asleep, 'must have dreamed something or recalled the previous day's stories, because she stretched deliciously in front of the stove and said:—No, freedom [i.e. Emancipation] is better!'

Two other aspects of the setting in time are significant in the story: times of the day and seasons of the year. The times of the day have the purely practical function of 'fixing' the typical activities of the peasants—milking and stove-kindling at dawn, harvesting and animal-minding in the heat of the day, bringing in the cattle and geese at sunset, cottage industries and story-telling in the evenings, restless and frustrated sleep at nights. But Chekhov always uses them to create moods: hope in the morning, vigorous activity in the noonday, anxiety or consolation in the evening, despair and the stark truth at night: small wonder that most of the scenes in *The Peasants* are set in the evening or at night; only the children are observed in the heat of the day and the other least articulate characters (Nikolai, Marya) or the most blindly optimistic (Ol'ga) in the morning.

The seasons of the year in the story share this archetypal function. The story, being an 'anatomy' of peasant life (the official censor, more perceptive than most, even referred to it as an 'article'), spans a whole winter. The early sections, in autumn, have the elegiac quality of a sombre resignation (of Ol'ga and

Nikolai, and, we feel, of Chekhov himself) to the stark facts of present-day peasant life; but winter brings, with Nikolai's death, a pitiless analysis of what is wrong and where the responsibility lies; and the spring thaw brings new hope and a new life—albeit back in the city—for Ol'ga and Sasha, and even a hope for the redemption of Kiryak. But the seasons of the solar year are also related to festivals of the Orthodox Christian calendar—Sundays, the fast for the Feast of the Dormition (August) or of the Protection of the Virgin (October), Christmas and Easter. This is where the setting in time develops its fully symbolic function, which we will return to later.

We have already considered some aspects of the general social framework, the accompanying social commentary, and the social role of some of the characters as defined by the story's background in time and place. The remainder of what we have to say on these topics will, perhaps, be best related simultaneously to the commentative, structural and symbolic functions of setting.

In his very explicit discussion on the last pages of the story about who is to blame for the peasants' wretchedness and demoralization (too explicit to be really Ol'ga's thoughts on the matter), Chekhov blames the ignorance and illiteracy, the greed and lack of self-respect of the peasants themselves, the arrogance and greed of officials and exploiters, but does not mention the landowners. Indeed, the only landowners we meet in the story are part of the setting. As we have seen, the river and meadows create a powerful opposition between the poverty and hopelessness of Zhukovo and the comfortable confidence of the village with the church opposite. When Ol'ga, through whose consciousness we perceive this opposition, goes to the church on the Sunday morning after her arrival, she sees the congregation step aside for the landowner's family. The two girls in white dresses and broad-brimmed hats and the plump pink boy in a sailor suit impress Ol'ga: 'From the first glance she decided that these were orderly, educated and beautiful people'. Appearing at the end of Section 2, they are clearly juxtaposed with the two girls and a son of the peasant family, who close Section 1—the sisters-in-law, Marya and Fekla, and Marya's brutal husband, Kiryak. The contrast is highlighted by Marya's quite different reaction to the 'beautiful people': 'But Marya scowled at them dismally and drearily, as if they weren't people who had come in but monsters that might crush her if she didn't get out of their way. And whenever the deacon intoned anything in a bass voice she imagined the shout "Ma-arya!"—and shuddered.' The land-owner's daughters only appear once more in the story, this time with the elder son who comes to help put out the fire. The 'burning house' *topos* recurs throughout nineteenth-century fiction as the dramatic moment that shows up, illuminates even, people in their true colours. In this scene the drunken or incompetent peasants have chaotically failed to put the fire out, and workers from the estate opposite have brought a proper fire-engine. They are led by a young student on horseback whose competence is explicitly juxtaposed with Kiryak's helplessness

But then from the lord's estate on the other side some foremen and workers arrived on two carts, bringing a fire-engine with them. A student arrived on horseback, wearing a white military jacket unbuttoned, very young. They began to hack with their axes and stood a ladder against the burning timbers and five men at once climbed up it, headed by the student who was red and shouting in a brusque husky voice, and his tone suggested that putting out fires was an everyday occurrence for him. They took the hut apart, log by log, dragged apart the byre, the wattle fencing and the nearest haystack.

—Don't let them break it!—angry voices could be heard in the crowd.—Don't let them!

—Kiryak aimed himself at the hut with a decisive air as if he intended to stop the outsiders from breaking things, but one of the workers turned him back and punched him in the neck. There was laughter, the worker punched him again, Kiryak fell over and crawled back into the crowd on all fours.

Two girls in bonnets had walked over from the other side, evidently the student's sisters. They stood some way off and watched the fire. The logs which had been dragged apart were no longer burning, but were smoking hard; the student, working the hose, directed the stream of water now at the logs, now at the peasants, now at the women struggling with pails of water.

—Georges!—shouted the girls reproachfully and in alarm.—Georges! [the name is pronounced here as in French].

The student's French name sums up the social distance between the folks 'over yonder' and the villagers, as do the two kinds of laughter in this episode: the girls' reproachful giggling as the masterful 'Georges' sprays the peasants with the hose, and the crowd's mocking laughter as the inept Kiryak makes a fool of himself.

As Donald Rayfield has pointed out,[25] the red glow of the fire, turning the sheep red and the doves pink (religious symbolism?) is the culmination of the imagery of sunset and redness, beginning with the first evening after Ol'ga's arrival in Zhukovo when she sees the setting sun reflected in the river

Sitting on the edge of the scarp, Nikolai and Ol'ga saw the sun setting, the sky, all gold and crimson, reflected in the river, in the church windows and through all the air which was soft and tranquil and inexpressibly pure as it never is in Moscow. And when the sun had set, the herd went past with bleating and lowing, geese flew home from the other side—and everything was hushed, the gentle light in the air dimmed and the evening gloom began to descend quickly.

But the gold and crimson light here has an apocalyptic quality as it glows in the river, the church windows and the pure air, while after the conflagration, or in the potter's fires on the steep slope below Zhukovo, it symbolizes the hellish elements in the peasants' lives. In both cases it is associated with gentle animals.

In both the scenes we have quoted the setting is used structurally to frame the key elements of peasant misery and ineptitude. In the first section the beatific evening light precedes a long description of the reunion of Nikolai's family, their wretched circumstances, and a violent scene from Kiryak, while the section ends with the cool bluish light of dawn and Fekla running bare-footed to her freedom. In the fire scene, once again Kiryak's ineptitude is framed by the competence of the student and the glow of the fire before and after it is brought under control.

The landowner's daughters and sons are part, then, of a landscape that is scarcely noticed by the peasants of Zhukovo, wrapped up in their care-ridden lives, and only glimpsed by Ol'ga, who has come to know and serve the gentry in the city. They are associated with the estate and church 'over yonder'. But the main characters in *The Peasants* also have their typical locations: as in *The Black Monk*, each of the characters has a typical setting, or 'sphere of influence', where his personality is best realized. The granny's sphere is the kitchen and larder, where she hides away all the fresh milk and decent food before serving the family with their fish-head soup and dry rye-crusts. For the grandfather and Kiryak it is the booze-hut, two doors away at the edge of the village, where they drown their sorrows and gain the courage to argue with granny or beat Marya. On the Sunday evening their pub songs are very neatly juxtaposed with the innocent dancing and singing of the girls in the meadow below (divided by the fires of the demonaic potter on the scarp)

> In the evening the potter on the scarp was firing pots. Down below in the meadow the girls were dancing in a ring and singing. An accordeon was playing. And over the river a solitary stove was burning and girls were singing, and from the distance this singing seemed gentle and harmonious. In and around the pub the peasants were making a racket; they were singing in drunken voices, all discordantly, and swearing so badly that Ol'ga just shuddered and said:
> —Oh, Lord! . . .

But this juxtaposed harmony and disharmony are at once brought together in one of those extraordinarily vivid and economical scenes in which Chekhov brilliantly fuses all the elements of his setting to epitomize a whole way of life

> It was after midnight, all the fires had died down on this side and over yonder, and down in the meadow and in the pub they were still celebrating. The old man and Kiryak, drunk, holding each other by the arm and bumping shoulders, went up to the barn where Ol'ga and Marya were in bed.
> —Leave her,—pleaded the old man,—Leave her . . . She's a harmless wench . . . It's a sin . . . She's not a bad wench.
> They both stood for a minute by the barn and moved on.
> —I lo-ove the flowers of the field!—the old man suddenly sang in a high

piercing tenor.—I l-ove to pluck them in the meadows! Then he spat, swore coarsely and went off to the hut.

(See Russian Texts, No. 125)

In between cursing and staggering, it is an innocent girls' song that the coarse old man sings after persuading Kiryak not to 'pluck' his long-suffering flower, Marya, yet again.

Marya's appointed place is in bed in the barn, whether hiding from Kiryak, yielding to him, or bearing his children. Nikolai's is in bed on the ledge above the stove: the safe, cosy centre of the home, the hide-away for frightened children, protected by hobgoblins and cockroaches, is the mark of his invalid status and the accompanying loss of status and respect (both ínvalid and inválid!). If Nikolai is trapped back into the ignominy of village life on the stove at the centre of the hut where he must spend his days and nights, no such symbolic prison can hold Fekla, the wife of his brother in the army. She is a free spirit, healthy, beautiful and selfish, who despises equally the shackles of rural and urban existence and is happily promiscuous among the bailiffs on the estate 'over yonder': her element is the river, where she bathes, washes clothes and fetches water, and this gives her both the mysterious supernatural quality of a water-nymph and an ability to exist in both of the worlds separated by the river

They approached the river. On the far side, right at the water's edge, a woman was standing and getting undressed.

—That's our Fekla,—said Marya, recognizing her,—She's been across the river to the master's yard. Been with the bailiffs. Such a hussy, and swearing —she's a terror!

Fekla, dark-browed, with her hair loose, still youthful and firm as a young girl, dived from the bank and pounded the water with her feet, and waves radiated from her in all directions.

—Such a hussy—a terror! repeated Marya.

Every time we meet Fekla it is in connection with water and knocking, and the stress is on her bare legs and her youthful beauty. Even when she has been stripped naked by the men 'over yonder' and has to beg Ol'ga to get her something to wear to get back into the hut, she knocks (*postuchal*) on the window, her teeth chatter (*stuchala zubami*), and she is radiantly, almost eerily, beautiful in the moonlight

Near the door, pressing herself to the wall, stood Fekla, stark naked. She was shivering with cold and her teeth were chattering, and in the bright moonlight she seemed very pale, beautiful and strange. The shadows on her and the glow of the moonlight on her skin seemed to stand out sharply and her dark brows and firm young breasts were outlined with a special clarity.

A similar consistency of physical description is reserved for that other free and slightly supernatural spirit of the story, General Zhukov's gnome-like retired chef, with his long beard and shining bald-patch

> A little old man of about eighty, with a long beard who looked like a gnome, not a local man, yet apparently something to do with the fire, walked around, hatless, with a white bundle in his arms; his bald-patch reflected in the fire.
>
> (See Russian Texts, No. 126)

The staccato syntax, with nominal and prepositional groups separated by commas, reflects the problem the observer (Ol'ga?) has in 'placing' the old man. This is compounded by the brilliant ambiguity of his role: 'not a local man' (*ne zdeshnii*)—and, perhaps, being gnome-like, not of this world at all 'somehow attached to the fire, perhaps even responsible for it' (*no, ochevidno, prichastnyi k pozharu*). If Fekla is a creature of the river, the boundary between the two worlds linked by the meadow, the old man is a creature of the *road*, which links both the old and the new (his memories of pre-Emancipation Russia) and the village and the city. As Ol'ga and Sasha make their way back to Moscow at the end of the story, he makes one more enigmatic appearance on the road

> At midday Ol'ga and Sasha reached a large village. Here on the broad village street they encountered the little old man, General Zhukov's chef. He was hot and sweating and his red bald-patch shone in the sun. He and Ol'ga did not recognize each other, then they both looked round at once, recognized the other, and without a word each went on his way.

One of the blessings of childhood is not to be defined by one's location, so Sasha and her 'opposite number', Mot'ka, the daughter of Marya, are free-ranging creatures, equally at home on a dirty warm stove-shelf and on a grassy sunlit slope. However, Sasha relates significantly to her setting wherever she is, and the innocent child's perception of landscapes frequently becomes a kind of social and moral comment on events and relationships. When she and her parents first enter the hut, one tiny laconic detail illuminates the whole way of life of which we learn later: Sasha's perception of the white cat becomes a kind of 'epiphany':[26]

'Down on the floor a white cat rubbed itself against the grate.

—Puss, puss!—Sasha called her over.—Puss!

—She can't hear,—said the little girl.—She's gone deaf.

—Why?

—Just is. They beat her.'

Sasha responds to animals because she is like 'a little wild animal that has been caught out in the field and brought into the hut'.

An important visual element in the setting turns out to be the main ally of this little tamed animal: the geese. Strings of white geese (paralleling the strings of dancing girls) nearly always decorate the green meadows and, like their setting, represent one of the positive forces in the story. For Sasha's granny they are a negative force, threatening her kitchen garden, but Chekhov humourously anthropomorphizes them into a group of busy villagers

> Granny posted Sasha beside her kitchen garden and told her to keep watch in case the geese got in. It was a hot August day. The publican's geese could have got into the garden by the back way, but at the moment they were going about their business, picking up oats around the pub, chatting peacefully, and only the gander raised his head up high as if to check whether the old woman was coming with her stick; some other geese might come up from down below, but at the moment they were grazing far away across the river, stretched out across the meadow like a long white garland.

When Sasha leaves her post, first to tell Mot'ka about churches and saints and doomsday, and then to roll with sensual delight down a grassy slope, Granny appears with her long stick to drive the geese out of the garden. When she seizes a switch and starts beating Sasha, the geese are no mere impartial observers: 'Sasha cried in pain and terror, but at that moment the gander, waddling from side to side and stretching out his neck, went up to the old woman and hissed something, and when he went back to his flock all the lady-geese greeted him approvingly: gaggle-gaggle!' This harmless piece of anthropomorphic humour fits in well with the child's perception of events and makes explicit the important role that nature has in the story as a moral commentator on adult human actions. Whenever the pastoral setting is described lyrically, it is as a counterpoint to some form of peasant brutality.

The seriousness and commitment to Nature as a positive force that runs through all Chekhov's stories and plays is well exemplified here. So often an apparent commitment to a character or an idea will be dispersed with a quick flick of his irony. It is as if the retiring and unassertive side of the writer will not permit too wholehearted a sympathy with the merely human or the merely rational. But Nature provides a standard, both moral and aesthetic, against which we may test the ring of Chekhov's moral conviction and his emotional involvement. And he is careful not to debase his currency with too overt moralizing or too pretty a natural description. Hence the strenuously prosaic insistence on describing nature in ordinary terms. As he told his brother Alexander in an often-quoted letter in 1886

> In my opinion a true description of Nature should be very brief and have a character of relevance. Commonplaces such as 'the setting sun, bathing in the waves of the darkening sea, poured its purple and gold, etcetera', 'the swallows flying over the surface of the water twittered merrily'—such commonplaces one ought to abandon. In descriptions of Nature one ought to seize upon the little particulars, grouping them in such a way that, in reading, when you shut your eyes, you get a picture.
>
> For instance, you will get the full effect of a moonlight night if you write

that on the mill-dam a little glowing star point flashed from the neck of a broken bottle, and the round, black shadow of a dog, or a wolf, emerged and ran, etcetera. Nature becomes animated if you are not squeamish about employing comparisons of her phenomena with ordinary human activities. [27]

There are two aspects to Chekhov's last point: like Turgenev, he is not squeamish about a bit of gentle anthropomorphism when it seems appropriate; on the other hand, he structures his stories in such a way that comparisons are inevitable between the beautiful, calm, stable phenomena of nature and the ugly, anxious, transient activities that men and women in society are prone to. Thus, Nature's role is both moral and aesthetic and the two are inseparable: whether providing a setting in sympathy with the action, or observing in ironic detachment, or even opposing the will and intentions of Man, the natural setting helps to forge the vital link between the thought and its expression. Through a dialectic of light and shade it makes dynamic the form with which Chekhov has enclosed the story.

This combination of the moral and aesthetic functions of natural settings in Chekhov's prose is nicely matched in the paintings of John Constable whose 'chiaroscuro of nature' as described by Kenneth Clark, worked in much the same way

By 'chiaroscuro of nature' Constable meant that some drama of light and shade must underlie all landscape compositions, and give the keynote of feeling in which the scene was painted . . . It is this sense of dramatic unity, as much as his feeling for the freshness of nature, which distinguishes Constable from his contemporaries. He recognized the fundamental truth that art must be based on a single dominating idea . . . In his greatest work naturalism is raised to a higher mode by his belief that since nature was the clearest revelation of God's will, the painting of landscape, conceived in the spirit of humble truth, could be a means of conveying moral ideas. [28]

—Nature takes on a religious dimension even in the episode of Sasha and the geese. As we know, the little girl was distracted from guarding the vegetables by her conversation about Doomsday. Her ideas about religion are all derived from her mother's highly ritualized faith and seem even more artificial because they are expressed largely in childish drama and a vocabulary full of diminutives (in italics here and in Russian text):

—The church is where God lives. People have lamps and candles burning, but God has *tiny little red green and blue* ikon-lamps, like *tiny eyes*. At night God walks around the church and he's got the Holy Mother with him and Nikolai the Wonder-Worker—tap, tap, tap . . . And the watchman gets scared stiff! E-eh, deary,—she added, copying her mother.—When Doomsday comes, all the churches will get carried off to heaven.
—Bells-and-all?—asked Mot'ka in a bass voice, stretching out each syllable.

—Bells and all. And on Doomsday all the good people will go to heaven and the angry ones will burn in the fire eternally and inextinguishably, deary. God will say to my mum and Marya too: you've never hurt anyone, so for that you turn right, into heaven; but he'll say to Kiryak and Granny: you turn left, into the fire. And anyone who has eaten during a fast will also be sent to the fire.

   ... *Little angels* flying in heaven and with their *tiny wings—flap, flap,* just like *teeny mosquitoes.*

Mot'ka thought for a little, gazing at the ground, and asked:

—Is Granny going to burn?

—She is, deary.

(See Russian Texts, No. 127)

Hell-fire and geese get fused in Sasha's dream that night, after she and Mot'ka have been soundly beaten and after Mot'ka has deliberately slopped some milk into Granny's plate of rye-crusts to make sure that she breaks the fast and qualifies for hell: ' ... As Sasha dozed off, she imagined the Last Judgement: a big stove like a potter's furnace was burning, and an evil spirit, with horns like a cow's, all black, was driving Granny into the fire with a long stick, just like she herself had been driving the geese.'

We have left until last our discussion of the church festivals as an aspect of the setting-in-time of *The Peasants*, partly because they have their own symbolic significance, but more particularly because the use of religion and reactions to Holy Writ on the part of the various characters are an important element in the symbolic and stylistic texture of the story. Just as the church-building with the five cupolas in the happy village across the meadows provides a visual focus for the social and moral counterpoint between life as it is and life as it could be, the church calendar and the Gospels are the focus of the moral and spiritual dialectic on which the story depends. Several critics have considered that *The Peasants* failed as a piece of narrative fiction because it lacked plot; [29] but the temporal structure provided by the solar and church calendars is very firm, so that every slight event and conversation gains an extra dimension in relation to these. In other words, the plot is more than just a chain of physical events; it is a moral dialogue between what is and what might have been. Sundays, fasting periods, a procession with a miraculous ikon, the Feasts of the Dormition, the Protection of the Virgin, the Annunciation not only fix temporal points through the eight winter months spanned by the story, but reveal the characters at their most typical and offer hope of an alternative way of life.

It is intriguing that Chekhov focusses on these particularly Orthodox feasts, relating mainly to the life of the Virgin, and only mentions in passing the universal Christian festivals of Advent, Christmas and Easter: perhaps, following the Slavophiles, he sees the salvation of this benighted Russia as having to be a specifically Russian salvation; he certainly wants to stress the special role of the Virgin in interceding on behalf of sinful man. One of the most treasured texts of mediaeval

Russian literature is 'The Journey of the Mother of God through Hell' (*Khozhdeniye bogoroditsy po mukam*), in which a tender Virgin Mary intercedes for sinners, and Chekhov's story is, on one level, a reworking of this legend; certainly, a recurrent phrase on the lips of Granny and Marya is 'Intercede for Christ's sake' (*Vstupítes' Khrísta radi*). Only Ol'ga, for whom religion is almost a profession, propounds to Marya those highly relevant messages of Christ's own teaching: 'Come unto me, all ye that labour and are heavy laden' (*priidite vse truzhdayuschiye i oberemenennye*) and 'Whosoever shall smite thee on thy right cheek, turn to him the other also' (*asche kto udarit tebya v pravuyu scheku, podstav' yemu levuyu*). But this Tolstoyan doctrine of non-resistance to evil is undermined by the whole story, by Chekhov's unusually explicit attack in the final section on the evil that is within the peasants themselves, and by the irony of his depiction of Ol'ga. As Donald Rayfield says

> Ol'ga is not merely an intermediary between the reader and this new cruel world. She is the bearer of an underlying Christian theme; deeply religious, she and her daughter are passionately fond of the New Testament, as much for its half-intelligible language as for its ethical message . . . More often her words affect the peasants unconsciously . . . She herself has poetic sensibility: it is the non-Russian slavonisms of the text, *ashche, dondezhe*, that move her to tears.[30]

On the one hand, then, all these positive qualities earn her the respect of the peasants of Zhukovo, who insist on addressing both her and Sasha by the respect-fully formal *vy*, and of the reader, for whom her awareness, dignity and sensitiv-ity are a welcome relief from the ignorance and brutality around her. On the other hand, the reader's positive view of her is gradually subverted by irony as the story progresses: there is comedy as well as poignancy in her tendency to burst into tears when she comes across an Old Church Slavonic word in the Gospel; in her reverential obsequiousness to the landowner's daughters, who are anything but 'cherubims'; in her petty-bourgeois speech and tea-drinking, mocked by Fekla; in her fussy nun's way of walking; and in the fact that her pre-occupation with church services, rituals and festivals actually cuts her off from reality

> Ol'ga often went off to church festivals and services in the larger villages nearby and in the local town, where there were two monasteries and twenty-seven churches. She was absent-minded and while attending church service she would completely forget about her family, and only when she got home would she suddenly make the joyful discovery that she had a husband and daughter, and then she would say, smiling radiantly:
> —God has sent me blessings!

The religious attitudes of each of the characters is summarized in the first part of Section 8 of the story. Up to this point old Osip's only contact with religion has been to cross himself before the portrait of General Battenberg which dominated the ikon corner in the hut of the village headman, Antip, and to try to wheedle some more time to pay his debts out of the same Antip: 'Grant me some divine kindness, your highness' (*Yavíte bozheskuyu milost', vashe vysoko-blagorodiye*). Now we are told explicitly that he never thought about God and dismissed the supernatural as women's concern. Granny, on the other hand, uses religious phrases constantly, but aggressively, inflicts strict observance of fasts on every-one around her, believes in the negative elements of hell-fire and eternal damna-tion, and replaces the prayers which she never remembers with lists of ikons. Marya and Fekla typify the attitude to religion of most of the peasants

> Marya and Fekla would cross themselves, fast every year, but understood nothing. The children were not taught to pray and nothing was said to them about God, no rules of behaviour were instilled into them, they were just forbidden to eat rich food during fasts. It was more or less the same in other families: hardly anyone believed, hardly anyone understood. At the same time everyone loved the scriptures tenderly and reverently, although there was no-one to read or explain, and because Ol'ga sometimes read the Gospel she was respected and she and Sasha were addressed by the polite 'you'.

All that survives of religion in peasant life—as in Chekhov's art—is the aesthetic element. But for Chekhov the aesthetic element is crucial, and it links religion with nature.

Section 8 begins with this discussion of the peasants' religious beliefs. This is framed by two brief but lyrical descriptions of the young girls of the village in their bright dresses going across the meadow to celebrate religious festivals: 'On Sundays when the weather was fine the girls would dress up and go off in a crowd to evensong, and it was a delight to watch them walking across the meadow in their red, yellow and green dresses.' To heighten the parallelism by a contrast, Chekhov follows this with a rather stark account of how they fasted for Lent and were fined by the priest if they broke the fast, then precedes the other description of the girls with a grotesque account of the excesses the villagers indulged in on a typical feast day. The next appearance of the girls is linked with that essential fusion of the spiritual, the moral and the aesthetic—a life-giving ikon. To heighten the incongruity, Chekhov reminds us of the village's nick-name

> And yet even in Zhukovo, in that Loutsville, there once occurred a real relig-ious celebration. It was during August when, throughout the whole prov-ince, they carried a life-giving ikon from village to village. On the day when it was due in Zhukovo, it was cool and overcast. Early in the morning the girls went off to meet the ikon in their bright festive dresses and brought it back towards evening in a procession led by the cross and singing, and just then they were ringing peals of bells across the river. A massive crowd of villagers

and outsiders jammed the street; noise, dust, pushing . . . And the old man, and Granny, and Kiryak—all stretched out their hands to the ikon, stared at it avidly and called through their tears:

—Intercede for us, little mother! Intercede for us!

Suddenly everyone seemed to realize that between earth and heaven was not just empty . . .

The one who *knows* that all is not empty between earth and heaven is Ol'ga. This knowledge is gained through her religion and through her perception of the beauty in nature. As she and Sasha leave Zhukovo to return to Moscow she stands once more on the scarp and looks across the meadows to the church: spring has come, the snows have melted, flooding the meadows and erasing the boundary between the villages; migrating birds have returned, and the bright sunset fills her with new hope

But somehow or other the winter came to an end. At the beginning of April warm days and frosty nights set in, winter would not yield, but one extra warm day tipped the balance at last—and the rivulets began to run, the birds struck up their song. The whole meadow and the bushes by the river were flooded by the spring waters, and between Zhukovo and the other side the whole area was already completely covered by an enormous lake on which, here and there, flocks of wild duck were taking wing. The spring sunset, ablaze, with magnificent clouds, every evening produced something extraordinary and new and unbelievable, precisely the sort of thing you can't believe in afterwards when you see those self-same colours and those self-same clouds in a painting.

The cranes were flying ever so swiftly and calling mournfully, as if calling one to follow them. Standing on the edge of the scarp, Ol'ga gazed for a long time at the flood, at the sun at the bright church which seemed to have grown younger, and the tears welled up and she could hardly breathe, she so passionately longed to go away somewhere, to follow where her eyes led her, even to the end of the earth.

(See Russian Texts, No. 127)

Turgenev's story started with a battle between light and darkness, in which the setting became a supernatural force threatening the tenuous thread of human life; Chekhov's ends with a battle between winter and spring in which the setting becomes a moral touchstone by which to evaluate human actions and a tenuous bridge from an unbearable reality to a potential better life. In both stories setting achieves thematic status.

NOTES TO CHAPTER 7

1. Robert Liddell, *A Treatise on the Novel* (London, 1947, p.110).
2. *Ibid*. p.115.
3. *Ibid*. p.117.
4. *Ibid*. pp.111-12.
5. D.S. Bland, 'Endangering the reader's neck: background description in the novel' *Criticism*, III, 1961, The Wayne State University Press; reprinted in Philip Stevick (ed.) *The Theory of the Novel* (New York, 1967, pp.313-31).
6. Claude Levi-Strauss, 'La geste d'Asdiwal', *Annuaire de l'Ecole Pratique des Hautes Etudes* (Sciences religieuse, 1958-59, pp.3-43); translated as 'The Story of Asdiwal', in Edmund Leach (ed.) *The Structural Study of Myth and Totemism* (London, 1967).
7. This problem is evident in Seymour Chatman's attempt to apply Barthes' categories in his analysis of Joyce's *Eveline*: 'New ways of analyzing narrative structure', *Language and Style*, 2, 1969, pp.1-36.
8. Roland Barthes, *S/Z* (Paris, 1970); translation by Richard Miller, (London, 1975).
9. For a fuller explanation and discussion see L.M. O'Toole, 'Dimensions of semiotic space in narrative' (*Poetics Today*, 4, 1980, pp.135-49); also, for more detail on the mathematical model, R.H. Atkin, *Multi-dimensional Man* (Harmondsworth, 1981).
10. Northrop Frye, *Anatomy of Criticism* (Princeton, 1957).
11. *Ibid*. p.100.
12. Robert Liddell, *op. cit.*, p.117.
13. Joseph Warren Beach, *The Concept of Nature in Nineteenth-Century English Poetry* (New York, 1936, p.4).
14. *Ibid*. p.5.
15. *Ibid*. pp.202-3.
16. Quotations and references are from I.S. Turgenev, *Sobraniye sochinenii v 10 tomakh*, I (Moscow, 1961, pp.75-91; author's translation).
17. Kenneth Clark, *Landscape into Art* (London, 1958, pp.20-1).
18. *Byliny* (Leningrad, 1954, p.107; author's translation).
19. A.V. Chicherin, '*Turgenev, ego stil*' (in *Masterstvo russkikh klassikov*, Moscow, 1969, pp.130-1).
20. I am taking it for granted here that even silent reading involves an unconscious partial articulation of the speech sounds represented by the print.
21. Quotations and references are from A.P. Chekhov, *Sobraniye sochinenii v 12 tomakh*, 8 (Moscow, 1962, pp.198-229; author's translation).
22. Thomas Bruford, *Chekhov and his Russia: a Sociological Study* (London 1947).
23. Thomas Winner, *Chekhov and his Prose* (New York, 1966, p.151).
24. See L.M. O'Toole, 'The Scythian factor' (in *Russian Literature*, forthcoming). As we show elsewhere (O'Toole, 1971), the wordless reaction of the 'dumb' Luker'ya may be the crucial peripeteia in Chekhov's *The Student*.
25. Donald Rayfield, *Chekhov: the Evolution of his Art* (New York, 1975, p.178).
26. See L.M. O'Toole, 'Narrative structure and living texture: James Joyce's *Two Gallants*' (*PTL: a Journal for Descriptive Poetics and Theory of Literature*, 1, 1976, pp.441-58) for a discussion of Joyce's concept of the 'epiphany' as a moment of sudden, synthesizing revelation in narrative.
27. L.S. Friedland (ed) *Chekhov: Letters on the Short Story, The Drama and Other Literary Topics* (New York, 1965, pp.70-1).
28. Kenneth Clark, *op. cit.*, p.89.
29. For instance, Rayfield, *op. cit.*: '*Peasants* reduces the element of plot to a minimum; only on reflection do we realize that it has a heroine through whom we see, hear and smell life . . . Even the seasonal structure is hardly noticeable: there are flashbacks from winter to summer,

a steady state of misery, and the overall picture is more static than in any other of Chekhov's late works' (pp.177-8); Thomas Winner, *op. cit.*: 'The work consists of a series of episodes which are only tenuously connected, but which create a total impression of peasant life' (p.151); Beverly Hahn, *Chekhov: a Study of the Major Stories and Plays* (Cambridge, 1977): '... there is no doubt that it projects only a rather flat image ... There is just sufficient individual characterization thereafter in the story to make us feel that some of the characters might have been really interesting with further development ... Here there is no real narrative line to take one's attention into other areas: simply a deliberate, *tour-de-force* rendering of what it means to live that primitive and squalid life. To give a sense of how far from the Tolstoyan ideal his "real" peasants are, Chekhov alternates his imagery of the extremely sordid conditions inside the hut with picturesque images of the surrounding countryside' (pp.153-4).

From this chapter it will be clear that I disagree with most of the points made by these authors, apart from Hahn's last sentence, which does not go far enough.

30. Donald Rayfield, *op. cit.*, p.179.

REFLECTIONS

WE ARE living in a cultural period when critics seem to be required to declare their allegiance to one or another of a large and growing number of competing schools of criticism. To command an audience you must say where you stand. Apart from a temperamental disinclination to being ideologically pigeon-holed in this way, I feel that every interesting critical method is partly eclectic and is bound to build on the achievements of its predecessors and competitors for public attention, and it seems a rather immature tendency in some schools that expects each new trend to supersede all others: 'Formalism' has been superseded by 'Structuralism' which has been superseded by 'The New Stylistics', or 'Post-Structuralism', or 'Phenomenology', or 'Hermeneutics', or 'Reader-Centred Criticism', or whatever the next 'New Wave' is to be. Each new set of critical preoccupations has made some useful contributions to the ongoing debate, and some have even produced insightful descriptions and interpretations of literary works, but too much of the discussion has been on a rarefied level of theoretical abstraction and too little has actually tested the competing methods on a particular work or group of works.

It is the author's conviction that most of the interesting theoretical questions emerge from problems of description and interpretation. One key theoretical question I shall have to return to, in view of my insistence on the study of the text itself, is: where is the text? On the page? In the social culture? In the writer's mind? In the reader's mind? The aesthetic assumption of my method is that every art-form has a unity and coherence of internal patterning that structures both the artist's act of communication and the reader's act of perception and understanding, and that even highly deviant forms like the modern novel are deviating from an assumed norm. Where this coherent patterning is to be found is no trivial question, and I want to take it up once more after considering briefly the approaches that are still most commonly found—if not always consciously adopted—in the teaching of literature in schools, colleges and universities.

When I was studying English and French literature at school and Russian literature at university, there was a tacit assumption that the main observations to be made about features in a text were in relation to the author's life: one read a biography or two, the relevant chapters of a literary history, and then expounded in essay form those aspects of the work that best fitted, or failed for some obvious reason to fit, the predicted patterns. This approach was—and *is*, for it is still remarkably widely practised—very easy to teach and very easy to learn, for the correlations drawn can be both impressionistic and unsystematic. They can also be quite naive. It is fraught with chronological assumptions about the direct relation between the features of the work and the age at which, and the Age in which, it was written. It is strongly subjective, both in terms of the priority accorded to the personality of the artist and in terms of the credence placed on the student-critic's individual response: critical maturity is measured in terms of one's 'feel for literature'.

Although I regard this as the least valid of the critical approaches I am discussing, I do not rule it out completely: no discussion of Turgenev's *Bezhin Meadow* can ignore the thirty-year-old writer's genuine social commitment in his depiction of the peasants as vital and dignified human beings in *A Sportsman's Sketches*, as compared with the pasteboard or slapstick peasants of earlier Russian fiction; we cannot comprehend the intensity of Kasatsky's spiritual search, his scorn for social conventionality, or his spasms of self-loathing unless we are aware of these elements in Tolstoy's make-up; the authenticity of Kovrin's megalomaniac symptoms and of Pesotsky's horticultural mania is enriched by our knowledge of Chekhov as a doctor and a gardener, especially in the 1880s. I have referred to these elements in relation to the three stories. But they are not of the first importance: our perception of the themes and our refraction of the heroes' experiences does not depend on our knowing these biographical facts; they are simply useful supplementary data which we can incorporate into our synthesis once the more purely structural analysis has been attempted: first the relations *within* the text, then the extra-textual correlations, where they are relevant.

The psychological approach which was first fashionable in the 1920s and 1930s has enjoyed a revived vogue in the 1970s. It has tended to choose the most accommodating authors—Dostoevsky, Kafka, Lawrence—and naively apply half-digested Freudian categories to the (psycho-)analysis of their novels. If the categories had to be expressed in rather obscure jargon—so much the better, as the vagueness of the correlations between the text and the artist's psyche would be less evident. This approach, too, was highly subjective. However, there has been an interesting shift in the theory: whereas the early psycho-analytical critics analyzed the work in relation to the workings of the writer's unconscious, its more recent proponents have focussed on the interplay between the text and what can be discovered of the *reader's* unconscious. This, indeed, is a kind of 'refraction' on one level. The danger is that it will lead to an overdetermination of the theme—the interpretation of every feature of the work according to a predetermined extra-textual assumption. While this may contribute to an interpretation of the short story, which we have defined as essentially 'centripetal', in the centrifugal form of the novel it always leads to over-simplification. As with the biographical approach, it can offer important supplementary evidence to enrich what we discover in the structure and linguistic texture of the work: we have drawn on some of Driessen's observations about Gogol's *The Overcoat* as a sexual fantasy, and this theme could be explored in much greater depth, but this would distract us from the far richer—and far more objectively describable— stylistic patterning in the story which, we have argued, epitomizes the theme. Dostoevsky is known to have had a profound effect on Freud's thinking, and at one stage in our analysis of *A Gentle Spirit* a psychological interpretation of the transactions between the hero and heroine, and between the narratorial voice and the reader (or Dostoevsky's constructed reader) seemed to be essential. Yet this could not be separated from the social, philosophical and religious drama of these transactions.

How central to criticism is a sociological approach? In discussing the stories by Turgenev, Korolenko, Chekhov and Gorky it would have been absurd *not* to have mentioned aspects of the writer's society that were relevant. The condition of the peasants ten years before the Emancipation of the Serfs in Turgenev compares significantly with their condition thirty-five years after the Emancipation as seen by Chekhov. For Korolenko, choosing as his central character a simple-minded native of the deepest backwoods of Siberia, the role of story-teller was inseparable from that of ethnographer. And for Gorky the social predicament of his 'twenty-six living machines' was essential for understanding the drama of their shattered ideal of beauty and purity. Once again, however, it would have been a serious distortion of the story to have interpreted its message as purely ideological, in the manner of the Soviet critics of the 1930s who were so eager to discredit the Formalist critics of the 1920s, whom they scarcely began to understand, but whose analyses had to be replaced by the slogans of 'Socialist Realism'. For them, *Twenty-Six Men and a Girl* was not a narrative experience, nor even a human document—it was a revolutionary placard. There have been other, less naive, sociologies of literature since, and they have a serious contribution to make to literary scholarship in general: the correlations between the formal-thematic elements of a work and the social-political features of the writer's society are of great interest provided they are not drawn too directly: an adequate semiotics of culture will allow for, and propose, various levels of mediation between the social institutions and the symbolic forms in which a society's artists encapsulate their social experience. Meanwhile, with such semiotics of culture only in its infancy, we must regard the sociological observation about the content and form of literary works—and the relations between content and form—as secondary to the analysis of the text itself.

The shift of interest in the last decade from the writer to the reader has been reflected in sociological criticism as well. A description of the social complexion of the readership of a work of fiction, both contemporary and in later periods, can tell us a great deal about its potential themes and why one view of the theme becomes dominant for any one society. The decline of Turgenev's reputation as society's political preoccupations overtook the ageing writer, or the vicissitudes of Dostoevsky's status, both in Russia and in the West, can give us valuable clues to important elements in their works that our own age may miss. The way a society refracts a work through the prisms of its own priorities tells us things about the work as well as about the society. And yet this, too, presupposes a structural analysis of the work itself that may be correlated with aspects of the social structure.

Ultimately, however, these sociological approaches are contributing to an account of literary evolution, and this, perhaps, is the major underlying theory that sustains all the critical approaches we have mentioned: not literature as a branch of biography, or psychology, or sociology, but as a branch of history. Most students of literature feel the need to adopt a chronological perspective even if they do not have one imposed on them, as is usually the case, by their syllabus. It is reassuring to plot the progress through decades of cultural history of literary themes, heroes, genres and styles. The dangers are that we will only notice the most obvious links and influences or will be trapped by the labels we too readily apply.

Some of the recurrent themes in the stories discussed in this book might be seen in this evolutionary way: 'the peasants', or 'rural versus urban life', or 'the search for a personal truth' are reflected in contrasting ways at different periods. But can we claim with confidence that this is an evolutionary tendency, rather than due to the social and psychological make-up of the writers? Can the relations of class and social power that we find in Chekhov's *The Peasants* or Gorky's *Twenty-Six Men and a Girl* really be seen as having evolved in any sense from those that we find in Pushkin's and Gogol's stories? Surely we have to start with the internal structure of these relations and their relevance in the interpretation of the individual work before we move to the grand generalizations of literary history. Many teachers of literature, and the books they adopt, work the other way round, from the general observations to their particular manifestations.

This tendency becomes an obsession when literary history focusses on the evolution of types of hero. The 'little man', the 'superfluous man', the 'underground man' and 'Socialist man' all recur endlessly in histories of Russian literature. And of course Akakiy Akakiyevich and Samson Vyrin and Postnikov do share the characteristics of the poor and put-upon in society; but the implications of their 'littleness' are quite different in Gogol's, Pushkin's and Leskov's stories. Silvio and Dostoevsky's narrator-hero and Kovrin all feel in some ways 'superfluous' in their contemporary society, but even in sociological terms the reasons for this alienation are quite distinct and in no sense is there a line of evolution linking the Pushkin, Dostoevsky and Chekhov stories. It is to avoid this kind of evolutionary pattern-making—as well as to illustrate contrasting structures—that we have resolutely avoided any chronological sequence in this book.

The history of genres may well be a valid approach to literary evolution, but classification and contrast in terms of the length or mode of publication of various types of fiction—the short story, the novella, the serialized novel, the novel proper ('Romantic', 'Realist', 'Naturalist', historical, science fictional, etcetera) is likely to be superficial unless it is done in terms of the kinds of structural features analyzed here. In other words, what is significant for literary comparison, between works, or genres, or between works of different literary cultures, is not broad genre characteristics, but precise differences in the handling of fable, plot or narrative structure, shifting tendencies in authorial stance; not the changes in character or setting as such, so much as the way these are constructed and incorporated into the composition of the work.

Short story writers, like novelists, often incorporate fragments of other genres into their narrative fictions. In fact, as we have seen, they often seem to be creating a dialogue between competing genres, literary and non-literary. Pushkin combines the thematic essay with the sentimental tale, Tolstoy—the external biography and didactic tract with the hero's stream of consciousness, Korolenko—the ethnographic description with the Christmas folk tale, Dostoevsky—the autobiography, the confession and the evidence for the defence. At this level of structure there are quite precise observations we can make about how the themes and structures and styles of these genres interact in our refraction of the whole text. This is where stylistics has a major contribution to make. New and revolutionary linguistic theories in the past twenty years have led to a revival of stylistics. And yet, however precise the linguistic description, one of the main tendencies in this enterprise has been the old-fashioned impressionistic one of trying to match stylistic features with aspects of the writer's personality or world-view (the 'style is the man' school of thought). The other has been to set up a spurious opposition between so-called 'literary language' and so-called 'everyday language' (the 'style as deviation from the norm' school of thought). But both these schools of thought make the mistake of interpreting literary choices on the linguistic level in relation to something outside literature.

Our point is that all linguistic choices in the short story have their function within the structure of the work itself: they are functional precisely because they incorporate aspects of social meaning into the thematic structure of each story. Silvio's military brusqueness is in contrast with the Count's aristocratic casualness as one element in the creation of narrative tension between them, as individual heroes and as representatives of social types; ultimately, the narrative tension grows out of the conflict of the dramatic roles: it is a matter of structural oppositions, not personal or social ones. And the same is true of the relationship between the speech of Akakiy Akakiyevich and the Person of Consequence, of Svinin and the Metropolitan, of Kasatsky and the merchant, of Kovrin and Pesotsky, of each of the peasant boys in *Bezhin Meadow*. It is equally true of the shifts in the language of the narrating voice: the coolly detached descriptions of Korolenko's ethnographer as compared with the purple prose which signals Makar's arrival at the palace of Judgement; Gogol's 'lyrical digressions' as compared with his outrageous word-play; the babbling clichés of Dostoevsky's narrator as compared with the profundity of his philosophical dilemma.

The effect of all these stylistic contrasts is to make the reader work imaginatively to recreate the worlds encapsulated in each linguistic register. And this brings us to the question with which we started this chapter: *where is the text?* The text must be in the mind of the reader: it is the product of the interaction between the structures the author has provided and the structuring energies of our minds. So each generation, each social group, each individual reader creates his own text; in fact, as I have suggested, each time we read, we create a new text, since our attention will focus on different facets of what we are reading, depending on our state of knowledge, sensitivity and mood. The model we are proposing is fashionable, then, in being reader-centred. It is a hermeneutic approach in so far as it concentrates on the interpretation of the literary text. It is a semiotic model in so far as it perceives and analyses the literary text as a complex of interacting, rule-governed signifying systems—our levels and dimensions. But whereas reader-centred criticism, hermeneutics and semiotics are fashionably supposed to have displaced and invalidated structuralism and formalism, I would maintain that they all depend on a thorough formal-structural analysis as a prerequisite for their associations and interpretations.

To finish, as we started, with our titles, I want to assert the priority of 'refractions' over 'reflections'. The schools of criticism discussed in this chapter—the biographical, the psychological, the sociological, historical, generic and stylistic —all have a contribution to make in general literary studies, but they are secondary in so far as they concern themselves with *reflections* of the writer, his world and his language in the literary work. Before we attend to these, we should describe and analyze and interpret as comprehensively as possible the *refractions* created by the reader's perception of narrative structure, point of view, fable, plot, character and setting.

RUSSIAN TEXTS

ЛЕСКОВ

1. но со стороны вздувшейся реки опять наплывают все
ближе и ближе стоны, и уже слышно бурканье и
отчаянное барахтанье.
-- То-о-ну!... Спасите, тону!
Тут вот сейчас и есть иорданская прорубь.
Конец!
Постников еще раз-два оглянулся во все
стороны. Нигде ни души нет, только фонари
трясутся от ветра и мерцают да по ветру,
прерываясь, долетает этот крик... может быть,
последний крик...
Вот еще всплеск, еще однозвучный вопль, и в
воде забулькотало.
Часовой не выдержал и покинул свой пост.

2. -- Посему надлежит заключить, что в сем деле не
все и не везде излагалось согласно с полною
истиной?...

... - Должно различать, что есть ложь и что
неполная истина...

... - Неполная истина не есть ложь. Но о сем
наименьше...

... - Святое известно богу, наказание же на теле
простолюдину не бывает губительно и не
противоречит ни обычаю народов, ни духу Писания.

3. Это был человек с так называемым "гуманным"
направлением, которое за ним было давно замечено
и немножко вредило ему по службе во внимании
высшего начальства.
На самом же деле Миллер был офицер
исправный и надежный..."

4. на службе всякая вина виновата;

закален крепким закалом;

чтобы на нее, как на парадный мундир, ни одна пылинка не села;

подкатят ему бревно под ноги, чтобы дать путь своему ближнему;

останется несмываемым пятном на его, Свиньина, репутации;

не оставить своего портрета в галерее исторических лиц государства Российского;

ГОГОЛЬ

5. доволен, что и себя не уронил, да и портного искусства тоже не выдал...

6. останавливала его мысль: ... не уронит ли он чрез то своего значения.

7. Он очень любил сильные эффекты, любил вдруг как-нибудь озадачить совершенно и потом поглядеть искоса, какую озадаченный сделает рожу после таких слов.

8. А значительное лицо, довольный тем, что эффект превзошел даже ожидание ...искоса взглянул на приятеля, чтобы узнать, как он на это смотрит.

9. Как вы смеете? Знаете ли вы, с кем говорите? Понимаете ли, кто стоит перед вами?
   Оставьте меня, зачем вы меня обижаете?

10. Нужно знать, что Акакий Акакиевич изъяснялся
большею частью предлогами, наречиями и, наконец,
такими частицами, которые решительно не имеют
никакого значения. Если же дело было очень
затруднительно, то он даже имел обыкновение
совсем не оканчивать фразы, так что весьма
часто, начавши речь словами: "Это, право,
совершенно того...", а потом уже и ничего не было,
и он сам позабывал, думая, что все уже выговорил.

11. Если ему случалось быть с ровными себе, он был
еще человек как следует, человек очень
порядочный, во многих отношениях даже не глупый
человек; но как только случалось ему быть в
обществе, где были люди хоть одним чином пониже
его, там он был просто хоть из рук вон: молчал,
и положение его возбуждало жалость, тем более,
что он сам даже чувствовал, что мог бы провести
время несравненно лучше. В глазах его иногда
видно было сильное желание присоединиться к
какому-нибудь интересному разговору и кружку, но
останавливала его мысль: не будет ли это уж очень
много с его стороны, не будет ли фамильярно, и не
уронит ли он чрез то своего значения? И
вследствие таких рассуждений он оставался вечно в
одном и том же молчаливом состоянии, произнося
только изредка какие-то односложные звуки, и
приобрел таким образом титул скучнейшего человека.

12. Какая именно и в чем состояла должность
значительного лица, это осталось до сих пор
неизвестным. Нужно знать, что одно значительное
лицо недавно сделался значительным лицом, а до
того времени он был незначительным лицом.
Впрочем, место его и теперь не почиталось
значительным в сравнении с другими еще
значительнейшими. Но всегда найдется такой круг
людей, для которых незначительное в глазах прочих
есть уже значительное. Впрочем, он старался уси-
лить значительность многими другими средствами...

13. 1. <u>Hyperbole</u>   a) <u>Adverbial</u>:

<u>весьма</u> недавно; местами <u>даже</u> <u>совершенно</u> в
пьяном виде; и <u>даже</u> шурин и <u>все совершенно</u>
Башмачкины; Он брал и <u>тут же</u> пристаивался
писать ее; рассказывали <u>тут же</u> перед ним
разные...истории; и колючие щелчки <u>без разбору</u>
по всем носам... <u>решительно</u> не знают; <u>совсем</u>
не оканчивать фразы, так что <u>весьма</u> часто...
а потом <u>уже</u> ничего не было и <u>сам</u> он
позабывал;

b) <u>Morphological</u>: (particularly
verb prefixes and suffixes):

над которым, как известно, <u>натрунились</u> и
<u>наострились</u> <u>вдоволь</u>; народ <u>наелся</u> и <u>отобедал</u>;
Акакий Акакиевич, <u>написавшись</u> <u>всласть</u>;

c) <u>Syntactic</u> (particularly
intensified negative contrast):

<u>ничего нет сердитее всякого рода</u>
департаментов; имя <u>никак не</u> искали... <u>никак</u>
<u>нельзя</u> было дать другого; Сторожа <u>не только</u>
<u>не</u> вставали с мест, ...<u>но даже не</u> глядели;
<u>Вряд ли где</u> можно было найти человека,
который <u>так</u> жил бы; <u>Мало сказать</u>... <u>Нет</u>...;
<u>не только</u> титулярным, <u>но даже</u> тайным...
<u>даже и тем</u>...; Напустила <u>столько</u> дыму, <u>что</u>
нельзя было видеть <u>даже и самых</u> тараканов;

2. <u>Qualification</u> (a mirror-image of hyperbole):

a) <u>Morphological</u> (particularly
diminutive and other modifying
suffixes):

низе<u>нько</u>го роста, <u>несколько</u> ря<u>боват</u>,
<u>несколько</u> ры<u>жеват</u>, <u>несколько</u> даже <u>на вид</u>
<u>подслеповат</u>, с <u>небольшой</u> лысиной на лбу;
вицмундир не зеленый, а <u>какого-то</u> рыжевато-
мучного цвета. Воротни<u>чок</u> на нем был
узе<u>нький</u>, низе<u>нький</u>; что-ни<u>будь</u> да прилипало...
или сен<u>ца</u> кус<u>очек</u> или какая-ни<u>будь</u> нит<u>очка</u>;

b) Syntactic

Чиновник нельзя сказать чтобы очень
замечательный; Когда и в какое время он
поступил в департамент и кто определил его,
этого никто не мог припомнить; наш северный
мороз, хотя, впрочем, и говорят, что он очень
здоров; с некоторого времени начал чувствовать,
что его как-то особенно сильно стало пропекать
в спину; он подумал, наконец, не заключается ли
каких грехов;

3. **Anti-climax** (often as much rhythmic as lexical

after a graded hyperbole):

низенького роста несколько несколько
несколько даже геморроидальным; И отец,
и дед, и даже шурин и все совершенно
Башмачкины ходили в сапогах; заплакал и
сделал такую гримасу, как будто бы
предчувствовал, что будет титулярный
советник; стал попивать довольно сильно по
всяким праздникам, сначала по большим,
а потом без разбору, по всем церковным,
где только стоял в календаре крестик;
столько дыму, что нельзя было видеть и
\ самых тараканов;

словом, даже тогда, когда все стремится
развлечься, --Акакий Акакиевич не
предавался никакому развлечению.

4. **Incongruity** (involving many of the other

devices we are examining):

Он имел особенное искусство vs. поспевать
под окно; только разве если, неизвестно
откуда взявшись, лошадиная морда помещалась
ему на плечо... vs. тогда только замечал...;
по лестнице, которая, надобно отдать
справедливость... vs. была вся умащена
водой, помоями...; хозяйка напустила столько
дыму в кухне, что нельзя было видеть даже и
самых тараканов; несколько под куражем, или
как выражалась жена его: "осадился сивухой,
одноглазый чорт";

5. <u>Puns</u>   a) <u>Etymological</u>:

Башмачкин ——— башмак

выисканным ——— не искали

советникам ——— не дают советов

значительное лицо ——— не уронит ли

значения

b) <u>Semantic</u>

произошел Акакий Акакиевич——произошло все
это кто определил его (technically, "appoint"
——"define") не на середине строки——скорее
на середине улицы ел кусок говядины с дуком
——ел все это с мухами и со всем тем, что ни
посылал бог на ту пору; холод пропекал в
спину——он был распечен генералом;

ДОСТОЕВСКИЙ

14. я в это слепо——безумно——ужасно верил

само имущее смятение——напрашивающееся на
смятение

О меня не любили никогда даже в школе——Меня
всегда и везде не любили

она была тиран——нестерпимый тиран души моей
——и мучитель

О, тогда я еще не понимал!——Я ничего, ничего
еще тогда не понимал!——До сегодня не понимал!

ведь это правда——то есть самая, самая
правденская правда.

15. А я хотел <u>широкости</u>, + я хотел <u>привить широкость</u>
прямо к <u>сердцу</u>,——<u>привить к сердечному</u> взгляду,
не так ли?

это был зверь, + это был припадок,———это был
зверь в припадке

16. Я хочу себя судить и сужу. Я должен говорить
pro и contra, и говорю.

17. Я ведь понимаю же теперь, что я в чем-то тут
ошибся! Тут что-то вышло не так... Вот план.
Но тут я что-то забыл или упустил из виду. Не
сумел я что-то тут сделать.

18. Теперь же песенка была такая слабенькая - о, не
то чтобы заунывная (это был какой-то романс),
но как будто бы в голосе было что-то надтреснутое,
сломанное, как будто голосок не мог справиться,
как будто сама песенка была больная.

19. Случай же в полку был хоть и следствием нелюбви
ко мне, но без сомнения носил случайный
характер. Я к тому это, что нет ничего обиднее
и несноснее, как погибнуть от случая, который
мог бы быть и не быть от несчастного скопления
обстоятельств, которые могли пройти мимо, как
облака. Для интеллигентного существа
унизительно. Случай был следующий.

20. Кто был я и кто была она... Вот пока она здесь -
еще все хорошо: подхожу и смотрю поминутно; а
унесут завтра и - как же я останусь один? Она
теперь в зале на столе, составили два ломберных,
а гроб будет завтра, белый, белый гроденапль, а
впрочем, не про то...

21. никто не ведает,   Но я стенал про себя

сколько я вынес,   про себя, и стоны
                           давил в груди

стеная над ней в   давил в груди даже от
    ее болезни   Лукерьи

22. Я не мог   предположить даже

представить   не мог,

23. он имел зуб на Безумцева; дело было не личное,
а касалось и полка, а так как офицеров нашего
полка тут был только я, то тем и доказал всем
бывшим в буфете офицерам и публике, что в полку
нашем могут быть офицеры не столь щекотливые
насчет чести своей и полка; после блестящего
мундира; И так - стыд так стыд, позор так
позор, падение так падение и чем хуже, тем лучше.

24. Тогда еще голос ее был довольно сильный, звонкий,
хотя неверный, но ужасно приятный и здоровый.
Теперь же песенка была такая слабенькая - о, не
то чтобы заунывная (это был какой-то романс) но
как будто бы в голосе было что-то надтреснутое,
сломанное, как будто голосок не мог справиться,
как будто сама песенка была больная.

25. Самое главное...

Главное ведь в том, что...

Я ведь понимаю же теперь.

И я понимал вполне мое отчаяние. О, понимал!

О, это было самое главное.

Главное, я не верил...

Я все видел, все до последней черты.

26. О, тогда я не понимал! Я ничего, ничего еще
    тогда не понимал! До сегодня не понимал!...
    Да и теперь не понимаю, и теперь ничего не
    понимаю.

27. А впрочем... а впрочем, что ж я об этом говорю!
    Глупо, глупо, глупо и глупо!

    О, дико, дико! Недоразумение! Неправдоподобие!
    Невозможность!

    А разве нет? Разве это правдоподобно? Разве
    можно сказать, что это возможно?

28. Господа, я далеко не литератор, и вы это видите,
    да и пусть, а расскажу, как сам понимаю.

29. Господа... если хотите знать... Ах, слушайте,
    слушайте!... Постойте, господа!... То есть,
    видите ли... Постойте... А? Как вы думаете?...
    Слушайте... Как бы это начать... Видите ли...
    Видите ли... Согласитесь... Это заметьте...
    Верите ли... Вы говорите... Видите, господа...
    Не знаю, понятно ли я выражаюсь... Повторяю, и
    опять повторяю... Еще скажу: о, конечно, никто
    не ведает... Прибавлю одно... Два слова прежде
    того... Знаете это... Слушайте и вникнете...
    О, поверьте...

30. Нет, послушайте, если уж судить человека, то
    судить, зная дело... Слушайте!
        Нет, возьмите-ка подвиг великодушия трудный,
    тихий, неслышный, без блеску, с клеветой, где

много жертвы и ни капли славы, - где вы,
сияющий человек, пред всеми выставлены подлецом,
тогда как вы честнее всех людей на земле, -
ну-так, попробуйте-ка этот подвиг, нет-с,
откажетесь!

31. Разумеется, она, тут же у ворот долго думала,
прежде чем сказала да. Так задумалась, так задумалась, что я уже спросил было: "Ну что ж?" -
И даже не удержался, с этаким шиком спросил:
"Ну что же-с?" - с слово-ерсом.

32. человек, дескать, прямой и изучил обстоятельства
дела; а я ведь "мстил же обществу",
действительно, действительно, действительно!
Постойте, разумеется, я ей о благодеянии тогда
ни полслова; напротив, о напротив: "это _я_, дескать, остаюсь облагодействован, а не _вы_."

33. "Правда: меня по приговору офицеров, <u>попросили
из полка удалиться</u>, <u>хотя</u>, <u>впрочем</u>, я сам уже
перед тем подал в отставку."

34. Да, они <u>присудили</u> как труса. Но я отказался от
дуели <u>не как</u> трус, а <u>потому что</u> не захотел
<u>подчиниться их тираническому приговору</u> и вызы-
вать на дуель, когда не находил сам обиды.
Знаете, - не удержался я тут, - <u>что восстать
действием против такой тирании и принять все
последствия - значило выказать гораздо более
мужества, чем в какой хотите дуели</u>.

35. Я <u>позвоили себе</u> усмехнуться на ее вещи. То есть
<u>видите ли</u>, я этого себе никогда не <u>позволяю</u>, у
меня с публикой <u>тон джентльменский</u>.

36. Я вступил в любезный разговор с необычайною
    вежливостью. Я ведь недурно воспитан и имею
    манеры. Я являлся как бы из высшего мира.

37. Тут-то я и заметил ее в первый раз особенно и
    подумал что-то о ней в этом роде, то есть
    именно что-то в особенном роде.

    для вас я особенно подчеркнул, и именно в не-
    котором смысле.

    у меня вдруг забродили некоторые на ее счет
    мысли. Это была третья особенная моя мысль об
    ней.

38. а потом: "согласна на все, и учить, и в ком-
    паньонки, и за хозяйством смотреть. и за боль-
    ной ходить, и шить умею", и т.д., и т.д., все
    известное!

ТОЛСТОЙ

39. Несмотря на свой выше обыкновенного рост,/он
    был красив и ловок. Кроме того, и по поведению
    он был бы образцовым кадетом,/если бы не его
    вспыльчивость. Он не пил, не распутничал и был
    замечательно правдив./ Одно, что мешало ему быть
    образцовым, были находившие на него вспышки
    гнева...

40. Когда же выпущенные кадеты являлись ему, он уже
    не поминал об этом, сказал, как всегда, что они
    все могут прямо обращаться к нему, чтобы они
    верно служили ему и отечеству, а он всегда
    останется их первым другом. Все, как всегда
    были тронуты...

41. Добившись одного, он брался за другое.

    добился до того... добился того...

    Кроме общего призвания жизни, которое состояло
    в служении царю и отечеству, у него всегда была
    поставлена какая-нибудь цель, и, как бы ничтожна
    она ни была, он отдавался ей весь и жил только
    для нее до тех пор, пока не достигал ее. Но как
    только он достигал назначенной цели, так другая
    тотчас же вырастала в его сознании и сменяла
    прежнюю. Это-то стремление отличиться и, для
    того чтобы отличиться, достигнуть поставленной
    цели, наполняло его жизнь.

42. Но очень скоро он увидал, что те круги, в
    которых он вращался, были круги низшие, а что
    были высшие круги, и что в этих высших
    придворных кругах, хотя его и принимали, он был
    чужой; с ним были учтивы, но все обращение
    показывало, что есть свои и он не свой. И
    Касатский захотел быть своим.

43. В Сибири он поселился на заимке у богатого
    мужика и теперь живет там. Он работает у
    хозяина в огороде, и учит детей, и ходит за
    больными.

44. Он встал во весь свой большой рост и стал перед
    нею, опершись обеими руками на саблю.
        -- Я только теперь узнал все то счастье,
    которое может испытать человек. И это вы, это
    ты, -- сказал он, робко улыбаясь, -- дала мне
    это!
        Он был в том периоде, когда "ты" еще не
    сделалось привычно, и ему, смотря нравственно
    снизу вверх на нее, страшно было говорить "ты"
    этому ангелу.
        -- Я себя узнал благодаря... тебя, узнал,
    что я лучше, чем я думал.
        -- Я давно это знаю. Я за то-то и полюбила
    вас.

> Соловей защелкал вблизи, свежая листва
> зашевелилась от набежавшего ветерка.

45. чем дальше и дальше шло время, тем строже и
строже он устанавливал свою жизнь.

с посетителями, которых все становилось больше
и больше...

Посетителей стало приходить все больше и больше...

слава отца Сергия распространялась дальше и
дальше...

Он думал о том, что он был светильник горящий,
и чем больше он чувствовал это, тем больше он
чувствовал ослабление, потухание божеского
света истины...

46. Если говорили, что он нужен был людям, что,
исполняя закон Христов любви, он не мог отказы-
вать людям в их требовании видеть его, что уда-
ление от этих людей было бы жестокостью, он не
мог не соглашаться с этим, но, по мере того как
он отдавался этой жизни, он чувствовал, как
внутреннее переходило во внешнее, как иссякал в
нем источник воды живой, как то, что он делал,
он делал все больше и больше для людей, а не
для бога.

47. Было даже время, когда он решил уйти, скрыться.
Он даже все обдумал, как это сделать. Он
приготовил себе мужицкую рубаху, портки, кафтан
и шапку. Он объяснил, что это нужно ему для
того, чтобы давать просящим. И он держал это
одеяние у себя, придумывая, как он оденется,
острижет волосы и уйдет. Сначала он уедет на
поезде, проедет триста верст, сойдет и пойдет
по деревням. Он расспрашивал старика солдата,
как он ходит, как подают и пускают.

48. Купец, усадив отца Сергия на лавочку под вязом,
    взял на себя обязанность полицейскую и очень
    решительно взялся прогонять народ. Правда, он
    говорил тихо, так что отец Сергий не мог слышать
    его, но говорил решительно и сердито:
        -- Убирайтесь, убирайтесь. Благословил, ну,
    чего же вам еще? Марш. А то, право, шею намну.
    Ну, ну! Ты, тетка, черные онучи, ступай, ступай.
    Ты куда лезешь? Сказано, шабаш. Что завтра бог
    даст, а нынче весь отошел.
        -- Батюшка, только из глазка на личико его
    взглянуть, -- говорила старушка.
        -- Я те взгляну, куда лезешь?

49. Так что, когда купец разогнал весь народ, он
    подошел к отцу Сергию и, став без всяких
    приготовлений на колени, громким голосом сказал:
        -- Отец святый, благослови дщерь мою
    болящую исцелить от боли недуга. Дерзаю
    прибегнуть к святым стопам твоим. -- И он сложил
    горсточкой руку на руку. Все это он сделал и
    сказал так, как будто он делал нечто ясно и
    твердо определенное законом и обычаем, как будто
    именно так, а не каким-либо иным способом надо и
    должно просить об исцелении дочери. Он сделал
    это с такою уверенностью, что даже и отцу Сергию
    показалось, что все это именно так и должно
    говорить и делать. Но он все-таки велел ему
    встать и рассказать в чем дело.

50. Купец рассказал, что дочь его, девица двадцати
    двух лет, заболела два года тому назад, после
    скоропостижной смерти матери, ахнула, как он
    говорит, и с тех пор повредилась. И вот он
    привез ее за тысячу четыреста верст, и она ждет
    в гостинице, когда отец Сергий прикажет привесть
    ее. Днем она не ходит, боится света, а может
    выходить только после заката солнца.
        -- Что же, она очень слаба? -- сказал отец
    Сергий.
        -- Нет, слабости она особой не имеет и
    корпусна, а только нерастениха, как доктор
    сказывал.

Если бы нынче приказал, отец Сергий, привесть
ее, я бы духом слетал. Отец святый, оживите
сердце родителя; восстановите род его --
молитвами своими спасите болящую дщерь его.

51. Если удавалось ему послужить людям или советом,
или грамотой, или уговором ссорящихся, он не
видел благодарности, потому что уходил. И
понемногу бог стал проявляться в нем.
    Один раз он шел с двумя старушками и
солдатом. Барин с барыней на шарабане,
запряженном рысаком, и мужчина и дама верховые
остановили их. Муж барыни ехал с дочерью
верхами, а в шарабане ехала барыня с, очевидно,
путешественником-французом.
    Они остановили их, чтобы показать ему les
pélérins, которые, по свойственному русскому
народу суеверию, вместо того чтобы работать,
ходят из места в место.
    Они говорили по-французски, думая, что не
понимают их.
    -- Demandez leur, -- сказал француз, --
s'ils sont bien sûrs de ce que leur pélérinage
est agréable à Dieu.
    Их спросили. Старушки отвечали:
    -- Как бог примет. Ногами-то были, сердцем
будем ли.
    Спросили солдата. Он сказал, что один,
деться некуда.
    Спросили Касатского, кто он?
    -- Раб божий.
    -- Qu'est ce qu'il dit? Il ne répond pas.
    -- Il dit qu'il est un serviteur de Dieu.
    -- Cela doit être un fils de prêtre. Il a
de la race. Avez vous de la petite monnaie?
    У француза нашлась мелочь. И он всем
роздал по двадцать копеек.
    -- Mais dîtes leur que ce n'est pas pour
les cierges que je leur donne, mais pour qu'ils
se régalent de thé; чай, чай, -- улыбаясь, --
сказал он, трепля рукой в перчатке Касатского
по плечу.
    -- Спаси Христос, -- ответил Касатский, не
надевая шапки и кланяясь своей лысой головой.

И Касатскому особенно радостна была эта
встреча, потому что он презрел людское мнение
и сделал самое пустое, легкое -- взял смиренно
двадцать копеек и отдал их товарищу, слепому
нищему. Чем меньше имело значения мнение людей,
тем сильнее чувствовался бог.

52. -- Во имя отца и сына и святого духа, -- послы-
шалось из-за перегородки. -- Уйди.

53. -- Бог благословит. Прости Христа ради.

КОРОЛЕНКО

54. Работал он страшно,/жил бедно, терпел голод и
холод. Были ли у него какие-нибудь мысли,
кроме непрестанных забот о лепешке и чае?
Да, были.
Когда он бывал пьян, он плакал. "Какая
наша жизнь, -- говорил он, -- господи боже!"
Кроме того, он говорил иногда, что желал бы все
бросить и уйти на "гору". Там он не будет ни
пахать,/ни сеять, не будет рубить/и возить дро-
ва, не будет даже молоть зерно на ручном жернове.
Он будет только спасаться. Какая это гора, где
она, он точно не знал; знал только, что гора эта
есть, во-первых,/а во-вторых, что она где-то
далеко, -- так далеко, что оттуда его нельзя
будет добыть самому тойону-исправнику...
Податей платить, понятно, он также не будет.

55. На самом краю слободы стояла небольшая юртенка.
Из нее, как и из других юрт, поднимался высоко-
высоко дым камелька, застилая белою, волную-
щеюся массою холодные звезды и яркий месяц.
Огонь весело переливался, отсвечивая сквозь
матовые льдины. На дворе было тихо.

56. Его жена, крепкая, жилистая, замечательно сильная
и столь же замечательно безобразная женщина...

57. Он хлопнул ее по плечу так сильно, что она по-
качнулась, и лукаво подмигнул. Таково женское
сердце: она знала, что Макар непременно ее
надует, но поддалась обаянию супружеской ласки.

58. В морозном воздухе раздался первый удар коло-
кола, когда Макар вошел в избу. Он первым
словом сообщил старухе, что у них в плашку
попала лисица. Он совсем забыл, что старуха не
пила вместе с ним водки, и был сильно удивлен,
когда, невзирая на радостное известие, она
немедленно нанесла ему ногою жестокий удар
пониже спины. Затем, пока он повалился на
постель, она еще успела толкнуть его кулаком в шею

59. Он шел уже долго. По его расчетам он давно
должен был уже выйти из Ямалаха и увидеть коло-
кольню, но он все кружил по тайге. Чаща, точно
заколдованная, держала его в своих объятиях.
Издали доносился все тот же торжественный звон.
Макару казалось, что он идет на него, но звон
все удалялся, и по мере того как его переливы
доносились все тише и тише, в сердце Макара
вступало тупое отчаяние.
        Он устал. Он был подавлен. Ноги
подкашивались. Его избитое тело ныло тупою
болью. Дыхание в груди захватывало. Руки и
ноги коченели. Обнаженную голову стягивало
точно раскаленными обручами.

60. (See following page)

ПУШКИН

61. 1. Кто не проклинал станционных смотрителей,
    2. кто с ними не бранивался? Кто в минуту гнева
    3. не требовал от них роковой книги, дабы
    4. вписать в оную свою безполезную жалобу на
    5. притеснение, грубость и неисправность? Кто
    6. не почитает их извергами человеческого рода,
    7. равными покойным подьячим или по крайней
    8. мере муромским разбойникам? Будем, однако,
    9. справедливы, постараемся войти в их положение
   10. и, может быть, станем судить о них гораздо

11. снисходительнее. Что такое станционный смот-
12. ритель? Сущий мученик четырнадцатого класса
13. огражденный своим чином токмо от побоев, и то
14. не всегда (ссылаюсь на совесть моих читателей).
15. Какова должность сего диктатора, как называет
16. его шутливо князь Вяземский? Не настоящая
17. ли каторга? Покою ни днем ни ночью. Всю
18. досаду, накопленную во время скучной езды,
19. путешественник вымещает на смотрителе. Погода
20. несносная, дорога скверная, ямщик упрямый,
21. лошади не везут -- а виноват смотритель.

60.

A	Макар и не заметил раньше, что на равнине как будто стало светать...	Makar's reactions: focus on light: end stress
B	И звезды погасли, а луна закатилась.	И + plural noun
C	И снежная равнина потемнела.	И + singular noun focus on darkness
1.	Тогда над нею поднялись туманы и стали кругом равнины, как почетная стража.	
2.	И в одном месте, на востоке, туманы и стали светлее, точно воины одетые в золото.	И + adv.
3.	И потом туманы заколыхались, золотые воины наклонились долу.	И + adv.
4.	И из-за них вышло солнце и стало на их золотистых хребтах и оглянуло равнину.	И + adv.
X	И равнина вся засияла невиданным, ослепительным светом.	И + singular noun (light)
Y	И туманы торжественно поднялись огромным хороводом, разорвались на западе и колеблясь понеслись кверху.	И + plural noun (sound)
Z	И Макару казалось, что он слышит чудную песню.	Makar's reactions: focus on sound

62. Легко можно догадаться, что есть у меня
    приятели из почтенного сословия смотрителей.
    В самом деле память одного из них мне
    драгоценна. Обстоятельства некогда сблизили нас
    и об нем-то намерен я теперь побеседовать с лю-
    безными читателями.

63. Вследствие сего смотрители со мной не церемо-
    нились, и часто бирал я с бою то,/что, во мнении
    моем, следовало мне по праву. Будучи молод и
    вспыльчив,/ я негодовал на низость и малодушие
    смотрителя, когда сей последний отдавал
    приготовленную мне тройку/ под коляску чиновного
    барина./ Столь же долго не мог я привыкнуть и к
    тому, чтоб разборчивый холоп обносил мне блюдом
    на губернаторском обеде./ Ныне то и другое
    кажется мне в порядке вещей. В самом деле, что
    было бы с нами,/ если бы вместо общеудобного
    правила: "чин чина почитай"/ ввелось в
    употребление другое, например, "ум ума почитай"?

64. ... Много могу я насчитать поцелуев,

    "С тех пор, как этим занимаюсь",

    но ни один не оставил во мне столь долгого,
    столь приятного воспоминания.

65. ехала в карете в шесть лошадей, с тремя малень-
    кими барчатами, и с кормилицей, и с черной мось-
    кою

66. "Так вы знали мою Дуню? -- начал он. -- Кто же
    и не знал ее? Ах, Дуня, Дуня! Что за девка
    была! Бывало, кто ни проедет, всякий похвалит,
    никто не осудит. Барыни дарили ее, та
    платочком, та сережками. Господа проезжие
    нарочно останавливались, будто бы пообедать аль
    отужинать, а в самом деле только чтоб на нее

подолее поглядеть. <u>Бывало</u>, барин, <u>какой бы сер-
дитый</u> ни был, при ней утихает и милостиво со
мною разговаривает. Поверите ль, сударь:
<u>курьеры</u>, <u>фельдегеря</u> с нею по получасу загова-
ривались. Ею дом держался: что прибрать, что
приготовить, за всем успевала. <u>А я-то</u>, старый
дурак, не нагляжусь, бывало не нарадуюсь; <u>уж я
ли не</u> любил моей Дуни, <u>я ль</u> не лелеял моего
дитяти; уж <u>ей ли</u> не было житье? Да нет, от беды
не отбожишься; <u>что суждено, тому не миновать</u>.

67. "Вот уже третий год, -- заключил он, -- как живу
я без Дуни и как об ней нет ни слуху ни духу.
Жива ли, нет ли, бог ее ведает. Всяко случается.
Не ее первую, не ее последнюю сманил проезжий
повеса, а там подержал, да и бросил. Много их
в Петербурге, молоденьких дур, сегодня в атласе
да бархате, а завтра, поглядишь, метут улицу
вместе с голью кабацкою. Как подумаешь порою,
что и Дуня, может быть, тут же пропадает, так
поневоле согрешишь да пожелаешь ей могилы..."

68. С этим словом он хотел в меня прицелиться... при
ней! Маша бросилась к его ногам. "Встань,
Маша, стыдно! -- закричал я в бешенстве, -- а вы,
сударь, перестанете ли издеваться над бедной
женщиной? Будете ли вы стрелять, или нет?"

69. Нас мало избранных, счастливцев праздных,
Пренебрегающих презренной пользой,
Единого прекрасного жрецов.

/Сильвио/: Отроду не встречал счастливца столь
блистательного! Вообразите себе молодость, ум,
красоту, веселость самую бешеную, храбрость
самую беспечную, громкое имя, деньги, которым не
знал он счета и которые никогда у него не перево-
дились, и представьте себе, какое действие должен был он произвести между нами. Первенство
мое поколебалось.

70.   Ты с этим шел ко мне
 И мог остановиться у трактира
 И слушать скрипача слепого! -- Боже!
 Ты, Моцарт, недостоин сам себя.

 Жизнь его, наконец, была в моих руках; я глядел
 на него жадно, стараясь уловить хотя одну тень
 беспокойства... Он стоял под пистолетом,
 выбирая из фуражки спелые черешни и выплевывая
 косточки, которые долетали до меня. Его
 равнодушие взбесило меня. Что пользы мне,
 подумал я, лишить его жизни, когда он ею вовсе
 не дорожит?

71. Утром ученье, манеж; обед у полкового коман-
 дира или в жидовском трактире; вечером пунш
 и карты.

72. Один только человек принадлежал нашему обществу,
 не будучи военным. Ему было около тридцати пяти
 лет, и мы за то почитали его стариком.
 Опытность давала ему перед нами многие
 преимущества; к тому же его обыкновенная угрю-
 мость, крутой и злой язык имели сильное влияние
 на молодые наши умы. Какая-то таинственность
 окружала его судьбу; он казался русским, а
 носил иностранное имя.

73. Однажды человек десять наших офицеров обедали у
 Сильвио. Пили по-обыкновенному, то есть очень
 много; после обеда стали мы уговаривать хозяина
 прометать нам банк... Сильвио имел обыкновение
 за игрою хранить совершенное молчание, никогда
 не спорил и не объяснялся. Если понтеру
 случалось обсчитаться, то он тотчас или
 доплачивал достальное, или записывал лишнее.
 Мы уж это знали и не мешали ему хозяйничать
 по-своему; но между нами находился офицер,
 недавно к нам переведенный. Он, играя тут же,
 в рассеянности, загнул лишний угол.

74. ...находился офицер, недавно к нам переведенный. Он, играл тут же, в рассеянности, загнул лишний угол. Сильвио взял мел и уравнял
счет по своему обыкновению. Офицер, думая, что
он ошибся, пустился в объяснения. Сильвио
молча продолжал метать. Офицер, потеряв
терпение, взял щетку и стер то, что казалось
ему напрасно записанным. Сильвио взял мел и
записал снова. Офицер, разгоряченный вином,
игрою и смехом товарищей, почел себя жестоко
обиженным и, в бешенстве схватив со стола
медный шандал, пустил его в Сильвио, который
едва успел отклониться от удара.

75. Имея от природы романтическое воображение, я
всех сильнее прежде сего был привязан к
человеку, коего жизнь была загадкою и который
казался мне героем таинственной какой-то повести.
Он любил меня, по крайней мере со мной одним
оставлял обыкновенное свое резкое злоречие и
говорил о разных предметах с простодушием и
необыкновенною приятностью. Но после несчастного вечера мысль, что честь его была зама-
рана и не омыта по его собственной вине, эта
мысль меня не покидала и мешала мне обходиться
с ним попрежнему.

ГОРЬКИЙ

76. Мы недолго ждали... Скоро спешной походкой, с
озабоченным лицом, по двору прошла Таня,
перепрыгивая через лужи талого снега и грязи.
Она скрылась за дверью на погреб. Потом, не
торопясь и посвистывая, туда прошел солдат.
Руки у него были засунуты в карманы, а усы
шевелились...
    Шел дождь, и мы видели, как его капли
падали в лужи и лужи морщились под их ударами.
День был сырой, серый -- очень скучный день.
На крышах еще лежал снег, а на земле уже
появились темные пятна грузи. И снег на крышах
тоже был покрыт бурым, грязноватым налетом.
Дождь шел медленно, звучал он уныло. Нам было
холодно и неприятно ждать...

Первым вышел с погреба солдат; он пошел по
двору медленно, шевеля усами, засунув руки в
карманы, -- такой же, как всегда.
Потом -- вышла и Таня. Глаза у нее...
глаза у нее сияли радостью и счастьем, а губы
-- улыбались. И шла она, как во сне,
пошатываясь, неверными шагами...
Мы не могли перенести этого спокойно.

77. мы выскочили на двор и засвистали, заорали на
нее злобно, громко, дико.

Мы смеялись, ревели, рычали.

78. ... И мы все говорили о нем и о будущих его
успехах у золотошвеек, которые, встречаясь с
нами на дворе, или обидно поджимая губы,
обходили нас сторонкой, или шли прямо на нас,
как будто нас и не было на их дороге. А мы
всегда только любовались ими и на дворе, и
когда они проходили мимо наших окон -- зимой
одетые в какие-то особые шапочки и шубки, а
летом -- в шляпках с цветами и с разноцветными
зонтиками в руках. Зато между собою мы
говорили об этих девушках так, что если бы они
слышали нас, то все взбесились бы от стыда и
обиды.

79. Но и ругались мы редко -- в чем может быть
виновен человек, если он полумертв, если он,
как истукан, если все чувства его подавлены
тяжестью труда?

80. Нас было двадцать шесть человек... наш хозяин
называл нас жуликами и давал нам на обед...
Нам было душно и тесно... Нам было тяжело и
тошно... она [печь] дышала на нас жаром...

81. живых машин, запертых в сыром подвале... в яму,
    вырытую пред нами и выложенную кирпичом... рамы
    были заграждены... стекла, покрытые мучной
    пылью... под тяжелым потолком, покрытым копотью
    и паутиной... в толстых стенах разрисованных
    пятнами грязи и плесени...

82. Нам было душно и тесно жить в каменной коробке
    под низким и тяжелым потолком, покрытым копотью
    и паутиной...   Нам было тяжело и тошно в толстых
    стенах, разрисованных пятнами грязи и плесени...

83. И целый день с утра до десяти часов вечера...
    И целый день...   С утра до вечера...   Изо дня в
    день... девять против девяти...

84. задумчиво и грустно мурлыкала кипящая вода в
    котле;

85. лопата пекаря зло и быстро шаркала о под печи,
    сбрасывая скользкие вареные куски теста на
    горячий кирпич.

86. ... Иногда мы пели, и песня наша начиналась так:
    среди работы вдруг кто-нибудь вздыхал тяжелым
    вздохом усталой лошади и запевал тихонько одну
    из тех протяжных песен, жалобно-ласковый мотив
    которых всегда облегчает тяжесть на душе
    поющего. Поет один из нас, а мы сначала молча
    слушаем его одинокую песню, и она гаснет и
    глохнет под тяжелым потолком подвала, как ма-
    ленький огонь костра в степи сырой осенней
    ночью, когда серое небо висит над землей, как
    свинцовая крыша. Потом к певцу пристает другой,
    и -- вот уже два голоса тихо и тоскливо плавают
    в духоте нашей тесной ямы. И вдруг сразу
    несколько голосов подхватят песню, -- она

вскипает как волна, становится сильнее, громче
и точно раздвигает сырые, тяжелые стены нашей
каменной тюрьмы...

Поют все двадцать шесть; громкие, давно
спевшиеся голоса наполняют матерскую; песне
тесно в ней: она бьется о камень стен, стонет,
плачет и оживляет сердце тихой щекочущей болью,
бередит в нем старые раны и будит тоску...
Певцы глубоко и тяжко вздыхают; иной неожиданно
оборвет песню и долго слушает, как поют
товарищи, и снова вливает свой голос в общую
волну. Иной, тоскливо крикнув: "Эх!" -- поет,
закрыв глаза, и, может быть, густая, широкая
волна звуков представляется ему дорогой куда-то
вдаль, освещенной ярким солнцем, -- широкой
дорогой, и он видит себя идущим по ней...

87. И -- ушла, прямая, красивая, гордая.
Мы же остались среди двора, в грязи, под
дождем и серым небом без солнца...

Потом и мы молча ушли в свою сырую
каменную яму. Как раньше -- солнце никогда не
заглядывало к нам в окна, и Таня не приходила
больше никогда!...

ТУРГЕНЕВ

88. - Ася, довольно тебе? - вдруг произнес за мною
мужской голос по-русски.
- Подождем еще, - отвечал другой, женский
голос на том же языке.

89. ... Гагин мне понравился тотчас. Есть на свете
такие счачтливые лица: глядеть на них всякому
любо, точно они греют вас или гладят. У Гагина
было именно такое лицо, милое, ласковое, с
большими, мягкими глазами и мягкими курчавыми
волосами. Говорил он так, что, даже не видя
его лица, вы по одному звуку его голоса
чувствовали, что он улыбается.
Девушка, которую он <u>назвал своей сестрою,</u>
<u>с первого взгляда показалась</u> мне очень

миловидной. Было что-то свое, особенное, в
складе ее <u>смугловатого</u>, круглого лица, с
небольшим тонким носом, <u>почти</u> детскими <u>щечками</u>
и черными светлыми глазами. Она была грациозно
сложена, <u>но как будто не вполне еще развита.</u>
Она <u>нисколько не</u> походила на своего брата.

90. Мне тогда и в голову не приходило, что человек
не растение и процветать ему долго нельзя.
Молодость ест пряники золоченные, да и думает,
что это-то и есть хлеб насущный; а придет время
-- и хлебца напросишься. Но толковать об этом
не для чего.

91. Мне было тогда лет двадцать пять, - начал Н.Н.
- <u>дела давно минувших дней</u>, как видите. Я
только что <u>вырвался на волю</u> и уехал за границу,
не для того, чтобы "<u>кончить мое воспитание</u>",
как говаривалось тогда, а просто мне хотелось
<u>посмотреть на мир божий.</u>

92. "Где нынче крест и тень ветвей над бедной
матерью моей!" - проговорила она вполголоса.
- У Пушкина не так, - заметил я. - А я хотела
бы быть Татьяной, - прдолжала она все так же
задумчиво.

93. - Ваш брат все знает... Я должен был ему все
сказать. - Должны? - проговорила она невнятно.
Она, видимо, не могла еще прийти в себя и плохо
меня понимала.

94. Я любил бродить тогда по городу; луна, казалось,
пристально глядела на него с чистого неба; и
город чувствовал этот взгляд и стоял чутко и
мирно, весь облитый ее светом, этим безмятежным
и в то же время тихо душу волнующим светом.

95. Весь этот день прошел как нельзя лучше. Мы
    веселились, как дети. Ася была очень мила и
    проста. Гагин радовался, глядя на нее. Я ушел
    поздно. Въехавши на средину Рейна, я попросил
    перевозчика пустить лодку вниз по течению.
    Старик поднял весла - и царственная река понесла
    нас. Глядя кругом, слушая, вспоминая, я вдруг
    почувствовал тайное беспокойство на сердце...
    поднял глаза к небу но и в небе не было покоя:
    испещренное звездами, оно все шевелилось,
    двигалось, содрогалось; я склонился к реке... но
    и там, и в этой темной, холодной глубине, тоже
    колыхались, дрожали звезды; тревожное оживление
    мне чудилось повсюду - и тревога росла во мне
    самом. Я облокотился на край лодки... Шепот
    ветра в моих ушах, тихое журчанье воды за кормою
    меня раздражали, и свежее дыханье волны не охлаж-
    дало меня; соловей запел на берегу и заразил меня
    сладким ядом своих звуков. Слезы закипали у меня
    на глазах, но то не были слезы беспредметного
    восторга. Что я чувствовал, было не то смутное,
    еще недавно испытанное ощущение всеобъемлющих
    желаний, когда душа ширится, звучит, когда ей
    кажется, что она все понимает и все любит...
    Нет! во мне зажглась жажда счастья. Я еще не
    смел назвать его по имени, - но счастья, счастья
    до пресыщения - вот чего хотел я, вот о чем
    томился... А лодка все неслась, и старик пере-
    возчик сидел и дремал, наклонясь над веслами.

ЧЕХОВ

96. Оставшись один, Коврин лег поудобнее и принялся
    за статьи. У одной было такое заглавие: "О
    промежуточной культуре", у другой: "Несколько
    слов по поводу заметки г.Z. о перештыковке
    почвы под новый сад", у третьей: "Еще об
    окулировке спящим глазком" -- и все в таком роде.
    Но какой непокойный, неровный тон, какой
    нервный, почти болезненный задор! Вот статья,
    кажется, с самым мирным заглавием и безразличным
    содержанием: говорится в ней о русской
    антоновской яблоне. Но начинает ее Егор Семеныч
    с "audiatur etc." и кончает -- "sapienti sat",

а между этими изречениями целый фонтан разных
ядовитых слов по адресу "ученого невежества
наших патентованных гг. садоводов, наблюдающих
природу с высоты своих кафедр", или г. Гоше,
"успех которого создан профанами и дилетантами",
и тут же некстати натянутое и неискреннее
сожаление, что мужиков, ворующих фрукты и
ломающих при этом деревья, уже нельзя драть
розгами.

97.   - Спасибо, Андрюша, что приехали. У нас
неинтересные знакомые, да и тех мало. У нас
только сад, сад, сад и больше ничего. Штамб,
полуштамб, - засмеялась она, - апорт, ранет,
боровинка, окулировка, копулировка... Вся, вся
наша жизнь ушла в сад, мне даже ничего, никогда
не снится, кроме яблонь и груш. Конечно, это
хорошо, полезно, но иногда хочется и еще чего-
нибудь для разнообразия. Я помню, когда вы,
бывало, приезжали к нам на каникулы или просто
так, то в доме становилось как-то свежее и
светлее, точно с люстры и с мебели чехлы
снимали. Я была тогда девочкой и все-таки понимала.

98. Она была ошеломлена, согнулась, съежилась и
точно состарилась сразу на десять лет...

99. Андрей Васильич Коврин, магистр, утомился и
расстроил себе нервы. Он не лечился, но как-то
вскользь за бутылкой вина, поговорил с
приятелем-доктором, и тот посоветовал ему
провести весну и лето в деревне. Кстати же
пришло длинное письмо от Тани Песоцкой, которая
просила его приехать в Борисовку и погостить.
И он решил, что ему в самом деле нужно про-
ехаться. ... потом ...отправился на лошадях
к своему бывшему опекуну и воспитателю Песоц-
кому, известному в России садоводу.

100. Она говорила долго и с большим чувством. Ему
почему-то вдруг пришло в голову, что в течение
лета он может привязаться к этому маленькому,
слабому, многоречивому существу, увлечься и
влюбиться, -- в положении их обоих это так
возможно и естественно! Эта мысль умиляла и
насмешила его; он нагнулся к милому,
озабоченному лицу и запел тихо:

"Онегин, я скрывать не стану,
  Безумно я люблю Татьяну..."

101. А когда я умру, кто будет смотреть? Кто будет
работать? Садовник? Работники? Да? Так вот
что я тебе скажу, друг любезный: первый враг в
нашем деле не заяц, не хрущ и не мороз, а
чужой человек.
        -- А Таня? -- спросил Коврин, смеясь.
-- Нельзя, чтобы она была вреднее, чем заяц.
Она любит и понимает дело.
        -- Да, она любит и понимает. Если после
моей смерти ей достанется сад и она будет
хозяйкой, то, конечно, лучшего и желать нельзя.
Ну, а если, не дай бог, она выйдет замуж?
-- зашептал Егор Самёныч и испуганно посмотрел
на Коврина. -- То-то вот есть! Выйдет замуж,
пойдут дети, тут уже о саде некогда думать.
Я чего боюсь главным образом: выйдет за
какого-нибудь молодца, а тот сжадничает и сдает
сад в аренду торговкам, и все пойдет к черту в
первый же год! В нашем деле бабы - бич божий!

102. Вид он имел <u>крайне</u> озабоченный, <u>все</u> куда-то
торопился и с таким выражением, как будто
<u>опоздай он хоть на одну минуту</u>, то <u>все</u> погибло!

103. как видишь, мороз, а <u>подними</u> на палке термометр
<u>сажени на две</u> повыше земли, там тепло...

<u>Как бы обширен ум ни был</u>, всего туда не
<u>поместишь</u>.

104. -- Кто это привязал лошадь к яблоне? --
      послышался его отчаянный, душу раздирающий
      крик. -- Какой это мерзавец и каналья
      осмелился привязать лошадь к яблоне? Боже мой,
      боже мой! Перепортили, перемерзили,
      перескверннили, перепакостили! Пропал сад!
      Погиб сад! Боже мой!

105. Таня чувствовала себя так, как будто любовь и
      счастье захватили ее врасплох, хотя с
      четырнадцати лет была уверена почему-то, что
      Коврин женится именно на ней. Она изумлялась,
      недоумевала, не верила себе... То вдруг
      нахлынет такая радость, что хочется улететь
      под облака и там молиться богу, а то вдруг
      вспомнится, что в августе придется
      расставаться с родным гнездом и оставлять отца,
      или бог весть откуда придет мысль, что она нич-
      тожна, мелка и недостойна такого великого
      человека, как Коврин, -- и она уходит к себе,
      запирается на ключ и горько плачет в продол-
      жение нескольких часов. Когда бывают гости,
      вдруг ей покажется, что Коврин необыкновенно
      красив и что в него влюблены все женщины и
      завидуют ей, и душа ее наполняется восторгом
      и гордостью, как будто она победила весь свет,
      но стоит ему приветливо улыбнуться какой-нибудь
      барышне, как она уж дрожит от ревности, уходит
      к себе -- и опять слезы.

106. Монах в черной одежде, с седою головой и
      черными бровями, скрестив на груди руки,
      пронесся мимо... Босые ноги его не касались
      земли. Уже пронесясь сажени на три, он
      оглянулся на Коврина, кивнул головой и улыб-
      нулся ему ласково и в то же время лукаво. Но
      какое бледное, худое лицо!

107. ... из-за сосны, как раз напротив, вышел
      неслышно, без малейшего шороха, человек
      среднего роста с непокрытою седою головой,

весь в темном и бо<u>с</u>ой, похожий на ни<u>щ</u>его, и на
его бледном, точно мертвом лице резко
выделялись черные брови. Приветливо кивая
головой, этот ни<u>щ</u>ий или <u>с</u>транник бе<u>сш</u>умно
подо<u>ш</u>ел к <u>ск</u>амье и <u>с</u>ел, и Коврин узнал в нем
черного монаха. Минуту оба смотрели друг на
друга -- Коврин с изумлением, а монах ласково
и, как и тогда, немножко лукаво, с выражением
себе на уме.

108. Черный вы<u>с</u>окий <u>с</u>толб, похожий на вихрь или
<u>с</u>мерч, пока<u>з</u>ался на том берегу бухты. Он <u>с</u>
<u>с</u>тра<u>ш</u>ною бы<u>с</u>тротой двигал<u>с</u>я чере<u>з</u> бухту по
направлению к го<u>с</u>тинице, <u>с</u>тановя<u>сь</u> в<u>с</u>е меньше
и темнее, и Коврин едва у<u>с</u>пел по<u>с</u>торонить<u>с</u>я,
чтобы дать дорогу... Монах <u>с</u> непокрытою
<u>с</u>едою головой и <u>с</u> черными бровями, бо<u>с</u>ой,
<u>ск</u>ре<u>с</u>тив<u>ш</u>и на груди руки, проне<u>сс</u>я мимо и
о<u>с</u>тановил<u>с</u>я <u>с</u>реди комнаты. -- Отчего ты не
поверил мне? -- спросил он с укоризной,
глядя ласково на Коврина.

109. У него пронеслось в памяти его прошлое, чистое,
целомудренное, полное труда.

110. -- Что ни говори, а кровь много значит. Его
мать была удивительная, благороднейшая,
умнейшая женщина. Было наслаждением смотреть
на ее доброе, ясное, чистое лицо, как у
ангела. Она прекрасно рисовала, писала стихи,
говорила на пяти иностранных языках, пела...
Бедняжка, царство ей небесное, скончалась от
чахотки.
      Не настоящий Егор Семеныч вздыхал и,
помолчав, продолжал: -- Когда он был мальчиком
и рос у меня, то у него было такое же
ангельское лицо, ясное и доброе. У него и
взгляд, и движения, и разговор нежны и изящны,
как у матери. А ум? Он всегда поражал нас
своим умом. Да и то сказать, недаром он

магистр! Недаром! А погоди, Иван Карлыч, каков
он будет лет через десять! Рукой не достанешь!

111. -- Я существую в твоем воображении, а вообра-
     жение твое есть часть природы, значит, я
     существую и в природе.

ТУРГЕНЕВ

112. Картина была чудесная: около огней дрожало и как
     будто замирало, упираясь в темноту, круглое
     красноватое отражение; пламя вспыхивая, изредка
     забрасывало за черту того круга быстрые отблески;
     тонкий язык света лизнет голые сучья лозника и
     разом исчезнет; острые, длинные тени, врываясь
     на мгновенье, в свою очередь добегали до самых
     огоньков: мрак боролся со светом. Иногда пламя
     горело слабее и кружок света суживался, из
     надвинувшейся тьмы внезапно выставлялась
     лошадиная голова, гнедая, с извилистой
     проточиной, или вся белая, внимательно и тупо
     смотрела на нас, проворно жуя длинную траву, и,
     снова опускаясь, тотчас скрывалась.

113. Не ясен сокол да напущает на гусей, на лебедей
     Да на малых перелетных на серых утушек --
     Напущает-то богатырь святорусский
     А на тую ли на силу на татарскую.

                         (Илья Муромец и Калин-Царь)

114. С самого раннего утра небо ясно; утренняя заря
     не пылает пожаром: она разливается кротким
     румянцем. Солнце -- не огнистое, не
     раскаленное, как во время знойной засухи, не
     тускло-багровое, как перед бурей, но светлое и
     приветно лучезарное -- мирно всплывает под
     узкой и длинной тучкой, свежо просияет и
     погрузится в лиловый ее туман. Верхний тонкий

край растянутого облачка засверкает змейками;
блеск их подобен блеску кованого серебра...
Но вот опять хлынули играющие лучи, -- и весело
и величаво, словно взлетая, поднимается могучее
светило.

115. Я добрался наконец до угла леса, но там не было
никакой дороги: какие-то некошеные, низкие
кусты широко расстилались передо мною, а за
ними далеко-далеко виднелось пустынное поле. Я
опять остановился. "Что за притча?... Да где
же я?" Я стал припоминать, как и куда ходил в
течение дня... "Э! да это Парахинские кусты!
-- воскликнул я наконец, -- точно! вон это,
должно быть, Синдеевская роща... да как же это
я сюда зашел? Так далеко?...

116. Между тем ночь приближалась и росла, как
грозовая туча; казалось, вместе с вечерними
парами отовсюду поднималась и даже с вышины
лилась темнота. Мне попалась какая-то неторная,
заросшая дорожка; я отправился по ней,
внимательно поглядывая вперед. Все кругом
быстро чернело и утихало, одни перепела изредка
кричали. Небольшая ночная птица, неслышно и
низко мчавшаяся на своих мягких крыльях, почти
наткнулась на меня и пугливо нырнула в сторону.
Я вышел на опушку кустов и побрел по полю
межой. Уже я с трудом различал отдаленные
предметы; поле неясно белело вокруг; за ним, с
каждым мгновением надвигаясь громадными
клубами, вздымался угрюмый мрак.

117. Странное чувство тотчас овладело мной. Лощина
эта имела вид почти правильного котла с
пологими боками; на дне ее торчало стоймя
несколько больших белых камней, -- казалось,
они сползлись туда для тайного совещания, --
и до того в ней было немо и глухо, так плоско,
так уныло висело над нею небо, что сердце у
меня сжалось. Какой-то зверок слабо и жалобно

пискнул между камней.

118. "Да где же это я?" -- повторил я опять вслух,
остановился в третий раз и вопросительно
посмотрел на свою английскую желто-пегую
собаку Дианку, решительно умнейшую изо всех
четвероногих тварей. Но умнейшая из
четвероногих тварей только повиляла хвостиком,
уныло моргнула усталыми глазками и не подала
мне никакого дельного совета.

ЧЕХОВ

119. Какие были деньги, свои и женины, он пролечил,
кормиться было уже не на что, стало скучно без
дела, и он решил, что, должно быть, надо ехать
к себе домой, в деревню. Дома и хворать легче,
и жить дешевле; и недаром говорится: дома
стены помогают.

120. -- И-и, касатка, -- говорила она, ложась на
сене рядом с Марьей, -- слезами горю не по-
можешь! Терпи и все тут. В писании сказано:
аще кто ударит тебя в правую щеку, подставь
ему левую... И-и, касатка!
    Потом она вполголоса, нараспев,
рассказывала про Москву, про свою жизнь, как
она служила горничной в меблированных комнатах.
    - А в Москве дома большие, каменные, --
говорила она, -- церквей много-много, сорок-
сороков, касатка, а в домах все господа, да
такие красивые, да такие приличные!

121. Однажды утром, -- это было уже в начале
сентября, -- Фекла принесла снизу два ведра
воды, розовая от холода, здоровая, красивая;
в это время Марья и Ольга сидели за столом и
пили чай.

-- Чай да сахар! -- проговорила ᵥₑₙ
насмешливо. -- Барыни какие, -- добавила она,
ставя ведра, -- моду себе взяли каждый день
чай пить. Гляди-кось, не раздуло бы вас с чаю-
то! -- продолжала она, глядя с ненавистью на
Ольгу. -- Нагуляла в Москве пухлую морду,
толстомясая! Она замахнулась коромыслом и
ударила Ольгу по плечу, так что обе невестки
только всплеснули руками и проговорили: -- Ах,
батюшки!

122. -- При господах лучше было, -- говорил старик,
мотая шелк. -- И работаешь, и ешь, и спишь,
все своим чередом. В обед щи тебе и каша, в
ужин тоже щи и каша. Огурцов и капусты было
вволю: ешь добровольно, сколько душа хочет. И
строгости было больше. Всякий себя помнил.

123. Она рассказала про свою госпожу, добрую,
богобоязненную женщину, у которой муж был
кутила и развратник и у которой все дочери
повыходили замуж бог знает как: одна вышла за
пьяницу, другая -- за мещанина, третью --
увезли тайно (сама бабка, которая была тогда
девушкой, помогала увозить), и все они скоро
умерли с горя, как и их мать. И вспомнив об
этом, бабка даже всплакнула.

124. Говорили о битках, котлетах, разных супах,
соусах, и повар, который тоже все хорошо
помнил, называл кушанья, каких нет теперь;
было, например, кушанье, которое приготовлялось
из бычьих глаз и называлось "поутру про-
снувшись".
    -- А котлеты марешаль тогда делали? --
спросил Николай.
    -- Нет.
    Николай укоризненно покачал головой и сказал:
    -- Эх вы, горе-повара!

125. Миновала полночь, уже потухли печи здесь и на
той стороне, а внизу на лугу и в трактире еще
гуляли.   Старик и Киряк, пьяные, взявшись за
руки, толкая друг друга плечами, подошли к
сараю, где лежали Ольга и Марья.
     -- Оставь, -- убеждал старик, -- оставь...
Она баба смирная...   Грех...
     -- Ма-арья! -- крикнул Киряк.
     -- Оставь...   Грех...   Она баба ничего.
     Оба постояли с минуту около сарая и пошли.
     -- Лю-эблю я цветы полевы-и! -- запел
вдруг старик высоким, пронзительным тенором.
--Лю-эблю по лугам собирать!
     Потом сплюнул, нехорошо выбранился и пошел
в избу.

126. Какой-то старик лет восьмидесяти, низенький, с
большою бородой, похожий на гнома, не здешний,
но очевидно, причастный к пожару, ходил возле,
без шапки, с белым узелком в руках; в лысине
его отсвечивал огонь.

127.   -- В церкви бог живет.   У людей горят лампы
да свечи, а у бога лампадки красненькие,
зелененькие, синенькие, как глазочки.   Ночью
бог ходит по церкви, и с ним пресвятая
богородица и Николай-угодничек -- туп, туп,
туп...   А сторожу страшно!   И-и, касатка, --
добавила она, подражая своей матери.   -- А
когда будет светопредставление, то все церкви
унесутся на небо.
     -- С ко-ло-ко-ла-ми? -- спросила Мотька басом,
растягивая каждый слог.
     -- С колоколами.   А когда светопредставление,
добрые пойдут в рай, а сердитые будут гореть в
огне вечно и неугасимо, касатка.   Моей маме и
тоже Марье бог скажет: вы никого не обижали и
за это идите направо, в рай; а Киряку и бабке
скажет: а вы идите налево, в огонь.   И кто
скоромное ел, того тоже в огонь.
     ... Маленькие ангелочки летают по небу и
крылышками -- мельк,мельк, будто комарики.

Мотька подумала немного, глядя в землю, и
спросила:
   -- Бабка будет гореть?
   -- Будет, касатка.

128. Но, как бы ни было, зима кончилась. В начале
     апреля стояли теплые дни и морозные ночи, зима
     не уступала, но один теплый денек пересилил,
     наконец, -- и потекли ручьи, запели птицы.
     Весь луг и кусты около реки утонули в вешних
     водах, и между Жуковым и тою стороной все
     пространство сплошь было уже занято громадным
     заливом, на котором там и сям вспархивали
     стаями дикие утки. Весенний закат, пламенный,
     с пышными облаками, каждый вечер давал что-
     нибудь необыкновенное, новое, невероятное,
     именно то самое, чему не веришь потом, когда
     эти же краски и эти же облака видишь на
     картине.
         Журавли летели быстро-быстро и кричали
     грустно, будто звали с собою. Стоя на краю
     обрыва, Ольга подолгу смотрела на разлив, на
     солнце, на светлую, точно помолодевшую церковь,
     и слезы текли у нее и дыхание захватывало
     оттого, что страстно хотелось уйти куда-нибудь,
     куда глаза глядят, хоть на край света.

BIBLIOGRAPHY

Alexandrescu, Sorin. 'Semantic Analysis of Faulkner's Characters.' *Semiotica*, 4, 1971, 37-51

Atkin, R.H. *Multidimensional Man*. Harmondsworth: Penguin Books, 1981

Bakhtin, Mikhail M. *Problemy poetiki Dostoevskogo*. Moscow,: Nauka, 1929 and 1963. Translation by R.W. Rotsel: *Problems of Dostoevsky's Poetics*. Ann Arbor: Ardis, 1973

Barthes, Roland. 'Introduction à l'analyse structurale des récits.' *Communications*, 1966, 8, 1-27. Translation in *New Literary History*, 6.3, 1974, 237-72

——. *S/Z*. Paris: Seuil, 1970. Translation by Richard Miller, London: Cape, 1975

Bayley, John. *Pushkin: A Comparative Commentary*. Cambridge University Press, 1971

Beach, Joseph Warren. *The Concept of Nature in Nineteenth-Century English Poetry*. New York: Russell & Russell, 1936

Bettelheim, Bruno. *The Uses of Enchantment*. Harmondsworth: Penguin Books, 1978

Bitsilli, P.M. 'K voprosu o vnutrennei forme romana Dostoevskogo' (On the internal form of a Dostoevsky novel). Sofia University, 1945. Reprinted in *Brown University Slavic Reprint*, IV, 1966

Blagoi, D.D. *Masterstvo Pushkina* (Pushkin's craftsmanship). Moscow, 1955

——. *Istoriya russkoi literatury v trekh tomakh* (A history of Russian literature in 3 vols.). Moscow-Leningrad: Nauka, 1958-64

Bland, D.S. 'Endangering the Reader's Neck: Background Description in the Novel'. *Criticism III*, Wayne State University Press, 1961

Bocharov, S.G. *Poetika Pushkina* (Pushkin's poetics). Moscow: Nauka, 1974

Booth, Wayne C. *The Rhetoric of Fiction*. University of Chicago, 1961

Bronzwaer, W.J.M. *Tense in the Novel: an Investigation of Some Potentialities of Linguistic Criticism*. Groningen: Walters-Noordhof, 1970

Bruford, Thomas *Chekhov and His Russia*. London, 1947

Cary, Joyce. *Art and Reality*. New York: Harper and Row, 1958

Chatman, Seymour. 'New Ways of Analyzing Narrative Structure'. *Language and Style*, 2, 1969, 1-36

——. (ed.) *Literary Style: a Symposium*. Oxford University Press, 1971

Chernyshevsky, N.G. 'Russkii chelovek na rendezvous' (Russian man at the rendez-vous). *Complete Works*, 5, Moscow, 1950

Chicherin, A.B. 'Turgenev, yego stil'' (Turgenev and his style). In *Masterstvo russkikh klassikov* (The craftsmanship of the Russian classics), Moscow, 1969

Chizhevskiy (Cizevskij), Dmitri 'Zur Komposition von Gogol's "Mantel"'. *Zeitschrift für slavische Philologie*, XIV, 1937, 63-94

Clark, Sir Kenneth. *Lancscape into Art*. Harmondsworth: Pelican Books, 1958

Driessen, F.C. *Gogol' as a Short Story Writer*. The Hague: Mouton, 1965

Eikhenbaum, Boris. 'Kak sdelana "Shinel'" Gogolya' (How Gogol's "Overcoat" was made). *Poetika*. Petrograd, 1919. Translation in *The Russian Review*, XX, 1963, 377-99

——. 'Problemy poetiki Pushkina'. In A.A. Volynskii (ed.) *Pushkin—Dostoevsky*, Petrograd, 1921

Eng, Jan van der. 'Le coup de pistolet. Analyse de la composition'. In J. van der Eng, A.G.F. van Holk, Jan M. Meijer. *The Tales of Belkin by A.S. Pushkin*. The Hague: Mouton, 1968

Erlich, Victor. *Russian Formalism: History—Doctrine*. The Hague: Mouton, 1969

——. *Gogol*. New Haven: Yale University Press, 1969

Fillmore, Charles. 'The Case for Case'. In A. Harms and E. Bach (eds) *Universals of Linguistic Theory*, New York: Holt, 1968

Forster, E.M. *Aspects of the Novel*. London: Edward Arnold, 1927

Friedland, L.S. (ed.) *Chekhov: Letters on the Short Story, the Drama and Other Literary Topics*. New York: Vision Books, 1965

Friedrich, Paul. 'Structural Implications of Russian Pronominal Usage'. In William Bright (ed.) *Sociolinguistics*. The Hague: Mouton, 1966, 128-64

Frye, Northrop. *Anatomy of Criticism*. Princeton University Press, 1957

Genette, Gerard. 'Discours du récit'. *Figures III*. Paris: Seuil, 1972, 67-282. Translation by Jane E. Lewin. *Narrative Discourse*. Oxford: Basil Blackwell, 1980

Gershenzon, M. *Mudrost' Pushkina* (Pushkin's wisdom). Petrograd: Nauka, 1918

Gifford, Henry. 'Anna, Lawrence and "The Law"'. *Critical Quarterly*, 1, No. 3, 1959

Goffman, Erving. *Frame Analysis: An Essay on the Organization of Experience*. New York: Harper Row, 1974

Goryachkina, M.S. *Satira Leskova* (Leskov's satire). Moscow, 1963

Gregory, Michael. 'Old Bailey Speech in *A Tale of Two Cities*.' *Review of English Literature*, VI, 2, 1966, 42-55

Greimas, A.J. 'La structure des actants du récit'. *Word*, 23, 1967, 221-38

Halliday, M.A.K. 'Linguistic Function and Literary Style'. In Seymour Chatman (ed.) *Literary Style: a Symposium*. Oxford University Press, 1971, 330-65

———. 'Categories of the Theory of Grammar'. *Word*, 17.3, 1961

Holquist, J.M. 'The Devil in Mufti: the Märchenwelt in Gogol's short stories'. *PMLA*, 82, 1967, 352-62

Jackson, Robert Louis. *Dostoevsky's Quest for Form*. New Haven: Yale University Press, 1966

Jakobson, Roman. 'Two Aspects of Language and Two Types of Linguistic Disturbances'. In Roman Jakobson and Morris Halle. *Fundamentals of Language*. The Hague: Mouton, 1956

———. 'Linguistics and Poetics: Closing Statement'. in Thomas A. Sebeok (ed.) *Style in Language*. Boston: MIT Press, 1960

Kayser, Wolfgang. *The Grotesque in Literature and Art*. Bloomington: Indiana University Press, 1963

Kozhevnikova, Kveta. 'Ustnaya spontannaya rech' v epicheskoi proze' (Spontaneous oral speech in epic prose). *Acta Universitatis Carolinae Philologica Monographia*, XXXII, Prague, 1970

Kristeva, Julia. 'Bakhtine, le mot, le dialogue et le roman'. *Critique*, 239, 1967, 438-65

Levi-Strauss, Claude. 'La geste d'Asdiwal'. *Annuaire de l'Ecole Pratique des Hautes Etudes* (Sciences religieuses), 1958-9, 3-43. Translation in Edmund Leach (ed.) *The Structural Study of Myth and Totemism*. London: Tavistock, 1967

Lezhnev, A. *Proza Pushkina* (Pushkin's prose). Moscow: Nauka, 1937 and 1966

Liddell, Robert. *A Treatise on the Novel*. London: Cape, 1947

Lodge, David. *The Language of Fiction*. London: Routledge, 1966

———. *The Modes of Modern Writing*. London: Edward Arnold, 1977

McHale, Brian. 'Free Indirect Discourse: a Survey of Recent Accounts'. *PTL: A Journal for Descriptive Poetics and Theory of Literature*, 3,2, 1978, 249-88

Meijer, Jan M. 'The Sixth Tale of Belkin'. In Jan van der Eng, A.G.F. van Hold and Jan M. Meijer. *The Tales of Belkin by A.S. Pushkin*. The Hague: Mouton, 1968, 110-34

Mendilow, A.A. *Time and the Novel*. New York: Deventer, 1952

Mirsky, D.S. *A History of Russian Literature*. London: Routledge, 1949

Mudrick, Marvin. 'Character and Event in Fiction'. *Yale Review*, L, Winter, 1960, 202-18

Nabokov, Vladimir. *Nikolai Gogol*. New York: New Directions 1958

O'Faolain, Sean. *The Short Story*. Cork: Mercier Press, 1972

O'Toole, L.M. 'Structure and Style in the Short Story: Chekhov's "Student"'. *The Slavonic and East European Review*, XLVIII, 114, 1971, 45-67

———. 'Linguistic Functions and the Study of Literary Style'. *Melbourne Slavonic Studies*, 5-6, 1971, 106-23

———. 'Narrative Structure and Living Texture: James Joyce's "Two Gallants"'. *PTL: A Journal for Descriptive Poetics and Theory of Literature*, 1, 1976, 441-58

———. 'Dimensions of Semiotic Space in Narrative'. *Poetics Today*, 4, 1981

———. 'The Scythian Factor'. *Russian Literature*, forthcoming

———. and Ann Shukman (eds.) 'A Contextual Glossary of Formalist Terminology'. *Russian Poetics in Translation*. Oxford: Holdan Books and Essex University, 1977, 4, 13-48

Pascal, Roy. *The Dual Voice: Free Indirect Speech and Its Functioning in the Nineteenth-Century European Novel*. Manchester University Press, 1977

Propp, Vladimir I. *Morfologiya skazki*. Leningrad, 1928 and Moscow, 1969. Translation *The Morphology of the Folktale*. Bloomington: Indiana University Press, 1958

Rayfield, Donald. *Chekhov: the Evolution of his Art*. New York: Barnes & Noble, 1975

Rhode, Eric. 'Dostoevsky and Bresson'. *Sight and Sound*, Spring, 1970, 82-3

Scholes, Robert. *Structuralism in Literature: An Introduction*. New Haven: Yale University Press, 1974

———. and Kellogg, Robert. *The Nature of Narrative*. Oxford University Press, 1966

Shklovsky, Viktor. 'Novella tain' (The mystery story). *O teorii prozy* (On the theory of prose), Moscow, 1925, 125-140

Shaw, J. Thomas. 'Pushkin's "The Shot"'. *Indiana Slavic Studies*, III, 1963, 113-29

Shukman, Ann. 'Ten Russian Short Stories: Theory, Analysis, Interpretation'. *Essays in Poetics*, 2,2, 1977

Slonimsky, A. *Masterstvo Pushkina* (Pushkin's craftsmanship). Moscow: Nauka, 1963

Todorov, Tzvetan. 'Les catégories du récit littéraire'. *Communications*, 8, 1966, 125-51

———. *Poétique de la prose*. Paris: Seuil, 1971

———. *Grammaire du Décaméron*. The Hague: Mouton, 1969

Tomashevskii, Boris. *Teoriya literatury (Poetika)*. (Theory of literature) Moscow-Leningrad, 1925. Translations: Part 1 in L. Lemon and M. Reis (eds.) *Russian Formalist Criticism: Four Essays*. Lincoln: University of Nebraska, 1965; Part 2 in L.M. O'Toole and A. Shukman (eds.) *Russian Poetics in Translation*, 5, 1978, Oxford: Holdan Books and Essex University

Tynyanov, Yurii. 'Dostoevskii i Gogol' (K teorii parodii)' (Dostoevsky and Gogol: towards a theory of parody) *Arkhaisty i novatory*. Leningrad: Nauka, 1930

Uspensky, Boris. *Poetika kompositsii*. Moscow: Iskusstvo, 1970. Translation by Valentina Zavarina and Susan Wittig. *A Poetics of Composition*. Berkeley: California University Press, 1973

Vinogradov, V.V. 'Stil' peterburgskoi poemy *Dvoinik*'' ' (The style of the St Petersburg poem *The Double*). *Dostoevskii I*. Petrograd, 1922, 211-57

———. *Stil' Pushkina* (Pushkin's style). Moscow: Nauka, 1941

Winner, Thomas. *Chekhov and His Prose*. New York: Holt, Rinehart & Winston, 1966

Wright, Andrew H. *Henry Fielding: Mask and Feast*. London: Chatto & Windus, 1965

INDEX

All figures in bold refer to main entries.